Regulation of Banks and Finance

Also by Carlos M. Peláez and Carlos A. Peláez

INTERNATIONAL FINANCIAL ARCHITECTURE: G7, IMF, BIS, Debtors and Creditors

THE GLOBAL RECESSION RISK: Dollar Devaluation and the World Economy

GLOBALIZATION AND THE STATE: Volume I

GLOBALIZATION AND THE STATE: Volume II

GOVERNMENT INTERVENTION IN GLOBALIZATION: Regulation, Trade and Devaluation Wars

FINANCIAL REGULATION AFTER THE GLOBAL RECESSION

Regulation of Banks and Finance

Theory and Policy after the Credit Crisis

Carlos M. Peláez and Carlos A. Peláez

First published 2009 by
PALGRAVE MACMILLAN

Palgrave Macmillan in the UK is an imprint of Macmillan Publishers Limited,
registered in England, company number 785998, of Houndmills, Basingstoke,
Hampshire RG21 6XS.

Palgrave Macmillan in the US is a division of St Martin's Press LLC,
175 Fifth Avenue, New York, NY 10010.

Palgrave Macmillan is the global academic imprint of the above companies
and has companies and representatives throughout the world.

Palgrave® and Macmillan® are registered trademarks in the United States,
the United Kingdom, Europe and other countries.

ISBN: 978–0–230–23903–6 hardback

This book is printed on paper suitable for recycling and made from fully
managed and sustained forest sources. Logging, pulping and manufacturing
processes are expected to conform to the environmental regulations of the
country of origin.

A catalogue record for this book is available from the British Library.

A catalog record for this book is available from the Library of Congress.

10 9 8 7 6 5 4 3 2 1
18 17 16 15 14 13 12 11 10 09

Printed and bound in Great Britain by
CPI Antony Rowe, Chippenham and Eastbourne

To Magnolia and Penelope

Contents

Illustrations

Figures

Tables

Abbreviations

AAA	Agricultural Adjustment Act
ABCP	Asset-backed commercial paper
ABS	Asset backed security
ADR	American depository receipt
ADTV	Average daily trading volume
AIM	Alternative investment market
APT	Arbitrage pricing theory
BCBS	Basel Committee on Banking Supervision
BHC	Bank holding company
BLS	Bureau of Labor Statistics
BOE	Bank of England
CAD	Current account deficit
CAP	Capital Assistance Program
CAPM	Capital asset pricing model
CAR	Capital asset ratio
CARS	Cumulative abnormal returns
CCI	Costs of financial intermediation
CD	Certificate of deposit
CDO	Collateralized debt obligation
CLO	Collateralized loan obligation
COSR	Cost of service regulation
D&O	Directors and officers
DIDMCA	Depository Institution Deregulation and Monetary Control Act of 1980
DUP	Directly unproductive profit-seeking activity
ECB	European Central Bank
ESB	Effective staggered boards
EU	European Union
FASB	Financial Accounting Standards Board
FDIC	Federal Deposit Insurance Corporation
FDICIA	FDIC Improvement Act
FHA	Federal Housing Administration
FHC	Financial holding company
FIRREA	Financial Institutions Reform, Recovery, and Enforcement Act of 1989

FOMC	Federal Open Market Committee
FPI	Foreign private issuer
FRBO	Board of Governors of the Federal Reserve System
FRS	Federal Reserve System
FSA	Financial Services Authority
FSF	Functional structural finance
FSLIC	Federal Savings and Loan Insurance Corporation
FSP	Financial Stability Plan
GAAP	Generally accepted accounting principles
GE	General equilibrium
GED	General equilibrium dynamic
GLBA	Gramm-Leach-Bliley Act
GSE	Government sponsored enterprises
HLT	Highly leveraged transaction
IASB	International Accounting Standards Board
IPO	Initial public offering
IRB	Internal ratings based
IRRC	Investor Responsibility Research Center
ISDA	International Swaps and Derivatives Association
IT	Information technology
LBO	Leveraged buyout
LCR	Least-cost resolution
LOLR	Lender of last resort
LSE	London Stock Exchange
LTV	Loan to value ratio
MBO	Management buyout
MBS	Mortgage backed security
MSA	Metropolitan statistical area
MTM	Mark to market
NIE	New institutional economics
NIRA	National Industrial Recovery Act
NLRA	National Labor Relations Act
NY	New York
NYE	New York stock exchanges
NYSE	New York Stock Exchange
OIS	Overnight index swap
OTC	Over the counter
OTS	Office of Thrift Supervision
PCA	Prompt corrective action
PCAOB	Public Company Accounting Oversight Board
PPIP	Public-Private Investment Program

R&D	Research and development
ROA	Return on assets
ROE	Return on equity
RTC	Resolution Trust Corporation
S&L	Savings and loan association
SB	Staggered board
SEIR	Structured early intervention resolution
SIV	Structured investment vehicle
SOX	Sarbanes-Oxley Act of 2002
SPE	Special purpose entity
SPV	Special purpose vehicle
SRO	Self-regulatory organization
SRP	Sale and repurchase agreement
TARP	Troubled Asset Relief Program
TPS	Trust preferred security
WPA	Works Progress Administration

Acknowledgments

This book provides an analytical review of regulation of banks and finance in the light of the credit/dollar crisis. We are highly indebted to Taiba Batool, Economics Editor of Palgrave Macmillan, for the encouragement of the project and for important improvements. We are most grateful to Gemma Papageorgiou at Palgrave Macmillan for steering the manuscript to publication. The team at Newgen Imaging Systems revised the manuscript with highly useful suggestions and competent typesetting for final publication.

We are grateful to many friends who helped us in this effort. A partial list includes Professor Antonio Delfim Netto, Ambassador Richard T. McCormack, Senator Heráclito Fortes, Professor Paulo Yokota and Eduardo Mendez. Magnolia Maciel Peláez, DDS, and Penelope Solis, JD, reviewed the manuscript providing many suggestions deriving from their long experience of health regulation, which is the subject of a joint project.

In writing this book we remembered dear friends and colleagues who helped and motivated in the interest on scholarly work and international affairs, Clay and Rondo Cameron and Otilia and Nicholas Georgescu-Roegen. We are solely responsible for the shortcomings and errors in this work.

CARLOS M. PELÁEZ AND CARLOS A. PELÁEZ
ATLANTIC CITY AND NEW YORK CITY

Introduction: Scope and Contents

As in previous crises, there is an ambitious, extensive, and heavy agenda of regulatory reform in parliaments, research circles, and government agencies. This book provides a comprehensive review of the analysis of finance, economics, and the law and economics that illuminates the past and current banking and financial regulations designed to prevent events such as the credit/dollar crisis and the global recession. The regulation of financial institutions and markets has occurred during financial crises and recessions. There is no theory and experience of financial regulation carefully applied to the credit/dollar crisis that orients parliaments and government agencies in designing new measures or changes in existing ones. The rush to regulation is largely motivated ad hoc by the existing official interpretation of what caused the financial crisis and what measures are required for its prevention. Academic and policy research typically follows regulation in an effort to provide rigorous analysis of policy and its effects on the functioning of the financial system.

The approaches of the economic theory of the state are analyzed in Chapter 1 to provide a framework of reference on why the government should intervene in the economy through collective action known as regulation. The two fundamental welfare theorems provide a foundation for the public interest view. The first theorem states that a Walrasian allocation results in optimum satisfaction and maximum efficiency, that is, in overall Pareto optimality. The second theorem states that every state of overall Pareto optimality can be converted into a Walrasian allocation by appropriate lump-sum transfers of resources. Collective action by the government is justified when there are Pareto-improving opportunities because of market failures, which are violations of the assumptions, or frictions, of the perfectly competitive allocation. The strongest current item in the regulatory agenda is the creation of a powerful systemic regulator to correct the market failure of financial instability caused by the counterparty financing of large, complex, and systemically important banks and financial institutions. The alternative private interest view posits that regulation fails in attaining its objective and is subject to capture by the regulated entities for their self-interest. This view explains the current financial crisis by government failure in the form of the impact of the Fed's zero interest rate during 2003–4 on the $221 billion yearly housing subsidy and the $1.6 trillion of nonprime mortgages guaranteed or acquired by Fannie Mae and Freddie Mac. The chapter covers the theory of second best, applied welfare economics, property rights, the new institutional economics, asymmetry of information, and the modified capture theory. It establishes the initial foundation of the role of finance in efficiency and growth, which with further elaboration of bank and financial functions provides the finance view or functional structural finance (FSF).

There are two general themes in Chapter 2. First, the nature of regulation is motivated by the analysis of financial guarantees and other general principles. This is followed by the theory of bank functions originating in the new microeconomics of banking. The emphasis throughout is in linking theoretical discovery with empirical research. Second, capital requirements and deposit insurance are considered in pure and empirical analyses. A separate section provides the general review of housing finance in the United States.

The first part of Chapter 3 focuses on the changes and structure of banking. There is review of vast literature on the impact of the technological revolution on banking and financial markets and how it has affected competition, eroding market power. The second part provides key analysis of central banking, both theory and empirical research. The final section provides the reservations on policy making originating in the Lucas critique of econometric policy models and the analysis of consistency of economic policy.

Chapter 4 is divided into interrelated parts. The first part focuses on investment banking and the reasons for its separation from commercial banking. There has been critically important research on the Glass-Steagall Act of 1933, the archetype of recession regulation. Empirical analysis of the market in the United States before the Glass-Steagall Act finds that there were no conflicts of interests by commercial banks in underwriting and that the public adequately discounted securities underwritten by commercial banks. The Glass-Steagall Act was unnecessary but it included Regulation Q that created harmful ceilings on interest rates, which eventually caused the exodus of banking away from the United States. There is an important research on underwriting and loan syndication that confirms the views on the Glass-Steagall Act. The chapter also analyzes theoretically and empirically two of the most contentious current issues: governance and incentive compensation. The principal/agent problem is resolved by efficient markets for capital, managers, and corporate control. Several sections deal with mergers and acquisitions. These are areas of intensive research in the field of law and economics.

The regulation of securities is considered in Chapter 5. The need for exit in the technological revolution leads to the analysis theoretically and empirically of leveraged buyouts (LBO). The regulation of new issues was an important part of the Securities Act of 1933, which has created significant research. There is evidence that the Securities Act of 1933 was influenced by elite investment banks that were concerned with erosion of their market power by the nationwide distribution of securities. The law and economics literature on insider trading raises intriguing issues on the theory and experience with restrictions on insider trading. The final set of sections focuses on the decision of going public, the Sarbanes-Oxley Act of 2002 (SOX) and the important research on the decision of cross-listing, which is critical in the analysis of the possible loss of competitiveness in finance of the United States.

The credit/dollar crisis and resulting global recession are analyzed in Chapter 6. The loss of output of the United States during the Great Depression accumulated to 25.7 percent during 1930–3. Forecasts of the loss of output of the United States in the current recession range from −2 to −4 percent. However, the experience of the Great Depression is frequently mentioned in the policy debate and the catchphrase, as in other recessions, is that these are the worst economic conditions since the Great Depression. Chapter 6 provides a comprehensive synthesis of research on the Great Depression organized in subsection on banks and money, debt deflation theories, financial market frictions, the gold standard, nonmonetary factors, wages and employment and growth theory, and the New Deal. A section analyzes two interpretations of the origins of the credit/dollar crisis: the view of systemic and prudential regulation versus the view on central banking and housing finance. Monetary and fiscal policies are reviewed before a final section on the agenda of regulation.

The conclusion is organized in terms of the two conflicting views on the causes of the credit/dollar crisis and their implications for the regulatory agenda. Notes, references, and the index complete the volume.

1
The Theory of
Regulation and Finance

Introduction

The objective of this chapter is to provide a general view of the theories of regulation followed by a final section on the role of finance in promoting efficiency and growth. The two main approaches are the public interest view, with emphasis on the need of government intervention to attain welfare improvements, and the private interest view, raising doubts about the effectiveness of regulation. The general theory of second best raises doubts as to the feasibility of determining welfare improving policies once the assumptions of the first best are violated. Applied welfare economics provides an engine for searching concrete information that could be useful in guiding policy. Property rights, transaction costs, and the new institutional economics (NIE) have changed the view of government intervention in markets. Asymmetry of information is an extremely important friction of the first best in financial markets. The capture theory has been modified by the analysis of the principal/agent problem and the assumption of imperfect information. The final section considers finance, efficiency, and growth. There is a summary of the main themes in the chapter.

The public interest view

Intervention by the government in economic affairs is justified and predicted by the public interest view because of the need to attain first-best efficiency and welfare when there are frictions or market failures. The foundation for analysis consists of the two theorems of welfare economics, considered in the first subsection below. The following subsection provides the analysis for the two neoclassical cases: monopoly and external economies. The final subsection considers market failure.

The first best

Adam Smith (1776) launched economics with his *Wealth of Nations*. This is a book rich in numerous analyses of the interactions of humans in economic affairs. It would be interesting to learn what Adam Smith would think of the contemporary interpretation of his concept of the invisible hand. The proposition is that individuals in seeking their self-interest promote the public good (Smith 1776, 477): "Every individual intends only his own gain, and he is in this, as in so many other cases, led by an invisible hand to promote an end which was not part of his intention." Perhaps it would be more appropriate to relate the ideas of Smith to the reaction during his times to mercantilism and excessive intervention by the state in economic affairs. Economists have concentrated in analyzing the conditions under which the allocation of resources in markets, without intervention by the state, would result on its own in maximum efficiency and optimum welfare or satisfaction. It took two centuries after Adam Smith to rigorously prove this proposition. There is no consideration by Smith of the static efficiency of the two fundamental theorems of welfare economics. The emphasis of Smith, according to Blaug (2007), is dynamic progress, which consists of growth of the total production of a firm or industry, resulting in growth of the economy.

The foundations of general microeconomic equilibrium were provided by Léon Walras in 1870 (Walras 1870 [1954]). The task of Walras was to provide the simultaneous determination of prices and quantities of goods and services by a system of simultaneous equations of demand functions by consumers, supply functions by producers, and identities of demand and supply. The arguments of the demand functions of a product are their own prices, prices of related commodities and consumers' income and tastes. The arguments of the supply functions were the costs of production, prices of productive services, and technology. Consumers maximize their utilities and producers their profits, taking prices as given; that is, under conditions of perfect competition. The work of Walras was a landmark in economics allowing the analysis of significant disturbances of economies (Duffie and Sonnenschein 1988, 567). The general equilibrium (GE) model is used by economists in numerous contemporary applications.

There are no definitive arguments in the work of Walras concerning the existence of a solution to his system (Arrow and Debreu 1954). The existence of a solution to the GE competitive model is meaningful for positive and normative purposes. The applicability of the model to reality requires consistency of the equations of the model and the conditions under which there is a solution. The definition of existence can proceed as follows (Duffie and Sonnenschein 1988, 567–8). For every commodity, the condition that aggregate demand less aggregate supply is zero results in the system of n excess demand equations z_i in n price variables, p_i:

$$z_i(p_1, \dots, p_n) = 0 \qquad i = 1, 2, \dots, n \tag{1.1}$$

The data of the economy are tastes, technology, the initial endowment or bundles of commodities of consumers, and firm ownership. There is no market power such that agents are price takers. Maximization of profits results in a unique production plan because the supply function for every firm is single valued. The aggregate demand of households depends on prices and income distribution and the aggregate household supply is the sum of initial endowments. There is a price vector, p^*, that balances demand and supply, under the data of the economy, if and only if p^* solves equation 1.1, that is, in GE all markets clear (Ibid, 578). By interaction of the demand functions of consumers and the supply functions of producers, the equilibrium price vector p^* depends on the basic data of the economy: tastes, technology, and endowments. The existence theorem verifies that equation 1.1 has a solution with nonnegative prices, that is, the existence of a Walrasian allocation.

The contribution of Arrow and Debreu (1954) consists of two theorems that specify very general conditions under which there is equilibrium in a perfectly competitive system. The first theorem states that there is equilibrium in a competitive system if every agent initially possesses a positive amount of every commodity that can be sold. The second theorem establishes the existence of a competitive equilibrium if there are types of labor with two specific properties. Each individual must be able to supply at least a positive amount of one type of labor; there is positive use for each type of labor in the production of goods. The uniqueness and stability of the solution to the competitive equilibrium were not considered by Arrow and Debreu (Ibid, 266) because of the need to define equilibrium and specify the dynamics of perfect competition.

Pareto optimal allocations occur when it is not possible to increase the utility, or level of satisfaction, of one individual without decreasing that of at least another. Walrasian equilibrium allocations are obtained by market-clearing prices. Markets clear when excess demands are zero. The fundamental welfare theorems establish the equivalence of Pareto optimal allocations and Walrasian equilibrium allocations.

The marginal conditions for Pareto optimality are obtained as solutions to the program of maximizing utility subject to constraints of resources and technology and that the utility of every other agent is fixed at a predetermined level (Duffie and Sonnenschein 1988, 576). The solution of the constrained maximization program yields the condition that the marginal rates of substitution in consumption are equal across individuals and also equal to the marginal rate of product transformation. The Walrasian equilibrium is obtained by maximization of utility for individuals and of profits by firms in terms of a common vector of product prices. The solution to the constrained maximization in consumption is that the marginal rate of substitution for each pair of commodities is equal to the ratio of commodity prices; the constrained maximization in production requires equality of the marginal rate of transformation to the commodity price ratio.

The marginal rate of substitution between a commodity A and another commodity B is the increase in consumption of A required to maintain unchanged satisfaction after a unit decrease in B when the amounts of other commodities are held constant (Arrow 1951, 507). The marginal rate of transformation between commodities A and B is the increase of output of A when there is a unit decrease in the output of B, with all other outputs of commodities remaining constant (Ibid, 507). Thus, Pareto optimality and Walrasian equilibrium have the same marginal conditions, being the basis for what Duffie and Sonnenschein (1988, 576) call the " 'marginal-this-equals-the marginal-that' proof of the basic welfare theorems." The statement by Arrow (Ibid) is that a necessary and sufficient condition for a Pareto optimum distribution is that the marginal rates of substitution between any two commodities be equal for every individual; a necessary and sufficient condition for maximum efficiency in production is that the marginal rate of transformation for every pair of commodities be equal for all firms (Ibid).

There is a separation of the relation of the Pareto optimum and the Walrasian equilibrium into two parts. The first fundamental theorem of welfare economics is the counterpart in contemporary economics of the Adam Smith statement that individuals promoting their self-interest promote the social good. The theorem states that Walrasian equilibrium allocations are Pareto optimal. The market clearing of the GE perfectly competitive model requires marginal conditions (equality of

rates of marginal substitution to relative commodity prices and equality of rates of product transformation to relative commodity prices) that
are exactly equivalent to those required by Pareto optimality. The perfectly competitive model results in a maximum of efficiency in the use
of available resources and existing technology in that it is not possible
to increase the output of one good without reducing that of another.
The perfectly competitive state results in an optimum of satisfaction in
the consumption of goods in that it is not possible to increase the utility
of one individual without reducing at least that of another. Resources
are used to provide the highest possible satisfaction to society with the
assumed distribution of income. Perfect competition is the first best of
efficiency and welfare. The second welfare theorem is concerned with
obtaining the efficiency of perfect competition while retaining influence on income distribution (Duffie and Sonnenschein 1988, 576). The
theorem states that it is possible to make lump-sum transfers of income
such that every Pareto optimal allocation can become Walrasian
equilibrium.

There is a simple intuitive explanation of the proof of the first welfare theorem (Ibid, 577). Consider the case of pure exchange of goods.
Every agent has an initial endowment and the preferences of each
agent define the economy. A nonnegative bundle of goods for each
agent is defined as an allocation and to be feasible it must be less
than or equal to the initial endowment. Assume first that there is an
initial Walrasian allocation obtained by maximization relative to the
nonnegative price vector, p. There is no other feasible allocation that
for the same satisfaction for each household (agent) can improve the
satisfaction for other households (agents). Suppose that there is such
an allocation, x_1, for the first individual, 1, and that the initial endowment of the ith individual is ω_i. Assume that this is the individual whose
welfare improves while that of others remains the same. Because of the
assumption that agents prefer more to less, the improving allocation
x_1 has quantitatively more of one or several of the commodities in the
bundle. Thus, agent 1 cannot afford x_1 at prices p because it exceeds
the value of its endowment:

$$px_1 > p\omega_1 \qquad\qquad\qquad (1.2)$$

Because every agent prefers more of every commodity than less, each
agent spends its endowment (income) to maintain its utility:

$$px_i \geq p\omega_i \qquad \text{for all } i \qquad\qquad\qquad (1.3)$$

The sum of the inequalities results in the left-hand side of prices multiplying bundles of goods, or expenditures, higher than the right-hand side of initial endowments, or income, because the allocations of all agents except 1 are at least equal to their initial endowments but that of 1 is higher. An allocation, or bundle of goods at a price vector, is feasible if and only if it is less than or equal to the initial endowment or income. Thus, the allocation that improves the welfare of agent 1 is not feasible and the exchange part of the first welfare theorem is proved. There is a similar proof for the production part; overall Pareto optimality of the Walrasian allocation is proved. Duffie and Sonnenschein (1988, 578) point to the simplicity of the argument, which follows from the definition of equilibrium and simple addition. However, they emphasize the important insight of the argument. An allocation that Pareto improves on a Walrasian allocation needs to possess higher value than the Walrasian allocation, thus being infeasible because it exceeds the initial endowment of the system. The method of Arrow (1951) and Debreu (1951), according to Duffie and Sonnenschein (578), provides deeper understanding of the relation between optimum welfare and efficiency, constituting a substantive improvement over the first-order conditions for an optimum. There is significant intuitive appeal. The Walrasian allocation cannot be further Pareto-improved without exceeding the budget constraint. Duffie and Sonnenschein (581–2) provide refined statements of the two welfare theorems that do not depend on certain restrictions used by Arrow.

Monopoly

Neoclassical economists consider two major frictions or distortions of assumptions of the first best that require intervention by the state. The two cases, monopoly and externalities (Pigou 1932), are considered below.

A French engineer, Henri Dupui (Hotelling 1938, 242–4), began the work on consumer surplus in 1844 that was subsequently elaborated by economists, including Marshall (1890) and Hicks (1939). In book three, chapter 6, Marshall (1890) observes that the price actually paid for a good, the market-clearing price where demand equals supply, is lower than what the consumer would be willing to pay, which is obtained from the demand curve. For every unit demanded from zero to the units corresponding to the market price the consumer obtains a benefit in that the price that he or she would be willing to pay given by the demand curve would be higher than what she actually pays for that unit, given by the market-clearing price. The difference between what the consumer would be willing to pay and what she actually pays is a surplus of satisfaction. The sum of all these surpluses is the consumer surplus. Similarly, the price a producer receives, or market price, is higher for every unit, at the market price, than the price at which she would be willing to sell it, read from the upward-sloping supply curve. The sum of all the differences between the price received or market-clearing price and the price at which she would have been willing to supply that unit is the producer surplus. The total surplus is the sum of the consumer and producer surpluses.

Figure 1.1 shows the analysis of taxation presented by Hotelling (1938, 243). The second fundamental theorem originated, according to Blaug (2007), in the classic work of Hotelling who argues that the deficits of marginal cost pricing should be financed by lump-sum taxes. These are the precursors of the lump-sum redistributions of the second fundamental theorem that can convert an efficient Walrasian allocation into an optimal allocation. It is a case of a Pareto-improving social policy. The assumption of perfect competition is still valid. The curve *dd'* is

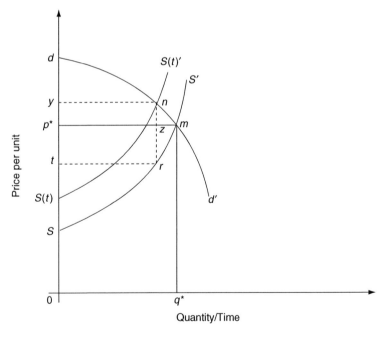

Figure 1.1   The analysis of consumer surplus

the market demand curve, obtained by summing all individual market demand curves. The *ss'* curve is the supply curve, obtained by summing all the individual supply curves, which in this case is equal to the sum of the marginal cost curves because of perfect competition. There is a market clearing at price *p** and quantity *q**. The consumer surplus is the area *p*dm* and the producer surplus is the area *p*sm*. The consumer surplus is the integral of the demand curve between the maximum price at *d* and the market price *p** at *m*:

$$CS = \int_{p^*}^{d} D(p)dp \tag{1.4}$$

Where *CS* is consumer surplus and *D(p)* is the demand curve, monotonic decreasing and single valued, and the integral is taken from *p** to *d*. Alternatively, the consumer surplus is the integral of the demand curve from the origin at 0 to *p** less what the consumers pay for the commodity, 0*p** multiplied by 0*q**, equal to the rectangle 0*p*mq**. The producer surplus is the rectangle 0*p*mq** less the integral of the supply curve from *s* to *p**:

$$PS = 0p^* mq^* - \int_{s}^{p^*} S(p)dp \tag{1.5}$$

Where *PS* is producer surplus, *S(p)* is the monotonic increasing, single-valued supply curve and the integral is taken from *s* to *p**. Suppose that the government introduces a unit tax of value *ty*. The supply curve would shift to *s(t)s(t)'*. The loss of consumer surplus would be the area of the curvilinear triangle *nzm* and the loss of producer surplus the curvilinear triangle *zmr*. These losses are called deadweight losses. The tax revenue is the tax per unit, *ty*, times the units taxed, *tr*, equal to the area of the rectangle *tynr*. The deadweight losses are commonly analyzed in the applications by means of linear demand and supply functions in which case the consumer surplus and producer surplus become triangles.

An important assumption of the first best is the absence of market power. Producers are price takers; that is, they accept the market price, having no power to influence it. This is not the case of a market with only one producer, a monopolist, which can restrict quantity to increase the price of its product. The output under monopoly is lower than that under perfect competition and the price under monopoly exceeds that of perfect competition. Figure1.2 shows the analysis of

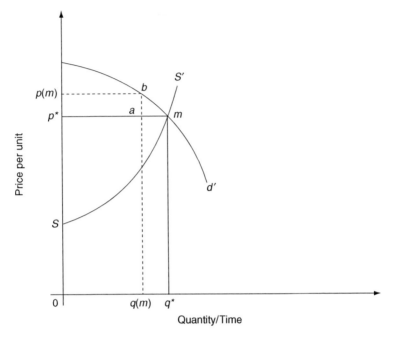

Figure 1.2 The analysis of monopoly

monopoly. The market clearing under perfect competition would occur at *m*, with price *p** and quantity *q**. The monopolist would set the price at *p(m)* with quantity *q(m)*. There is a deadweight loss measured by the curvilinear triangle *abm*. Tullock (1967) introduced the concept of the monopolist's rectangle, *p*abp(m)*, which is a measure of resource misallocation in seeking protection for the creation and maintenance of the monopoly, discussed below in a separate section on rent-seeking. Market power is another classic case for government intervention, which can consist of regulation, taxation, or direct state ownership.

There is natural monopoly, according to the technological definition, when a firm can produce a single homogeneous product at any level of output at lower cost than the combination of two or more firms (Joskow 2006, 8). Consider a market with demand function for a homogeneous product and price *p* (Ibid.):

$$Q = D(p) \tag{1.6}$$

There are k firms producing individual output of q_i for total output of

$$Q = \sum_{i}^{k} q_i \tag{1.7}$$

The cost function for each firm is identical, $C(q_i)$. There is a natural monopoly when (Ibid.)

$$C(Q) < C(q_1) + C(q_2) + \dots + C(q_k) \tag{1.8}$$

That is, there is less cost in producing the entire output Q with one firm than dividing production among several firms. Firms are subadditive at output Q when they have this property at that specific output Q. When firms have this property for the entire demand for the product $Q = D(p)$, they are globally subadditive. A necessary condition for the existence of a natural monopoly is that the cost of production of the good is subadditive at output Q (Ibid, 9).

There are economies of scale when the average cost declines throughout a range of output, say, from 0 to $q_i = Q$ (Ibid). The cost function is subadditive over this output range. Economies of scale are a sufficient condition for the technological concept of natural monopoly. Joskow (Ibid) illustrates the concepts with the firm having total cost function:

$$C_i = F + cq_i \tag{1.9}$$

And average cost:

$$\frac{C_i}{q_i} = \frac{F}{q_i} + c \tag{1.10}$$

Average cost is declining as output increases because of the term F/q_i. The average cost is higher than marginal cost:

$$\frac{F}{q_i} + c > \frac{dC_i}{dq_i} = c \tag{1.11}$$

Economies of scope occur when it is cheaper to produce two or more products in one firm than in two or more firms (Joskow 2006, 11–2). Consider the case of a firm producing two products, q_1 and q_2 with cost function $C(q_1, q_2)$. There are N vectors of two products $q^i = (q_1^i, q_2^i)$ with the property that $\Sigma q_1^i = q_1$ and $\Sigma q_2^i = q_2$. The condition for the cost function to be subadditive is for all N vectors of products (Ibid, 12):

$$C\left(\sum q_1^i, \sum q_2^i\right) = C\left(\sum q^i\right) < \sum C(q^i) \qquad (1.12)$$

This means that it is cheaper to produce both products in one firm than in multiple firms.

The existence of subadditive costs creates a case for government intervention to prevent suboptimal outcomes of more than one producer. The case for entry and price regulation on the basis of natural monopoly requires major economies of scale together with perpetuating sunk costs that constitute a significant part of total costs (Ibid, 27). The strongest case for regulation to ameliorate monopoly prices occurs in the presence of significant barriers to entry and if unregulated prices can be maintained by the monopolist well above marginal cost and average cost (Ibid, 37). The stronger the entry barriers and the more inelastic the demand for relevant products, the stronger the market power enjoyed by the monopoly.

Externalities

The divergence of private and social costs resulting from externalities considered by the classic bees example of Meade (1952) is explained by Bator (1958, 359–60) by means of a simple two-product model and only a labor input, L. The output of apples, A, depends only on the use of labor, L_h, with production function:

$$A = A(L_h) \qquad (1.13)$$

But the output of honey, H, depends on its use of labor, L_h, and also on the output of apples, A:

$$H = H(L_h, A(L_a)) \qquad (1.14)$$

The constrained maximization of the product transformation function provides the familiar equality of value marginal product, the multiple of the price of honey, p_H, times the marginal physical product of labor in producing honey, $\partial H/\partial L_h$, to the remuneration of labor, w (Ibid, 359):

Value marginal product of labor in honey production
= $p_H(\partial H/\partial L_h) = w$ = labor remuneration.

The producer of honey adds an additional unit of labor up to the point where the value marginal product is just equal to the remuneration paid.

However, the profit-maximizing condition for A has two terms:

$$p_A = \frac{dA}{dL_a} + p_H \left(\frac{\partial H}{\partial A} \frac{dA}{dL_a} \right) = w \tag{1.15}$$

where p_A is the price of apples. In the case of apples, the profit-maximizing decision would not be efficient unless the effect of apples on honey is zero; that is, if $\partial H/\partial A = 0$. In the presence of the positive externality of apples on honey output, the use of labor in apple production, L_a, would be less than optimal (Ibid).

Under perfect competition, the marginal cost of the apple producer is (Bator 1958, 360)

$$MC_A = \frac{w}{dA / dL_a} \tag{1.16}$$

The marginal cost of the honey producer is

$$MC_H = \frac{w}{\partial H / \partial L_h} \tag{1.17}$$

The ratio of the marginal costs $(\partial H/\partial L_h)/(dA/dL_a)$ is equal to relative prices. However, the marginal rate of transformation under no intervention differs from relative prices (Ibid):

$$\frac{\partial H / \partial L_h}{dA / dL_a} = \frac{p_A}{p_H} + \frac{\partial H}{\partial A} \tag{1.18}$$

Bator concludes that equality of prices to marginal costs does not result in Pareto efficiency. Prices determined in free markets will diverge from social marginal cost. The result suggests Pigou (1932) taxes on negative externalities and subsidies on positive externalities. Cheung (1973) analyzes the system in Washington State in the United States showing that contracts between beekeepers and farmers have existed for very long periods. The externalities in the case of bees are not a relevant example because they are internalized through agreements among the parties without government intervention. Muth et al. (2003) analyze government intervention in honey.

Market failures

Regulation can be defined as using legal instruments to implement goals of social and economic policies (Hertog 1999, 223). The government alone has the power to coerce by using instruments that can be enforced with penalties, which can take many forms, such as fines, public dissemination, prison terms, court injunctions, and even the closing of business. Economic regulation can be of the structural form, to regulate markets in the presence of market power, such as entry and exit rules and licensing (Ibid, 224). Conduct regulation restricts market behavior with measures such as price controls, minimum quality standards, and others. Social regulation is oriented toward protection of the environment, labor, and consumers with measures such as safety regulations (OSHA), disclosure of product content (fats and cholesterol), control of substances (DEA), and prohibitions of discrimination in employment and housing. There is a distinction between theories of positive and normative regulation. Positive theories intend to explain the economic need of regulation and its consequences while normative theories attempt to rank types of regulation by efficiency, according, for example, to their costs and benefits.

Public interest is defined as the optimum allocation of scarce resources to satisfy competing private and social ends, the definition of price theory (Robbins 1935) with the inclusion of the collective good. Under ideal conditions, free markets result in optimum allocation but this is not the case in practice because of different conditions than in the theory of perfect competition. The public interest view contends that government regulation can correct resource misallocation caused by imperfections such as market power, unbalanced and missing markets, and undesirable results. Collective action can be superior to individual action in enforcing contracts and ensuring property rights with lower transaction costs (Hertog 1999, 225). Table 1.1 classifies the types of market failures, the potential policies, and their intentions.

There has been criticism of the public interest view. The market can compensate itself for many of the alleged market failures. The theory is weak in that it is relatively simple to find unlimited number of market failures and very difficult to rank them for priority action (Hertog 1999, 231; Peltzman 1989). The theory of market failure assumes prohibitive transaction costs in the free market but zero costs by government regulation, which can be implemented with total efficiency. The existence of imperfections causes regulation to distort multiple markets in addition to those with imperfections. The correction of one or a few market failures, say, by setting prices equal to marginal costs, does not attain a second-best solution. The theory of second best postulates that once there is a distortion of the first best, the satisfaction of additional marginal conditions need not move the economy to a better outcome. The asymmetry of information appears to apply only to the private sector as if the government were omniscient and had command of all the

Table 1.1 Failures, policies, and consequences of public interest regulation

Failure	Policy	Intentions of Policy
Imperfect competition		
Price > Marginal Cost	Barriers to entry/exit	Fair price
Lower output	Anticollusion norms	Higher output
	Price regulation	
	State ownership	
Unbalanced market		
Excess capacity	Diminish number of	Stabilize output and
Price level < total costs	producers	employment
	Macro policies	
Information		
Missing information	Licensing	Consumer protection
Asymmetric	Self-regulation	Quality of products
information	Misleading rules	Financial/economic stability
Adverse selection	Advertising bans	Depositor and shareholder
Moral hazard		protection
Prudential supervision		
Prudential regulation		
External effects		
MSC > MPC	Pigou taxes and	Lower output of negative
Excess output	subsidies	externality
MSB > MPV	Safety regulation	Higher output of positive
Insufficient output		externality
Public goods		
Not produced	Collective provision	Higher economic efficiency
Free-rider problems		
Undesirable results		
Unequal distribution	Minimum wages	Social efficiency

Source: Hertog (1999).

information required to ameliorate the effects of missing markets or asymmetric information and effectively enforce the rules.

There is a more sophisticated version of the public interest view that does not assume perfect foresight and effectiveness by the government (Hertog 1999, 235). Regulation could still attain more efficient outcomes than the private sector or private negotiation by economic agents. The government could obtain information less expensively and more effectively through coercion, such as in banking supervision and in data banks on car accidents. The revised theory still assumes that market failures exist and that the government can ameliorate them more effectively than private contracting. Regulation would still be the efficient solution for market failures.

The private interest view

The possibility of government failure, considered in the first subsection, could restrict collective action to improve social welfare. Economic analysis is used in the private interest view by considering the factors that determine demand and supply of government intervention or regulation. Optimization of self-interest by politicians and regulators provides alternative analysis of collective action.

Government failure

The correction of market failures by designing policies that attain efficient allocation appears quite difficult. Once the economy is in the world of second best, policy design may be frustrating. The authorities would need perfect information; that is, the regulators must be omniscient and omnipotent, similar to the benevolent dictator of welfare economics. The possibility of government failure is actively debated in the technical and policy literature.

There may be a fallacy in the analysis of market failures. Pigou is careful in outlining the difficulties of determining in practice the measures to correct for externalities. Other writers may be excessively enthusiastic in comparing intervention by a government that never makes mistakes with a "blackboard" or textbook case of market failures. This is the "Nirvana Fallacy," comparing theoretical markets that have imperfections with flawless government intervention (Demsetz 1969). If the markets fail because of imperfect information, government intervention will also fail for the same reason. There is no superiority of information by the government in intervention. For example, there is no reason why government-owned banks would give fewer loans to defaulting companies than privately owned banks.

The process of diagnosis of market failures, the "double market failure test," analyzes the problems caused by the failure and nonmarket problems that may occur by the effort to ameliorate it (Zerbe and McCurdy 1999, 2000). That is, the policy analyst considers the problems and the consequences of actions to remedy them. The solution should cause the least possible interference with the market. The US determined by Executive Order 12866 in 1993 that federal officials conduct an economic analysis of proposals for regulation, assessing if the problem is a "significant market failure."

The costs required to transfer, establish, and maintain property rights are called transaction costs (Ibid). They consist of the costs of negotiation, contracts, lawsuits, and others. In practice, they are not zero. Trades would be undertaken if transaction costs were zero or less than the potential gains of trading. There is market failure when the trades do not occur. There is market failure when the value of the unpriced externality exceeds transaction costs. Transaction costs without evident price are ubiquitous, the same as externalities. Thus, there are large numbers of market failures. For example, if inefficient breach of contract is encouraged by law, it produces an externality. The concept of market failure can lead to almost unlimited intervention by the government. Transaction costs exist when there is nonmarket failure in the form of ineffective bureaucratic amelioration of market failure. However, nonmarket failure costs are not powerful in preventing government intervention.

A market failure occurs when market institutions do not allocate resources in such a way as to result in Pareto optimality. Government intervention requires assessing if the market is not allocating resources efficiently and if government intervention can improve on the performance of the market with benefits that exceed the costs of intervention (Winston 2006, 2). There is government failure when intervention was not required and in cases when a different form of intervention than the one followed would have been more efficient. Intervention should be altered when economic welfare is reduced or resources allocated in a way that is significantly different than the one suggested by the standard of efficiency. While theory can provide optimum policies to correct market failures, the evaluation of government failure requires solid empirical evidence. In the past century, the US government has intervened with antitrust policy and regulation to restrict market power and ameliorate imperfect information and externalities. The government has also provided or financed social services that could not be provided by the private sector.

Winston (2006, 14) researched the available empirical evidence in scholarly research and concluded that US policies did not increase consumer welfare in the case of monopolies, mergers, and collusion. The regulation of agriculture and international trade actually produced significant deadweight losses in transfers from consumers to producers. Scholarly research also shows that US markets are relatively competitive with deadweight losses of 1 percent of GDP, but without excluding distortions of price originating in regulation and trade protection. There is the counterfactual issue of whether the markets would have been more competitive had there not been antitrust and regulation efforts. The research results show that significant competition in the United States eroded monopolies, created difficulties for collusion, and resulted in mergers that increased efficiency or had no effects.

The cost of inefficiencies caused by the government in intervention to ameliorate market failures is in the hundreds of billions of dollars (Ibid, 73–4). In cases of actual existence of market failures, there were successes at the expense of diminishing significant benefits, and there were reductions of welfare in various instances. Government failures occur because policies are erroneous or ineffectively implemented, being subject to influence by interest groups against the general social interest. There are cases when there is evidence favoring government measures but politics and ineffectiveness of the relevant agencies prevent sound policy and implementation. Frustrated with the lobbying for regulation by certain types of business, Milton Friedman (1999) identified a suicidal impulse of parts of the business community.

The economic theory of regulation

This theory is the essence of the private interest view of regulation with predictions that are different than those of the public view. The public view predicts that regulation will occur in response to market failures. The excess profits charged by a monopolist or the externalities of pollution cause the government to intervene to find an efficient allocation that cannot be obtained in a free market. The private interest view claims that the regulated industrialists, politicians, and government officials interact to create regulatory agencies and measures to optimize their self-interests.

The state has a unique resource in its power to coerce (Stigler 1971, 4–5). Taxation permits the government to seize money. The state does not require the consent of individuals and companies to organize resources and take decisions of households and companies. Thus, an industry can capture the state to increase its profits. The industry may obtain four different types of favors from the government (Ibid, 4–6):

- Direct subsidy of money
- Restriction of entry in the industry by a rival
- Interference with substitutes and complements
- Price-fixing

The theory of economic regulation of Stigler integrates economic and political analysis (Peltzman 1989, 1). The departing proposition is that politicians are the same as other individuals in maximizing their own interests. Thus, interest groups can provide financial support to politicians or regulators to influence the nature of regulation.

In Stigler's formalization of the economics of regulation, the objective function for maximization includes attaining and maintaining power (Ibid, 6–7). The representative politician has the power of deciding the variables in regulation such as prices, number of firms, and others. Votes and money are the two objects of choice in the utility function of politicians. Groups may vote for or against the representative politician depending on the effects of a regulatory measure. The politician prefers decisions that result in favorable votes because his or her goal is obtaining and maintaining power. There are multiple forms by which regulatory decisions can secure campaign funding, free efforts to get out the vote, bribes, or well-remunerated political appointments.

The representative politician values wealth and knows that the successful election bid requires campaigns that have financing and qualified staff. Thus, the politician will focus on the consequences of regulatory measures for obtaining votes as well as money for electoral purposes. The essence of Stigler's theory is that the representative politician does not maximize the welfare of the constituency but rather his or her very own. Optimization of aggregate welfare is important only in increasing the economy to obtain a larger share of its growth. In short, the politicians and regulators exchange regulatory measures for votes and money. The delivery of the benefits requires some form of group organization.

There are two restraints or costs in Stigler's theory: costs of organization and information (Peltzman 1989, 7–8). The group acquiring the regulation must deliver the required campaign resources and voters must have the information. The existence of these costs suggests how the benefits of regulation are acquired by the producers. In a market with potential for regulation, the number of buyers is typically large while the number of sellers is small. In the extreme, there is only one producer in a natural monopoly and millions of consumers. The process of organization and its costs will be typically high for many consumers. It is also more difficult to organize collective action of many consumers because of the possibility of free riding: many will not pay the costs hoping that they will obtain the benefits for free because others will pay their part (Olson 1965).

The target of regulation is one or a few producers operating in monopolistic or oligopolistic markets. These producers do not have to create costly organizations to raise the funds required to bid for the regulatory measures because they are individually, financially strong. The producers will likely win the bidding for regulatory measures because of the strength of their financial position and the ease of organization. Regulatory capture is more likely by producers than by consumers. Regulatory measures will be designed to maximize the self-interest of the producers, politicians, and regulators instead of the welfare of society. Regulators force producers to subsidize certain consumers with rents created by regulation. Regulation not only creates a cartel of surface transportation for railroads but also imposes the continuance of passenger service at high losses for the companies (Peltzman 1989, 9).

The contribution of Stigler (1971) is labeled as the economic theory of regulation by Posner (1974, 343) to distinguish it from earlier theories of capture of regulation. The distinguishing characteristic is the formal consideration of demand and supply of regulation. Its link with the earlier capture theories of political science is that economic regulation is designed to promote the interests of groups with effective political pressure.

The critical concept in Peltzman (1976, 211, 1989, 10) is that the regulatory body is not captured by a single economic interest. The maximization of utility by the politician derives from the typical marginal conditions of price theory, allocating benefits across groups. There need not be pure producer protection if consumers can provide votes or money. In other words, the politicians allocate favors among groups of consumers and producers so as to maximize their utility.

The politician in the Peltzman (1976, 222) model maximizes majority or power, M, defined as (Bó 2006, 206):

$$M = M(p, \pi) = M(p, c(q)) \tag{1.19}$$

In this equation, p is the price paid by consumers, π the profits, c production costs, and q output. The increase in prices paid by consumers tends to decrease the popularity of the politician; the first derivative of function M with respect to price p is negative, $M_p < 0$. An increase in profits tends to increase the capacity of producers to mobilize resources or votes favoring the politicians, such that $M_\pi > 0$. Peltzman (1989, 10–1, 1976, 222) emphasizes diminishing returns, such that $M_{pp} < 0$ and $M_{\pi\pi} < 0$ (Bó 2006, 206). There are also no cross-effects of prices and profits, such that $M_{p\pi} = 0$. Profits can increase with costs, such that $f_p \geq 0$, at a decreasing rate, $f_{pp} < 0$, and profits decrease with costs, $f_c < 0$. In accordance with standard utility analysis, the politician maximizes power, $M (p, \pi)$, subject to the constraint $\pi = f(p, c)$, or maximizes L

with respect to p, π and λ (Peltzman (1976, 222), where λ is the Lagrange multiplier:

$$L = M(p, \pi) + \lambda(\pi - f(p,c(q))) \tag{1.20}$$

The first-order condition is (Peltzman 1976, 222; Bó 2006, 206)

$$M_p + M_\pi \frac{df}{dq} = 0 \quad \text{or} \tag{1.21}$$

$$M_p = -M_\pi \frac{df}{dq} \tag{1.22}$$

The interpretation of the first-order conditions is as follows (Bó 2006, 206). At a relatively high price under monopolistic conditions, the regulator/politician will decrease the price in an effort to obtain votes from consumers. In accordance with neoclassical economics, the regulator/politician will continue to lower prices until the marginal gain in votes or power is equal to the marginal loss of power resulting from dissatisfying producers. The increase in prices from a competitive equilibrium would occur until the gain in benefits to industry is equal to the marginal loss of votes of consumers. In this model, the price of the politician/regulator would be somewhere in the middle of pure monopoly price and perfectly competitive price.

In the economic approach to political behavior of Becker (1983, 372), the competition among pressure groups to obtain political influence determines the equilibrium value of taxes, subsidies, and other benefits. Expenditures of time and money increase political influence by exerting political pressure. In equilibrium, there is maximization of the income of all groups by optimal spending on political pressure constrained by expenditure productivity and the behavior of other groups. Each group maximizes the income of its members under the Cournot-Nash assumption that the increase of political pressure by one group does not affect the expenditures of other groups. There is a critical political budget equation of the amounts paid in taxes and received in subsidies:

$$n_s G(R_s) = S = n_t F(R_t) \tag{1.23}$$

in which n_s is the number of members receiving subsidies, n_t is the number of members levied by taxes, R_s is redistribution to each s, R_t is redistribution away from each t, F is the function of the revenue of a tax on R_t and G is the cost of providing R_s. An important feature of Becker

(Ibid, 374–5) is that *F* includes the deadweight costs of taxes in affecting hours worked, investment, and others. *G* includes the deadweight costs resulting from distortions of subsidies on hours worked, investment, and others. The determinants of political equilibrium in the Becker model are as follows: the effectiveness of each group in exerting pressure, the impact of additional pressure on their influence, the number of members in each group, and the deadweight costs of taxes and subsidies.

The model of Becker (Ibid, 373) explicitly considers the impact on the competition for influence of the distortions caused by taxes and subsidies, known as deadweight costs. The taxed groups are stimulated to lower taxes by deadweight costs while the subsidized groups are discouraged from raising subsidies. The model can also explain traditional government intervention because of market failures without the concepts of social welfare functions and benevolent planners. The competition among pressure groups explains government measures that increase efficiency, such as public goods and taxes on pollution, because the groups that benefit from measures that increase efficiency have advantage over those adversely affected by the measures.

The critical variables in the Becker model are deadweight costs of taxes and subsidies that affect the allocation of time between work and leisure, investment, consumption, and other behavior. The deadweight costs typically increase at an increasing rate in response to increases in taxes and subsidies. Pressure by the subsidized group is discouraged after an increase in deadweight costs because tax revenue provides a lower subsidy. However, pressure by the taxed group is encouraged after the increase in the deadweight cost of taxes because tax reduction has a lower effect on the revenue available for subsidy. The conclusions of Becker (Ibid, 395) emphasize intrinsic advantage in competing for influence. Subsidized groups try to compensate their intrinsic disadvantage by efficiency, optimal size, or smooth access to political influence. The pressure of taxpayers diminishes if deadweight costs to taxed groups decline with the decrease of the tax per person resulting from an increase in the number of taxpayers. Groups that are small relative to taxpayers have an advantage in obtaining subsidies. This is the case of farmers in rich countries and urban dwellers in poor countries.

The second best

The second best is defined by Lipsey (2007) as any situation in which the first best cannot be attained. There are assumptions in the two fundamental welfare theorems. When these assumptions are violated, the

Walrasian allocation is not efficient and it is not possible with lump-sum redistributions to convert any Walrasian allocation to an optimum Pareto allocation. The violation of an assumption is now commonly called a "market failure." Earlier literature referred to the violations as distortions. Lipsey and Lancaster (1956) and Lipsey (2007) refer to them as "sources of divergence," abbreviated to sources. Consider the older use of distortion. The second-best optimum for a given distortion is defined by Lipsey and Lancaster and Lipsey as "the setting of that source [distortion] that maximizes the value of the objective function, given settings on all the other existing sources [distortions]"(Lipsey 2007, 352). The general theory of second best proposes that distortions are ubiquitous such that it is almost always impossible to attain the first best. The irremovable distortion in the theory stands for the significant number of distortions that makes the first best unattainable.

Distortions can be created by private agents or by the state and can also occur exogenously (Ibid, 353). Some proposals for intervention claim that exogenous distortions are part of the state of nature and that the role of the government is to remove them to move the economy to the Pareto optimum. An example by Lipsey (Ibid, 353–4) is that private agents remain rationally ignorant when the cost of acquiring information exceeds the value to the agent. The state could acquire the information at an average cost lower than those of agents and provide it to the agents if the costs to the state are lower. Examples such as this one show that not all distortions are created by policy, a proposition by some authors to justify restoring first best conditions by means of piecemeal policy. Lipsey (Ibid) lists numerous static distortions that would make the first best unattainable: uncompetitive market structures, differentiated products, location in space of lumpy firms, non-auction labor markets, incomplete and asymmetric information, positive and negative externalities, missing markets, and utility functions in which there are arguments of the consumption of others. This is not an exhaustive list. A dynamic distortion arises out of endogenous technological change that is characterized by uncertainty in the sense of Knight (1921), which consists of the lack of a probability distribution that permits the estimation of expected returns from investment in research and development (Lipsey 2007, 355).

Ubiquitous distortions led Lipsey (Ibid) to conclude that economics does not have a GE model without institutions and the combination of perfectly free markets that depicts a modern industrialized economy. There are no theoretical arguments or empirical evidence suggesting that such economies are statically efficient. The proposition that the government can improve on the existing allocation is a judgment.

There is no model incorporating the distortions. Lipsey (Ibid) argues that it is not possible to define resource allocation once endogenous technological change is assumed because its expected returns cannot be calculated in the absence of probability distributions. Thus, in practice, there is no knowledge of the necessary and sufficient conditions for efficient allocation of resources. The calculation of the second best may be more difficult than that of the first best because there is no GE model that incorporates some or all of the distortions. Thus, it is unfeasible to calculate the second-best optimum allocation for a distortion that can be changed by policy (Ibid, 356). The removal of a distortion directly by policy improves welfare only in the abstract model of a state of nature with only one distortion. For example, price and entry regulation of a natural monopoly may increase output toward that of perfect competition while also increasing pollution, soiling even more the laundry of the classical example of negative externality.

A major conclusion of Lipsey (Ibid, 358) is that general policy rules for piecemeal policy improvements are not feasible in a world of second best full of distortions. There are three types of objections to piecemeal policy improvements raised by Lipsey (Ibid, 359). Type I objections refer to proposals in which only one distortion is considered, as for example taxes, and only two items in this distortion, one item assumed and another item that policy can change. The results of policy may be significantly altered in models incorporating more than one source and more items. Type II objections refer to the reliance in proposals of unrealistic assumptions that do not provide guidance for practical policy. The policy proposals based on market failures of the first-best model are as unrealistic as the assumptions of the first best. Type III objections refer to the exclusion of the effects of technology, which Lipsey (Ibid) considers a major problem because small induced changes in the growth rate can have major cumulative effects on GDP.

The conclusion by Lipsey (Ibid, 361) is that economists analyze policy with models that omit distortions that can alter results significantly. The acceptance that piecemeal models can improve on existing allocations depends on judgments on the validity of those models. Lipsey (Ibid) encourages the use in policy of formal models (derived from mathematically checked logic), "appreciative theorizing" (rigorously derived verbal arguments), relevant evidence, and unavoidable judgments. The applications must be relevant to the context and narrower than considering the welfare of the entire society. It is possible that canned advice based on first base theory could cause more harm than the alleged distortions it intends to ameliorate.

Applied welfare economics

The recommendation of Lipsey (2007) is that there is value in applied welfare economics, or what is called project evaluation or cost-benefit analysis. Harberger (1971, 785) proposed three basic postulates for applied welfare economics. The value of a unit of a good for a demander should be measured by the competitive demand price. The value of a unit for a supplier should be measured by the competitive supply price. The costs and benefits of a group, such as a nation, should be added in the evaluation of projects, programs, or policies without considering who receives the benefits.

The postulates relate to a contested issue in economics about the use of consumer surplus in the measurement of welfare. Critics argue that consumer surplus (1) requires the assumption of constant marginal utility of real income; (2) does not consider the distribution of income; (3) allows only for small changes in variables; (4) ignores changes in income distribution; and (5) is surpassed by more rigorous revealed preference analysis. However, Harberger proposed that consensus on the three postulates would further the interests of applied welfare economics.

The postulates are, according to Harberger (1971, 795), simple, robust, and inherited from a long tradition in economics. Their simplicity is in the use of basic economic analysis and the availability of required data. The robustness originates in the ability to define a full optimum. It is possible to introduce taxes and subsidies to ameliorate distortions such as monopoly and pollution. The analysis incorporates the excess of marginal social benefit over marginal social cost per unit of economic activity and the effects of changes in policy variables such as taxes and subsidies. Most distortions found in practice can be analyzed.

Harberger argues that the practical usefulness of economic advice does not originate in a desire for elegant economic optimum analysis. The economist, according to Harberger (Ibid), "is more likely to be asked which of two alternative agricultural programs is better, or what resource-allocation costs a given tax increase involves, or whether a certain bridge is worth its cost. And to be relevant, his answer must recognize the existence of many distortions in the economy, over whose presence neither he nor his client have control." Typically, the practical question involves ranking alternatives in terms of their potential damage and benefits. Harberger argues that the three postulates provide solutions equivalent to more elegant optimization exercises.

Harberger and Jenkins (2002) summarize the state of the art in applied welfare economics as follows. The three principles of Harberger (1971) are accepted. The demand price is a measure of the benefit while the supply price is a measure of the cost. Efficiency considerations dictate that it does not pay to engage in activities where supply price (extra cost) exceeds demand price (extra benefit). Similarly, it pays to expand into activities where extra benefit (demand price) exceeds extra cost (supply price).

Distortions introduce a wedge in costs and benefits, as argued by Harberger and Jenkins (2002). Taxes constitute the most common case. Consider that p^d is the demand price gross of tax, p^s is the supply price net of tax, the tax per unit is 10 percent and ΔC is the increase of the service as a result of the project. The net gain (benefit less cost) of the project is $p^d 1.1\Delta C$ less $p^s \Delta C$ equal to $.1 p^s \Delta C$, as p^d equals p^s. That is, when quantity increases with a tax, there is a welfare benefit equal to $.1 p^s \Delta C$, and there is a loss if there is a decrease in quantity. A subsidy to production has the opposite effect: there is a loss if quantity increases, an added cost, and a gain if quantity decreases, a cost reduction. Table 1.2 summarizes the effects of taxes and subsidies.

Define D_i as equal to p_i^d less p_i^s, which is positive for a tax and negative for a subsidy, and maintain the change in quantity as ΔX_i. The general expression of Harberger and Jenkins (2002) for external effects is $\Sigma_i D_i \Delta X_i$ with the sum over all i. In the case of no distortions in a competitive efficient allocation, the sum of external effects is zero because the D_i are all zero. The expression also simplifies evaluation, concentrating on existing distortions and not in all economic activities, to compute the overall effect of distortions.

The analysis of applied welfare economics uses the concept of sourcing (Harberger and Jenkins 2002). An increase in demand for a good eventually translates in the world market for the commodity. The source is world demand and supply: an increase in demand will reflect

Table 1.2   Effects of taxes and subsidies

External effect	Wedge	Change in quantity
Quantity increases		
$T_i \Delta X_i > 0$	$T_i = p_i^d - p_i^s > 0$	$\Delta X_i > 0$
$S_i \Delta X_i \Delta < 0$	$S_i = p_i^s - p_i^d < 0$	$\Delta X_i > 0$
Quantity decreases		
$T_i \Delta X_i < 0$	$T_i = p_i^d - p_i^s > 0$	$\Delta X_i < 0$
$S_i \Delta X_i > 0$	$S_i = p_i^s - p_i^d < 0$	$\Delta X_i < 0$

Source: Harberger and Jenkins (2002).

in increased supply from producers, in reduced demand by other consumers, or a combination of both.

Suppose there is an economic project in which part of the purchases are from demanders and must be valued at the gross or tax including price and another part is from newly generated supply that must be valued at the net of tax supply price. It is possible to derive the following formula (Ibid):

$$p_j^d = p_j^m + f_1 T_j^d - f_2 T_j^s \tag{1.24}$$

The economic price for the *jth* good, p_j^d, is equal to the market price for the *jth* activity p_j^m, plus the adjustment upward for the tax on demanders, $f_1 T_j^d$ (where f_1 or sourcing coefficient is $-\eta/(\varepsilon - \eta)$, η is the negative price elasticity of demand and ε the positive price elasticity of supply and T_j^d the tax on demanders) less the downward adjustment for the tax on suppliers, $f_2 T_j^s$ (where f_2 is $\varepsilon/(\varepsilon - \eta)$ and T_j^s the tax on suppliers). The explanation of the expression is that the new demand by the project generates a negative externality that displaces other demanders via the tax on demanders. The project stimulates new supply, generating a positive externality via the tax on suppliers. The expression merely states that the economic price of a good is the market price with adjustments by the weighted average of the sourcing coefficients.

A typical problem found in reality is a multiplicity of tariffs on imports and subsidies on exports. The approach allows the derivation of the opportunity cost of foreign exchange, E^*, as a weighted average of sourcing factors of the taxes on t_i, the taxes on the ith imports, and z_j, the subsidies on the jth imports (Ibid):

$$E^* = \sum_i f_i E_m (1 + t_i) + \sum_j f_j E_m (1 + z_j) \tag{1.25}$$

$E_m(1 + t_i)$ is the domestic currency price of a dollar of the ith import inclusive of the *ad valorem* import tax t_i, $E_m(1 + z_j)$ the domestic currency price of the jth export inclusive of the *ad valorem* export subsidy z_j, and the f_i and f_j are respectively the sourcing factors of displacing the ith import with tax t_i and stimulating the jth export with subsidy z_j. The weights f_i and f_j are fractions and must add to one. The expression can be simplified to (Ibid)

$$E^* = E_m (1 + \sum_i f_i t_i + \sum_j f_j z_j) \tag{1.26}$$

It expresses the opportunity cost of foreign exchange as the market exchange rate, E_m, adjusted by the weighted average of distortions in the form of import duties and export subsidies. There is, not without controversy, the expression for the opportunity cost of capital (Ibid):

$$\omega^* = \sum_i f_i \rho_i + \sum_j f_j r_j \tag{1.27}$$

The expression states that the opportunity cost of capital, ω^*, is equal to the weighted average of the marginal productivity of capital in the ith good, ρ_i, and the market rate of interest in the jth market, r_j, weighted by the appropriate sourcing factors, accounting for the payment of capital, f_i, and the loss of revenue to the government because of the displacement of investment, f_j.

Cost-benefit analysis consists of the set of methods allowing the ranking of options of policy by economic analysis on the basis of their benefits and costs (Boadway 2006, 1). In some cases, such as a water development project at the local level, partial equilibrium analysis may be sufficient. More complex GE models may be required when analyzing taxes, subsidies, and regulation that affect various markets. The concern is with the economic welfare of households. Political science may consider other important aspects.

Value judgments are kept to a bare minimum of three general principles. The preferences of a household determine its welfare. An increase of welfare is Pareto optimal in that the well-being of an individual increases without reducing that of another. There are no external concerns, such as freedom, nondiscrimination, and so on, other than the economic welfare of individuals in the ranking of alternative policies. There is the assumption of a social welfare function in the sense of Bergson (1938) and Samuelson (1947), in which welfare increases in all arguments. There are specific restrictions in the social welfare function and resulting complication for cost-benefit analysis (Boadway 2006, 2–6).

There is an expression for the welfare loss of a tax (Ibid, 7–8):

$$\Delta W = -R_d(consumer\ surplus\ loss) - R_s(producer\ surplus\ loss) \\ + R_g(increase\ in\ government\ revenue)$$

The imposition of a tax causes loss in consumer and producer surplus, measured as triangles in a model of linear demand and supply and a rectangle of gain in government revenue. The redistributive weights R_d, R_s and R_g represent the effects of redistribution of income caused by the tax. The shares of individuals in different income groups are represented by the demand R_d and supply R_s weights and the share of government in revenue collected from different income groups is represented by the weight for government R_g. The method can be applied to any type of change in policy.

The basic analysis of project evaluation consists of calculating the net present value of the project. Consider a project that begins in time period 0 and ends at T, where t is the index of time, B are the benefits, C the costs, and r the constant social discount rate (SDRT), then present value is obtained by the formula (Ibid, 10):

$$PV = \sum_{t=0}^{T} \frac{B_t - C_t}{(1+r)^t} \qquad (1.28)$$

It is possible to rank policies by their PV to make choices. A policy with positive present value is socially desirable. However, there is a difficult decision as to how positive a project should be. The variables are subject to estimation error, not only the costs and benefits but also the discount rate. This process is typical in private sector companies that are making capital budgeting decisions. There are situations in which there is a maximum capital budget and the present value calculations have to be used to work within the budget. Another complication is the extension of projects over multiple time periods, making comparisons more difficult. Standard practice consists of using current consumption as the measuring rod of costs and benefits. Shadow prices may be used for such things as the cost of labor when there are distortions, which is the typical case.

The calculation of present value requires adjustments for inflation. For purposes of simplification, assume a constant rate of inflation per period of π. The conversion of nominal to constant benefits and costs is obtained as follows (Ibid, 12):

$$b_t = \frac{B_t}{(1+\pi)^t} \text{ and } c_t = \frac{C_t}{(1+\pi)^t} \qquad (1.29)$$

The nominal interest rate, i, must follow:

$$(1 + i) = (1 + r)(1 + \pi) \qquad (1.30)$$

Thus, the net present value can be rewritten in real terms as

$$PV = \sum_{t=0}^{T} \frac{b_t - c_t}{(1 + i)^t} \tag{1.31}$$

Property rights

The neoclassical analysis of externalities did not include property rights and transaction costs. The *first case* considered by Coase (1960) is that of the pricing system working effectively *with liability for damage and without costs*. In this case, the damaging business has to pay for the cost of the damage and he explicitly assumes that there are no costs of transactions. The importance of the work of Coase is to incorporate these costs in the decision by firms, revealing their implications for allocation and public policy. The costs consist of almost everything that is not included in the costs of physical production and transportation. They include the costs of negotiation, legal counsel, litigation, and enforcement of judgments, among many. If there are no such costs, the party that is liable would bargain with the other party and enter into an agreement that would internalize the externalities. Thus, transaction costs are the expenses incurred in bargaining the effects of externalities or could be considered as the costs of internalizing the externalities. The discovery in this case of liability and no transactions costs is that if property rights are well-defined and there are no transaction costs, the perfectly competitive market would attain efficient allocation without need of government intervention. Coase does not claim that this case occurs in reality but simply uses it to place in relief the neglect of the costs by neoclassical economics and how they affect property rights and a solution to the problem. It is not a new theorem but rather the qualification of an important proposition of neoclassical economics.

The *second case* considered by Coase maintains the assumption of no transaction costs. However, in this case there is no rule of liability for damages. The pricing system has no liability for damage and no transaction costs. In this case, there may still be bargaining between the parties in the externality but a solution is uncertain. The competitive pricing system may or may not internalize the externalities.

Coase states that the assumption of no transaction costs is used in the first two cases but that he considers it to be very unrealistic. He proceeds to describe the types of transaction costs. These costs include discovering the party for the transaction, communicating the desire to bargain and the terms of bargaining, engaging in the negotiations to reach a settlement, drafting the contract, ascertaining by inspection that there is compliance with the terms of the contract, and many other transaction activities. Coase contends that these transaction costs are quite high in the real world. He argues that these costs could be sufficiently high such that they would preclude the transactions hypothesized in the model with no transaction costs. Coase argues that in cases of high costs the government may use its coercion powers to force a solution. However, he is careful to state that such a solution is not costless because the government also faces costs, which in some cases may be extremely high. The arrangements to find a solution may differ from case to case.

An interpretation of Coase, according to Glaeser and Shleifer (2003, 422), is that a market economy that is functioning adequately and has well-defined property rights needs only common law to solve the problems of social harm. Glaeser and Shleifer (Ibid) argue that the reasoning followed by Coase (1960) does not lead to the superiority of strict private litigation. Efficiency could be attained by multiple regimes: private litigation, regulation, a combination of private litigation and regulation, or no form of government intervention. Glaeser and Shleifer provide a model to analyze the desirability of alternative regimes and apply it to the analysis of the rise of the regulatory state in the United States in 1877–1917.

The new institutional economics

The work of Coase (1937) is credited with the beginning of the NIE (Coase 1998, 72). It originated in dissatisfaction with conventional or mainstream economics. The NIE argues that economists merely formalized the work of Adam Smith during 200 years after the publication of his book in 1776. While this is an exceptional achievement, the impressive theoretical development, according to the NIE, is lacking in factual support.

Economic welfare depends on the flows of goods and services and in turn on productivity. Adam Smith showed how productivity depended on specialization. Coase (Ibid, 73) contends that exchange makes specialization possible and that the productivity of the economic system is enhanced by lower costs of exchange, or transaction costs. These costs depend on institutions: the legal system, the political system, the social system, culture, education, and others. Economic performance is determined by institutions, which provide relevance and importance to the NIE.

Table 1.3   Stages of economic institutions

Stage	Institutional characteristics
I Embeddedness	Informal institutions, customs, traditions, norms, religion
II Institutional environment	Game rules: property (polity, judiciary, bureaucracy)
III Governance	Game play: contract, relating governance structures and transactions
IV Allocation/employment	Prices, quantities, incentives

Source: Williamson (2000).

There are two distinguishing characteristics in the NIE, the claims that institutions are important and that they can be analyzed by economic theory. Williamson (1985, 1994, 1998, 2000) considers that the second characteristic distinguishes the NIE from the initial US institutionalists. The focus is not on the traditional economic concerns of allocation but the use of economic tools to analyze how institutions developed the way they did.

Table 1.3 shows the stages of institutional development that require different forms of social analysis (Ibid, 596–8). Institutional research is concerned with the two intermediate stages: institutional environment and governance. The final stage is the subject of the theory of choice or mainstream economics.

The research on the economics of property rights focuses on the issues of the second stage of institutional environment. According to a strand of thought, proposed by Coase, the system of private enterprise needs property rights to function adequately. The user of a resource has to remunerate the owner. There must be definition of property rights and a process of arbitration of disputes for optimum allocation of resources.

An important characteristic of the NIE is the criticism of ideals based on omniscience, benevolence, nil transaction costs, and similar assumptions. The works of Coase and Demsetz challenged the proposition of omniscient and benevolent governments that could ameliorate all market failures. All forms of organization are subject to failures, including markets and the government.

An important characteristic of the work of Coase (1960) is the critique of the comparison of the actual world with idealized constructs, such as resource allocation in perfectly competitive models. Williamson (2002, 439) explores the public policy consequences of such comparison. The argument by Coase is that the concern with the ideal models led to the view that market failures are ubiquitous but that government failure never or seldom occurs. The important intellectual consequence is the abandonment of the truly important research agenda on the comparison of actual structures of organization with the recognition that all are flawed.

The analysis of Coase (1937) leads to the concept of the firm as a governance structure (Williamson 1998, 75). Governance and transactions are aligned in accordance with their economies of transaction costs, requiring descriptions of transactions, governance structure, and the process of economizing transaction costs. The fundamental transaction of transaction-cost economics is vertical integration. There are multiple consequences for policy arising from labor, capital, corporate governance, regulation/deregulation, multinational, and public sector transactions.

Asymmetry of information

The model of perfect competition requires perfect information. All agents have the same information on prices, technology, credit, and so on. Several economists writing after 1970, Akerlof (1970, 2003), Spence (1973, 2002), Stiglitz and Weiss (1981) and Stiglitz (2002), focus on incorporating in models asymmetry of information consisting of the assumption that some agents have information that others do not possess. These efforts prove that in case of imperfect information, the free market does not attain Pareto optimality on its own. Thus, there is the possibility that collective action may implement Pareto-improving policies.

There is a critique of the efficiency of competitive markets because of imperfect information (Stiglitz 1994). According to this view, the fundamental welfare theorems asserting that competitive markets are efficient do not provide any guidance on financial markets that produce, process, disseminate, and use imperfect information. There are conceivable forms to improve efficiency by means of government intervention in financial markets. Market failure originates in costly information. Information is more important in financial markets than in those of goods. According to Stiglitz, information is a public good. Thus, there is a role for government intervention to provide enough information that would not be provided under free financial markets.

There are seven market failures in the analysis of Stiglitz:

- *Monitoring.* The information on the soundness of a financial institution is valuable to investors and depositors, being a public good.

- *Monitoring externalities*. The selection and monitoring by a financial institution may encourage other lenders, causing a positive benefit. Similarly, unsound creditors may cause difficulties in the raising of capital, creating a negative externality.
- *Bankruptcy and insolvency*. There are externalities of financial problems. The failure of one or several institutions may cause credit problems for borrowers.
- *Missing and incomplete markets*. Adverse selection and moral hazard inhibit trade and efficiency.
- *Imperfect competition*. The imperfect nature of information causes imperfect competition in financial markets that significantly depend on information.
- *Pareto inefficiency*. Imperfect information causes Pareto inefficiency in financial markets because of the breakdown of the assumption that information is exogenously obtained.
- *Uninformed investors*. There may be improvements in markets if government requires greater disclosure of information needed by investors.

The modified capture theory

The extensions of the theory of capture with asymmetric information can include three actors: the politician (principal), the regulator, and the firm (agent). Bó (2006) surveys the available models. There is not yet sufficient evidence on regulatory capture. However, the redistributive consequences of capture could be significant when there is transfer of income from consumers to firms (Ibid, 226).

Industrial organization is defined by Laffont (1994, 507) as the study of the economics of the firm or industry when competition is not perfect. In this view, regulation is the normative public economics of industrial organization.

There has been dissatisfaction with cost of service regulation (COSR). Laffont (Ibid, 508–9) outlines the major criticism of COSR. There are several characteristic aspects of COSR. The regulator allows that prudent investors operate with a rate of return on investment above the market rate. Prices are equal to costs that include allocation for capital return. There is a regulatory lag period in which prices remain fixed until the regulator, consumers, or the firm initiate a new process of reviewing prices. This review constitutes a process of checks and balances in which the regulator arbitrates the desires of high prices by firms and of low prices by consumers.

There are several criticisms of COSR considered by Laffont (Ibid). Allocating fixed costs among products is quite difficult in practice, resulting in confusing prices. The equality of prices and average costs reduce the incentives to cost minimization. Similarly, there are no incentives for quality improvements. The cost and procrastination of the process have been also criticized. Laffont (Ibid, 509) finds that the lack of a clear normative framework is a major theoretical deficiency. However, he finds some advantages. The checks and balances of the COSR are more realistic than the assumption of a benevolent planner. The pricing method diminishes the possibility of bankruptcy of the firms. The capital formula creates a long-term commitment of the firm or industry.

An important objective of the theory of regulation, according to Laffont (Ibid, 510), is to incorporate the notion that regulators are limited by the lack of information on the regulated firms. The theory of regulation shifted with its reformulation as an agency problem with stress on the role of asymmetries of information and the use of incentive theory. The regulated firms are the agent and the state or regulatory authority is the principal. The canonical model of Laffont specifies the cost function of a natural monopoly in the form of a multiproduct firm:

$$C = C(\beta, e, q_1, ..., q_n) + e^* \tag{1.32}$$

The cost C is observable, q_k is the production level of good k with $k = 1, ..., n$, β is adverse selection or cost parameter known only by the firm, e is a moral hazard variable or nonobservable action of the firm and e^* is a random variable. The utility function consists of

$$S = S(\theta, s, q_1, ..., q_n) \tag{1.33}$$

Where θ is a parameter capturing private information of the firm or of consumers and s is the effort level of the firm or of consumers.

Finance, efficiency, and growth

Adam Smith referred to the role of finance in terms of a parable (Levine 1997, 701). Specialization was the driver of economic growth that Smith observed during the industrial revolution. The transition to specialization from a barter economy required a medium of exchange, provided by money. The early characterization of economic development was the movement away from the subsistence to the money economy, which is not far from the parable of Smith.

The parable of Levine (Ibid, 701–2) focuses on the need for the entrepreneur to escape the constraints of self-generating resources to obtain the appropriate risk, liquidity, intertemporal allocation, and volume of resources provided by financial markets and institutions. External financing is the key opportunity and function provided by financial markets that permit individuals and even large corporations to escape the constraints of self-generated capital. External finance requires financial markets and institutions and makes a significant difference in modern technologically and organizationally driven economic growth. Levine (Ibid) argues that the functions of financial intermediation cannot be considered in isolation, except for specific analysis, but rather must be taken together to identify how they promote the two channels of capital and technological accumulation (see Becsi and Wang 1997).

Property rights are defined by Levine (2005b, 62)] for purposes of analysis as a general combination of policies, legal and political systems, and informal norms that jointly define and protect private property. There is equal and fair application of the law to all members of society and there are limits to the interference of the government in private contracting. Levine (Ibid, 61) argues that the protection of property rights results from a balance of an active government defining and enforcing property rights, facilitating private contracting, and applying the law fairly to all with sufficient constraints that prevent government coercion and expropriation.

There are two currents of research on the origin of property rights surveyed by Levine. First, the law view argues that the traditions of the legal system shape property rights in early historical periods. Property rights are influenced by legal systems transplanted from England, France, Germany, and Scandinavia. French and English law systems are the more widely used. The French legal system originated in the Napoleonic codes designed to implant the will of the state in reaction to the corruption of judges. The English system crystallized during the Glorious Revolution at the turn of the seventeenth century that ended the confiscation by the Crown and protected property rights by the separation of powers, restricting expropriation by the state. North and Weingast (1989) analyze the external economies of protection of property rights of government creditors that led to development of banking because of similar protection of the rights of private creditors. Summerhill (2007a,b) finds that protection of rights of creditors in Brazil's Empire did not result in financial development. Cameron

(1961, 1967, 1972, 1992) shows how banks were critically important in the early stages of industrialization. There were early contributions by Gurley and Shaw (1955, 1960) and Goldsmith (1969).

The second school of thought considered by Levine (2005b) is the endowment view. The simultaneous occurrence of events in economic samples also prevents identification of clear causal relations in the origins of property rights. Critics of the law argue that other factors created economic growth and prosperity leading to the protection of property rights. Endowments of multiple types—geography, natural resources, indigenous populations, climate, and so on—determined the pattern of income distribution that was critical in influencing the type of protection of property rights. For example, income distribution was less concentrated, population larger, and property rights better protected in New England than in colonies in South America characterized by concentration of income in extractive activities, lower population, slavery, and resulting in poorer protection of property rights. The endowment view postulates that historical patterns of protection of property rights are self-propagating over centuries. The conclusion of Levine (Ibid) is that the two views, and multiple others, are not mutually exclusive. The difficulty in isolating cause and effects in samples of social variables prevents definitive conclusions.[1]

The large literature surveyed by Levine (2005a) supports the existence of a strong positive association between long-term economic growth and the functioning of the financial system. There are important qualifications of these results and conflicting views. However, Levine finds that the weight of the evidence supports the view that financial intermediaries are important in explaining growth even controlling for simultaneous bias. An important microeconomic result is the facilitating role of financial development on external finance. It is difficult to conclude from this vast literature that the financial system has a passive role in economic growth; that is, that financial development is simply triggered by economic growth, which is in fact determined by other factors.

There are theoretical models of endogenous growth that include the role of financial development (Bencivenga, Smith, and Starr 1995; Levine 1991). A sample of the literature on growth and finance is surveyed below.

The operational definition of financial development by King and Levine (1993, 718) is by means of the following indicators:

- *Traditional financial depth*: The overall size of the formal system of intermediation captured by the ratio of liquid liabilities to GDP.

- *Differentiation of financial institutions engaged in intermediation*: The importance in allocation of domestic credit by deposits banks relative to the central bank measured by the ratio of domestic assets of deposit banks to domestic assets of deposit banks plus the central bank.
- *Distribution of assets by the financial system*: Measured by (1) the ratio of credit to nonfinancial private firms to total credit (excluding credit to banks) and (2) the ratio of credit to nonfinancial private firms to GDP.

King and Levine (Ibid, 719–20) analyze the channel by which financial development influences growth in terms of two sources of growth:

- *The rate of physical capital accumulation*: Measured by two indicators, the per capita growth rate of physical capital and the ratio of investment to GDP.
- *Efficiency in social allocation of capital*: Measured as the growth residual by controlling for capital accumulation or total productivity growth.

King and Levine estimate the following regression on averaged data 1960–89 for 77 countries (Levine 2005a):

$$G_j = \alpha + \beta F_i + \gamma X + \varepsilon \tag{1.34}$$

where F_i is the value of the ith indicator of financial development averaged in 1960–89, G_j is the jth growth indicator averaged in 1960–89, and X is a matrix of conditioning information controlling for other factors related with economic growth.

Models of endogenous growth incorporate the analysis that more liquid stock markets increase the interest in investing in projects with long-term gestation because investors can recover their funds in case they need them before the projects mature (Bencivenga, Smith, and Starr 1995; Levine 1991). Liquid stock markets promote investment in long-term projects with higher returns, contributing to economic growth. Levine and Zervos (1998) analyze the empirical association between stock market development and economic growth, physical capital accumulation and productivity growth with a sample of 42 countries during 1976–93, controlling with many factors including banking development.

The results of Levine and Zervos suggest that there is a robust positive association of stock market and banking development with current and future rates of economic growth, capital accumulation, and productivity growth, even after controlling for many factors. There is consistency of the empirical results with the view that enhanced trading of productive technologies promotes efficient allocation of resources, physical capital accumulation, and faster economic growth (Levine and Zervos 1998, 554). Significant regression coefficients for both stock market and banking development indicate that the services provided by banks differ from those furnished by stock markets. Theory can further develop the idea that banks and stock markets originate and develop simultaneously, providing different types of financial services.

The results of King and Levine (1993) suggest strong, positive association between the financial development indicators and the growth indicators with economically large coefficients. They examine the possibility that finance merely follows growth by examining if financial depth predicts the indicators of economic growth, physical capital accumulation, and productivity. The regressions show that financial depth in 1960 is a good predictor over the following 30 years of the growth indicators after controlling for various factors. In addition, there is an economically large relation between initial financial development and growth.

The work of Schumpeter (1911 [1934]) emphasizes the critical role of banks in allocating savings to the most productive economic activities (Beck, Levine, and Loayza 2000). Banks influence economic development by allocating savings but not necessarily by changing the rate of savings. The hypothesis of Beck, Levine and Loayza is that the analysis of Schumpeter (1911 [1934]) postulates that banks influence growth of productivity and technological change. Schumpeter analyzed long periods of displacement of the equilibrium of the perfectly competitive model by waves of innovation. Banks financed the early stages of industrialization (Cameron 1967, 1972). A competing hypothesis considered by Beck, Levine, and Loayza is that the role of banks consists of raising domestic savings rates and attracting foreign capital. In addition, Beck, Levine, and Loayza attempt to determine empirically if the level of development of banking could help to explain cross-country differences in total factor productivity. The specific subject of empirical inquiry is whether the level of development of banking has an impact on private savings rates and on growth of real per capita GDP, capital per capita, and productivity per capita. The essence of the inquiry is to explore the Schumpeter view by analyzing the channels through which banks affect economic growth. The strategy consists of determining the effects of banks on capital accumulation, private savings rates, and productivity growth to follow these effects on growth of per capita GDP.

Beck, Levine, and Loayza use two econometric techniques designed to control the simultaneous bias arising from the joint determination of banking sector development, on the one side, and capital accumulation, total factor productivity growth, and private savings rates, on the other. In the first technique, they use a cross-sectional instrumental variable estimator, averaging data for 63 countries in 1960–95. The dependent variables used are growth of real per capita GDP, growth of productivity, and private savings rates. The independent variables in the regressions are banking sector development and a set of variables designed to control for other determinants of economic development. Legal origin is used as an instrumental variable with the objective of extracting the exogenous component of banking sector development. The second technique also eliminates simultaneous bias originating in effects of individual countries. The dataset is a panel with data averaged in each of the five-year periods during 1960–95. The econometric method permits consistent and efficient estimates of the effects of banking development on productivity and savings factors of growth. Beck, Levine, and Loayza conclude that banks have a strong determining positive influence on growth of GDP per capita and on growth of productivity. The results support the view of Schumpeter that the level of banking development has an important role in determining the rate of economic growth through effects on productivity growth and technological change. There are no equivalently strong conclusions on the effects of growth of capital per capita and changes in the savings rate.

The objective of Demirgüç-Kunt and Maksimovic is to probe whether the lack of development of legal and financial systems restricts firms in their investments in opportunities that potentially promote profitable growth. They develop a financial planning model of the firm with three assumptions: constant ratio of assets to sales, constant profit rate per unit of sales, and equality of economic depreciation rate to that reported in financial statements. The external financing needs, EFN_t, of a firm growing at g_t percent in year t are given by two components (Demirgüç-Kunt and Maksimovic 1998):

$$EFN_t = \text{required investment for a firm growing at } g_t$$
$$+ \text{ available internal capital for investment}$$
$$= g_t{}^*Assets_t - (1 + g_t)^*Earnings_t{}^*b_t \tag{1.35}$$

The internally financed growth rate, IG, is obtained by equating equation (1.35) to zero, solving for g_t and denoting by ROA the firms' ratio of earnings after taxes and interest to assets, or return on assets (Ibid):

$$IG_t = \frac{(ROA_t * b_t)}{(1 - ROA_t * b_t)} \qquad (1.36)$$

Because IG_t is convex and increasing with the returns on assets of the firm, higher growth rates can be financed internally by more profitable firms.

The maximum short-term growth rate, *SFG*, is the maximum rate of growth of a firm reinvesting all earnings and borrowing sufficient short-term resources to maintain unaltered the ratio of short-term borrowing to assets (Ibid). According to this definition, the firm does not issue equity or borrow long term to finance growth. The maximum short-term growth rate is given by (Ibid)

$$SFG_t = \frac{ROLTC_t}{(1 - ROLTC_t)} \qquad (1.37)$$

The variable $ROLTC_t$ denotes the ratio of earnings after tax and interest to long-term capital.

Using the above model for a sample of 30 countries, Demirgüç-Kunt and Maksimovic find that active stock markets and developed legal systems are important factors facilitating growth of firms. Firms in countries with compliance with legal norms and active stock markets can obtain external funds, not generated internally, to grow faster. The conclusion is that economic growth is facilitated by development of financial markets and institutions.

There are conflicting theoretical predictions on the relationship of regulation, concentration, institutions, and bank efficiency (Demirgüç-Kunt, Laeven, and Levine 2004, 594). The view of concentration claims that restrictions to competition and monopolistic power result in a few banks with adverse effects on efficiency. The view of the efficient structure proposes that more efficient banks gain market share because they have lower costs. The institutional view claims that powerful elites influence regulation to restrict competition and enjoy resulting rents. Demirgüç-Kunt, Laeven, and Levine analyze the relationship of regulation, market structure, and institutions with information on 1400 banks in 72 countries. They define the costs of intermediation of banks by two measures: the net interest margin or the ratio of net interest income less interest expenses to interest bearing assets and overhead expenditures or the ratio of bank overhead costs to total assets. The regression equations are of the following type (Ibid, 598):

$$Net\ Interest\ Margin_{i,k} = \alpha + \beta_1 C_i + \beta_2 B_{i,k} + \beta_3 R_i + \beta_4 M_i + \beta_5 I_i + \varepsilon_{i,k}$$
(1.38)

where i is the index for countries, k the index for banks, C_i is a measure of concentration of banks in country i, $B_{i,k}$ a vector of characteristics specific to bank k in country i, R_i a vector of regulatory restrictions on banks, M_i a vector of macroeconomic and financial system control variables, I_i a vector of indicators of institutional development, and $\varepsilon_{i,k}$ the residual.

There are two revealing conclusions by Demirgüç-Kunt, Laeven, and Levine (2004, 618–9). First, bank regulations are significant in explaining the cost of financial intermediation. Various types of bank regulation, such as restrictions of entry, regulation of bank activity, and interference with the conduct of banking business, increase net interest margin. Second, it is not possible to consider bank regulation in isolation from broad institutional factors. The regulation of banks is conditioned by broader national institutions related to protection of property rights and the freedom of competition in economic activities.

Summary

There is no general theory of the state in economics that would provide concrete principles on the need and effectiveness of intervention in economic affairs. There are multiple approaches. The appeal to data, as common in economics, does not provide a definitive conclusion. There is significant consensus that financial development is important in static efficiency, or optimum resource allocation, but less generalized agreement on the role of finance in economic growth.

2
Functions and Regulation of Deposit Banks

Introduction

This chapter provides the analysis of the functions of deposit banks and two important types of regulation on required capital and deposit insurance. There is a preliminary section on the arguments in favor and against regulation. Chapter 3 covers the remaining types of regulation of deposit banks, which are market power and prudential supervision.

Regulation

This section provides general issues regarding regulation of financial institutions: whether regulation should be there or not. Financial guarantees are rich in explaining the types of regulation.

Financial guarantees are ubiquitous in the real world and their analysis is critical to understanding financial regulation (Merton and Bodie 1992). There are financial guarantees in loans and other debt-related contracts. Commercial banks, insurance companies, brokers, clearing agencies of exchanges, and many other financial intermediaries provide guarantees. States and the federal government also provide financial guarantees. The federal government has provided deposit insurance since the 1930s. The government sponsored enterprises (GSE), Fannie Mae and Freddie Mac, under conservatorship after 2008, provide guarantees on mortgages and mortgage-backed securities. The federal government has also provided guarantees on student loans. Sometimes guarantees are explicit; there are also implicit guarantees such as that of the parent company on the bonds issued by a subsidiary. The too-big-to-fail doctrine of the US Federal Reserve System (FRS) is an implicit guarantee that an institution with risk of affecting the entire financial system, having potential secondary effects on production and employment, will be rescued by the monetary authorities.

There is an implicit guarantee in the issue of every loan as shown by the following identity, valid in functional and valuation meaning (Ibid, 88):

$$L^{Risky} + G_L = L^{Default\ free} \tag{2.1}$$
$$L^{Risky} = L^{Default\ free} - G_L \tag{2.2}$$

where L^{Risky} is the loan with risk, $L^{Default\ free}$ the default-free loan, and G_L the loan guarantee. The lender of dollar-denominated loans to any other party than the US government, which issues the money in repayment of its obligations, implicitly sells loan guarantees. Lending consists of two distinct activities: default-free lending and risk-bearing of default by the lender.

There are three ways in which a financial intermediary can insure against default the customers that are holding its liabilities (Ibid, 90). First, investors can provide the intermediary with insurance capital by acquiring its equity or subordinated debt. Ratios of total capital of banks to assets, including regulatory capital requirements by the Basel Committee on Banking Supervision (BCBS), constitute an example of regulation providing guarantees of the liabilities of financial intermediaries such as deposits. Second, a third party may provide the guarantee. This private sector guarantor would work best when the risk insured by the guarantee can be diversified, such as mortality risk in insurance companies, or hedges in capital markets, such as hedging FX, equity, or interest rate risks. Insurance of municipal bonds by bond insurers and swap guarantees constitute an example of private sector guarantees. Third, the liabilities of the intermediary to its customers can be guaranteed by the government. This third form applies when the risks are not diversifiable or hedged in capital markets. This is the case of supervision by central banks to control bank runs with lender of last resort (LOLR) functions, open market operations, and other instruments.

Guarantors make profits by mixing adequate premiums while controlling operating costs and losses from shortfalls (Ibid, 91). Suppose for simplicity no administrative costs, if $V > E$, where V is the value of collateral assets and E the promised payment, the guarantor earns the premium without making any payments. However, the guarantor must pay $E - V$, or shortfall, when $V < E$. Denoting the premium by P and the interest rate for investment of the premium by r, the profit function of the guarantor is (Ibid)

$$P(1 + r) - \max[0, E - V] \qquad (2.3)$$

The expected profit of the guarantor, π^e, is the premium plus interest less the shortfall times the probability of shortfall, θ (Ibid):

$$\pi^e = P(1 + r) - \theta(E - V) \qquad (2.4)$$

There are three forms by which guarantors manage their portfolios of guarantees (Ibid, 91–100). First, the guarantor monitors the insured institution. For example, the broker marks to market (MTM) frequently the position of the customer borrowing on margin. This is an ideal case because the broker has control of the position and can seize it and sell it, obtaining the funds to repay the broker's lender. In addition, the broker can call more margin value, which is equivalent to increasing capital of the insured bank in the case of bank capital requirements. Second, the guarantor can force the insured institution to restrict the assets it holds. For example, the Basel capital requirements require measurements of credit and market risk and effective processes for their control to preserve capital and soundness of financial institutions. Third, the guarantor can impose risk-based premiums. For example, there are proposals for measuring deposit insurance premium by the Federal Deposit Insurance Corporation (FDIC) by the individual risks of banks. There are hurdles in implementing this proposal because of the large number of banks and the imprecision of estimates of fair value of deposit insurance.

The banking industry has been heavily regulated by the federal government and states. This tight regulation was evident by the second half of the 1970s in the segmentation of various financial activities (Black, Miller, and Posner 1978, 379). Banks under federal regulation could not underwrite securities with the exception of certain municipal bonds, engage in affiliation with securities companies and firms underwriting insurance, and could not provide long-term mortgage loans except with significant restrictions. There were strict restrictions on branching within and across states; there were requirement of approval by regulatory authorities in cases where establishing a new branch or acquiring a bank was authorized. Bank holding companies (BHC) provided a vehicle for some flexibility. Offices of BHCs and their nonbanking subsidiaries could open offices where branches of banking subsidiaries could not be established because of limitations of branching in state statutes. BHCs increased competition and broadened the services provided to consumers.

The relations between lenders (banks) and borrowers (clients) provide meaningful analysis for banking regulation (Ibid, 385). Banks do not intend to influence the conduct of business by their clients but instead prevent borrowers from benefiting at the expense of the shareholders of the bank by channeling loan proceeds in the form of dividends, increasing the business risks, or pledging part of the assets to another lender. The bank monitors the client to prevent that it increases its value in the customer relation relative to that of the bank. The loan is originally evaluated before disbursement and subsequently monitored.

There are two widely used forms to diminish the administrative costs in lending (Ibid). First, banks try to maintain a significant value of the assets of the borrower in relation to the loan. The parallel measure in bank regulation is the concern with capital relative to risk-weighted assets. Second, low-risk collateral may be used in guarantee of service of the loan. The conflict of interest between the borrower and the lender leads the bank to restrict risky investments by the client, supervising the corporation's activities (Ibid, 402). The parallel measure in bank regulation is identifying, measuring, and controlling risks to ensure asset quality. An important approach is to assume that bank regulators protect the interest of the depositors who are viewed as lenders to the bank. Bank regulators can use methods similar to those that banks use in their relations with borrowers. The costs of supervision and the effectiveness of protection of depositors (creditors) of banks and mitigation of risks from BHCs can be enhanced by increasing bank capital requirements (Ibid). There is no parallel in bank/client relations for the macroeconomic risk of bank runs. The regulatory measure in preventing runs has consisted of insuring deposits.

The relations of a bank with a corporate borrower with affiliated firms can illustrate the regulation of BHCs (Ibid, 403). Typically, BHCs do not increase the risk to banks, which are likely more secure with BHC affiliation. The lender would change capital requirements in accordance with changes in the type of business of the affiliated company but would not restrict those businesses. Protection of depositors and the insurance fund with minimum cost suggests regulation of the BHC and its subsidiaries only to protect depositors from risk originating in the business of the corporation and affiliates. Black, Miller, and Posner (Ibid) reject the option of imposing capital requirements on the BHC. Capital requirements on the BHC would protect from risk originating in its nonbanking activities, reducing the likelihood that creditors of the BHC could seek assets of the bank. Adjustment of bank capital for these risks eliminates the need for capital requirements of the BHC. The focus of policy is on the activities of the BHC that can increase the risk of operations of the bank. The correct policy is to regulate the financial structure of the bank.

The approach of Black, Miller, and Posner is that BHCs by themselves do not necessarily increase the risks of bank affiliates. They provide a combination of two policies to ameliorate such a risk, if it were to exist at all. First, the FDIC could eliminate the ceiling on insured deposits; that is, all deposits irrespective of value of principal would be insured. Full insurance of deposits would eliminate the possibility of a run on banks because of failure of the BHC. There would be no loss to depositors because of the increasing risk of a bank originating in its BHC. There would still be risk to the FDIC of a bank's failure. The proposal of full insurance would be complementary to policies designed to reduce specific risks relating to the BHC structure. Second, the FDIC could have a structure of premiums increasing with the risks of the BHC to an affiliated bank.

There are practical limitations of required monitoring to measure risks and determine risk premiums of deposit insurance. Banks would have an incentive to control risks because of the lower risk premium of deposit insurance. Black, Miller, and Posner (1978, 407) argue that the risk-premium deposit insurance would not prevent banks from becoming insolvent, which is not likely a valid goal of policy. However, tying insurance premiums to risk may encourage risk controls by BHCs and affiliated banks.

The unregulated banking system would attain an optimal allocation under assumptions of individual endowments of wealth, competitive markets, infeasibility of the government improving administrative efficiency, and lack of externalities (Benston and Kaufman 1996, 688). In the view of Benston and Kaufman (Ibid), prudential supervision should only have the role of ameliorating the negative externalities resulting from deposit insurance sponsored by the government. Dow (1996) argues in favor of banking regulation. Dowd (1996) defends *laissez-faire* banking and Boot and Thakor (1993) model of the self-interest of regulators. Benston and Kaufman (1996, 689–90) argue that private insurance companies may not be superior to the government in sponsoring deposit insurance. There are three negative externalities in banking. First, bank runs may spread to otherwise solvent banks. Second, the failure of a bank can cause economic distress in the form of lower production and employment. Third, taxpayers and prudently managed banks may bear the costs of government-sponsored deposit insurance.

The first survey of the monumental sample of Barth, Caprio, and Levine (2006) is for 1998–9, covering over 100 countries with information on 200 regulatory and supervisory practices. The second survey is for 2003–4, covering 50 more countries and 100 new questions. The samples provide comprehensive information on world banking and regulation. The analysis proceeds on the basis of two approaches to banking regulation.

First, the public interest view postulates that high costs of obtaining information and enforcing contracts distort the incentives and effectiveness of monitoring and disciplining of banks by the private sector (Barth, Caprio, and Levine 2006). A powerful official banking regulatory agency would have incentives and the capacity to effectively monitor and discipline banks, ameliorating the market failures of information and contracting and improving on the market allocation.

Second, the private interest view postulates that regulators are not different from other agents and maximize their self-interest instead of those of society as a whole (Ibid). The official regulators of the public interest view would divert credit to politicians and elites in power. Private-sector bankers have the incentives, resources, and organization as a small group, manipulating regulation in optimizing their self-interest. Politicians with ultimate control of the process will strengthen official regulation with resulting inefficiency and corruption in lending. The policy alternative of the private interest view is effective rules of disclosure and sound private contracting that would permit the private sector to do what the regulators do not accomplish. The private interest view does not propose *laissez-faire* but rather strong legal and regulatory conditions required to restrain the costs of information and contract enforcement.

The analysis of the worldwide sample supports the predictions of the private interest view that disclosure to the public increases credit to the private sector and the efficiency of bank intermediation, reducing corruption in lending (Ibid). Stricter regulation on information disclosure would permit enhanced private sector monitoring, reducing bank corruption. Disclosure rules would enhance the capacity of private investors in influencing sound bank governance. Generous deposit insurance lowers private-sector monitoring, leading to excessive risk-taking by bankers and higher probability of financial crises. Powerful official regulators do not appear to strengthen efficiency in banks or in decreasing banking fragility. There are no benefits from regulation such as government ownership of banks and restrictions on bank activities and entry of new banks. Restrictive regulation coincides with bank inefficiency, lower levels of banking development, and increasing bank fragility.

The critical issue of political economy is why countries choose a regulatory system. Barth, Caprio, and Levine provide an answer by means of two-stage least squares estimation of the following system:

$$Bank\ Regulation = \alpha + \beta * Political\ System + \delta X + u \qquad (2.5)$$
$$Political\ System = \gamma Z + \varepsilon \qquad (2.6)$$

They use five measures of bank regulation for individual analysis: an index of private monitoring, entry applications denied, official supervisory power, activity restriction, and government-owned banks. They use four measures of differences in political systems for individual analysis: executive constraints, executive compensation, executive openness, and accountability. The control variables in the second stage regression, X, are legal origin dummy variables for legal tradition of British common law, French Civil law, or German Civil law. The instrumental variables, Z, used to extract the exogenous component of the political system are latitude, independence, initial executive constraints/competition/openness, and religious composition.

The political economy results of Barth, Caprio, and Levine are revealing. Countries adopting bank supervisory and regulatory practices focusing on information disclosure have more open, competitive, and democratic political systems. The regressions indicate a large impact of political institutions on banking system policies. There is less likelihood that countries with open, competitive, and democratic political system will deny a high percentage of entry applications of new banks than countries with more autocratic political systems. There is no clear relation between political system indicators and power of bank supervisors. Limits on bank activities and systems of large government-owned banks are more likely in autocratic regimes, confirming the view that those regimes design regulation to channel credit to the ruling elite.

Bank functions

Contemporary analysis focuses on the functions performed by banks: monitoring of borrowers, providing liquidity services, and transforming illiquid assets into immediately liquid assets. There is a preliminary section on the microeconomics of banking.

Table 2.1 Schematic primary deposit bank balance sheet

Assets	Liabilities
Loans and investments	Deposits
Net holdings of defensive assets	Shareholders' equity
Defensive position	
Required reserves	

Source: Tobin (1982, 497).

Microeconomics of banking

The primitive commercial bank holds loans and investments with relatively longer terms and characterized by illiquidity in that they cannot be converted readily into cash except in some cases at a discount. This is the category of assets labeled loans and investments in Table 2.1, following Tobin (1982, 496–7). This model applies to the primitive banks instead of banks buying and selling large assets relatively matched in terms to liabilities. It is the model behind significant part of analysis of traditional monetary policy. The deposits on the liability side are immediately convertible into cash, such as demand deposits, or short-dated. To meet unexpected conversion of demand deposits into cash, the primitive commercial bank holds defensive assets in excess of required reserves. Tobin (Ibid, 497) defines the basic accounting identity of the primitive commercial bank as

$$D, Deposits + E, shareholders' equity = kD, Required reserves$$
$$+ R, defensive position + L, loans and investments \qquad (2.7)$$

where the reserve ratio is a fraction, $0 < k < 1$.

The net holding of defensive assets is equal to the excess of defensive assets over required reserves, or defensive position. The bank counts with this defensive position to comply with required reserves in case of unexpected withdrawal of deposits or unusual increase in demand for loans (Ibid). The bank uses many options, such as withdrawal of deposits in other banks, not refinancing fed funds overnight loans, borrowing on sale and repurchase agreements (SRP) of treasury bills, or outright sale of the bills. In this simplified model, Tobin (1982, 498) considers three critical bank decisions, concentrating analysis on disposable assets:

- first, the values of the portfolio of loans and investments and the net defensive position;

- second, the holding of primary or secondary reserve assets, and the value of short-term borrowing;
- third, the structure of the loan and investment portfolio.

Disposable assets are given by

$$D + E - kD = R + L = Disposable\ assets \qquad (2.8)$$

The disposable assets can be divided between the defensive position R and loans and investments L. If the remuneration to the defensive position R is r and the bank's revenue is $P(L)$ on the investment portfolio of size L (net of administrative costs and allowance for default), deposits are D_0 beyond the bank's control and equity is fixed at E, the bank attempts to (Tobin 1982, 500)

$$Maximize\ P(L) + rR \qquad (2.9)$$

subject to the balance sheet constraints:

$$L + R = E + (1 - k)D_0 \qquad (2.10)$$

If the marginal revenue from loans exceeds r, $P'(L) > r$, the banks grow the loan and investment portfolio with the only limitation of its ability to finance a negative defensive position. If $P'(L) < r$, the banks maintain all deposits and equity in defensive assets. The maximum revenue occurs at the loan position L^* corresponding to equality of the marginal revenue from the loan, $P'(L)$, to the marginal revenue from the defensive position, r, with the second-order condition of $P''(L) < 0$ (Ibid, 501). The analysis extends easily to the existence of fixed costs in deposit.

The prohibition of interest on deposits or equivalent agreements among financial institutions conferred rents on banks that would otherwise be enjoyed by depositors in the form of higher paid interest (Ibid, 506). Banks may also enjoy rents in acquiring deposits similar to the monopolistic rents obtained in lending. Technology and deregulation have significantly reduced these rents. In the absence of limits on interest, banks acquire deposits until the marginal value of each deposit class is equal to the marginal cost; that is, when the addition to net revenue of a marginal dollar of deposit is equal to the increase in cost. If the marginal value exceeds the marginal cost, the bank will seek to increase deposits by raising the interest rate. The effective interest rate includes nonmonetary benefits given to depositors, such as services and preferred treatment. The effective cost to the bank includes a variety of administrative costs, promotion expenses, investment on attractive facilities, and others.

Reality is more complex with the banking firm taking decisions on the level of its loans and investments before knowing the future level of its deposits. That is, banks like other economic agents make decision on illiquid claims on the basis of uncertain future streams of income. Banks must consider major withdrawals even with low probability (Ibid, 507). In the past, and during the credit/dollar crisis after 2007, solvent banks failed because of illiquidity. Not even the LOLR has eliminated this specter, as shown by the aggressive extension of the rediscount window by the Fed and other central banks from deposit to nondeposit financial institutions and from treasury and agency securities to a large variety of securities. The banking firms must take into account that increases in loans and investments increase the special costs resulting from a negative defensive position. The expected or opportunity costs of providing loans and investments must consider the decline in the expected defensive position and safety margin of the bank. The special costs of meeting a negative defensive position add to marginal and total expected costs of banking. In the Tobin (1982, 510–1) model with uncertainty, maximum expected total revenue is maximized for a level of loans and investments by the condition that the marginal expected revenue is equal to the marginal expected costs of the defensive position.

There are three forms of incompleteness of contracts considered by Rajan (1998). The first type is *external incompleteness*, occurring when the environment of legal and property rights is not conducive to detailed contracting. In this case, it may not be possible to enforce property rights in the same way as in systems where judges are incorruptible and the bankruptcy system is effective and transparent. The second type is *intrinsic incompleteness*. For example, creditworthiness is very difficult to verify in court and changes in accordance with conditions that are quite difficult to anticipate. The third type is *deliberate incompleteness*, with contracts deliberately incomplete to avoid worse outcome relative to writing complete contracts. Incomplete contracts result in bargaining with focus on how the institutional framework determines the rights and powers of various parties in the bargaining process.

An important example by Rajan (Ibid, 533–4) is the clear right of the depositor to the deposits but the unwritten claim of the borrower to drawing the line of credit. The borrower's right to the credit was deliberately left unwritten or incomplete because of the potentially onerous burden on the bank. The bank kept the option between reputation and monetary capital. The reputation of the bank is the result of past investments by the institution, clients, and employees. This reputation cannot be replicated by an anonymous market player. Rajan (Ibid, 534) argues that banks constitute a second-best institutional form providing payment, savings, and credit functions in a setting of incomplete contracts.

Monitoring

Banks issue secondary assets, deposits, to acquire primary assets, loans (Diamond 1996, 52). Lower costs of monitoring provide comparative advantage to banks in asset services. Monitoring by a principal can improve contracts by saving on contracting costs. Delegated monitoring consists of banks acquiring private information on the borrower to provide an asset service funded by issuing unmonitored deposits. It explains why investors prefer to participate in projects of borrowers by means of deposits.

If the cost of monitoring a company's project is K, a large number of lenders per borrower, m, would incur a cost of $m \times K$ unless it delegates to a bank. If S denotes the cost without monitoring and D the incentives to the monitor or costs of delegation, delegated monitoring is successful if (Diamond 1996, 54, 1984, 398)

$$K + D \leq \min[S, m \times K] \tag{2.11}$$

The key objective is finding the organizational structure and form of contracting that results in minimum costs of delegating monitoring to a financial intermediary. The optimal contract is obtained by maximizing the expected return of the entrepreneur given the minimum expected return to depositors in the form of the competitive interest rate (Diamond 1984, 396). The optimal contract is a debt contract with smallest face value that provides depositors with the expected competitive interest rate and a non-pecuniary bankruptcy penalty (Ibid, 396–7). Examples of penalties are time consumed in bankruptcy proceedings and reputational loss of the manager in bankruptcy.

Banks can centralize monitoring, reducing the costs of duplication of monitoring by many lenders (Diamond 1996). Diversification of loan portfolios is the financial engineering function of banks that reduces significantly the risks of liquidation of banks permitting them to issue unmonitored deposit contracts. The agency incentive problem occurs because the bank obtains private information from the borrower

(Diamond 1984, 399). The bank could argue that the payments from the entrepreneur are lower than actual, paying a small value to depositors. There must be incentives for the bank to pay depositors. Suppose there are N entrepreneurs, $i = 1, ... N$. Assuming independent and identically distributed entrepreneurial projects, the cost of delegation per entrepreneur, D_N, decreases monotonically with N. The deadweight penalties occur only in the extreme left-hand tail of the probability distribution of project returns. The probability of a project falling in the tail decreases monotonically. Diamond (1984, 401) proves the proposition that if the projects of entrepreneurs are bounded and independently distributed:

$$D_N \to 0 \text{ as } N \text{ grows without bound, } N \to \infty \qquad (2.12)$$

That is, diversification reduces the incentive costs of delegation. Demand deposits are not monitored because the bank (agent) assumes full responsibility for the deposits and is assigned the penalties resulting from payment to depositors (principals) that are lower than face value plus the competitive interest rate. Diversification results in low probability of the bank incurring penalties and permits the bank to observe privately the information obtained in monitoring without sharing it. The incentive contract is highly levered debt with bankruptcy penalties. The debt is riskless asymptotically, as $D_N \to 0$ when $N \to \infty$.

Diamond (Ibid, 409) concludes that financial intermediaries permit better contracts and attaining Pareto superior allocations. The prediction of the model of delegated monitoring is the existence of financial intermediaries with significant diversification, having capital structure consisting mostly of debt (deposits) and characterized by low default probability. Some of the projects financed by banks may have common association with the rate of growth of the economy, exchange rates, interest rates, and other similar variables. Diamond (Ibid, 410) argues that there is a case for banks to hedge interest rate risk in derivative markets. The incentive constraints of risk sharing within the bank suggest that there should not be regulation preventing them from hedging risks in derivative markets (Ibid). An alternative would be forcing borrowers to hedge. As diversification increases without bound, bank deposits become riskless. Regulation restricting diversification, as for example single-branch banking, can increase the risk of bank failures, creating the pressure for deposit insurance (Diamond 1996, 64).

Liquidity

An important issue in analysis and regulation is if banks provide functions of liquid deposits and lending that could be provided independently (Kashyap, Rajan, and Stein 2002). Money market funds could provide liquid deposits by investing in short-term, highly rated investments that are marked to market daily. Investors have normally converted a principal of $1 of deposits in a cash withdrawal of at least $1. There are minimal if any principal/agent problems in money market funds because of the matching of deposits with marketable assets of highest quality. In contrast, there may be higher incentives for bank managers as agents to take excessive risk relative to what would be desired by investors and depositors as prudent. There could be arguments that the money market fund would be more efficient in providing liquidity because of the lack of deadweight costs, such as the double taxation of interest to bank equity holders as costs and then as dividends. The money market fund does not have the costs of monitoring opaque companies to provide them loans. Moreover, banks have additional costs of regulation, including capital requirements, required reserves, and costs of holding precautionary liquidity for emergencies.

The deposit banks exist because of an important general function, the provision of liquidity, which has important synergies between deposit taking and lending (Ibid). The consideration of credit lines or commitment loans is critical to understanding the synergies of deposit and lending activities. A line of credit is drawn by clients as unexpectedly as demand deposits. The synergy is the division of the overhead costs of banking between the liquidity provision to depositors and to clients that draw on their lines of credit. Banks that have highest liquidity are precisely those that engage in providing commitment loans. In contrast, finance companies and other financial intermediaries do not engage typically in providing liquidity through lines of credit.

Theoretically, a bank could perfectly match the maturity of its assets, such as loans, and liabilities, such as deposits. For example, the bank can lend to customers for terms of three months and borrow through deposits maturing simultaneously in three months. The interest income of the bank would be the interest rate received from the loans less the interest rate paid on the deposits. The bank would still require prudential capital to compensate for credit risk; that is, the possibility that in three months the borrower of the loan defaults. The matched book of assets and liabilities does not include liquidity risk because the loan contracts and the deposit contracts have specific maturity clauses in which the borrower repays the bank the proceeds of the loan plus interest and the depositor has the right to receive the principal plus interest. In this example, the bank has matched the liquidity, eliminating liquidity risk. Any bank would scarcely remunerate capital with a continuously matched book of assets and liabilities. Yield curves are typically upward sloping, with shorter maturities yielding less than longer ones. Profitable bank management requires mismatching assets and liabilities, borrowing short-dated money and lending for longer maturities. The interest income is the much higher spread of the higher rates received on assets with longer maturities less the much lower rates paid on short-dated money.

The important departing analysis of Diamond and Dybvig (1983), explained in simpler form by Diamond (2007), is the mismatch of liquidity by banks. Banks obtain funds from demand deposits that can be withdrawn at any time and lend these funds in the form of loans that are difficult to sell at a price without discount. The bank funded with demand deposits has a key mismatch of liquidity. The definition of a bank run by Diamond and Dybvig (1983) and Diamond (2007, 189) is when an excessive number of depositors attempt to withdraw simultaneously. The motivation of depositors to withdraw can originate in the expectation that the bank may fail. In a bank failure, depositors may lose all or most of their deposits. The bank run occurs where there is a generalized expectation by depositors that the bank could fail. There need not be any truth in that expectation. Even false news in the media could cause a bank run as long as it creates the generalized expectation in depositors.

Transformation services

The services provided by banks are illustrated in Table 2.2. On the asset side, banks provide services to borrowers, consisting of granting them loans and evaluating and monitoring them. On the liability side, banks provide traditional services to depositors, in the form of holding deposits, clearing transactions, maintaining an inventory of currency and facilitating the payment of goods and services (Diamond and Dybvig 1986, 57–8). The column in the middle shows the transformation service, involving the asset and liability sides of the balance sheet, of converting monitored illiquid, risky loans, and investments into unmonitored demand deposits.

The larger banks have more demand for loans and monitoring capacity than smaller banks. Thus, smaller banks sell their excess liquidity in unsecured overnight loans of excess reserves at the fed, named fed funds, to the larger banks. Diamond and Dybvig (1986, 58) argue that there is a transformation service of large banks, converting illiquid

Table 2.2 Services provided by banks

Assets	Liabilities
Provided to borrowers	*Provided to depositors*
Loan	Deposit holding
Evaluation (reduce adverse selection)	Transactions clearing
Monitoring (reduce moral hazard)	Currency inventory
Approval	Payment for goods and services
→Transformation→	
Converting illiquid loans into liquid deposits: liquidity creation	

Source: Diamond and Dybvig (1986).

loans and investments into liquid fed funds. There is no similar transformation service by smaller banks that sell their excess reserves. The
fed funds rate is an important price of liquidity. However, there is no
insurance against bank runs in the fed funds market. The rise in counterparty risk, such as in the credit/dollar crisis after 2007, may cause
the sale of fed funds to less risky institutions, or even the holding as
reserves, to avoid unsecured loans during the failure of institutions,
as it occurred to United States and foreign financial institutions in the
case of the failure of Lehman Brothers in 2008.

The initial evaluation of a borrower by a bank intends to limit adverse
selection (Diamond and Dybvig 1986, 58–9), which occurs when banks
choose unsound projects for financing and do not finance sound projects. The subsequent monitoring of the loan prevents moral hazard, or
the use of the financing for riskier, unsound activities, such as borrowing for an industrial project and investing in high-risk commercial real
estate. Monitoring services by banks reduce the diversification costs of
risk-sharing by investors and the evaluation and monitoring costs.

The transformation services link the asset and liability sides of the
balance sheets of banks (Ibid, 59). The collection of information on the
borrowers is centralized in a financial intermediary with diversification of assets among companies and industries. Because the information collected is private, the assets of the banks are special in that they
are not traded and are illiquid. The securitization of loans changed the
real-world conditions of bank loans that are classified according to their
credit rating and packed in traded securities. There is still a transformation function in the form of SRPs of asset-backed securities (ABS) that
convert illiquid assets, such as mortgages, auto loans, and credit card
receivables, into liquidity. The analysis of Diamond and Dybvig extends
smoothly to this new state of nature of structured products. The bank

run occurs when the liquidation value of the loan portfolio is less than the value of the liquid deposits (Ibid, 63).

The liquidity run on the financial company engaging in SRPs occurs when there is expectation by a counterparty that the value of the security offered in guarantee of the SRP less the haircut could exceed the sale value in case of default of the repurchase agreement. Such expected collapse of resale value would break the transformation function of converting an illiquid ABS at a significantly lower value. The transformation function of assets into liquidity improves information sharing but not if the liquidation value is less than the value in the SRP agreement. As in the Diamond and Dybvig (1983) bank run, the liquidity run occurs as counterparties try to avoid a loss of their capital. Diamond and Dybvig (1986, 63) argue that lines of credit by banks constitute part of the transformation service: banks guarantee the conversion of illiquid assets of borrowers into cash. The SRPs of the structured investment vehicles (SIV) of the credit/dollar crisis were insured of liquidity risk with guarantees by bank credit lines that could provide liquidity in case of failure of refinancing the collateralized debt obligations (CDO) and other structured products. These lines of credit are subject to runs if the counterparties expect others to withdraw refinancing (see Diamond and Dybvig 1986, 63).

Optimal regulation would require policies that take into account their effects on the asset services provided by banks (Ibid, 59). The regulatory policies should maintain incentives for banks to grant loans to sound projects and engage in optimal monitoring and disincentives to discourage lending to unsound projects. Deposit insurance with government participation and coordination is a policy designed to prevent bank runs. There are incentives for banks to take high risks and correspondingly high profits with the possibility of eliminating downside risks with deposit insurance. Banks with this type of moral hazard would pass on the risks of unsound lending to the deposit insurance authority but would appropriate the gains of profitable risky lending. It is quite difficult to design variable-rate deposit insurance programs because of the opacity of risk activities of banks. The purpose of the rediscount window is to provide liquidity to sound assets by the central bank during periods of stress of deposits.

Capital requirements

The foundation for analysis of banks is the fragility of demand deposits, which are subject to runs. Regulation has consisted of imposing minimum capital requirements on banks. Classic empirical analysis explores the counterfactual that bank capital requirements substitute for deposit insurance and have not been better than unrestricted decisions on capital. The risk-based international capital requirements of Basel II constitute the global standard.

Bank fragility

There are four players in the theory of banking, the entrepreneur (borrower) with a project, the banker lending to the entrepreneur, the depositors holding balances in the bank, and the investors holding claims in bank capital (Diamond and Rajan 2000). The entrepreneur has a project and specific abilities to manage it that are superior because he or she can extract higher cash flows than anyone else. However, the entrepreneur can only commit his or her human capital to the project on a spot basis. The project is illiquid because the entrepreneur can withdraw his or her human capital before completion. The banker cannot obtain full value in liquidation. The banker has specific knowledge in extracting the highest value in liquidation that he or she developed in evaluating and monitoring the project from the beginning. The financial asset created by borrowing from the bank, a loan, has similar illiquidity as the project in that the loan cannot be sold at full value reflecting prospective discounted cash flows. The illiquidity of the bank's financial asset originates in the inability to commit human capital of the entrepreneur or the banker.

Diamond and Rajan (2001b, 289) argue that a bank financed with demand deposits constitutes a device to tie human assets to capital to create liquidity. The difficult, illiquid asset of the project of the entrepreneur can be converted into liquidity by the special collection skills of the relationship banker. The bank can provide liquidity to the borrower by borrowing with demand deposits from its lenders, thus not being forced to liquidate the assets or sell them at discount, interrupting the entrepreneur's project (Ibid). There is a basic fragility in this device. Banks commit to convert deposits sequentially in the order in which the request is made. If the bank tries to capture rents without passing on full collections to depositors, it will face a bank run. The sequential nature of the demand deposits can provoke a self-fulfilling run. The fragility of the bank capital structure permits it to borrow the full value of the illiquid financial asset into which the project of the entrepreneur was transformed. The bank creates liquidity on both sides of the balance sheet (Ibid).

Diamond and Rajan (2000, 2432) argue that banks maximize the volume of credit extended with a deposit capital structure that is rigid and fragile because of the threat of bank runs. Under uncertainty, the decline in value of the assets below the value of deposits can trigger a loss of confidence that results in a bank run. The bank faces a trade-off of credit and liquidity relative to the cost of bank runs.

There is a claim, capital, that is softer in renegotiation (Ibid, 2433). Demand deposits that can be sequentially withdrawn are subject to collective action and, as such, are not renegotiable. Capital can be considered not only as equity in the bank but also as long-term debt in which case rights to holders only accrue in the event of default. Capital provides a buffer against shocks of asset values. There are three tradeoffs of more capital. First, the banker can increase the rents from lending. Second, the bank has a buffer against sudden changes in asset values. Third, the bank can extract more from borrowers.

The economy modeled by Diamond and Rajan (Ibid, 2434) has entrepreneurs and investors, two periods and three dates, 0, 1, and 2. The discount rate is zero and all agents are risk neutral. The projects of entrepreneurs require initial investment of $1 at date 1 and end at date 2. The returns of the projects in terms of cash flows are C^H with probability q^H in state H and C^L with probability $(1 - q^H)$ in state L. The human capital of the entrepreneur is required to generate the cash flows. Without the human capital of the entrepreneurs, the assets have random value $\tilde{Y}$ with realization Y^s in state s until C^s is produced. The value of the asset then collapses to zero. The contract specifies the payments due from the entrepreneur to the bank, P_t, and the assets that the banker can seize in the event of default by the entrepreneur. Because of specific ability originating in evaluating and monitoring the project from the beginning, the banker obtains Y^s in liquidation while the rest can obtain only βY^s, with $\beta < 1$. The following assumption ensures that the banker will use specific skills in at least one of the states to make the loan worthwhile:

$$q^H Y^H + (1 - q^H)X^L > 1 + \beta[q^H Y^H + (1 - q^H)X^L] \qquad (2.13)$$

The following result is obtained by Diamond and Rajan (Ibid, 2442):

If Min $[P_2, Y^s] < d$, where d is the value of deposits, there will be a bank run, and depositors will receive

$$\tfrac{1}{2}\text{Min}\,[P_2, \beta Y^s] + \tfrac{1}{2}\text{Min}\,[P_2, Y^s] \qquad (2.14)$$

The demand deposits cannot be negotiated and the failure to obtain their full value d triggers collective action in the form of a run. If

$$\text{Min}\,[P_2, Y^s] \geq d \qquad (2.15)$$

there is no run. Depositors are paid d. Additional conditions determine the payments to capital and the banker.

In the two possible states at date 2, the bank can have low deposits, $d = Y^L$, or high deposits, $d = Y^H$. Assuming $Y^L < \beta Y^H$, a low level of deposits in 2, $d_2 = Y^L$, can result in risk-free or safe deposits, with payment to depositors and other claimants of (Ibid, 2443)

$$D^{Safe} = q^H\left[\frac{1+\beta}{2}\right]Y^H + \left(1-q^H\right)Y^L \tag{2.16}$$

The operation of the bank with a high level of deposits, $d = Y^H$, could result in a bank run if the realization is Y^L. The payment to depositors and other claimants in the risky situation is (Ibid, 2444)

$$D^{Risky} = q^H Y^H + \left(1-q^H\right)\left[\frac{1+\beta}{2}\right]Y^L \tag{2.17}$$

The bank can pay depositors and other claimants no more than

$$\text{Max}\{D^{Safe}, D^{Risky}\} \tag{2.18}$$

If $Y^L \geq \beta Y^H$, D^{Risky} is unaltered, and (Ibid, 2443)

$$D^{Safe} = q^H\left[\frac{\left(Y^H - Y^L\right)}{2}\right] + Y^L \tag{2.19}$$

The following result is obtained by Diamond and Rajan (Ibid, 2443):

Condition, if	Relation	
$q^H Y^H < (1 - q^H)Y^L$	$D^{Safe} > D^{Risky}$	(2.20)
$Y^L \leq q^H Y^H$	$D^{Risky} > D^{Safe}$	(2.21)
$Y^L > q^H Y^L \geq (1 - q^H)Y^L$	There is a β^* for which $D^{Safe} > D^{Risky}$ if and only if $B < \beta^*$	(2.22)

The bank raises more external financing with a capital structure with safe deposits than with a capital structure with risky deposits if $D^{Safe} > D^{Risky}$. The rent to the banker with low deposits is lower than the costs of a run. Rent occurs in high-deposit states. Thus, the capital structure with highest ex ante value is that with relatively fewer deposits when difficult times are expected and higher deposits when better times are expected (Ibid, 2443). The level of deposits can be considered as a leading indicator of the economy. An important implication of the model of Diamond and Rajan (Ibid, 2444) is the explanation of the decline of capital ratios, from 55 percent in the 1840s to approximately 10 percent currently. After an increase in the liquidity of project, β, there are proportionately more deposits in the capital structure that increases upfront value. In terms of collateral, banks are especially valuable when the collateral value of assets, $\beta E[\tilde{Y}]$, is low but the capacity of the bank in collection is important. In the model of Diamond and Rajan (Ibid, 2445), the bank can pledge in addition to existing collateral, $\beta E[\tilde{Y}]$, an extra value:

$$\text{Max}\{D^{Safe}, D^{Risky}\} - \beta E[\tilde{Y}] \qquad (2.23)$$

The model of Diamond and Rajan (2001b, 317) uses abstract concepts such as loans and demand deposits that would exist only in traditional deposit banks. The concepts and results do extend to modern financial institutions. The loans in the model capture the complex positions, on and off the balance sheet, of current financial companies. The management of these complex positions to maturity requires the skills of bankers. Demand deposits can be seen as representing guarantees of liquidity, including loan commitments, irrevocable letters of credit, and demand deposits (Ibid). The analysis can be interpreted as a comparative advantage of financial institutions in managing complex positions and providing guarantees of liquidity. The functions of managing positions and providing liquidity guarantees complement each other when the value added is already embedded in the positions and the skills of the banker are principally used in transfers instead of in creating additional value. The rents of the bank suffer the most during a run. The bank obtains low-cost financing by means of issuing claims convertible into cash on demand.

The extension of the analysis to the credit/dollar crisis is straightforward. The function of skills in management of the banks is illustrated by the SIVs. The banks created off-balance sheet SIVs with illiquid financial assets based on cash flows of underlying mortgages in the form of CDOs, extremely complex in pricing and financing. The financial asset, such as mortgages, was based on an illiquid physical asset, a house. The returns of the CDOs were magnified by dividing them in tranches—equity, mezzanine, and senior—according to increasing priority in absorbing defaults of the underlying loan, such as mortgage-backed securities (MBS). The tranches had decreasing yields in accordance with their higher risk as measured by the credit rating.

The function of creating liquidity is illustrated by the financing of the structured products. On the basis of the strength of their balance sheets, banks issued commercial paper of the SIV, with the liquidity guarantee of bank letters of credit. This commercial paper was financed in SRPs, which were rated AAA because of the credit rating of the guarantor, the bank. The increasing default of mortgages resulted in an increase in counterparty risk. Banks faced increasing difficulty in refinancing maturing SRPs and had to honor the letters of credit issued to the SIVs. Eventually, the SIVs had to be incorporated into the balance sheet of banks in the form of writedowns of the CDOs. The failure of banks to refinance commercial paper of the SIVs was the equivalent of the bank run in the models of Diamond and Dybvig (1983) and Diamond and Rajan (2000, 2001a,b).

Banks were hit by the liquidity demands of their counterparties. The liquidity shock extended to many segments of the financial markets—interbank loans, asset-backed commercial paper (ABCP), high-yield bonds, and many others—when counterparties preferred lower returns of highly liquid safe havens, such as treasury securities, than the risk of having to sell the collateral in SRPs at deep discounts or holding an illiquid asset. The price of an illiquid asset is near zero. Finding MTM prices of the complex assets became quite difficult and was delayed by efforts such as a super SIV financed by major banks in which illiquid SIV assets would be held until counterparty risk diminished. Eventually, banks sequentially wrote down assets aggressively. Mutual funds are not subject to runs because their assets are MTM daily (Diamond and Rajan 2001b, 317). This is a primary reason why money market funds cannot create liquidity: their assets are MTM daily and are highly liquid. Deviations from highly liquid marketable assets in portfolios of money market funds in the form of illiquid, depreciating liabilities of failing investment banks triggered runs in September 2008.

The model of Diamond and Rajan (2000, 2444–5) implies that there is a capital structure (level of deposits and capital) that maximizes what the bank can pledge to investors. Increasing the required capital of banks can make them safer. However, the increase in capital requirements increases the banker's rents, reduces the amounts that the bank can pledge to claimants, and increases the effective cost of bank capital. Suppose there is rigid capital requirement that prevents raising more deposits in the future, the maximum amount that the bank could pledge to claimants would decline from $\max\{D^{Safe}, D^{Risky}\}$ to $[(1 + \beta)/2]E[\tilde{Y}|s_1]$ because more capital is required. The horizon of the banker would then be shortened, causing the use of the liquidation option. The effects on borrowers are uneven, creating a credit squeeze on cash-poor borrowers and diminishing the pressure on cash-rich borrowers. In the case of abrupt increase in very strict capital requirements, there could be a run on the bank if maturing deposits exceed what the bank can pledge (Ibid, 2445). There could also be adverse effects of failure to fund investment projects with longer gestation periods.

Empirical analysis

Bank capital in the Peltzman (1970, 1965) model has two roles. First, bank capital cooperates with inputs of labor and deposits in the production of bank services, such as liquidity, brokerage, accounting, information, and others. Second, bank capital attracts deposits by means of insurance against declines in bank assets below the value of deposits. Bank equity capital is 10 percent or less of total resources and its major returns derive from its role in insuring deposits. The main purpose of capital investment in banks is in attracting deposits that are used to buy assets but few assets are acquired with bank equity capital (Peltzman 1970, 1).

The objective of Peltzman (Ibid, 2) is the most critical but difficult issue in empirical economics: the design and test of a counterfactual. In this case, the counterfactual is the analysis of current effects of regulation on bank capital investment and what would have been bank capital investment without regulation. The method is to provide and measure a model of the independent market determinants of bank capital investment. The success of regulation is evaluated by whether it improved on the outcome attained by the market without intervention.

The Banking Acts of 1933 and 1934 affected bank capital investment significantly by the introduction of deposit insurance and regulation through the FDIC (Ibid, 4). The FDIC strengthened the role of the federal government in banking regulation by imposing federal regulation of state banks that insured their deposits. After FDIC no bank desiring to insure deposits could escape federal regulation. To the extent that deposit insurance substitutes for bank capital, the FDIC created incentives for banks to reduce capital investment.

The equation for empirical estimation used by Peltzman (Ibid, 10) is

$$\%\Delta C = \beta_0 + \beta_1\pi^e + \beta_2\pi^a + \beta_3 RD + \beta_4 C/D \\ + \beta_5\%\Delta D^e + \beta_6\%\Delta C^R + u \tag{2.24}$$

where $\%\Delta C$ is the percentage change in bank capital, π^e is the expected rate of return on capital in banking, π^a is the expected rate of return on alternative investments for bank capital, *RD* is the default risk of bank portfolios, *C/D* is the ratio of capital to deposits, $\%\Delta D^e$ is the expected annual rate of growth of deposits, $\%\Delta C^R$ is the percentage change of bank capital desired by regulators, and *u* is a random variable. The sample used by Peltzman (Ibid, 21–4) was obtained from banks in 49 states in 1963, 1964, and 1965.

The empirical results of Peltzman answer two important issues of his research objective. First, there is support for the proposition that banks substitute deposit insurance for bank capital. Second, there is no support for the proposition that banks behaved differently without regulation than they actually did under capital regulation.

The regression equation used by Mingo (1975, 1113) is a variation of that of Peltzman (1970, 10):

$$\%\Delta C = \beta_0 + \beta_1 \left(\frac{NI}{C} \right)_{t-1} + \beta_2 \left(\frac{US}{D} \right)_t + \beta_3 \left(\frac{C}{D} \right)_t + \beta_4 \%\Delta C_{at-3}$$
$$+ \beta_5 \%INS + \beta_6 ABC + \beta_7 MEMBER + u \qquad (2.25)$$

The left-hand variable, $\%\Delta C$, is the percentage change in bank capital. The term $(NI/C)_{t-1}$ is the ratio of net income to capital in the prior period as proxy of the expected rate of return. The term $(US/D)_t$ is the ratio of holdings of government securities to total deposits net of cash, as a proxy for the default risk of the portfolio. The term $(C/D)_t$ is the ratio of capital to total deposits net of cash. The percentage growth in total deposits in the prior three years is denoted by $\%\Delta C_{at-3}$. The term *%INS* is the percentage of deposits insured by the FDIC to total deposits. The term *ABC* is the negative inverse of the ratio of bank capital to the capital desired by regulators. Finally, *MEMBER* is a dummy variable equal to one if the bank is a member of the FRS or zero otherwise.

The sample of Mingo (1975, 1115) is obtained from 323 banks drawn randomly from 32 states in 1970 with stock variables measured as averages of 1969–70. The results support the contention that banks substitute deposit insurance for capital and that regulators have not attempted to reduce this substitution effect. However, Mingo finds that lower ratios of actual capital to capital desired by regulators in one period are followed by increases of capital in the subsequent periods. The magnitude of the effect of regulation is relatively large and regulators appear to concentrate their efforts on banks with the worst capital adequacy. The average bank experiencing a decline of 10 percent in the ratio of actual capital to the level desired by regulators engages in an 11 percent increase in capital investment.

There is a simultaneous equation model of demand factors affecting the stock demand for capital c^d and the flow supply of capital $(dc/dt)^s$ considered by Dwyer (1981). The lower case letters denote logarithms of the variables. As the cost of capital paid by the bank π increases, the quantity of capital demanded by the bank decreases because of adjustments in the pecuniary and non-pecuniary rates paid to deposits and reduction of assets. The model has three equations: demand, supply, and the fixing of level of capital at any time, and three endogenous variables: c, dc/dt, and π. Dwyer estimates the model with times series data using the method of three-stage least squares. The results support the substitution by banks of deposit insurance for capital conditional on the hypothesis that the Banking Acts of 1933 and 1935 created rents captured by bank owners. The time series data do not permit the separation of both hypotheses. Thus, the cross-section estimates are decisive.

A data set of 80,000 bank-year observations for almost all insured banks in 1983–9 is used by Berger (1995) to explore the empirical association between bank capital asset ratios (CAR) and return on equity (ROE). The analysis consists of regressions of CAR and ROE on three years of lagged CAR and ROE and several control variables. The results show positive Granger (1969) "causality" in both directions. Berger (1995, 433) is cautious in alerting that the results are merely "gross statistical associations" that do not necessarily test for causality. Moreover, as all econometric relations, the structures existing in a given time dimension affected by regulation and exogenous shocks may not exist in other time periods under different factors. The usefulness of this empirical research is in helping to find theories that are consistent with the data. The positive Granger causality from earnings to capital is consistent with the addition of retained earnings to equity. The positive Granger causality from capital to earnings is consistent with the reduction of the costs of uninsured deposits. Banks may have paid higher premiums on uninsured funding because of expectations of bankruptcy and the deadweight costs of liquidation. Banks increasing capital in response to higher than optimal expectation of liquidation appeared to have experienced lower rates on uninsured funds and resulting higher earnings.

On October 21, 1996, the Board of Governors of the Federal Reserve System (FRBO) allowed BHCs to include in tier 1 capital a debt/equity hybrid, trust preferred securities (TPS). On February 28, 2005, the FRBO revised the risk-based capital rule that permits the limited inclusion of TPS in the tier 1 capital of BHCs (FRBO2008BHC, 4060.3):

> Until March 31, 2009, the aggregate amount of qualifying cumulative perpetual preferred stock (including related surplus) and qualifying

trust preferred securities that a banking organization may include in tier 1 capital is limited to 25 percent of the sum of the following *core capital elements*: qualifying common stockholders' equity, qualifying noncumulative and cumulative perpetual preferred stock (including related surplus), qualifying minority interests in the equity accounts of consolidated subsidiaries and qualifying trust preferred securities.

The BHC creates a special purpose vehicle (SPV), which holds all its common equity (Benston et al. 2003, 303). The SPV sells investors preferred stocks in the form of TPS, lending the sale proceeds to the BHC as junior-subordinated debt that is similar to the TPS. The only asset of the SPV is this loan. The corporate form of the SPV is a trust under Delaware or other state law. The trust is taxed as a partnership. The interest on the loan is paid as dividend income to the holders of the TPS. Registered TPS with the SEC can deduct interest payments in contrast with dividends that are paid from earnings after taxes. Benston et al. analyze the issue of TPS by BHCs during 1996–9; they find that early issuers of TPS enjoyed significantly positive cumulative abnormal returns (CARS) in intervals after first issue in 1996 when the FRBO allowed their use as tier 1 capital. The 65 BHCs filing a TPS with the SEC experienced positive additional abnormal returns primarily because of their use as tier 1 capital. The motivation for issuing TPS was adding to tier 1 capital without issuing expensive common stock, providing clear benefits to stockholders of BHCs. Benston et al. (Ibid, 319) proposed the inclusion of subordinated debentures in addition to TPS as part of tier 1 capital. Subordinated debentures have the same tax-avoidance properties as TPS but lower issuance costs.

International capital requirements

The risk components of the international ratings-based approach (IRB) of Basel II (BCBS 2004) are probability of default, *PD*, loss given default, *LGD*, exposure at default, *EAD*, and effective maturity, *M*. In some cases, banks may have to use a measure of risk component provided by supervisors. In others, banks may use their own internally generated measures. An essential element of IRB is calculation of unexpected losses, *UL*, and expected losses, *EL*. The framework uses risk-weight functions to calculate capital requirements for *UL*. The process is described in BCBS (2005) and is based on technical contributions by Merton (1974), Gordy (2002), and Vasicek (2002).

Table 2.3 shows some risk weights for *UL* calculated by Basel II risk weight functions. Calculations assume *LGD* of 45 percent and maturity of 2.5 years. There appear to be lower risk weights for residential

Table 2.3   IRB risk weights for unexpected loss

PD	Corporate	Residential Mortgages	Other retail	Revolving Retail
0.03%	11.30%	4.15%	4.45%	0.98%
5%	112.27%	82.35%	125.45%	103.41%
10%	146.51%	113.58%	142.69%	158.47%
20%	188.42%	140.62%	189.41%	222.88%

Note: *LGD* = 45%, Maturity = 2.5 years, Turnover for corporates = €5 million.
Source: BCBS (2004, 197).

mortgages, which has been a factor in commentary on Basel II. There is an evident sensitivity to probability of default, *PD*.

In theory, the concept of regulatory capital should be obtained by maximization of a social welfare function that explicitly considers costs, such as increase in the cost of credit, and benefits, like the reduction in the probability of bank failure, resulting from regulation of bank capital (Elizalde and Repullo 2007, 88). In practice, regulatory capital is the charges stipulated in the IRB of Basel II. An objective of Basel II is to align regulatory and economic capital. Economic capital is defined by banks as that which would cover bank losses with a probability or confidence level that corresponds to a desired external rating. Elizalde and Repullo (Ibid, 87) define economic capital for practical analysis as the level that would be chosen by the bank in the absence of regulation. Actual capital is the level maintained by the bank in the presence of regulation.

Using the definitions of regulatory and economic capital, Elizalde and Repullo find that there is no direct relationship between these two levels of capital. Regulatory capital is related to the level of confidence of the regulator but economic capital is associated with the margin of intermediation and the cost of bank capital. When bank capital is costly, economic capital is below regulatory capital; for low costs of bank capital, economic capital is above regulatory capital. In practice, banks choose actual capital instead of economic capital based on whether initial capital is higher or equal to the minimum stipulated by regulation and on the rule for closing banks that are seriously undercapitalized (Ibid, 112). The BCBS (2009Jan; Wellink 2009Mar) is in the process of modifying Basel II in response to the credit/dollar crisis, which is considered in Chapter 6.

Deposit insurance

The fragility of the capital structure of banks caused by demand deposits has resulted in regulation imposing government-sponsored deposit insurance. Narrow banking is an alternative that would separate the lending and deposit functions of banks. Option methods can provide measurements of the fair value of deposit insurance.

Narrow banking

The instability of banks and its impact on the real economy can be eliminated by means of narrow banking, as proposed by Simons (1948). The proposal of 100 percent reserves in banks was viewed by Simons as enforcing legislative restrictions on the terms of borrowing and lending. It was only part of more comprehensive proposals on financial reform. Fisher (1936) vigorously adopted the proposal (Allen 1993). The policy objective of replacing fractional reserves with full reserves would be to eliminate the role of banks in creating money, centralizing the money creation function in monetary authorities (Allen 1993, 705; Graham 1936, 428–9 and references in his footnote 2). Graham (1936, 440) proposed government monopoly of the money supply with banks lending as other financial institutions based on capital, debenture borrowing, and time deposits. The view of Friedman (1967, 3) is that the proposals of financial reforms of Simons (1948) were unnecessary and in the wrong direction, preventing financial diversification and lower costs of capital required for higher capital formation. Friedman (1967, 4) finds some value in the proposal for entirely different reasons in that it could provide more freedom for banks that at the time of his writing in the 1960s were constrained by regulation implanted during the Great Depression.

A contemporary exposition of the 100 percent reserve proposal is that banks limit their lending to long-term resources, such as capital and preferred long-term securities, while investing all proceeds of demand deposits in the form of money market funds. Restriction of lending to capital would be a form of attaining this objective. These proposals are similar to a fully insured bank (Diamond and Rajan 2001b, 318–9). The main problem of runs is the interruption of productive projects of entrepreneurs as banks liquidate loans during runs. There would be no runs if bank deposits were fully insured by the government. The fully insured bank would not create liquidity. The excess of deposits over the market value of loans would constitute a subsidy by the institution ensuring deposits. The commitment function of banks, or providing liquidity to borrowers with productive projects, would be as limited under fully insured banks as in the all capital bank. The volume of lending would be lower under regimes similar to the all capital bank than in the fragile demand deposit of banks modeled by Diamond and Rajan.

In practice, not all deposits are insured (Ibid, 319). Banks have multiple liabilities that are similar to demand deposits, such as large deposits, commercial paper, and interbank borrowing. The credit/dollar crisis has shown that large depositors can create crises of illiquidity, identical to the runs in the models of Diamond and Dybgiv (1983) and Diamond and Rajan (2000, 2001b). A counterpart of the liquidity runs of this type is the closing of the ability to raise capital by rapid movement of the stock price to zero of institutions suffering liquidity squeezes. Measures such as the rediscount window, open market operations, and deposit insurance were unable to prevent the failure of some of the largest financial institutions in the United States in 2008.

Deregulation

In 1983–90, 1150 US commercial and savings banks, about 8 percent of the industry in 1980, failed, almost twice more than between creation of FDIC in 1934 through 1983 (Benston and Kaufman 1997, 139).[1] In addition, over 900 savings and loans associations (S&L), or about 25 percent of the industry, were closed or merged by the Federal Savings and Loan Insurance Corporation (FSLIC) or placed in conservatorships. The Financial Institutions Reform, Recovery and Enforcement Act of 1989 (FIRREA) abolished the insolvent FSLIC, creating the Resolution Trust Corporation (RTC) and the Savings Association Insurance Fund (SAIF) and providing $150 billion of taxpayer funds to resolve insolvent S&Ls. The threat of banks economically insolvent or close to insolvency prompted Congress to enact the 1991 FDIC Improvement Act (FIDCIA). Commercial banks recovered with record profitability by 1995 and few banks were classified as undercapitalized. The recovery of the thrift industry was much slower. FIRREA also introduced the new regulator of S&Ls, the Office of Thrift Supervision (OTS).

FDICIA implemented partially the philosophy of structured early intervention resolution (SEIR) in the form of prompt corrective action (PCA) and least-cost resolution (LCR) (Benston and Kaufman 1997, 146, 1996, 695–6; see Mishkin 1992; White 1989). FDICA specified five zones of capital/asset ratios to which regulators quickly assigned percentages. Regulators would take corrective actions when capital/asset ratios entered zones of peril that could indicate possible insolvency. Regulators also moved to resolution at the lowest possible costs. Although the standards of SEIR were not followed in practice, regulation experienced improvement.

There were problems with US regulation and banking practices identified by Mishkin (1992). The key problem of deposit insurance is moral hazard. Depositors do not monitor banks if they are assured of the safety of their deposits and also do not penalize them by withdrawing deposits when symptoms of a bank's stress become evident. Examples of excessive risks by banks in the 1980s were loans to emerging countries and to commercial real estate. Mishkin (Ibid, 135) also finds adverse selection caused by deposit insurance in attracting into banking entrepreneurs with business models favoring excessive risk. Bank franchises became more valuable to entrepreneurs with high risk preferences than to those with inclination to controlling risks.

Banks in the United States experienced significant transformation because of regulatory and technological factors (Berger et al 1995, 56). The regulatory factors include reduction of reserve requirements, various changes in capital requirements by the Basel accords, deregulation of deposit accounts, increase of bank powers, and relaxation of restrictions on interstate and intrastate banking. Technological innovations include more rapid communications facilitating the transfer of funds. Financial innovations have been important in risk transfer with securitization and derivatives.

In the 1980s, restrictive bank regulation undermined the competitiveness of US banks (Calomiris 2002, 16). Competition affected banks from domestic sources, such as securities markets and finance companies, and from entry of foreign banks in US markets as well as diminished competitiveness in foreign markets. Freer capital flows and technological advances in communications and information eroded US banking competitiveness. Politicians reacted to the pressure on US banks by engaging in deregulation.

The first change in regulation in the 1980s was the elimination of the interest rate ceiling on bank deposits (Berger et al. 1995, 178–9). Restrictions on the rate that intermediaries could pay depositors had existed since the Banking Act of 1933. Regulation Q established ceilings on the rates paid by banks on time deposits and other regulations prohibited payment of interest on demand deposits. The objective of the Bank Act of 1933 was to restrict competition within banking to strengthen banks while also preventing banks to finance stock market transactions by the market of call loans (Calomiris 2002, 16). Senator Carter Glass intended to prevent the transfer of reserves to New York banks during periods of low demand for loans because he believed banks became vulnerable to stock market cycles (Ibid). During the stagflation of the 1970s banks experienced significant disadvantage as the maximum nominal interest rate lagged behind accelerating and unpredictable inflation. The situation worsened with the second oil shock in 1980, causing inflation that raised market interest rates to two-digit levels.

The Depository Institution Deregulation and Monetary Control Act of 1980 (DIDMCA) incorporated significant changes (Berger et al. 1995). Banks were authorized to open new accounts that could pay interest on overnight funds. DIDMCA also mandated the phasing out of Regulation Q interest rate ceilings by March 1986. The Depository Institutions Act of 1982 authorized banks to offer money market deposit accounts without incurring reserve requirements and exempt from ceilings of Regulation Q.

The Bank Act of 1935 required the FRS to impose reserve requirements on deposit banks (Ibid, 83). The FRS managed reserve requirements during the 1960s and 1970s. Banks borrow money from depositors and other sources. Part of that money is withheld as reserve requirements. The increase in inflation and interest rates during the 1960s and 1970s increased the cost of borrowed funds deposited as reserves, causing significant stress on the banking industry. During the 1980s and 1990s, legislation and FRS policy relaxed the burden of reserve costs on banks.

The Federal Reserve Act imposed limitations on the types of assets that could be discounted by the Fed but the Glass Steagall Act authorized advances by Federal Reserve Banks (FRB) to member banks on any asset (Friedman 1970, 22). The Banking Act of 1933 prohibited payment of interest on demand deposits and imposed limits on interest rates paid on time deposits issued by commercial banks. These measures were motivated by the belief that the banking panic of the Great Depression originated in unsound banking in the form of high-risk loans by banks trying to obtain sufficient revenue to pay competitive rates on deposits (Ibid, 18). The reduction of competitive pressure would reduce the occurrence of unsound banking. Subsequently, controls were influenced by the pressure to direct credit to mutual savings banks and savings and loan associations that complained of unfair competition from commercial banks that prevented them from financing housing. These controls were unimportant when implicit rates on demand deposits were at or below zero percent and when market rates on time deposits were below those imposed by Regulation Q (Ibid, 15). The interest-rate controls became important already in the 1960s and increasingly during the rise in inflation and the stagflation of the 1970s.

The imposition of controls of interest rates over a long period permitted banks to find ways of evading and avoiding them. Banks avoided the zero interest imposition on demand deposits by providing services to customers and loans at less than market rates (Ibid, 24). The rise in market rates of certificates of deposits above Regulation Q rates in the second half of the 1960s triggered compensatory reaction by banks. The growth of money market banks occurred through the invention of the large certificate of deposit (CD) that provided the funding for the increasing volume of loan demand. Friedman (1970, 25) finds that CDs declined from $24 billion in mid-December 1968 to less than $12 billion in the beginning of October 1960. There was no decline in banks' total liabilities because of the rise in liabilities on which the banks could pay a market rate in the euro-dollar market (Friedman 1970, 25). The banks paid market rates on CDs by accounting them as "due from head office" in the balance sheets of their European offices. The head office changed the liability "due to foreign branches" for "due on CDs" (Friedman 1969). The future was predicted by Friedman (1970, 26–7):

> The banks have been forced into costly structural readjustments, the European banking system has been given an unnecessary competitive advantage, and London has been artificially strengthened as a financial center at the expense of New York.

The controls were unfair to people with lower incomes and wealth who received rates on their savings below those that would prevail in a free market and had almost no other alternative allocation for their savings (Friedman 1970, 27). The argument that the poor are net borrowers does not justify the reduction of their real savings and their ability to improve their wealth. There were also effects on the efficiency of the capital markets in the form of erroneous signals.

Neoclassical policy argues in favor of control of monopolies because of welfare improvements resulting from marginal cost pricing. However, Winston (1998, 91) argues that the regulated industry is characterized by inefficiency. The deregulation of an industry causes firms to innovate in marketing, operations, and technology, eliminating the inefficiencies caused by regulation. This process of moving to efficiency can take significant periods of time. Regulation also causes rigidity in the response of companies to shocks such as recession, inflation, and stagflation. The growth of efficient firms causes concentration in industries (Demsetz 1973). Stiroh and Strahan (2003) analyze how the deregulation of the banking industry in the United States in 1976–94 affected competition.

Stiroh and Strahan argue that the more efficient banks gain market share after deregulation with the association strengthening more than five years after deregulation. The proxy for efficiency is relative performance, measured as either profits or costs. As in industrial deregulation, there is a period of gestation of increasing competition after deregulation. The more efficient banks grew while the worst performing ones shrank. Deregulation introduces a competitive shock in banking. There is also evidence suggesting that bank expansion into new markets occurs by acquisition of better-managed banks and increasing competition with those with poorer management. Stiroh and Strahan (2003, 804) conclude that the transfer of assets from less efficient to better-managed banks was a clear benefit of deregulation.

Banking consolidation accompanied deregulation as smaller banks were acquired by larger institutions. Entrepreneurship could be frustrated if the banking system did not have the relationship with innovators provided by smaller banks. Black and Strahan (2002, 2829) find that there was significant increase in new incorporations in deregulating states. Deregulation increased competition in banking through consolidation with resulting decrease in the importance of smaller banks. The research of Black and Strahan (2002, 2829) suggests that bank size created diversification benefits with reduction of the costs of delegated monitoring that exceed the potential comparative advantage of smaller banks in developing long-term relationships with clients. The evidence suggests that consolidation and the decline in the share of small banks helped instead of harming entrepreneurs.

In the model of Diamond and Dybvig (1983), deposit insurance can prevent a bank run based on unfavorable expectations of depositors. Cooper and Ross (2002) introduce moral hazard in the form of imprudent investments by banks and failure of monitoring by depositors. Without monitoring by depositors, banks engage in risky investments. Both banks and depositors are willing to hold high-risk portfolios. Cooper and Ross conclude that appropriately designed capital requirements complement deposit insurance in attaining a first-best outcome. The model fits the experience of the S&Ls of the 1980s: inadequate capital requirements combined with deposit insurance and competition for deposits after relaxation of Regulation Q resulted in high-risk portfolios.

The objective of Jeon and Miller (2007) is to determine if the deregulation of interstate and intrastate banking influenced the rates of new charters (birth), failure (death), and merger (marriage). They use a sample of US commercial banks during 1978–2004. The major conclusion is that deregulation increased consolidation or mergers but not entry or exit. They also find a demonstration effect that consolidation can result temporarily in new charters but not in entry or exit and that exits lead to mergers. Intrastate and interstate deregulation of banking and branches has driven consolidation, considered both at the national and state levels. Consolidation has been slower than expected. Entry of new banks has softened the reduction in the number of banks.

The credit crunch would consist of a leftward shift in the supply of loans by banks while keeping constant the riskless interest rates and the quality of potential borrowers (Bernanke and Lown 1991, 207). The evidence suggests that there was a "capital crunch" after 1987 concentrated in several states, especially in New England. The real estate collapse in that region was the likely cause of the decline in bank capital and lending. Bernanke and Lown (1991, 238) conclude in favor of eliminating the remaining restrictions on interstate banking existing at the time. Relaxation of interstate banking would permit banks to smoothen their operations through geographical diversification.

There is evidence of a capital crunch in New England during the early 1990s (Peek and Rosengren 1995). Banks may shrink instead of issuing new equity because of asymmetry of information. There are no incentives for bankers to reveal their problems. Potential investors may not buy bank equity at normal economic returns because of the fear of dilution of current equity holders. Because equity cannot be issued at prices that are acceptable to bankers, shrinking is the only alternative to the banks. The sample of New England of Peek and Rosengren (1995) indicates that some banks in New England chose shrinking to recover capital/asset ratios because of pressures of regulation on financial markets and the preferences of bankers. Banks provide credit to small and medium businesses where information is private. Shrinkage because of capital crunch can reduce bank lending that is not provided by other lenders, or a credit crunch.

Fair valuation

Under periodic examinations by the FDIC, Merton (1977) shows that loan guarantees have an isomorphic correspondence with common stock put options. Thus, option-pricing techniques (Black and Scholes 1973; Merton 1973) can be used to value deposit guarantees. If the guarantor audits only at the end of a finite period, the analysis can be extended to demand-deposit guarantees or deposit insurance. Merton (1978) extended the model by allowing for surveillance or auditing costs and random auditing times. He finds that the surveillance costs are paid by depositors and the holders of equity pay for the put option component of the deposit guarantee.

If the FDIC finds during the examination that the bank is insolvent, it can close it, liquidate it, or arrange a purchase-and-assumption transaction with a solvent institution (Marcus and Shaked 1984, 448). Insured depositors are guaranteed by the FDIC and there is even protection for uninsured depositors in a purchase-and-assumption transaction. Deposits in a bank are similar to a debt claim with maturity equal to the length of the examination interval. Let B_τ be the level of deposits at the time of the next examination, which is the face value if the deposits are left in the bank, A_τ the value of the assets and T the effective maturity of the debt or time until the next administration. The claim on equity at maturity is worth $A_\tau - B_\tau$ if $A_\tau > B_\tau$ (Ibid). The bank is declared insolvent if $A_\tau < B_\tau$, defaulting on the debt and holders of equity receive zero. Assuming that the value of the bank follows a diffusion process, Merton (1977) shows that the fair market value of the insurance provided by the FDIC, I, at time 0, is (Marcus and Shaked 1984, 448–9)

$$I = B_\tau e^{-r\tau}[1 - N(x_2)] - e^{\delta\tau}A_0[1 - N(x_1)] \tag{2.26}$$

where δ is the dividend rate per dollar of bank assets, r is the risk-free interest rate, $N(\cdot)$ is the cumulative normal distribution, x_1 is $[\ln(A_0/B_\tau) + (r + \sigma^2/2 - \delta)T]/(\sigma\sqrt{T})$, σ is the instantaneous standard deviation of the rate of return of the asset A, and x_2 is equal to $(x_1 - \sigma\sqrt{T})$. The equation is the same at that of a put option with exercise price B_τ on a stock with current value A_0, paying the dividend rate δ. Marcus and Shaked (1984, 449) argue that the interpretation of equation (2.26) is that the deposit insurance gives depositors an option to sell to the FDIC their claims on the bank at the price of B_τ.

The sample used by Marcus and Shaked (1984, 452) is of 40 large banks that accounted for 25 percent of total US demand deposits in 1980. There are limitations that bank assets, A, and the standard deviation of returns, σ, are not observed directly. In addition, the distribution of bank returns may not be distributed normally. There is also the assumption that all deposits are protected because of the purchase and assumption transaction in case there is insolvency. The estimates of Marcus and Shaked (Ibid, 454) after adding the administrative expenses of FDIC are fair premium rates of the 40 banks of $145 per million in 1979 and $126 per million in 1980, compared with the actual rate of $333 per million. The FDIC premium is expensive but there is the restriction of assuming normality of stock returns. The results also show significant variation among the 40 banks.

Government sponsored enterprises

The charter of the national mortgage associations or GSE contains a declaration of five purposes for which they are authorized by Congress (12 USC § 1716):

1. Providing stability in the secondary market;
2. Responding appropriately to the private capital market;
3. Continuing assistance to the secondary market for residential mortgages;
4. Promoting national access to mortgage credit;
5. Orderly managing and liquidating mortgage credit throughout the United States, minimizing adverse effects to the residential mortgage market and losses to the federal government.

The charter requires that the GSE "support the secondary market for residential mortgages, assist mortgage funding for low- and moderate-income families and be attentive to the geographic distribution of mortgage funding, including underserved areas" (Jaffee and Quigley 2007, 109). The retained portfolio of MBS of the GSE is not required to satisfy their charter obligations and its unhedged interest-rate risk "creates a large risk for the US Treasury and a systemic risk for US capital markets" (Ibid, 110). Thus, the GSE constitute a threat, which materialized in 2007–9, and not a guarantee of the stability of the US residential mortgage market. The net income of Fannie Mae in 2008 was a loss of $58.7 billion and that of Freddie Mac $50.1 billion. The technical literature reaches consensus that "affordable housing goals have not substantially increased homeownership among low-income families" (Jaffee and Quigley 2007, 111). However, An et al. (2007) find beneficial effects of the goals in neighborhoods.

There are various types of large federal subsidies to the GSE. First, some subsidies to the GSE derive from their federal charters, which result in treatment as federal agencies instead of for profit companies (Jaffee and Quigley 2007, 120). Thus, the GSE are exempt from state and local income taxes and registration requirements and fees with the SEC. The US Treasury provides the GSE a line of credit of $2.25 billion and they use the Fed as fiscal agent. The debt of the GSE can be purchased by the Fed in open market operations and is eligible as collateral for public deposits and in unlimited investment by federally chartered banks and thrifts. Second, the major part of the federal subsidy originates in the implicit guarantee of their debt and MBS by the federal government.

That guarantee materialized in the credit/dollar crisis after 2007. The total subsidies to housing in the United States amounted to $221.1 billion in 2006 composed of "$37.9 billion in government outlays for low-income housing assistance, $156.5 billion in federal tax expenditures for housing and $26.7 billion in credit subsidies, including the GSEs and the VA)" (Ibid, 123).

There are three proposals for the regulation of the GSE (Jaffee 2009). First, the guarantee function would be relocated to a new, independent agency of the federal government and the retained portfolio of assets would be returned to shareholders without any link to the federal government. Second, the GSE model would be maintained with regulatory changes to prevent unsound balance sheets and systemic risk. Third, the originating financial entities would issue covered bonds collateralized by the cash flows of the mortgages to create incentives for sound origination of mortgages, which may have been weakened by independent layers of origination, servicing and funding, or placement of MBS with investors.

Fannie Mae and Freddie Mac relaxed credit-risk management and drastic changes were required. The losses of Fannie Mae in the first three quarters of 2008 amounted to $18 billion of which about $17 billion resulted from the credit losses in the guaranty book (Raines 2008, 8). Significant part of the losses, about 70 percent, originated in the guaranteeing of high-risk Alt-A loans, with insufficient information and documentation, and in lesser magnitude by subprime loans; the former Chief Credit Officer of Fannie Mae depicts the role of the GSE in the housing event as follows (Pinto 2008):

> There are approximately 25 million subprime and Alt-A loans outstanding, with an unpaid principal amount of over $4.5 trillion, about half of them held or guaranteed by Fannie and Freddie. Their high risk activities were allowed to operate at 75:1 leverage ratio. While they may deny it, there can be no doubt that Fannie and Freddie now own or guarantee $1.6 trillion in subprime, Alt-A and other default prone loans and securities. This comprises over 1/3 of their risk portfolios and amounts to 34% of all the subprime loans and 60% of all Alt-A loans outstanding. These 10.5 million unsustainable, nonprime loans are experiencing a default rate 8 times the level of the GSEs' 20 million traditional quality loans. The GSEs will be responsible for a large percentage of an estimated 8.8 million foreclosures expected over the next 4 years, accounting for the failure of about 1 in 6 home mortgages. Fannie and Freddie have subprimed America.

Summary

Bank functions reveal the critical analysis of banking services: the monitoring of the assets, the liquidity services of the liabilities, and the transformation of illiquid assets into liquid liabilities. The fragility of the transformation function opens the essential analysis of bank runs. Banking regulation provides excellent illustrations of the main currents of regulatory thought, the private interest view, and the public interest view.

3
Deposit Bank Market Power and Central Banking

Introduction

This chapter provides the analysis of two areas of significant regulation of banks. First, there are multiple mechanisms to restrict market power in banks. The main topics covered in various sections are market structure, entry, and market power. Second, government intervention in banking is proposed for stabilization of the economy. The main topics covered are the general principles of central banking, the transmission of monetary policy, inflation targeting, and the Lucas Critique and consistency of optimal plans. The text is completed with a brief summary.

Banking competition

The two fundamental welfare theorems cannot be applied directly to banking (Vives 2001). There are evident violations of the assumptions. Retail banking is characterized by frictions that create entry barriers, such as reputation, branch network, and switching costs. Corporate banking also creates entry barriers in established relationships and asymmetric information that provide advantage of information to bankers with long-established relations. These frictions permit the exercise of market power by banks. Vives argues that certain measure of rivalry is required in banking to promote innovation and efficiency. The rapid changes in banking resulting from deregulation and technological change require adaptation of competition and regulation. Vives finds dangers in both excessive competition and excessive market power. There are different levels of competition in banking, which is a multiproduct industry. Institutional characteristics of regulation and bank soundness influence the optimum level of competition. The continuing improvements in processing information and in electronic transactions raise concern of frictions and market power, requiring active competition policy. There is intensive competition in global wholesale and investment banking suggesting natural oligopoly as the equilibrium market structure (Ibid). There may be a limited or no role for competition policy in wholesale and investment banking. The following subsections consider the critical issues of marker structure, entry, market power, and the relation of concentration to financial stability.

Market structure

Early research on market structure and power is centered on the structure-conduct-performance paradigm (Berger et al. 2004a). More recent research considers the efficiency hypothesis. There are numerous references on the structure-conduct-performance approach.[1]

There has been significant technological change affecting banks since 1980 (Berger 2003; Berger and Mester 2003). Banks and other financial institutions use information technology (IT) intensively both in the back office, in the form of processing transactions electronically at decreasing costs, and in the front office, in the form of providing faster services of higher quality to clients. In addition, banks develop and use financial technology intensively for their own risk management and product development and also for their clients. The measurement of bank productivity by the Bureau of Labor Statistics (BLS) consists of the ratio of numbers of transactions, an output, to labor, an input, which may not capture many effects of technological improvement (Berger 2003, 157–8; Berger and Mester 2003). The index does not state outputs that are intensive in the use of capital, where IT advances occurred. It does not accurately portray the business of banking because of the focus on transactions instead of on intermediation. The index may not include all the labor input because of outsourcing of services to credit bureaus and so on.

An enhanced measurement of productivity in banking is obtained by econometric research on cost and profit functions at the individual bank level (Berger 2003; Berger and Mester 2003). The typical banking cost function is as follows (Berger 2003, 158):

$$\ln C = f_c(\ln w, \ln q, \ln z, \ln v) + \ln u + \ln \varepsilon \tag{3.1}$$

where C denotes variable costs, f_c is the log cost function corresponding to the best-practice frontier, business conditions are denoted by w, variable input prices, q, variable output quantities, z, fixed input and output quantities and v, environmental variables, u is an inefficiency factor with value of zero for best-practice firms and positive for other firms, and ε is the random error with mean zero.

It is possible to decompose the predicted gross change in costs from time t to $t + 1$, C_{t+1}/C_t, into three multiplicative components (Berger 2003, 159; Berger and Mester 2003):

$$\frac{C_{t+1}}{C_t} = \left\{\frac{\exp f_{t+1}(x_1)}{\exp f_t(x_t)}\right\}\left\{\frac{\exp \ln u_{t+1}}{\exp \ln u_t}\right\}\left\{\frac{\exp f_{t+1}(x_{t+1})}{\exp f_{t+1}(x_t)}\right\} \qquad (3.2)$$

where x is the vector of business conditions (w, q, z, v) and t is the cost function or the mean value for a set of variables at time t. The first term in parentheses captures the movement of the best-practice frontier, the second term the change in inefficiency, and the third term the changes in business conditions. The change in total cost of the industry from time t to time $t + 1$, $C_{t\,t+1}$, is represented by using the average business conditions, average inefficiency, and zero random error, decomposed into the three multiplicative components (Berger and Mester 2003):

$$\Delta TC_{t\,t+1} = \Delta BP_{t\,t+1} {}^*\Delta IN_{t\,t+1} {}^*\Delta BC_{t\,t+1} \qquad (3.3)$$

where BP is the component of best practices, IN is the inefficient component, and BC is the component of business conditions. Berger and Mester (2003) obtain a similar decomposition for the profit function of banks, under standard profit maximization and alternative profit maximization. The analysis of performance of firms is enhanced by using profit maximization instead of cost minimization because it provides better description of the objective of managers and owners who consider revenues as well as costs. Thus, the change in total gross profit $\Delta TP_{t\,t+1}$ from t to $t + 1$ is obtained in the form of (Ibid):

$$\Delta TP_{t\,t+1} = \Delta BP_{t\,t+1} {}^*\Delta IN_{t\,t+1} {}^*\Delta BC_{t\,t+1} \qquad (3.4)$$

The sample of Berger and Mester for 1984–97 is characterized by significant changes in technology, regulation, competition, and business conditions (Berger 2003). It contains annual information for nearly all US commercial banks, concentrating on 1984, 1991, and 1997. This period was also characterized by significant variation in economic variables relevant to banking, such as interest rates. An important empirical finding is the worsening of bank cost productivity in 1991–7 together with significant improvement in profit productivity. The findings support the consistency of the hypothesis that banks maximize profits not only by increasing revenue but also by reducing costs. More products of higher quality were offered by banks, raising their costs but with strong revenue-increasing effects. Banks can capture the returns of new technology with resulting profit increases. Competition eventually decreases the returns, with the process being repeated with successive innovations. Continuing innovation increases the returns of banks that adopt them but they need not necessarily be the same banks (Berger and Mester 2003).

Most of the results found by Berger and Mester occurred in merging banks. They experienced the greatest deterioration in cost productivity and also the most significant improvements in profit productivity. It is likely that merging banks took higher risks and obtained correspondingly higher profits by exploiting diversification gained in mergers.

The theory of contestability provides analysis of monopolistic markets with potential entry of firms (Baumol, Panzer, and Willig 1982; Baumol and Willig 1986). The simple threat of entry may cause the incumbent monopolist to set price equal to average cost. The conditions of perfect contestability require a potential rival with an equal cost structure; potential entrants calculate profits of entry at the prices of the incumbent firm; and there are no barriers to entry or exit.

Contestability theory can be used by the government to protect consumers and smaller firms from market power by large firms. It can also provide larger firms the freedom to attain efficiency, promoting entrepreneurship. Baumol and Lee (1991, 1) argue that the concept of perfect contestability is a model of ideal markets. In these idealized conditions, there are no costs to entry and exit. The constant potential entrance forces incumbents to behave properly. Because sunk costs are zero, there are always stimulating returns that can be realized by an entrant in lowering excess prices and costs of incumbents. In perfect contestability, there are no waste and inefficiency, excess profits, and predatory pricing.

The objective of contestability theory is to provide a theoretical and analytical framework of markets that have few producers with market power because of economies of scale (Baumol and Lee 1991, 2–5). The technological characteristic of output in these markets is increasing returns; that is, output increases at an increasing rate. Economists characterize this situation as a production function that is initially convex or mathematically that its second derivative is negative. As a result of increasing returns, average costs of these producers decline for a long range of output. The technological characteristic of increasing returns is what determines market power. The producer that is selling in the market has already benefited from decreasing average costs: the large initial fixed cost is divided among more units of production. The cost of the first units produced by a new firm in the market would be that fixed cost divided by these few units, thus much higher than the cost of the established producer.

Declining costs typically occur in industries where there are large fixed investments that are required for initiation of business (Baumol and Lee 1991). Average cost, or total cost divided by output, decreases from initially high levels as investment is spread over increasing units of production. These investments are typically indivisible; that is, a large lump sum of money is required to start production. Consider the establishment of a railroad. Before starting to sell services, the railroad makes heavy investments in buying the rights to go through land, setting the rails, building stations, and others. The first entrant in the market has the advantage of having already made the investment. There would be a long lag before a competitor would start business. That competitor would face very heavy average costs initially and could not face the lower prices that the established producer could offer.

An important concept in contestability theory is the nature of investment. There are investments that have sunk costs (Ibid). The laying of the rails in the railroad is a good example. They cannot be transferred from the west to the east. A locomotive need not be considered sunk cost because it could conceivably be transferred from one location to another.

The fact of entry is not critical to the theory. What is crucial is merely the threat of entry (Ibid). Consider a situation in which the incumbents are pricing above average cost, thus appropriating economic rents. The threat of entry of new producers in the market would moderate the behavior of incumbents. If they maintained prices that resulted in noneconomic profits, entrants would be attracted to the market. These entrants would lower prices, causing losses of clients to the incumbents. There would be a deterrent to the incumbents to price above average cost because of the threat of entrants in the market attracted to the profits. The fact that a market is contestable may result in conduct by firms that is different from that in traditional analysis of market power. Price would tend to approximate average cost, or production would take place at the intersection of the demand and average cost curves. This is the first benefit of contestability: the lack of excess prices and profits (Ibid, 3). Entrants would drive the prices and profits to levels about the same as those that would prevail under perfect competition.

There is a proposal to combine the insights of Coase and contestability theory into a unified regulatory framework (Bailey 1999). Contestability theory suggests the unbundling of activities to identify parts of the market that exhibit harm, which should be the subject of regulation. The parts of the market that pose no harm should be allowed to function independently of government intervention. The parts with harm should not be regulated with remedies without proper analysis and providing adequate incentives. The government should limit its intervention, promoting corrections that permit the improved functioning of markets.

Stiglitz (1987) contends that the theory of contestability rests on the specific assumption of zero sunk costs. He argues that the theory is invalid even in the presence of small sunk costs. There are other arguments that question the theory of contestability.

The reduced form revenue equation of a profit maximizing firm in standard comparative statistics is used by Panzar and Rosse (1987) to obtain a test of monopoly. Claessens and Laeven (2004) apply this test to banking systems in many countries. The following equation is estimated by OLS and GLS from reduced-form revenue equations pooling samples for each country (Ibid):

$$\ln P_{it} = \alpha + \beta_1 \ln W_{1,it} + \beta_{2,it} \ln W_{2,it} + \beta_{3,\,it} \ln W_{e,it} + \gamma_1 \ln Y_{1,it} \\ + \gamma_2 \ln Y_{2,it} + \gamma_3 \ln Y_{3,it} + \delta D + \varepsilon_{it} \tag{3.5}$$

where the variables are as follows: P_{it} is the ratio of gross interest revenue to total assets as proxy for output price of loans; $W_{1,it}$ the ratio of interest expense to total deposits and money market funding as proxy for input price of deposits; $W_{2,it}$ the ratio of personnel expense to total assets as proxy for input price of labor; $W_{e,it}$ is the ratio of other operating and administrative expenses to total assets as proxy for input price of equipment/fixed capital. The subscripts denote bank, i, and year, t. The three Y terms are controls variables for (1) the ratio of equity to total assets, (2) the ratio of net loans to total assets, and (3) the logarithm of total assets, controlling for possible effects of size. Dummy variables are denoted by D.

The Panzar and Rosse (1987) H statistic would be zero for monopoly and one for competition. It is the sum of the elasticities of the reduced-form revenue equation given by equation (3.5) (Claessens and Laeven (2004):

$$H = \beta_1 + \beta_2 + \beta_3 \tag{3.6}$$

The Panzer and Rosse model is for equilibrium. Claessens and Laeven conduct tests for equilibrium and for competitive environment.

The selected sample of Claessens and Laeven consists of 35,834 bank-year observations, with 4479 banks on average per year. It covers 50 countries in 1994–2001. The results indicate that less restriction on activities in banking and more foreign banks are associated with more competition in banking systems. The restriction of entry of commercial banks reduces competition in banking. Claessens and Laeven conclude that the most significant pressure of competition is openness to new entry in banking. There is no evidence of negative association of concentration with competitiveness in banking. The results suggest that contestability is more important for competition than structure.

Economic theory predicts that market power results in lower output at a higher price, reducing firm growth, what Beck, Demirgüç-Kunt, and Maksimovic (2004) denominate as the structure-performance hypothesis. The information-based hypothesis predicts a positive or nonlinear relation between market power and loan access for opaque borrowers in the presence of asymmetries of information and agency costs. The equation of Beck, Demirgüç-Kunt, and Maksimovic has financing obstacle as the dependent variable and concentration as the explanatory variable. There are additional explanatory variables: government, foreign ownership, exporting firm, number of competitors, manufacturing, services, size, inflation, and growth. The firm data are obtained from firm survey replies of more than 10,000 firms in 80 developed and developing countries. The data on bank ownership and regulatory structure are from the first sample of Barth, Caprio, and Levine (2006).

The results of Beck, Demirgüç-Kunt, and Maksimovic (2004) find that concentration in banking increases obstacles to firm financing, with stronger effects for small and medium firms relative to larger firms. The relationship holds for low-income countries but becomes nonsignificant for middle-income and rich countries. The relationship between concentration and financing obstacles is reduced or becomes nonsignificant for high institutional development, efficient credit registry, and participation of foreign-owned banks. There are stronger effects of concentration on firm financing obstacles in countries implementing rigid restrictions on banking activities, interference with the banking system, and larger share of government-owned banks.

Entry

The original reason for granting banking charters was to finance the sovereign and obtain revenue from possible rents obtained by the banks. Analysis of the history of banking charters suggests two broad avenues for countries abandoning charters for revenue (Grossman 2001). Countries with established central banks controlling the money supply in early times had less strict banking regulations. Countries in which banks provided means of payments adopted earlier and comprehensive banking codes. Entry restriction can occur because of technical factors or by barriers created by law.

The United States had virtually free banking incorporation in the century before 1935 (Peltzman 1965, 11–2). The federal and state banking authorities operated independently of each other. There was competition among the federal and state authorities such that when one denied the application for a bank charter the other granted it. This period ended in the 1930s with the belief that excessive concession of charters had been an important cause for the banking crises during the Great Depression. The Banking Act of 1935 required that the FRS, in admitting a new state bank, and the Comptroller of the Currency, in chartering a new national bank, must meet an administrative needs criterion on the financial history and condition of the bank, future earnings potential, and the needs of the community that the bank serves. The FDIC was also required to meet the same requirement prior to insuring a new nonmember state bank. The Banking Act of 1935 gave the federal regulators an effective veto power on the policies of chartering by states.

The link between entry and capital investment is (Peltzman 1965, 14)

$$B = \frac{C}{S} \qquad (3.7)$$

where B denotes the number of banks, C capital invested in banking, and S average capital size per bank. Taking natural logarithms of both sides of equation (3.7) and differentiating with respect to time (Ibid, 14):

$$\left(\frac{1}{B}\frac{dB}{dt}\right)^* = \left(\frac{1}{C}\frac{dC}{dt}\right)^* - \left(\frac{1}{S}\frac{dS}{dt}\right)^* \qquad (3.8)$$

This equation decomposes the change in the number of banks into a change in the stock of capital, or the rate of investment, and a change in the capital size per bank. The asterisks denote intended changes. The major role of capital in banking is insurance against insolvency caused by sequential withdrawal of deposits. The relation of capital to deposits is captured by (Ibid, 21):

$$C = kD^\alpha \qquad (3.9)$$

where C is capital, D deposits net of cash assets, α a positive constant, and k the ratio of C to D^α.

The determinants of the intended change in capital investment are expressed as (Ibid, 35):

$$\left(\frac{1}{B}\frac{dB}{dt}\right)^* = \psi\left(\pi, \left[\alpha\left(\frac{1}{D}\frac{dD}{dt}\right)^E\right], \ln k, \mu, \pi^0, R, u\right) \tag{3.10}$$

where π denotes the expected rate of return of capital, D the deposits net of cash, the superscript E expected, k the ratio of capital to deposits, μ the risk of capital loss, π^0 the expected rate of return in alternative investments, R the regulation, and u the random errors. The rate of change in the number of banks can be expressed as new entries, E_t, mergers and acquisitions (M&A), M_t, and the rate of bank suspensions and liquidations net of reopening, X_t (Ibid, 25):

$$\left(\frac{1}{B}\frac{dB}{dt}\right) = E_t - M_t - X_t \quad \text{or} \tag{3.11}$$

$$E_t = \left(\frac{1}{B}\frac{dB}{dt}\right) + M_t - X_t \tag{3.12}$$

Combining equation (3.11) with equation (3.12) yields the expression:

$$E_t = \psi\left(\pi, \left[\alpha\left(\frac{1}{D}\frac{dD}{dt}\right)^E\right], \ln k, \mu, \pi^0, R, u\right) - \left(\frac{1}{S}\frac{dS}{dt}\right) + M_t + X_t \tag{3.13}$$

The operational form of this equation is used by Peltzman to test the effects of regulation on entry.

The data used by Peltzman are for 1921–62, considering two subperiods, 1921–35 and 1936–62, which captures the implementation of the Banking Act of 1935. The rate of increase in number of banks in 1935–62 was 0.6 percent per year compared with estimates of the rate of 1.2 percent per year that would have occurred had there not been changes in the regulation of entry. Peltzman calculates that in the worst case the rate of new bank formation would have been 0.9 percent per year, 50 percent higher than under entry restrictions. During 1936–62, 2272 new banks were formed, for a yearly average of 84. Peltzman calculates that in the absence of restrictions 4500 new banks would have been created. Regulation reduced the creation of new banks by 2200.

In analysis of the electric industry, Stigler and Friedland (1962, 2) propose the evaluation of regulation as to whether it shifts significantly demand and supply curves in the industry to affect output and prices. Peltzman (1965, 14) focuses on a central issue of counterfactual in economics, which is measuring "the difference between the number of banks actually entering and the number which would enter without regulation." Edwards and Edwards (1974) argue that the analysis of Peltzman (1965) distorts the evaluation of entry regulation in two ways. First, Edwards and Edwards (1974, 445–51) contend that there is an error of ignoring the indirect effects of regulation. Entry restriction increases the expected profit rate in banking, causing overestimation of the impact of regulation on new entry of 45 percent. Second, regulatory behavior is not modeled correctly. The Banking Act of 1935, according to Edwards and Edwards (1974, 452), has a primary objective of preventing a high rate of failure in banking. The Banking Act of 1935 has an additional objective for regulators to consider the availability and quality of banking services. In the view of Edwards and Edwards, bank failures are likely to occur when actual and expected profits are low. High profit rates are found in noncompetitive markets, coinciding with unsatisfactory banking services. Regulators are likely to ease restrictions of entry when the expected profit rate increases and tighten restrictions when the expected profit rate declines. In implementing the Banking Act of 1935, the maximization of the self-interest of regulators in the form of prestige and power of their agencies would dictate easing of restrictions in the presence of high profits and tightening when expected profits decline. Edwards and Edwards measure an overestimation of the effects of entry of bank formation of 12 percent because of ignoring the correct regulatory model. They argue that the results coincide with the public interest view that regulation is motivated in promoting the public good instead of the capture theory of optimizing the self-interest of the regulated industry, the banks in this case.

The results of Peltzman (1965) on the reduction of entry in banking by the Banking Act of 1935, according to Burton and Settle (1992, 511), are largely confirmed by subsequent contributions by Edwards and Edwards (1974), Ladenson and Bombara (1984), and Throop (1975). The view of banking restriction by the Banking Act of 1935 ignores that 22 states softened restriction on branching in 1931–5 (Burton and Settle 1992, 512). Branches are substitutes for new banks and may have reduced the rate of entry of new banks. Burton and Settle (1992) use the operational models of Peltzman (1965), with appropriate control variable for the branching relaxation and supplementary analysis for entry in the states with unit banking. They conclude that their results are consistent with the hypothesis that banking entry was determined by the same factors existing before the Banking Act of 1935.

The relaxation of restrictions on intrastate branching, and in lesser form of interstate branching, which began in the 1970s was followed by significant improvements in the efficiency of banks (Jayaratne and Strahan 1998). After relaxation of restrictions on statewide branching, banks experienced a decline in losses of 29 basis points in the short run and 48 basis points in the long run. The accompanying decline in operating costs was 4.2 percent in the short run and 8 percent in the long run. These results are obtained by controlling business cycles in the states. The evidence suggests that most of the benefits were passed on to consumers, with declines in average loan rates of 19 basis points in the short run and 30 basis points in the long run. Increases in bank profitability were small and generally insignificant. In 1992, calculations suggest that borrowers saved about $6 billion in the form of lower loan rates. Relaxation of entry restrictions through branching deregulation triggered efficiency improvements as the better-performing banks grew at the expense of banks with high costs and low profits.

The impact of de novo bank entry in isolated markets, characterized by one, two, or three banks, resulted in higher costs and benefits (McCall and Peterson 1977, 1588). The study could not measure the effects of free entry but rather relaxation of entry conditions under current chartering and regulatory practices. McCall and Peterson create a singular sample from all banks in 1966–9 in isolated, rural markets with less than four banks and experiencing *de novo* unit or branch banking. Each bank experiencing *de novo* entry is paired with a control bank with similar characteristics except entry in its market. The sample included pairs of de novo entry and control banks in states with entry in unit banking systems and in branching systems in the two years prior to entry and the five years following entry. In states with restrictive branching regulation, the entry of *de novo* banks in rural, nonmetropolitan, monopoly or oligopoly markets affected profitability and the interest rate policies of banks in a major way. The effects occurred immediately and through the five years after entry. Depositors benefited from higher interest rates and competitor banks were not affected. There were no similar impacts in states with less restrictive branching regulation.

Agency costs in banking occur when management chooses units of preferred expenses in excess of what is required for optimal operations and manages banks with suboptimal risk-taking (Rose 1992, 326). Agency costs would be reduced by markets for capital, labor, and corporate control. Restrictions on bank entry and operations can increase agency costs. Rose uses a sample of 6444 banks in 22 states implementing significant relaxation of entry restrictions in 1969–87. Relaxation of restrictions was followed by reductions in noninterest costs for overhead and other operating expenses relative to total operating costs and on an employee basis. The reduction of entry barriers was also followed by an increase in accepting portfolio risks. There were increases in labor productivity and in dividends on common stock.

Small community banks provide a significant part of credit to small businesses but disappear in industry consolidation by merger, acquisition, or failure (DeYoung 2003). The disappearance of a small bank reduces the supply of credit to small businesses. *De novo* small banks with new charters can replace that segment of the supply of lending. After 1995, more than 1000 small *de novo* banks were created in the United States, providing loans to small businesses. The issue addressed by DeYoung is the fragility of these small *de novo* banks that causes the exit over the long run. The sample used covers 1664 new commercial banks that obtained charters during 1980–5 before the industry shocks of the 1980s and early 1990s. The control sample includes 2371 small established commercial banks serving the same geographical market as the newly chartered banks. In the initial period of operation *de novo* banks were as likely to fail as similar established banks. However, over time they consumed their start-up capital and were more likely to fail or be acquired than established banks. The rate of failure of *de novo* banks increased to about five times that of established banks, declining after a decade to the normal industry levels. There was a higher likelihood of failure of new banks established during the bank failures of 1984–5 than in 1981–4. *De novo* and established banks failed for similar factors, such as aggressive lending, inferior cost control, and use of noncore deposits. Both groups of banks were more likely to fail because of adverse environmental conditions, such as intensifying competition and lower economic growth, but *de novo* banks show significantly higher rates of failure in adverse external conditions.

Conduct and market performance in a product market segment or locality can be affected by (1) the number of competitors, (2) the average size of firms, and (3) the distribution between small and large firms (Cetorelli and Strahan 2003, 3). These three characteristics can determine capital accumulation and economic growth that measure the contribution of the segment or locality to economic welfare. The objective of Cetorelli and Strahan is to analyze empirically the relationship of banking concentration and regulation on competition in the product market segments. They use panel data beginning in 1977, when state-level deregulation began, and ending in 1994, when geographic restrictions on banking were relaxed by the Riegle-Neal Interstate Banking and Branching Efficiency Act. The estimated equation has several measures of industry structure as explained variables with bank dependence, banking competition, control variables, and fixed effects as explanatory variables.

The results of Cetorelli and Strahan reveal positive association of banking competition in local US markets with number of establishments, average establishment size, and higher share of small establishments through the entire size distribution. This evidence is consistent with the hypothesis that banks with market power create an entry barrier to producers possibly to protect their existing clients. Thus, market power can inhibit entrepreneurial development. Banking policy takes different shapes worldwide (Cetorelli and Strahan 2003). In the United States, bank mergers have been reshaped to prevent undesirable concentration in local markets. During the historical period, the United States restricted entry by unit banking and branching and interstate restrictions. The political economy is favorable to regulatory restrictions if there are benefits of appropriating rents for both incumbent banks and firms, which is the case of prohibitions of entry of foreign banks (Rajan and Zingales 2003).

There are potential advantages of firms that enter the market early, or early movers, and firms that enter later, or entrants (Berger and Dick 2007). The early mover may enjoy an advantage in the form of a barrier to entry that can prevent erosion of rent. The various factors are related to the fixed-cost investment decisions of the banks. On the demand side, there are costs for depositors in switching their accounts to other banks. There are sunk costs and scale economies on the side of supply. The early movers make fixed investments in attracting clientele. The costs are fixed because building and advertising do not depend on the number of consumers that are served or accessed by the branch and are sunk because they cannot be recouped. Consumers of the bank services become captive to the early movers because of the costs of switching to other banks. A significant part of the potential clientele of banks is captive in slow population environments prevailing in the advanced countries. Thus, entrants must attract clients from the non-captive segment of the population.

The unique data set of Berger and Dick covers 10,000 bank entries during 1972–2002 that identifies entry and exit date of all banking firms at the level of Metropolitan Statistical Area (MSA). They classify the banks into four groups in entry ranges from the past five years to 20 years. The econometric research considers the period 1992–2002 to analyze banks in all categories. The data cover 318 markets and over 8000 bank entries in the 11-year period. The main regression equation is (Berger and Dick 2007)

$$MS_{i,m,t} = \sum_j \beta^j OE^j_{i,m,t} * OE^j_{i,j,t} + \alpha^* IN_{1972} + \gamma_m + \eta_i + \tau_t + \upsilon_{i,m,t} \qquad (3.14)$$

where MS is market share of the ith bank in the mth market at time t for the jth order of entry, OE is the order of entry in the ranges of years, IN_{1972} denotes the early movers that had entered in 1972 or earlier, γ_m is a market fixed effect, η_i is a bank specific effect, τ_t is a year effect, and $\upsilon_{i,m,t}$ is a random disturbance. A second equation is specified to examine if the method of entry, such as M&A or *de novo* branches, is significant.

The results of Berger and Dick suggest that early movers have larger deposit shares, controlling for firm, market, and time effects. The later entrants have lower market shares than earlier entrants. The 1972 incumbents have the largest advantage in market share. Entrants can reduce their disadvantage if they enter by M&As instead of by de novo branches or charters. Strategic investments in large branch networks enhance the strength of early entrants in markets.

Market power

There are various approaches to analyzing the inefficiency of firms in concentrated industries. A significant part of the efforts of monopolists would not be in increasing output but rather in finding the optimum level of output restriction, as analyzed by Hicks (1935, 8). The variation around monopoly maximum profit may be low, depending on the slopes of the marginal revenue and marginal cost curves. Hicks (Ibid) argues that the subjective costs of adapting output to maximum profit may exceed the minor gains that could be realized. Monopolists are likely to have rapidly rising subjective costs. Thus, Hicks (Ibid) states that monopolists "are likely to exploit their advantage much more by not bothering to get very near the position of maximum profit, than by straining themselves to get very close to it. The best of all monopoly profits is a quiet life." This cost efficiency of monopoly is labeled as the "quiet life" hypothesis (Berger and Hannan 1998).

The method of applied welfare economics measures the cost of monopoly in terms of the welfare losses of consumer and producer surpluses resulting from a higher price and lower output relative to perfect competition. Harberger (1954) calculated the welfare losses caused by monopoly in US manufacturing during 1924–8 at less than 1 percent. These results conflict with neoclassical economics that considers the monopoly problem to be quite important. Lax management in firms in concentrated industries is analyzed by Williamson (1963). The degree of competition and motivational factors were considered by Leibenstein (1966) in explaining the contradiction between low profits and welfare losses in concentrated industries and neoclassical analysis of monopoly. Less than perfectly competitive firms would lack the motivation for effort summarized in the concept of X-efficiency that could explain low profits and welfare losses. The firm with market power could spend significant part of its excess profits in maintaining and enlarging those profits, as proposed by Tullock (1967, 2003) in the concept of the Tullock rectangle. The waste of monopoly profits in seeking legal protection of market power would be different in nature from the redistribution of wealth from consumers to monopolists. Trade barriers in developing countries provide the background for the concept of rent-seeking, which is the waste of resources found by Krueger (1974) (see Posner 1975). The concept was refined by Bhagwati (1982) in the concept of directly unproductive, profit-seeking activities (DUP) that seeks to explain losses from protectionism. The theory of the firm of Jensen and Meckling (1976) considers expense-preference behavior as an important agency cost of the separation of ownership and management (Berle and Means 1932). The low welfare losses of monopoly found by Harberger (1954) were confirmed in banking by Rhoades (1982).

The loss of efficiency because of concentration could exceed the deadweight losses of applied welfare economics, as argued by Berger and Hannan (1998, 454), because the efficiency losses would apply to every unit produced by concentrated firms while the welfare losses apply only to the output foregone because of higher prices. There are several sources of inefficiency in banking resulting from higher prices derived from market power (Berger and Hannan 1998, 455):

- *Quiet life*. This is the application of the proposition of Hicks (1935). Because of the cushion of the price under market power relative to competition, managers may permit increases in unit costs. The motive is consumption of the price difference while still passing on to owners benefits from the rents.

- *Expense preference.* This is the agency cost of the theory of the firm (Jensen and Meckling 1976). Managers may spend excessively in inputs, such as leisure, that maximize their utility functions. Another agency cost is taking risks that are lower than optimal.
- *Rent-seeking.* Managers may use excess profits in obtaining, maintaining, or enlarging market power (Tullock 1967; Krueger 1974; Bhagwati 1982).
- *X-efficiency.* Lack of managerial motivation, pursuit of goals other than profit maximization, and general X-efficiency concepts of Leibenstein (1966) may result in lax cost minimization.

There are two empirical models used by Berger and Hannan (1998): one to measure cost inefficiency and the other to measure welfare losses. They use an ownership sample of 233 banks and a full sample of 5263 banks in the United States during 1980–9. The cost function used in the first empirical model consists of the following equation (Berger and Hannan 1998, 457; see Berger and Mester 1997):

$$\ln C_{it} = \ln C_i(Y_{it}, w_{it}) + \ln x_i + \ln v_{it} \tag{3.15}$$

where t is time, C is operating costs, $C(Y, w)$ a cost function, Y an output quantity vector, w an input price vector, x_i an efficiency factor, and v a random error. The average residual, $\ln x_i^a$ for each bank, provides an estimate of $\ln x_i$. The second equation of the empirical model is (Berger and Hannan 1998, 456)

$$EFF_i = f(CONC_m, X_i) + \varepsilon_i \tag{3.16}$$

where i is the subscript for firm, EFF_i is a measure of the efficiency of the ith firm obtained from the cost function in equation (3.15), $CONC_m$ is a measure of concentration in the market m of operation of the ith firm, and ε_i is an error term.

The equation used for the measurement of the welfare loss in the second empirical model is (Ibid, 463)

$$WTL = (1/2)*PQ*\eta*\pi^2 \tag{3.17}$$

WTL is the welfare triangle loss, *PQ* is the product of prices *P* and quantities *Q* in the products in which the bank has market power, η is the elasticity of demand or supply in the case of deposits, and π is the proportionate change in price $\Delta P/P$ resulting from market power. Panagariya (2002, 175) provides the following formula to measure the cost of a tariff as proportion of GNP:

$$\frac{\text{Cost of protection}}{\text{GNP}} = (\tfrac{1}{2})\alpha\eta\rho^2 \qquad (3.18)$$

where α is the ratio of imports to GNP at the equilibrium with tariff, η is the absolute value of the arc elasticity of demand for imports in the movement from a protected equilibrium to a free-trade equilibrium, and ρ^2 is the square of a number less than unity. Panagariya argues that the calculations with this formula will likely provide low magnitudes. He reports that the numbers found in the early studies of the 1960s were quite low, less than 1 percent of GNP, and other subsequent calculations with GE models also provide relatively low numbers, in the range of 0.5 to 2 percent of GNP. The formula shows that the rate of increase of the cost of protection increases with the tariff. Panagariya (2002, 175) refers to a cost of 2.5 percent for a 50 percent tariff calculated by Harberger for Chile in the 1950s. Empirical measurements of welfare losses are typically quite low.

The empirical research conclusion of Berger and Hannan (1998) is that market power permits banks to avoid minimization of costs without being forced to exit the industry. The higher operating costs caused by market concentration exceed significantly the triangle-measured loss of welfare, by perhaps as much as a multiple of 20. An alternative measure of loss of efficiency shows that it exceeds the triangle welfare loss by a multiple of three.

Concentration and stability

A general equilibrium model is developed by Boyd, De Nicoló, and Smith (2004) to analyze the differential impact of competitive and monopolistic banking systems on the probability and effects of banking crises. It is not possible to analyze the probability of banking crises under competition or monopoly independently of the rate of inflation or monetary policy. A banking crisis occurs when reserve assets drop below their optimal level after withdrawal by depositors. There is higher probability of a crisis under monopoly than under competition if the nominal interest rate, or rate of inflation, is below a certain threshold. The probability of a crisis under competition is higher when inflation exceeds the threshold. The intuitive explanation consists of considering two effects. The monopolistic bank can increase expected profits by restricting its cash reserves, which would result in a higher probability of exhausting reserves, or a banking crisis, compared with competitive banking. This effect dominates at low levels of nominal interest rates or inflation below the threshold, resulting in higher crisis probability under monopoly. Returns to depositors are lower under monopolistic banking. This effect will dominate when nominal interest rates or inflation are higher, resulting in lower crisis probability under monopoly. In addition, the probability of output losses is higher under competition than under monopoly. The profit motive of the monopolist results in economizing the liquidation of assets except cash, thus not interrupting production. The final result of Boyd, De Nicoló, and Smith (2004) is that increases in the rate of inflation increase the probability of banking crisis under both competition and monopoly.

Cross-country data for 79 countries and 50 crises are used by Beck, Demirgüç-Kunt, and Levine (2003) to probe the effects on banking system fragility of bank concentration, bank regulation, bank ownership, and the general competitive/institutional environment. They find that systemic banking crises are less likely to occur in concentrated banking systems, even when controlling for multiple macroeconomic, regulatory, and institutional factors. Banking systems are destabilized by entry barriers and restrictions of banking activities. There is greater likelihood of systemic banking crises in environments of denial of entry in banking and tight restrictions of banking business lines. There is less likelihood of banking crises in countries promoting competition throughout the economy.

Central banking

This section provides the structure of analysis of central banking. There is an introductory subsection on general principles of central banking. The following subsection analyzes the mechanism of transmission of monetary policy through the credit channel and the financial accelerator. Many central banks have adopted the method of inflation targeting. The final subsection analyzes the important contributions of the critique of the use of econometric models in policy simulation and the time consistency of optimal policy.

Introduction

A general principle of central banking is derived by Bernanke (2000) from three historical episodes. First, the Great Depression could have been only a moderate decline in economic activity if the Fed had not increased interest rates to arrest an outflow of gold. Second, the Lost Decade of Japan in the 1990s could have been shorter in duration and lower in magnitude if the monetary authorities had not increased interest rates and took early measures to recover economic activity. Third, the stock market decline of October 19, 1987, was better managed by the provision of liquidity by the Fed, maintaining stability in stock exchange and futures markets. Based on these episodes Bernanke (2000) concludes that "history proves that a smart central bank can protect the economy and the financial sector from the nastier side effects of a stock market collapse."

The Fed combines in the same institution supervisory and central bank responsibilities. Bernanke (2007, 62) finds economies of scope in supervision and financial stability functions in the form of information, expertise, and powers. The supervisory functions of the Fed provide significant information on financial markets and institutions that is useful in design and implementation of monetary policy. The authority of bank examinations and the staff to conduct them has proved effective in taking remedial actions through the central banking function. Providing liquidity after 9/11, for example, relied on the knowledge of the management of key institutions, funding positions, financial positions, risk management, and capacity in evaluating collateral to provide funding. Bernanke (Ibid, 65) also provides similar examples in situations such as the Long Term Capital Management and Drexel Burnham Lambert.

Monetary policy distinguishes among policy goals, instruments, and intermediate targets (Bernanke and Mishkin 1992, 188). The goals or objectives of monetary policy vary among central banks, with the European Central Bank (ECB) focused on inflation. The US FRBO (2005) and the Federal Open Market Committee (FOMC), according to the Federal Reserve Act Section 2A, "shall maintain long run growth of the monetary and credit aggregates commensurate with the economy's long run potential to increase production, so as to promote effectively the goals of maximum employment, stable prices, and moderate long-term interest rates." The operating procedure of central banks consists of the choice of instruments and the methods by which they control them (Ibid). Instruments are variables that the central bank influences in the very short-term of a day or week. In practice, it is the choice of price or quantity that the central bank could attempt to fix by open market operations (Friedman 1990). The central bank policy rate, such as the fed funds rate in the United States, is the main policy instrument of central banks. The central bank policy rate is a proxy for the marginal cost of bank funding. Intermediate targets are variables that the central bank cannot control on a daily basis and are not policy goals but can be used to guide policy. Monetary aggregates, for example, can be considered intermediate targets (Bernanke and Mishkin 1992, 188).

The use of rules or discretion in monetary policy has been the subject of significant concern in economics, including the gold standard (Fischer 1990). A simple function of economic or monetary conditions determines a monetary rule (Bernanke and Mishkin 1992, 184). Friedman (1960) proposed a simple rule of growth of the money supply by a predetermined annual percentage. The advantage of rules is avoiding shocks caused by surprises, permitting a lower steady-state rate of inflation (Bernanke and Mishkin 1992, 184; Kydland and Prescott 1977). The advantage of discretion is that it allows the central bank to adjust policies in accordance with unforeseen circumstances in contrast with prior commitment to a specific rule. The choice of rules and discretion has been largely theoretical.

Bernanke and Mishkin (1992, 184–5) propose a pragmatic approach based on the analysis of monetary policy in six industrialized countries during 1973–91. Although admitting the limitations of case studies, they find normative and positive hypotheses that are subject to further analysis in the form of positive theories of central banking and empirical verification. The positive hypotheses found by Bernanke and Mishkin are as follows:

- *Crisis focus.* Central banks pursue multiple objectives but focus on those relating to current crises.
- *Inflation and targets.* Money growth targets are adopted during inflation, to help in choosing policy and to signal the intention to take tough measures.
- *Hybrid rules and discretion.* Central banks appear to follow rules in designing policy in medium- and long-term dimensions but retain the flexibility of discretion in addressing short-term concerns.

The normative hypotheses found by Bernanke and Mishkin consist of differences in the nature of monetary policy between less and more successful central banks. This cross-section analysis helps to derive lessons of design and execution of monetary policy. The most important normative hypothesis found by Bernanke and Mishkin is that Central banks have followed both rules and discretion but without accelerating inflation. For example, the implementation of medium-term money growth targets while engaging in exchange-rate stabilization in the short term coincided with stable inflation.

The transmission of monetary policy

The most important first step in the analysis of central banking is the determination of whether impulses of monetary policy affect output and prices. This is a difficult task. Romer and Romer (2004) provide a fresh approach by measuring a new indicator of monetary policy. An important hurdle is the confusion of endogenous movements in conventional measures such as the stock of money and the fed funds rate. Another distortion is the relation of the measure of monetary policy with the anticipatory forecasts of the Fed. Romer and Romer use qualitative information on FOMC meetings in 1969–96 and quantitative measurements in deriving a new series of the "intended funds rate" changes. The objective is to purge the endogenous components from the actual measurement of monetary policy. The effects on output and prices of both the intended and actual indicators of monetary policy are measured. The results of Romer and Romer (2004, 1056) indicate strong relationship between shocks of monetary policy and industrial production. Industrial production begins to fall five months after a tightening shock, reaching a minimum in about two years. The impact is strong and highly significant: a one percentage point tightening is related with a decline in industrial production of 4.3 percent. Tightening monetary policy is associated with declining inflation but with longer lag. A one percentage point tightening is associated with almost no change in inflation in the first 22 months, when it declines steadily. In 48 months, a one percentage point tightening decreases inflation by 6 percent.

Movements in real output follow monetary impulses with a lag that may extend for two years or more (Bernanke and Gertler 1995, 27). The credit channel of monetary policy is not an independent explanation but rather a mechanism that enhances the transmission of monetary policy. Endogenous changes in the premium of external finance amplify the effects of monetary policy on interest rates. The external premium is the difference between the costs of obtaining external finance, such as by the issue of equity or debt, and the opportunity costs of using retained earnings.

Frictions in the credit markets create a wedge between the expected returns of lenders and the costs to potential borrowers (Ibid, 28). The frictions consist of imperfect information, search for borrowing opportunities, costly writing, and enforcement of contracts (Hall 2001, 443). Potential lenders do not have the same information about the true financial position of borrowers. Loans may be extended to borrowers who are not creditworthy or denied to sound borrowers, which is adverse selection, or used by borrowers in projects with much higher risk than contracted with lenders, which is a moral hazard. A change in interest rates causes a change in the same direction in the premium of external finance. The borrower may use internal finance up to a certain level. The supply of external finance after that level may become more inelastic as the lender tries to compensate for the frictions by charging higher interest rates for credit (Ibid, 444–5). That is, there would be a higher premium for external finance. If there is an increase in interest rates, supply may become even more inelastic because of the higher risk of default perceived by lenders. The external premium would increase even more. A decrease in interest rates would result in less inelastic supply, decreasing the premium of external finance because of lower perceived risk of default. Firms that finance a larger portion of the project with internal finance or that can post higher collateral may experience a lower premium of external finance.

There are two explanations of how monetary policy affects the premium of external finance (Bernanke and Gertler 1995, 29). First, the balance sheet channel postulates that change in monetary policy alter the balance sheets and income statements of borrowers, affecting such variables as net worth, cash flow, and liquid assets. Second, the bank lending channel analyzes how the monetary policy impulse has effects on the supply of loans by depository institutions. The balance sheet channel is much better established than the bank lending channel. Bernanke and Gertler (1995) propose a more general view of the existence of a credit channel without assigning greater relative importance to the balance sheet of bank lending routes. Monetary policy consists of changing short-term interest rates with less impact on long-term interest rates. Thus, the finding by Bernanke and Gertler (1995, 29) of impact on variables that reflect longer-term decisions is somewhat intriguing:

> The earliest and sharpest declines in final demand occur in residential investment, with spending on consumer goods (including both durables and nondurables) close behind.

The net worth of a borrower, consisting of the sum of liquid assets and marketable collateral, is inversely associated with the premium of external finance. With stronger net worth the borrower may use a higher proportion of self-generated funds in investment and spending, relying less on external funds (Bernanke and Gertler 1995, 35). This behavior explains collateral and down payments in borrowing arrangements. Increasing interest rates weaken the balance sheets of borrowers by raising short-term interest rates and by causing declines in the marketable value of assets that could be used as collateral. Declining interest rates strengthen borrowers' balance sheets by decreasing short-term costs and increasing asset values. The investment and spending decisions of borrowers are affected by changes in their balance sheets. The financial accelerator argues that endogenous procyclical movements in the balance sheets of borrowers may amplify and propagate business cycles (Ibid, 35).

A model of intercompany lending by Kiyotaki and Moore (2002, 46) analyzes lending contagion through balance-sheet effects. First, there are indirect effects as fluctuation of asset prices affect the value of real loan collateral. At the end of the period of financing, the assets held are equal to the ratio of net worth to the difference between asset and collateral prices. If there is a shock to a group of firms related by similar collateral, the net worth of constrained firms declines, decreasing asset demand and user costs. The decline in user costs causes a decline in asset prices. All firms in the group suffer a capital loss on their assets, shrinking net worth. Firms reduce current investment, resulting in future lower revenue, net worth, and investment. Kiyotaki and Moore (Ibid, 49) argue that there is an intertemporal multiplier effect being processed through asset prices. The effects propagate to other firms than the one that first experienced the shock. Second, default has direct effects through credit chains. The disruption of production in some firms causes similar effects on other firms, causing a generalized decline of output.

The bank lending channel operates when banks experience difficulty in obtaining external finance, that is, deposits and other funding (Hall 2001, 445). Firms would compete for a smaller pool of available lending funds, increasing the loan rate. Larger firms may find alternative sources of financing but smaller ones may not be able to replace bank loans for other external sources of financing. According to Hall (Ibid), "the resulting tightening in loan supply under the bank lending channel is often termed a credit crunch." The important characteristic of the credit crunch is the widening differential between borrowing costs for firms and policy interest rates of the central bank. The cost and/or availability of finance in the form of loan spreads and volumes are indicators of the credit crunch, which were widely monitored in the credit/dollar crisis after 2007–8. Other sources constraining external financing of banks can originate in shocks in the economy, such as increasing debt defaults and collapse of stock prices of banks, and in regulatory changes, such as increases in capital requirements (Ibid, 446). These shocks can reduce the elasticity of supply of external financing of banks, causing a credit crunch.

The essential proposition of the lending view is that central banks can shift loan supply functions of banks (Kashyap and Stein 2000, 407). The withdrawal of bank reserves by the central bank, for example, could cause contraction of bank loans, which would increase the cost of external finance to firms that depend on bank loans. The lending channel assumes frictions in the form of nonapplicability of the proposition of Modigliani and Miller (1958). The first proposition of Modigliani and Miller is on the value invariance of financing the firm (see the second proposition in Miller and Modigliani 1961). The capital structure is the choice of debt versus equity to finance the firm, or the ratio of debt to equity. Under no costs of bankruptcy, the value of the firm is independent of the ratio of debt to equity. Under the Modigliani and Miller invariance of financing banks would be indifferent in funding by means of deposits that are insured and subject to reserve requirements, on the one hand, and other sources of funding that are not subject to reserve requirements and are not insured, on the other hand. A simple example is the trade off between demand deposits, which are both insured and subject to reserve requirements, and wholesale certificates of deposits, which are neither insured nor subject to reserve requirements. In this frictionless world, the monetary impulse would simply alter the relative proportion in funding of sources that are subject to reserve requirements relative to those that are not.[2]

Banks issue equity and debt to individual investors to fund loans to firms that are dependent on bank loans. The critical friction in banking is the asymmetry of information on the assets of the banks between bankers and investors that may result in adverse selection (Stein 1998, 466). There are no frictions if the bank can fund loans with insured liabilities that are subject to reserve requirements. Constraints on the issue of insured liabilities can result in adverse selection as the banks resort to noninsured funding. In the presence of frictions, the central bank can influence the spread of loan rates over the rates on open market securities (Ibid, 467). The withdrawal of bank reserves by monetary policy forces banks to increase their funding of uninsured deposits that are affected by adverse selection; this substitution causes contraction of aggregate bank lending and resulting increase in the relative cost of bank loans. In addition, banks demand reserves at the central bank to issue insured deposits. The central bank can influence rates in the bond market by affecting the demand for bank reserves (Ibid).

The significant diversification of financial instruments, with the rise of credit risk transfer vehicles, raises doubts about the frictions of insured and uninsured funding sources of banks. Significant portions of bank lending are funded by structured products, such as ABS. The credit/ dollar crisis after 2007–8 could be interpreted as amplified by unprecedented rise in perceived counterparty risk in SRPs. Counterparty risk is a manifestation of adverse selection. However, the events may not provide support for the bank lending channel because the action of the central banks consisted of using all available measures in monumental doses to reduce counterparty risk with limited and much delayed effects.

Empirical results showing that monetary policy is followed by effects on output could be interpreted in various ways. There is a critical identification problem. The contraction in loans may not be the consequence of monetary policy constraining the ability of banks to fund with insured deposits but rather the result of an inward shift of loan demand schedules (Kashyap and Stein 2000, 408). There are also competing theoretical propositions, such as the balance sheet channel that Bernanke and Gertler (1995) find to be of greater relative importance.

An approach to testing indirectly the lending channel is to consider the shifts in the composition of external finance by firms (Kashyap, Stein, and Wilcox 1993, 1996). There are two necessary conditions for the working of the lending channel. First, banks consider securities and loans as imperfect substitutes on the asset side of their balance sheets; tightening of monetary policy would contract loan supply by banks. Second, firms consider loans and nonbank financing as imperfect substitutes; contraction of loan supply would have effects on the production side of the economy. The empirical results of Kashyap, Stein, and Wilcox (1993) suggest that changes in monetary policy affect the structure of loans and commercial paper, which then appears to affect investment.

An approach is to consider differences in banks in the capacity to obtain uninsured funding when faced with reduction of reserves caused by central bank monetary policy. Less liquid banks may be forced to reduce assets after withdrawal of reserves by open market sales while those with stronger balance sheets may be able to replace the loss of liquidity. The first hypothesis of Kashyap and Stein (2000, 409) is that $\partial^2 L_{it}/\partial B_{it}\partial M_t < 0$, where the subscripts i and t denote banks and time, L_{it} measures bank lending, B_{it} measures balance sheet strength, and M_t is an indicator of monetary policy. The cross-sectional derivative $\partial L_{it}/\partial B_{it}$ expresses the sensitivity of lending constraint at any time t, intensifying during periods of tight money. The time series derivative $\partial L_{it}/\partial M_t$ is a measure of the sensitivity of lending activity to central bank policy, intensifying for banks with weaker balance sheets. Kashyap and Stein test a second hypothesis that smaller banks have weaker balance sheets, experiencing stronger effects from reserve withdrawals by the central bank. Kishan and Opiela (2000) also test the lending channel by analysis of individual bank data.

The data set of Kashyap and Stein (2000) consists of quarterly income statements and balance sheets of all reporting banks in 1976–93, for a total of 961,530 bank quarters. They conclude that monetary policy has greater influence on smaller banks with less liquid balance sheets.

Prices of assets acquired with borrowing may fluctuate more widely in response to changes in fundamental factors. The ability to borrow with collateral is the key factor that causes the fluctuation of these assets. The amplifying effect on regional house prices is processed through the decline of demand for houses resulting from the impairment of the ability to borrow against assets with declining prices (Lamont and Stein 1999). There are three types of potential repeat buyers in the theoretical framework used by Lamont and Stein (1999, 500). First, unconstrained movers are families that are never in pressure to sell their homes but may sell if there are advantages, such as new jobs, better schools, and others. These families demand houses as a decreasing function of price, performing a stabilizing role. Second, constrained movers may not have sufficient money to provide a larger down payment. The demand for housing for this group is an increasing function of prices because they could sell the house to obtain part of the down payment for another house. Third, constrained nonmovers do not have resources to acquire a new house and have no influence on house prices. The basic proposition of Lamont and Stein (1999, 500) is that there must be a high ratio of constrained movers to unconstrained movers for leverage to have significant impact on house prices. The implication is that there is meaningful price impact of leverage in regions with a high proportion of homeowners with high loan to value (LTV) ratios.

The data set of Lamont and Stein (1999, 501) covers 44 metropolitan areas in 1984–94. The endogenous nature of leverage at the city level requires estimation with instrumental variables. They find a significant and economically meaningful correlation between leverage at the city level and the elasticity of response of house prices to shocks of per capita income.

The housing market provides the empirical evidence for testing the endogenous mechanism of the financial accelerator by Almeida, Campello, and Liu (2006). In most countries, there is a down payment constraint in obtaining a mortgage loan. Suppose that the down payment is a fraction, τ, of the value of the house, P. Mortgage banks impose this constraint on borrowers to ensure recovery of the principal lent in case of default. Thus, the loan, L, cannot exceed a fraction, λ, of P, where λ equals $1 - \tau$. The maximum LTV ratio, L/P, is provided by λ (Ibid, 325). That is,

$$\lambda = LTV \le \frac{L}{P} \tag{3.19}$$

It is easier for households to borrow to finance spending the higher LTV ratio. In reality, $\lambda < 1$ constitutes a quantity constraint of down payment or collateral on households. The affordability or income constraint is the limit of the yearly service of the mortgage, equal to loan payment plus property taxes plus insurance, to a specific fraction of the household's expected future income per year. For example, in the United States, there is a limit of the expenditures on housing of 28 percent of yearly income. If the house value is $100 with a down payment of $30, the expenditures on the loan plus taxes and insurance is 10 percent of the value of the mortgage or $7, then the minimum household income to qualify for the house is $25 equal to $7/.28 (Ibid, 327).

There are three empirical propositions tested by Almeida, Campello, and Liu. First, in case of binding collateral constraint, the sensitivity of housing prices to housing demand increases with increases in the maximum LTV ratio offered to households. Second, in case of binding collateral constraint, the sensitivity of new mortgage borrowing increases after increases in the maximum LTV ratio offered to households. Third, the driver of the sensitivity of housing prices to housing demand shocks is the country-years in which there is less likelihood of a binding income or affordability constraint.

The sample used by Almeida, Campello, and Liu (2006, 328) is obtained from 26 countries during 1970–99 for housing data and GDP per capita, which is the driver of the empirical tests. Their results show that in countries with higher maximum LTV ratios both housing prices and new mortgage borrowings are more sensitive to aggregate income shocks. In countries where the income or affordability constraint is less likely to bind, there is higher sensitivity between LTV ratios and income. There is a procyclical effect of debt capacity on housing prices processed by the collateral constraint. There are stronger procyclical effects of debt capacity in countries with high LTV ratios.

Inflation targeting

There are two ingredients of inflation targeting, according to Bernanke (2003). First, inflation targeting consists of a monetary policy framework.

It originated in the substitution of intermediate money growth goals, such as by the Bundesbank (central bank of Germany), with inflation goals. The Bundesbank used money growth targets consistent with its desire of maintaining inflation around 2 per cent per year. Explicit intermediate inflation targets began to be used by several central banks in the 1990s. The monetary policy framework of inflation targeting is characterized (Bernanke 2003, 9; Bernanke and Mishkin 1997, 106) as "constrained discretion." Monetary policy is constrained by the intermediate, quantitative goal of attaining a given annual percentage inflation of, say, 2 percent per year. Discretion is exercised in the short term when needs arise to maintain output resulting in full employment. The central bank must have credibility about inflation control to effectively use discretion to attain the short-term objective. Credibility by the central bank is attained, according to Bernanke (2003), by anchoring inflation expectations. Central bank credibility was eroded, in this view, in the 1970s, when excessive monetary expansion sanctioned the higher oil prices after 1973, causing deep recession during 1973–5, and another recession in 1982 when the interest rate in the United States rose to nearly 20 percent to break inflation. The great moderation of the past two decades (Rogoff 2006), in the form of lower volatility of output and inflation but continuing high volatility of financial variables, such as prices and rates of financial assets, could be explained by the enhanced credibility of central banks (Bernanke 2003). The lowering of the fed funds to nearly zero in 2003–4 and in 2007–8, with a major commodity shock in the second episode, were feasible, according to an interpretation of this view, because of the credibility of the Fed in controlling inflation. As in all economics, there are likely other factors explaining the lack of inflation after monumental doses of monetary impulses with older and newer policy instruments. In 2003–4, the monetary impulse of zero rates may have been a key factor in the rise of asset prices, such as houses and stock market valuations. In 2007–8, monetary impulses may have fed the rise in commodity prices in futures markets.

Second, the inflation targeting policy has an important communication strategy (Bernanke 2003, 10; Bernanke and Mishkin 1997, 106). The central bank must effectively communicate inflation goals to the executive and legislature, the financial markets and the public. The goals must have a quantitative percentage specification of maximum inflation, a time framework, and periodic releases of forecasts. The communication strategy is designed to enhance the credibility of the central bank. An inflation report consists of a technical document, showing the analytical and empirical background of the inflation target and its execution.

Policy makers would not implement a mechanical policy rule but could informally operate a rule requiring judgment (Taylor 1993, 198; see Asso, Kahn, and Leeson 2007 for the evolution of thought). In this framework, the policy makers would recognize the responses of the general instrument in the policy rule. Pure discretion would require the resetting of policy instruments in every period. The policy rule is a permanent contingent plan that ends only with a cancellation clause (Taylor 1993, 1999). Thus, a policy rule is meaningful if it is operated during a significant period of time.

The quantity theory of money, $MV = PY$, where M is the money stock, V income velocity, P prices, and Y output, was used by Friedman and Schwartz (1963) in the analysis of US economic history (Taylor 1999). There is a close connection between the policy rule of Taylor (1993, 1999) and the quantity equation. The functional form of velocity is $V(r, Y)$, where r is the interest rate. The substitution of V in the quantity theory of money equation yields a relation between r and P and Y. This leads to an expression of r as a function of two variables, the price level, P, and real output, Y. Assuming a linear relation of the interest rate with the logarithms of the price level and output, making the price level and output stationary by considering the first difference of the price level or inflation and the deviation of output from a possibly stochastic trend and abstracting from lags, Taylor (1993, 1999) derives the following equation:

$$r = \pi + gy + h(\pi - \pi^*) + r^f = (r^f - h\pi^*) + (1 + h)\pi + gy \qquad (3.20)$$

where r is the short-term interest rate, π the inflation rate or percentage change in P, y the percentage deviation of real output Y from trend, and g, h, π^* (inflation target) and r^f (real rate of interest) are constants.

There are relevant conclusions in the analysis of the history of monetary policy in the United States by Taylor (1999). The policy rule complements the analysis by Friedman and Schwartz (1963). There is response of interest rates to inflation and real output according to a monetary policy rule that is implied in various monetary systems. US economic history is characterized by major changes in the monetary rule accompanied by major changes in economic stability. Taylor (1999) argues that the analysis of the reasons of monetary policy changes suggests that they influenced economic outcomes instead of the reverse proposition. A good policy rule in historical experience is the one in which the interest rate response to inflation and real output is more aggressive, that is, $h > 0$, and $(1 + h)$ is higher. For example, the interest rate was insufficiently low in the late 1960s and 1970s, accommodating the oil price increase with higher inflation. There was lower inflation with an output cost after the excessive tightening in the early 1980s. The great moderation observed recently (Rogoff 2006) was accompanied by more aggressive policy, higher *(1 + h)*, that promoted price stabilization with output growth. There was a learning process of central bankers together with institutional changes and investments in new ways of analyzing policy.

The inflation target framework of the Bank of England (BEO) consists of constrained discretion (Bean 2003). In practice, the BEO decides on the policy measures for adjusting to shocks and in the rapidity of implementing the target after deviations. The Chancellor of the Exchequer, acting as principal, provides each year to the agent, the BOE, a "remit," specifying the desired rate of inflation, measured by the harmonized index of consumer prices (HICP). This remit also specifies the economic policies of the government in maintaining stable levels of economic growth and employment. Bean (2003, 487) provides an example in the form of maximizing the expected value of a quadratic loss function:

$$L_t = E_t \left[\sum_{k=0}^{k=\infty} \beta^k \frac{\left\{ L(\pi_{t+k} - \pi^*)^2 + \lambda(y_{t+k} - y_{t+k}^*)^2 \right\}}{2} \right] \tag{3.21}$$

The supply side is represented by a new Keynesian forward Philips inflation curve (Bean 2003, 487; see Clarida, Galí, and Gertler 1665, 2001):

$$\pi_t = \beta E_t \pi_{t+1} + \kappa(y_t - y_t^*) + u_t \tag{3.22}$$

In these equations t is time, π is inflation, π^* the desired rate of inflation, y the output, y^* the potential output, u a supply shock, and β, λ and κ parameters. With $\pi > 0$, inflation targeting is flexible, considering both inflation and the output gap as targets entering the loss function (Svensson 2003, 431).

The optimum plan requires the satisfaction of the first order conditions for all $k \geq 0$ (Bean 2003, 487):

$$E_t \pi_{t+k} = -\left(\frac{\lambda}{k} \right) E_t [(y_{t+k} - y_{t+k}^*) - (y_{t+k-1} - y_{t+k-1}^*)] \tag{3.23}$$

The equation means that the optimal plan requires that the marginal rate of transformation between output and inflation that is embodied in the supply schedule is equal to the marginal rate of substitution that is embodied in the loss function. As Bean (2003, 487) observes, the optimal plan "ensures that inflation will be brought back to target, but at a rate that recognizes the consequences for activity."

The approach of flexible inflation targeting consists of stabilizing inflation around a relatively low level while policy is concerned in maintaining output close to potential output (Svensson 2003, 426). The simple instrument rule approach is based on the Taylor (1993) rule. A variant of this approach advises that the rule should be only a guide-line and not a firm commitment. Svensson (2003, 428) argues that the use of simple instrument rules is incomplete, allowing deviations from the rule but without specifying rules for determining appropriate deviations. This approach would be insufficiently concrete for practical applications.

In practice, central banks have not committed to simple instrument rules or their various variants. An alternative approach is by means of tar-get rules specifying the objectives to be attained, the levels of the targets, and the explicit or implicit loss function, considering information avail-able to the central banks and their judgment, that would be minimized (Svensson 2003, 429). This approach would incorporate all information, in particular the use of judgments. An optimal targeting rule consists of an operational expression of the condition of equality of the marginal rates of transformation and marginal rates of substitution between the target variables. Central banks collect significant amounts of information using various types of judgment and forecast key variables. The approach fol-lowed in practice may be considered as inflation forecast targeting (Ibid, 466). The policy instrument is managed in such a way that the inflation forecast based on available information and judgment corresponds to the inflation target with limited variation of the output gap.

The Lucas Critique and consistency

The Lucas (1976) Critique argues that econometric models are useful in short-term forecasting but that simulations using these models do not provide valuable information on the evaluation of alternative economic policies. The issue is not the deviations between the estimated and actual structure *before* the policy change. The problem is the deviation between the prior actual structure and the structure that is valid *after* the policy impulse. In the theory of economic policy, the following dif-ference equation determines the motion of the economy (Lucas 1976):

$$y_{t+1} = f(y_t, x_t, \varepsilon_t) \tag{3.24}$$

where y_t is a vector of state variables, t a time index, x_t a vector of exogenous forcing variables, and ε_t identically distributed random shocks. The task of empirical research is to estimate the function f. The practical problem is estimating the values of a vector θ of fixed parameters, using (Ibid):

$$f(y, x, \varepsilon) = F(y, x, \theta, \varepsilon) \tag{3.25}$$

There is no difficulty in estimating θ because the past values of x_t are observed. Forecasting requires inserting forecasted values of x_t into F. Policy can be evaluated with knowledge of F, θ, and future values of x_t. The central assumption of the theory of economic policy is whether (F, θ) will remain stable after changes in the forcing sequence $\{x_t\}$.

The evaluation of policy is conducted by choosing the current value of policy, x_0, and future values, $x_1, x_2, \ldots$, and inserting them in (F, θ). The validity of this method requires assuming that there is no systematic change of (F, θ) with the choice of $\{x_t\}$. Lucas argues that the knowledge of dynamic economic theory leads to the conclusion that this assumption is not justified. Some view on the path of future variables that concern economic agents is required, together with other factors, in obtaining the decision rules corresponding to (F, θ), such as supply and demand functions. The assumption of stability of (F, θ) under alternative policy rules is equivalent to assuming that the views of economic agents are not altered by changes in policy shocks. Lucas argues that the structure of econometric models is determined by optimal decision rules, such as demand and supply functions, which vary systematically with the changes in policy. Thus, the structure of econometric models may be altered by changes in policy. The policy process would require reestimation of the structure and future changes in policy, altered again by changes in expectations by economic agents, and so on (Kydland and Prescott 1977, 474).

One of the examples of Lucas (1976) refers to temporary investment tax credits to stimulate the economy during recessions (Chari 1998, 183). Firms may postpone investment when they anticipate the tax credit moving through the political process, accentuating the recession that policy intends to ameliorate.

An important result of the Lucas (1976) critique is leading to an articulated research program (Chari 1998, 183). The program would specify the structural model and policy regime in which the economy is believed to operate. The policy regime consists of a function prescribing the policies corresponding to every economic state. The model assumes agents that are aware of the policy regime. The model is then taken to data to find the policy regime and actual details. It is only possible to understand policy effects by choosing among alternative rules. Decisions on monetary policy require that the authorities know the change in future expectations in response to the policy impulse. If the policy impulse is within the current policy regime, it is possible to predict the effects of the policy. It is quite difficult to uncover the policy regime. It is possible to provide advice in choosing among alternative policy rules (Ibid).

Optimum control theory is an elegant and powerful method in analyzing dynamic systems but it is not suitable for dynamic economic planning, according to an important proposition by Kydland and Prescott (1977, 473). It is not even adequate when there is a well-defined, generally agreed fixed social objective function. The social objective function will not be optimized even when planners implement the best discretionary policy on the basis of the current situation. If current outcomes and the movement of the state of the system depend only on past policy decisions and the current state, optimal control theory is an appropriate tool. This is not likely the case in dynamic economic systems. The current decisions of economic agents are sensitive to their expectations of future policy impulses. Optimal control theory is appropriate for policy design if the expectations of future policy impulses by economic agents are not sensitive to the future policy plan. It is quite likely that economic agents will guess the forthcoming policy impulse if they understand the structure that determines the decision rules embodied in supply and demand functions. The expectations of economic agents on future policies affect their current decisions after changes in the social objective function. While this is consistent with optimal control theory all that is required is that agents have some knowledge of the likely change of attitudes of policy makers resulting from changing economic conditions. Calvo (1978) extends the analysis of the time consistency of optimal policy to a monetary economy.

After the information revolution with multiple financial/economic press vehicles covering markets worldwide economic agents are quite aware of the likely path of future economic policy in response to deteriorating or improving economic conditions. The speed of adaptation of expectations of economic agents on future policy in response to the current environment has become likely almost instantaneously. The Lucas (1976) critique is becoming even more relevant with the electronic dissemination of financial/economic information. Circumventing the Lucas critique requires an infinite loop of iterations of recalculating the structure in response to changes caused by expectations of future policy.

The two-period case illustrates the principle of Kydland and Prescott (1977, 476) that the optimal plan is inconsistent. Consider the fixed social objective function depending on the decisions of economic agents, ψ_i, $i = 1,2$, and the policy decisions, ρ_i (Ibid):

$$S = S(\psi_1, \psi_2, \rho_1, \rho_2) \tag{3.26}$$

The optimal plan is obtained by maximizing (3.26) subject to

$$\psi_1 = \Psi_1(\rho_1, \rho_2)$$

and

$$\psi_2 = \Psi_2(\psi_1, \rho_1, \rho_2) \tag{3.27}$$

The Ψ_i denominate functions of agents' decisions. The plan is consistent if ρ_2 maximizes the social objective function (3.26), given the past decisions, ψ_1, ρ_1, and the constraint (3.27). If the functions are differentiable and there is an interior solution, Kydland and Prescott (1977, 476) obtain the necessary conditions for consistency:

$$\left(\frac{\partial S}{\partial \psi_2}\right)\left(\frac{\partial \Psi_2}{\partial \rho_2}\right) + \frac{\partial S}{\partial \rho_2} = 0 \tag{3.28}$$

The effects of the consistent policy at 2, ρ_2, on ψ_1, are ignored. The first order condition for the optimal decision rule is (Kydland and Prescott 1977, 476) :

$$\left\{\left(\frac{\partial S}{\partial \psi_2}\right)\left(\frac{\partial \Psi_2}{\partial \rho_2}\right) + \frac{\partial S}{\partial \rho_2}\right\} + \left\{\frac{\partial \Psi_1}{\partial \rho_2}\left[\frac{\partial S}{\partial \psi_1} + \left(\frac{\partial S}{\partial \psi_2}\right)\left(\frac{\partial \Psi_2}{\partial \psi_1}\right)\right]\right\} = 0 \tag{3.29}$$

The first term in braces on the left hand of (3.29) must be zero to meet the consistency condition in (3.28). The consistency condition (3.28) is met if the second term in braces in the left hand (3.29) is zero, which can occur in two different ways (Ibid). First, the effect of the policy ρ_2 on the decisions of economic agents ψ_1 is zero, that is, $\partial \Psi_1/\partial \rho_2 = 0$. Economic agents do not change their decisions on the basis of anticipations of economic policy in the next period. Second, the term in the square brackets in the second term in braces is zero, that is, $[\partial S/\partial \psi_1 + (\partial S/\partial \psi_2)(\partial \Psi_2/\partial \psi_1)] = 0$. This means that the effects of changes in S by ψ_1 directly or indirectly through ψ_2 are zero.

There is a revealing example by Kydland and Prescott (1977, 477). Suppose there is an area that is highly exposed to risk of life and property because of flooding. The optimum social outcome is that no houses be built in that area. If there were a policy commitment by the government not to provide costly flood prevention devices, no rational economic agent would ever live and build in that risky area. However, if economic agents surmised that the government would provide dams and levees to prevent floods and then rescue lives and compensate property losses after a flood, people would live and build in flood-doomed areas. The example illustrates how anticipations of future policy, flood prevention, and physical/pecuniary rescue jeopardize the optimum social outcome of not placing lives and property in jeopardy.

Summary

The relaxation of interstate and intrastate restriction promoted competition in banking services. There is less concern in banking regulation on market power. After two decades of sustained economic growth with low inflation and volatility of output and inflation, there was significant consensus that central banks had mastered the dual, conflicting, and elusive mandate of prosperity without inflation (Burns 1958). The credit/dollar crisis has demystified central banking, leading to a search for new rules on systemic regulation, procyclicality, and cross-border cooperation considered in Chapter 6. The regulatory approach depends on the view of the origin, propagation, and strength of impact of the credit/dollar crisis.

4
Investment Banking, Governance, Mergers, and Compensation

Introduction

This chapter and the following deal with the issues of regulation of financial institutions engaged in transactions with securities. The first section of this chapter considers the market structure of banking in relation to securities: universal, conglomeration, or specialized. The Glass-Steagall Act constitutes regulation during difficult times. Underwriting and loan syndications are important activities of investment banking. Governance is critical to the protection of rights of stakeholders in corporations. Mergers and acquisition raise intriguing issues of entry, corporate law, and takeover defenses.

Market structure

There are advantages and disadvantages in universal banking (Benston 1994; Saunders and Walter 1994). The universal bank engages in the entire range of financial activities: taking funds from the public to lend, underwriting, and brokerage of securities and insurance. The universal bank may own equity in nonfinancial firms, voting on the shares it owns and by delegation on the shares of others and electing its employees as members of the boards on which they hold equity (Benston 1994, 121). Financial conglomerates are financial institutions engaged in all types of financial activities: traditional banking, insurance and securities underwriting, and brokerage (Vander Vennet 2002, 254).

The US system imposed specialized banking with the Glass-Steagall Act of 1933 (Benston 1990), separating investment and commercial banking, which is discussed below. The Bank Holding Company Act and the National Banking Act prohibited US banks from engaging in insurance, real estate brokerage, and other financial services (Benston 1994, 122). Restrictions on banking in the United States, particularly of large banks, originate in the reservations of many of the founding fathers, with the exception of Alexander Hamilton (Hamilton 1780; Cowen, Sylla and Wright 2006; Peláez 2008). According to Sylla and Wright (2006, 656):

> Alexander Hamilton, US Secretary of the Treasury during 1789–1795, had absorbed important lessons of financial history during the previous decade. On the basis of what he had learned, Hamilton formulated a comprehensive plan to give the United States a modern financial system. He then executed the plan during his term of office.

There are seven issues concerning universal banks (Benston 1994). First, the failure of one or more universal banks could have systemic effects, causing the failure of other financial institutions and affecting the production of the economy. However, Benston (1994, 124) finds that only 10 of the 9440 banks that failed during the Great Depression were not specialized unit banks. Second, directed lending for industrial and economic policy can be accomplished through specialized institutions. Directed lending has caused financial instability such as in the United States in housing by Fannie Mae and Freddie Mac or by development banks in emerging countries. Third, universal banks could frustrate the unique system of the United States in protecting minority shareholders. The legal environment explains the type of financial system chosen by countries (La Porta et al. 1997). Fourth, universal banks could crowd out specialized banks because of economies of scale and scope. Fifth, there are also potential harmful effects of related lending (La Porta et al. 2003; Maurer and Haber 2005, 2007). Here, there is also an issue of financial stability because the bank could provide riskier "related loans" to the nonfinancial company that has equity stake in the bank. Sixth, there is no reason why universal banks would engage as alleged in practices that are detrimental to consumers. Seventh, there is the conflict of interest of issuing inferior securities of clients likely to default to redeem their debt to the bank and pass on the credit risk to the investors buying the securities.

The Second Directive of the European Union (EU) allowed conglomeration and universal banking with implementation by all member states (Vander Vennet 2002, 255). The directive of the EU defines credit institutions broadly according to the German model of universal banking. There are no limits to the creation of conglomerates because banks, investment houses, and insurance companies can hold unlimited equity participations in each other. There are limits in stock participation in nonfinancial companies because of capital requirements. The new rules stimulate the restructuring of banks, with some specializing further and other diversifying.

Benefits to consumers, clients, and stockholders would be realized if the combination of diverse financial activities has positive effects on costs and/or revenues (Ibid, 256). Costs would be lower if the conglomerate resulting from various financial services benefits from economies of scope and scale. Diversification and cross-selling of financial products could improve revenue generation of the conglomerate. The reputation effects or market power of conglomeration could lower funding costs. Information gathering from combining initial evaluation and monitoring of traditional banking and equity sharing could have positive effects in the performance of universal banks. There are also potential benefits in the form of increasing X-efficiency. Sheltering of specialized institutions in an ineffective market of M&As could create agency costs.

The operational definition of Vander Vennet (2002, 260) classifies banks into three categories based on observed functional diversification and universality. The financial areas of operation are traditional banking, insurance, and securities. First, specialized banks operate traditional banking or the transformation of deposits into loans. Second, financial conglomerates are engaged in at least two of the areas of financial services. Third, universal banks engage in diversified financial services, holding equity share in nonfinancial companies. The sample consists of data from 2375 banks in 17 countries of the EU in 1995 and 1996 (Ibid, 261). These banks accounts for more than 85 percent of total bank assets in their countries. There are three empirical approaches. First, the various bank categories are analyzed by the stochastic cost and profit frontier. Second, specialized banks are analyzed relative to specialized banks in terms of the relationship of profitability and a set of market and bank characteristics. Third, the relation of profitability and the capacity in dealing with moral hazard is analyzed with stock market data.

The conclusions of Vander Vennet illuminate the issue of relative performance of universal and specialized banks. There is no evidence of disadvantage of specialized banks relative to financial conglomerates in traditional intermediation. There is more efficiency of conglomerates relative to specialized banks in nontraditional banking activities. There is significantly higher average operational efficiency relative to specialized banks, with also domination in profit efficiency. The empirical analysis suggests a relation of the profit efficiency of universal banks to their access to inside information through equity participation.

It is difficult to define and enforce property rights when information is nonexcludable but not a public good as it is the case of intermediation (Anand and Galetovich 2000, 358). On a normative basis, financiers with market power collect information that reduces the costs of free riding in information gathering by other entities. This view is in contrast with the policy efforts to reduce entry barriers and promote price competition. Free riding could occur in investment banking in various ways, such as by firms deserting to a competitor after their creditworthiness has improved and by attracting employees from rival investment banks. There is human capital in information gathering that is not transferable: investment bankers specialize in a few companies and develop close personal contracts. The migration of an investment banker can possibly result in the transfer of business to the new employer. Contracts may be incomplete and ineffective in preventing free riding of information in investment banking.

In the models of Anand and Galetovich (2000), the short-run gains of free riding on the information obtained by other intermediaries are lower than the long-term profits obtained in cooperative arrangements. The model provides for the endogenous determination of market structure, size of intermediaries, and prices. If information is nonexcludable, the analysis of market structure must proceed at two levels: (1) the local level of each deal and (2) the aggregate level of the market. After intermediaries incur the expenses to collect information, local monopoly is required to maintain incentives of collecting information. The determination of prices is the result of bilateral bargaining instead of competition among intermediaries. Local monopoly is not determined by technology but by a market structure required for self-enforcing the commitment not to free ride (Anand and Galetovich 2000, 360). The market shares of intermediaries must be similar because if they become very large for one intermediary they will be too small for others in such a way that the gains from free riding will exceed the long-term gains of cooperation. If too many intermediaries enter the market, the share of each one will be too small, discouraging cooperation. Intermediation markets would tend to become natural oligopolies.

The experience of investment banking in the long term is consistent with the model of Anand and Galetovich (2000, 378–84). First, the market structure of investment banking has been characterized in underwriting by stable market shares; no dominant bank and changing identities of top firms over time. The top banks maintained stable shares, with the industry leader not having more than 20 percent of the market. The industry has been very profitable, with pretax return on equity of large investment banks on average around 30 percent during 1981–91. An oligopolistic structure was maintained over the long term. Second, there is evidence supporting cooperation at the deal level. Underwriting fees have remained stable over the long term. Lead banks typically choose another bank from the top six to co-manage the issue. There have been stable long-term relationships between firms and their investment bankers. Third, the nonexcludable property of information is shown by the high premium paid to employees who can make or break the business of the investment bank. Anand and Galetovich (Ibid, 394) conclude that it is difficult to extrapolate antitrust policies and regulation from markets with excludable products to markets of intermediation in which information is not a public good but is nonexcludable.

The Glass-Steagall Act

The internal structure of firms is of importance to theory, regulatory policy, and the concern of the NIE with the nature of the firm. Regulation could impose structures on firms to ameliorate market failures and solve conflicts of interest. Kroszner and Rajan (1997) analyzed theoretically and empirically the structure of US investment banking by commercial banks before the 1933 Glass-Steagall Act forced banks to exit securities underwriting.

The combination of lending and investment banking can lead to conflicts of interest based on information asymmetries. There could be moral hazard in that the commercial side of the business could force the investment banking side to issue securities of companies in difficulties, misrepresenting their actual financial state to the public and using the proceeds from the issue of securities to repay the loans to the commercial part of the bank. Knowledge of the financial state of companies could lead to adverse selection as banks could "cherry pick" the sound clients, leaving the others to be financed in the securities markets.

The contribution of Kroszner and Rajan (1997) for the period before the Glass-Steagall Act analyzes a sample of 43 internal departments and 32 securities affiliates of commercial banks and trusts involved in investment banking underwriting of 906 securities. They find evidence that outsiders recognize the conflict of interest between commercial and investment banking. The prices of securities underwritten by the internal departments of banks, perceived as having higher potential conflict of interest, were discounted relative to those of securities underwritten by independent affiliates, with lower perceived conflict of interest. They conclude that internal structure matters in the competitive edge and market perception of companies. The results support the contention that analysis and empirical research of the functioning of the firm is potentially promising. Competitiveness and lack of externalities in the form of implicit or explicit deposit insurance ensure that banks evolve naturally to the effective structure without regulatory rules.

The Glass-Steagall Act of 1933 prohibited commercial banks to engage directly or through affiliates in underwriting, holding, or dealing in corporate securities. The motivation for this legislation was the alleged conflict of interest that would arise from the combination of lending by a commercial bank with the underwriting of securities. Legislators were also concerned with the higher risk of banking resulting from the combination of commercial and investment banking activities. There is a trade off between the economies that banks gain by information on their clients resulting from the combination of banking and underwriting of securities and the doubts on the quality of issues originating in the suspicion of conflicts of interest (Kroszner and Rajan 1994).

Banks recently suffered loss of prime clients with the advent of markets for corporate fixed-income securities, beginning with commercial paper. A similar loss of clients occurred in the 1920s. The data of Kroszner and Rajan (1994, 813) show that the number of national and state banks, including their affiliates, engaged in the securities business jumped from 277 in 1922 to a high of 591 in 1929, at the onset of the Great Depression. The motive for engaging in securities was not the appropriation of gains from the conflict of interest in underwriting second-rate securities but rather a reaction to maintain business opportunities. During 1921–9, the issue of all types of securities by bank affiliates was $1127 million compared with $1649 million for investment banks. There was no significant difference in the quality of securities issued by banks and investment banks. During 1921–9, 54.9 percent of the bonds underwritten by bank affiliates were of investment grade level compared with 47.4 percent for investment banks, with 18.8 percent below investment grade for bank affiliates versus 28 percent for investment banks. The nonrated bonds underwritten by affiliates of banks were 26.3 percent of the total versus 24.6 percent for investment banks. The sample of Kroszner and Rajan is particularly useful. During 1921–33, before the Glass-Steagall Act, banks and investment banks competed for the securities business on equal bases. There was little regulation and common entry and exit from the business. The market also exhibited significant dynamism.

The hearings in Congress that led to the Glass-Steagall Act presented arguments that banks systematically fooled naïve investors about the actual quality of securities that had inferior performance. The economic argument is that banks benefited from asymmetry of information. The banks had information on the deteriorating quality of certain firms, engaging in conflict of interest by promoting the issuance and underwriting of securities of those firms to use the proceeds to cancel their loans to the banks. The public subsequently suffered losses as the securities underperformed, a fact anticipated by banks. Moreover, banks had access to large pools of funding from naïve depositors. Kroszner and Rajan (1994, 815) label this possibility as the "naïve-investor" hypothesis: the worst performance would have been by low-quality securities, underwritten by bank affiliates; the public had little information about these securities.

The data gathering, calculation, classification, and testing of Kroszner and Rajan (1994, 819–20) provide strong evidence for refutation of the "naïve-investor" hypothesis: "affiliate-underwritten issues defaulted statistically less often than ex ante similar investment-bank-underwritten issues. The differences in default rates are greatest for the non-investment-grade issues." That is to say, there was no effort by bank affiliates to intentionally fool the public with the underwriting of low-quality issues. These scholars also verified that the results were statistically robust.

The experience of 1921–33 shows that the securities underwritten by bank affiliates were of higher quality than those underwritten by investment banks. In fact, the difference in performance of underwritings by bank affiliates and investment banks is stronger in the case of lower-rated securities where banks could have had greater potential conflict of interest originating in being privy to information not available to the public. Kroszner and Rajan (1994, 829) conclude that "the focus of legislative action on protecting the investing public from the effects of conflicts of interest has been misplaced." The combination of commercial and investment banking in one universal-type bank did not result in defrauding of the public.

The credit-rating agencies placed a discount, as in lemons in the secondary market for automobiles, on securities in which there could have been the alleged conflict of interest. Kroszner and Rajan (1994) found that bank affiliates avoided these companies, the opposite behavior had they been interested in exploiting their information by selling low-quality securities to the unsuspecting public.

There are three identifiable factors of the repeal of the Glass-Steagall Act (Barth, Brumbaugh, and Wilcox 2000). First, academic research demonstrates that the combination of banking and securities under-writing in the same group did not cause the banking problems of the Great Depression. Second, the limited securities activities allowed to banks in the 1990s did not result in banking problems. Third, new tech-nology allows the rapid use of information from one company to benefit another; there was an increase in the profitability of selling insurance and securities products to households and businesses. The Gramm-Leach-Bliley Act (GLBA) of November 12, 1999, reformed the restric-tions imposed by the Glass Steagall Act of 1933 and the Bank Holding Company Act of 1956 (Ibid). However, American banks still lack the full flexibility of their competitors in other advanced countries. Single holding companies can offer banking, securities and insurance, much the same as before the Great Depression.

The barriers of activities between banks and other financial entities had been eliminated by regulatory decisions and earlier legislation. Thus, GLBA can be viewed as ratifying and amplifying changes instead of as revolutionary (Ibid, 196; Harvard Law Review 1997). GLBA created a new entity, the financial holding company (FHC), which is autho-rized to operate in activities that are "financial in nature or incidental to financial activities or even complementary to financial activities" (Barth Brumbaugh, and Wilcox 2000, 194). The Fed must determine if the activities are not likely to create substantial risk to the safety and soundness of banks. The structure of regulation continues, with the Fed regulating only member banks. By the principle of functional regu-lation accepted by GLBA similar activities are regulated by the same regulator. According to functional regulation, the regulation of federal and state banking is by federal and state banking regulators; securities activities are regulated by federal and state securities regulators; and insurance activities are regulated by state insurance regulators.

The main benefit of GLBA for banks is gains from economies of scope (Ibid, 198). The costs of gathering, processing, and evaluating informa-tion can accrue once and then be distributed among many categories of financial services. There could be low marginal cost for banks in distrib-uting securities and insurance services through already existing tech-nology, staff, and delivery channels. The modern industrial revolution in the form of jumps in technology applicable to banking operations, such as data processing and electronic communication channels, may generate significant economies of scope. The overhead in back office, administration, and IT can be spread over a wider range of financial ser-vices. Finance predicts that under certain conditions diversification may reduce the volatility of returns. If there is lower correlation of returns of various bank activities, risk, or the standard deviation of returns, may decline, resulting in more stable broad banks (Ibid). Banks may pass on to consumers lower fees for a broader range of financial services. There are two potential adverse effects. First, there is the recurring problem of higher risk activities. Second, the combination of insured deposits with investment banking and insurance may give broader banks a strong competitive edge relative to other financial institutions.

Four hypotheses can be tested on the GLBA (Mamum, Hassan, and Son Lai. 2004, 335–6). First, GLAB creates positive wealth effects for all segments of the financial sector. Economies of scope were foregone because of the Glass-Steagall Act (Benston 1994, 126). Second, banks benefit the most from GLBA. The large customer base of banks ensures that they will benefit the most from economies of scope and scale. Third, the reduction of risk from diversification should diminish systematic risk in the financial industry. Fourth, GLBA is a *de facto* law for large financial institutions that have the resources to enter into new allowed activities. Using a sample of 389 firms affected by GLBA, Mamum, Hassan, and Son Lai (2004) find benefits for all segments, banking, insurance, and brokerage, with largest gains for banking. The diversification opportunities appeared to have diminished systematic risk.

Underwriting

There is a trade off in the underwriting of debt securities by a commercial bank in the potential conflict of interest of having a lending relationship with the issuer and a benefit in the enhanced information resulting from that relationship (Gande et al. 1997, 1176–7). The enhanced information of commercial banks could provide a certification benefit to the issues they underwrite. The fed authorized certain banks to establish Section 20 subsidiaries of the BHCs to underwrite corporate securities (Roten and Mullineaux 2005, 243–4). The data used by Gande et al. (1997, 1198) consists of 670 fixed-rate US nonconvertible debt issues underwritten by the top 20 underwriters during 1991–5. An important concern is whether universal banking would result in less availability of credit to smaller firms. The empirical results indicate that Section 20 units underwrite larger proportions of small-size issues than is the case of investment banks. The certification role of Section 20 units is consistent with the lower yields (higher prices) of issues with lower credit rating in which the affiliated commercial bank retains a significant stake. There is no conflict of interest in the empirical result of no significantly higher yield spreads of debt issues to refinance existing debt, in which the affiliated commercial bank has a lending stake, between underwriting by the Section 20 unit and investment banks.

The Big Bang reform of financial markets in the United Kingdom in 1986 provides a long period of information to test whether there is conflict of interest by commercial banks in underwriting debt securities (Hebb and Fraser 2003). The United Kingdom had a banking system with separation of the securities segment from deposit banking. This system is different from universal banking in the European continent where banks engage in all financial activities and can hold securities of nonfinancial entities. The rulebook of the London Stock Exchange (LSE), instead of legislation, constrained banks from engaging in securities activities by restricting members to partnerships (Ibid, 82–3). The change was provoked by the government threatening to refer the LSE rulebook to the Restrictive Trade Practices Court. The changes in the rules known as the Big Bang authorized outside ownership of 100 percent of member security firms. Major UK and foreign banks entered into the UK securities segment. The regulatory measure, the Financial Services Act of 1986, established agencies of regulation and self-regulation. By the end of 1986 almost one-half of the 200 independent stock exchange member firms had become part of a large financial conglomerate.

There are two hypotheses tested by Hebb and Fraser (2003, 83–4) on the UK experience. First, the conflict of interest hypothesis postulates that banks shift risks from the existing loan of a client to the bond it underwrites. The ex ante rates on these bonds will be higher and the *ex post* performance worst. Second, the certification of value hypothesis postulates that banks gather more information on the issuers than investment banks, thus certifying the quality of the underwritten bonds. Investment banks may be less inclined or able to gather information. The *ex post* performance of issues underwritten by commercial banks will be superior relative to that of issues underwritten by investment banks. The results of Hebb and Fraser indicate that there is no difference for as long as three years in the buy and hold returns of issues underwritten by commercial and investment banks. There is no evidence supporting the conflict of interest hypothesis.

There is more sensitivity to asymmetry of information in equity than in debt (Ibid, 69). Equity is subject to stronger variation than fixed-income debt. The conflict of interest and certification of value arguments depend on asymmetry of information. A sample is constructed with new issues underwritten by commercial and investment banks, matching industry, date of issue, and size of order. The results indicate significantly greater uncertainty in underwritten issues by banks about the issue's true value. There appears to be market perception of risk in issues underwritten by commercial banks. There is no support for the certification of value of new equity issues underwritten by commercial banks. With a sample for 1995–9, Roten and Mullineaux (2005) find relatively lower costs for initial public offerings (IPO) of smaller issues in underwriting by commercial banks relative to investment banks. There is not sufficient information to conclude on comparative advantages.

Loan syndication

There were 1300 commercial loan syndications led by investment banks in the United States during 1996–2003 for total funding of $768 billion (Harjoto, Mullineaux, and Yi 2006). This syndication activity permits the analysis of the difference in lending practices of commercial and investment banks. The advantage of commercial banks in offering cheaper rates of interest on loans appears highest in multiple ways except in regulation. The sources of advantages are (Harjoto, Mullineaux, and Yi 2006, 50–2)

- *Funding type.* The core deposits of commercial banks provide inexpensive, reliable, and stable funding. A significant portion consists of insured deposits at low rates because of the risk-free feature of deposit insurance. There are additional costs of insurance premiums and regulation.
- *Regulation.* Deposit banks are subject to regulation in the form of reserve ratios on deposits and capital ratios on risk assets. Investment banks are not regulated in the same way as commercial banks.
- *Relationships.* Commercial banks monitor clients in close relationships, diminishing information asymmetry and adverse selection. Investment banks are focused on transactions.
- *Product bundling.* Commercial banks benefit from their relationships with clients by offering with the loans a bundle of additional services, such as cash management, pension management, or underwriting services. The economies of scope permit lower rates.
- *Mark-to-market.* Investment banks are more likely to package loans in ABS and sell them. Securities are MTM. Commercial banks have larger portions of their loans under book value accounting, having less market risk and permitting more generous pricing.

The econometric analysis of Harjoto, Mullineaux, and Yi (2006) provides interesting results. The lending of investment banks is to firms that are leveraged and less profitable than those receiving loans from commercial banks. The terms of investment banks are longer than those of commercial banks with less likelihood of loan-commitment contracts, supporting the view that investment banks focus on transactions relative to relationships. The spreads of investment banks exceed those of commercial banks by 64 basis points but the difference shrinks when syndications are co-arranged with commercial banks. Harjoto, Mullineaux, and Yi reject the hypothesis that the loan pricing models of commercial and investment banks are identical. On the basis of credit ratings, investment banks charge less for credit risk than commercial banks; the inclusion of other variables weakens this result.

Relationship banking is defined by Boot (2000, 10) as lending provided by a financial intermediary with two activities. First, the lender invests in obtaining information, frequently proprietary, that is specific to the customer/borrower. Second, the intermediary engages in multiple interactions with the same customer over time and/or across products to evaluate the profitability of its lending. A traditional interpretation of investment banking is as brokering or matching of buyers and sellers of the securities of a firm. In this activity, investment banks merely facilitate transactions and value added in the capacity to reduce costs of search and matching. Relationship banking is different from simple brokering but investment banks face credit and placement risk in underwriting securities, which is similar to lending in relationship banking (Boot 2000, 10–11). The range covering at one extreme bank loans and at the other public debt issues includes syndicated loans somewhere in the middle; syndicated loans can be viewed as a hybrid of bank loans and public debt markets (Dennis and Mullineaux 2000). Syndicated loans may receive credit enhancement by the reputation of the managing agent (Ibid). The functions of relationship banking are carried into structured credit products through the credit enhancement of the securitized loans by the originating bank. The proprietary information of banks in relationship banking continues to have a key role in credit risk transfer.

The borrower is likely to reveal more information in relationship banking than in transactions and the lender would have incentives in investing in information gathering, resulting in a Pareto-improving exchange of information (Boot 2000, 12). Banks reduce asymmetry of information between borrowers and lenders. There are four features of contracts in relationship banking that can improve welfare. First, there is flexibility in the form of discretion in renewals, using information that can facilitate long-term contracting. Second, potential conflicts of interest and agency costs can be better controlled by extensive covenants that are possible because of the seniority of bank debt. Third, collateral can be monitored by the relationship financier, strengthening the proximity of the relation. Fourth, borrowers can obtain loans that are unprofitable for the bank in the short term, allowing intertemporal transfers in loan pricing; relationship banking is an important source of funds for de novo borrowers (Ibid, 12–3). There are two categories of costs of relationship banking. First, there is a soft-budget constraint in the form of unwillingness of banks to take tough actions on the borrower viewed as a long-term client. Second, there are rents in the information monopoly of the bank realized when the firm can pay higher fees for loans (Ibid, 16).

The syndicated loan occurs when two lenders jointly provide funds to a borrowing company (Sufi 2004, 2). There are similarities and differences between debt underwriting and loan syndication (Lee and Mullineaux 2004, 110–1). The borrowing corporation contacts one or several financial entities that would commit to the full amount of a relatively large funding. The lead institution in the syndication negotiates the deal with the borrower, subsequently preparing a descriptive memorandum of the transaction and meeting with potential participants in the lending or underwriting group. The arranger of the loan identifies the entities that would be invited to participate and acts as the bookrunner of the transaction. The arranger specifies the brackets of the participation, in round millions of dollars. Institutions taking larger brackets receive titles, such as manager and co-manager. The differences originate in the banking relationship. The borrower identifies potential participants on the basis of past banking relationships, taking special care in the selection because of the potential need of dealing with participants in a future restructuring. There are also restrictions on resale of participations because of the potential needs to restructure with unknown lenders.

Governance

The separation of ownership and management of a firm has been a source of inquiry in economics (Adam Smith 1776; Berle and Means 1932; Jensen and Meckling 1976). The analysis focuses on the difference between the optimum solution provided by free markets in the first-best competitive allocation and the existence of control decisions within firms (Coase 1937). The doubt is why shareholders around the world entrust their wealth to managers of firms that may optimize their self-interest instead of that of shareholders. If there had not been significant success in management, then investors would choose opportunities different than equity and debt in joint-stock companies. An important departure is the theory of the firm of Jensen and Meckling (1976) seeking analysis in terms of the conflict of interest of agents maximizing their welfare instead of that of the shareholders that entrusted them with their wealth. A complete theory of the firm, according to Bolton and Scharfstein (1998, 103), would have to include the Berle and Means (1932) separation of ownership and control together with the Coase (1937) view of integration and organizations.

Stigler and Friedland (1983) test with modern econometric methods the data on corporations used by Berle and Means (1932). The conclusion is that there is no significant difference in executive compensation or in the use of assets to generate profits between the management-controlled companies and the owner-controlled companies in the companies used by Berle and Means. Separation of shareholder ownership and managerial discretion does not substantiate the exploitation of owners by managers alleged by Berle and Means.

The modern corporation with layers of managers and divisions in vertical integration, such as the case of GM, had only begun at the time of the writing by Berle and Means (1932). Economies of scale and scope in the modern factory system based on the assembly line and organizational innovations provided rents. The insight of their work is mostly in the endurance of that corporate model (Rajan and Zingales 2000). The account by Sloan (1963) is significantly responsible for that endurance (Rajan and Zingales 2000). Modern corporations experienced substantial concentration of power, creating significant organizational rents in strict command-and-control regimes with vertical communication through middle management. The highest rewards were reaped at the top of the hierarchy, motivating junior and middle management to acquire the skills to climb through the organization.

Managers derive satisfaction from perquisites such as larger offices with views, more expensive computers than those required, contribution to favorite charities, acquisition of inputs from friends, and the like (Jensen and Meckling 1976). A significant number of these perquisites provide nonmonetary satisfaction. Consider the vector $X = \{x_1, x_2, \ldots x_n\}$ of quantities of factors and activities, x_i, which provide non-pecuniary satisfaction to the manager. For the firm (Ibid):

$$B(X) = P(X) - C(X) \tag{4.1}$$

where $B(X)$ is the net dollar benefit to the firm of ignoring the impact of X on the manager's utility and, thus, equilibrium wage, $P(X)$ is the total dollar value to the firm obtained from X, and $C(X)$ is the total dollar cost of the x_i. If the optimum level of X is X^*, without taking into account the effects of X on the manager's satisfaction and equilibrium wage, the optimum level of factors and activities is given by (Ibid)

$$\frac{\partial B(X^*)}{\partial X^*} = \frac{\partial P(X^*)}{\partial X^*} - \frac{\partial C(X^*)}{\partial X^*} = 0 \tag{4.2}$$

If the manager uses activities and factors, X, providing non-pecuniary satisfaction above the optimum level, X^*, such that $X \geq X^*$, which states that at least one component of X exceeds the corresponding one in X^*, then $F = B(X^*) - B(X) > 0$ is a measure of the dollar cost to the firm of using non-pecuniary benefits providing utility to the manager in excess of the optimum. If X^m denotes the factors and activities providing the manager maximum utility, then $F = B(X^*) - B(X^m)$, where F is the current market value of the flow of expenditures by the manager on desired non-pecuniary benefits.

The firm is a set of contractual agreements to reduce agency costs resulting from the derivation of satisfaction by the manager from the use of non-pecuniary activities and factors (Ibid). Consider the optimum value of the firm, V^*, obtained in the perfectly competitive model without frictions or agency costs by the optimum investment I^*. The manager has a share of α in the firm's equity. The shareholders invest in monitoring costs, M, and impose bonding costs, b, on the manager. If M', b', α', and I' denote the optimum values with non-pecuniary benefits of F', then agency costs A are given by the divergence of the Pareto-optimum solution from the optimization of utility from non-pecuniary factors and activities (Ibid):

$$A(M', b', \alpha', I') = (V^* - I^*) - (V' - I' - M' - b') \tag{4.3}$$

Statutory and common law and the capacity of devising contracts determine agency costs, which are as real as other costs. Neoclassical theory ignored transactions costs, which can be as high as one half of GNP. Positive agency costs would prevent the market from attaining Pareto optimality. Economic growth with joint-stock corporations with limited liability required the delegation by many owners to professional managers. Comparing the model of no frictions and zero agency and transaction costs with reality is probably part of the Nirvana fallacy of Demsetz (1969) of comparing theoretical markets with flawless government intervention (Jensen and Meckling 1976). As in the case of transactions costs of Coase (1960) and subsequent literature in law and economics, the solution consists of finding contractual arrangements that protect the property rights of minority shareholders. The alternative could consist of state-owned enterprises that would be plagued by agency costs, unless the absurdity of the Nirvana fallacy was accepted in such a way that government managers do not derive satisfaction from non-pecuniary activities and factors.

A critical distinction of US securities markets is the strong protection of minority interests. Recent research has shown the vital link of the law to the development of capital markets. The econometric research of La Porta et al. (1998) provides interesting conclusions on investor and creditor rights in relation to families of legal rules. There is much stronger protection of rights of investors in countries where the legal rules originate in the tradition of common law than in that of civil law, with the tradition of French civil law being the worst and those of German-civil-law and Scandinavian countries falling in-between. There is strong protection of investors of all types in common-law countries. Using a sample for 49 countries, La Porta et al. (1997) analyze external finance in terms of origin of the legal system, strength of legal protection of investor rights, and quality of enforcement of laws. The results show that the legal environment is important for developing a country's capital markets. Legal protection of investors by laws and their enforcement encourages them to exchange funds for securities, broadening capital markets. The lowest development of capital markets is in countries with civil-law systems, especially worst in French civil-law systems. La Porta et al. (2006) studied securities laws in 49 countries in relation to the issue of new securities. They conclude that securities laws contribute to improving markets because they facilitate private contracting. The existence of a focused and independent regulatory enforcer does not show statistical significance in developing capital markets. Larger stock markets are positively associated with disclosure requirements and liability standards that allow investors to recover losses. The emphasis on market discipline and private litigation of common law, in the form of private contracts and standard disclosure, explains the stronger development in countries with that legal regime.

The surviving organization form is the one that can deliver products at the lowest price that covers costs (Fama and Jensen 1983a, 327). The control of agency costs is a critical determinant for the survival of an organization form. There are two types of costs incurred in controlling agency costs. First, there are costs of drafting, monitoring, and bonding contracts among agents that have conflicting interests. Second, there is a residual loss because the benefits are lower than the costs of fully enforcing the contracts. There are residual claimants or residual risk bearers in organizations that absorb the impact of the difference between stochastic inflows of resources and promised payments (Ibid, 328). Common stock shareholders in open corporations contribute wealth in exchange for the residual claim to the value of the corporation. The corporation is a "nexus of contracts" or rules of the game, written or unwritten, establishing hierarchies in the decision process, defining residual claims, and creating mechanisms that control agency problems in decisions (Fama and Jensen 1983b, 321).

The decision process in an organization is depicted by Fama and Jensen (Ibid, 321–2) as consisting of initiation of the decision, ratification, implementation, and monitoring. The initiation and implementation are lumped into the category of *decision management*; the ratification and monitoring are considered in the category of *decision control*. There are two hypotheses proposed by Fama and Jensen (1983b). First, decision systems that separate decision management from decision control accomplish the separation of residual risk from decision management. Second, restriction of residual claims in a few agents is accomplished by combining decision management and decision control in a few agents. A key distinction in the framework of Fama and Jensen (1983a,b) is the diffusion of residual risk bearing, which is high in complex organizations with many shareholders, such as the open corporation, but can be concentrated, as in small and medium companies. Size is not as important as the separation of the human capital required for decisions from the residual risk bearing. In open corporations, there are many residual risk bearers who delegate decision management to professional managers, giving rise to agency problems in the form of conflicting interests of owners and managers. When risk bearers also have the human capital for decision management, as in the law firm, there is delegation to managing partners but less opportunity for agency problems.

Organizations such as the open corporations alleviate the agency problem by establishing hierarchies for decision management and decision control (Fama and Jensen 1983b). This can be illustrated by risk management in financial institutions and is incorporated in the Basel II capital requirements (Peláez and Peláez 2005, 2008a,b,c). The financial institution develops a risk management process. For example, traders can take decisions in positions based on risk guidelines proposed by a risk management area that is independent and reports to senior management. This process provides rules of the game to avoid rogue traders attempting to maximize their bonuses in conflict with the preservation of capital functions of the senior management. Monitoring is conducted by accounting and auditing areas that are also separated from traders taking risk decisions. Ratification of the key decisions and rules of the game of risk management of the financial institutions is the responsibility of the board of independent directors who also exercise the monitoring or oversight of the key decisions. The discipline of this system in the Fama and Jensen (1983b) framework is by the stock prices in organized stock markets. In addition, the market for corporate control and the job market for managers also exercise control over the agency problems of corporations. The legal system determines the overall rules of the game in the form of common law applying to governance and takeovers.

The classical corporation theory of Berle and Means (1932) is based on the argument that technology creates the need for large firm size, requiring investment by many shareholders. The agency problem originates in the separation of ownership and control by managers who may promote their self-interest instead of those of the owners. Roe (1991) provides a political theory of the corporation and finance in the United States. The alternative ownership by concentrated institutional holding of equity was prohibited by law in response to the public distrust of corporate ownership by banks, insurance companies, and pension funds. The law "foreclosed" alternatives to the Berle and Means (1932) corporation. A corporation in an enterprise of persons and assets, seeking profits under rules (Eisenberg 1989). Corporate organs or officials determine these rules by unilateral actions. The rules are determined by markets, contracts or other types of agreements, and the law. There are three categories of rules: enabling (providing legal effect to adopted rules), default rules (governing specific issues unless other rules are adopted), and mandatory (governing defines rules that cannot be altered).

Corporate governance consists of legal and contractual mechanisms used by investors in minimizing the agency costs of managers (Easterbrook 2002, 733). These mechanisms are important when they have lowest costs in restricting management. There would not be need for governance mechanisms if there were effective controls provided by the market for corporate control, the market for managerial services, and the product market. In research on finance, corporate governance consists of the means by which the investors in corporations obtain returns on their investment (Shleifer and Vishny 1997, 737). While investors obtain returns without contributing in other ways to the corporation, research focuses on the adequacy of solutions to the issue of corporate governance and the possible improvements. In the model with no frictions, competition in product markets would eliminate agency costs as firms maximize profits. The existence of sunk costs reveals the need for governance mechanisms, which are economic and legal institutions that can be modified through the political process (Ibid, 738). Corporate governance could also be defined as the actions and institutions dealing with adverse selection and moral hazard (Tirole 2001). Sound governance consists of selecting the most competent managers and making them accountable to investors. Economists focus on ways to implement shareholder value instead of its legitimacy.

Governance is synonymous with authority and power, words which are absent in standard economics where markets allocate resources without frictions (Zingales 1998). Following Williamson (1985), Zingales (1998) considers a governance system as a set of complex constraints that arise in a relationship, which determine the ex-post bargaining over generated quasi-rents. The initial contract setting rules for this bargaining is likely to be incomplete because it cannot anticipate completely how to divide the rents in every possible state of nature. The decisions were made ex ante at the time that investment was sunk compared with the ex-post distribution of the quasi rents. Corporate governance, according to the definition of Zingales is the complex set of rules shaping ex-post sharing of the quasi rents obtained from the operation of the firm.

The corporate model of vertical integration with command-and-control hierarchies resulting in organization rents has changed with horizontal specialization and the rise in relative importance of human capital relative to inanimate capital (Rajan and Zingales 2000), which is reshaping the theory of the firm (Zingales 2000) and corporate governance (Rajan and Zingales 2001). This transformation is evident in many activities, with finance providing an important example. In the older financial company, the charter provided the authority and the corresponding capacity to create rents. The development of modern finance with option pricing formulas by Black and Scholes (1973) and Merton (1973, 1974, 1998) created methods of fair pricing of complex products. Trading, structuring, and developing these products require significant talent and investment in human capital. The charter of a bank may not be valuable unless there is the capacity to hire, retain, and reward sophisticated human capital, which is a sunk cost belonging to the individuals and not to the company. Hierarchies of vertical integration break down with this importance of human relative to inanimate capital. Financial companies are increasingly resembling law firms, in which the knowledge and reputation of the attorneys is the main (human) capital of the firm. The governance system and the distribution of quasi-rents are changing to different models of bargaining. Technology and globalization have created the new horizontal specialization, in which production tasks are outsourced within countries and offshored (Feenstra 1998, 2007; Feenstra and Hanson 1999). The classic absorption of Body Fisher by GM in the 1920s strengthened the command-and-control hierarchy of the modern corporation (Bolton and Scharfstein 1998). Horizontal specialization is reversing governance in the sense of power toward horizontal bargaining as it occurred before GM acquired Fisher Body, creating new models of bargaining for quasi rents.

The effective corporate governance system requires some combination of legal protection and large investors (Shleifer and Vishny 1997, 769). Larger investors are required to put pressure on managers for distribution of profits. Concentrated investors require some rights, such as voting rights or the power to pull collateral, to impose their power on managers. There must also be legal protection of rights of minority shareholders to prevent their exploitation by management and large investors. An extensive system of rules protects large and minority investors, including protection of minority shareholders, election of directors without interference by management, and class-action lawsuits for violation of fiduciary duty.

There are various arguments in favor of state ownership and management of economic activities because of monopoly and external economies. The arguments of agency theory apply to state-owned companies (Ibid, 768). Ownership is highly centralized, with powerful discretion, while the cash flow benefits are dispersed across the entire population, with hardly any organized rights. The managers of state-owned companies respond to political interests with disregard of social welfare issues. Discretion is not used to optimize profits and operations but rather to favor personal interests of bureaucrats. State-owned companies have been among the most inefficient organizations, creating major problems in government budgets that are socialized in the form of taxes.

Financial globalization can be defined as free international trading of financial assets (Stulz 2005). In a model with only one friction in the form of impediments to the free flow of financial assets among countries, the removal of the friction causes an increase in aggregate welfare. After removal of the friction, asset prices, portfolio choice, and corporate financial policy are independent of the country, or the country

Table 4.1 Sample of research on corporate governance

Reference	Results
Aggarwal et al. 2007	An index of firm-level governance shows that the value of foreign firms decreases when its index level declines relative to that of the comparable US firm.
Coffee 1999	Analyzes governance in the privatization of transition economies.
Doidge et al. 2004	Country characteristics, such as economic/financial development and the openness of the home country, together with investor protection by the state are more important than firm characteristic in determining a firm's governance.
Dyck et al. 2007	Analyzes the reputation and regulatory consequences of reporting governance abuse in the media.
Faleye 2004	Proxy contest is an alternative to takeovers. Proxy fight targets have 23 percent more cash than comparable companies.
Ferris et al. 2003	Directors serving in more than one board attract other directorships but their monitoring is not affected by multiple appointments.
Glassman and Rhoades 1980	There are higher profit rates in owner-controlled banks relative to manager-controlled banks.
Griffith et al. 2002	There is no evidence of a relation of CEO ownership and bank performance, suggesting management entrenchment or other factors.
Hannan and Mavinga 1980	Management-controlled banks tend to spend more on preferences of managers than owner-controlled banks in similar situations.
La Porta et al. 2000	Tests using a cross-section sample of 4000 companies in 33 countries support the outcome theory by which minority shareholders exert pressure on insiders to distribute cash.
La Porta et al. 2002a	Tests using a sample of 539 companies in 27 advanced countries provide evidence of higher valuation in countries with enhanced protection of rights of minority shareholders and in firms that have higher ownership of cash flow by the controlling shareholder.
Morck et al. 1989	Concludes with sample of 455 of the S&P 500 firms that boards monitor performance of firms in the industry, taking appropriate action, but are reluctant to penalize adverse shocks to the entire industry or economy.
Pagano and Volpin 2005	There is significant negative correlation between the proportionality of the voting system and shareholder protection in a panel of 45 countries; there is positive correlation with employment protection in a panel of 21 OECD countries.
Romano 1991	Analyzes shareholder lawsuits, concluding that they provide a weak but not ineffective vehicle of corporate governance.
Shleifer and Vishny 1986	Develops a model in which a large minority shareholder can advance monitoring of the management of a company.
Williamson 1984	Analyzes the contractual terms of each constituency and the firm.
Williamson 1988	Analyzes debt governance on the basis of rules and equity governance on the basis of discretion.

irrelevance proposition. The neoclassical capital model postulates that capital flows to the regions of highest marginal returns, resulting in efficient allocation of resources for the world. Stulz (2005) explains the fact that financial globalization has had limited impact by means of a twin-agent problem. The first problem is the use of corporate discretion to promote self-interest of insiders. Second, state rulers use their discretion to improve their self-interest. The problem of corporate discretion by insiders occurs in firms closely controlled by a few large shareholders and with poor protection of investors. This governance/protection structure explains home bias or the tendency to hold only securities of the country and not originating in other countries (Dahlquist et al. 2003).

Regulation and the system of governance failed to prevent the corporate scandals of the turn of the millennium (Jensen 2005). The checks and balances of the agency problem do not function perfectly in the case of overvalued equity. Equity is overvalued in the market when the company cannot produce earnings statements that support the market price of the stock; overvaluations were significant. Jensen (2005, 10–1) finds that Enron was valued in the market at $70 billion when it was worth $30 billion. Corporate cultures were redesigned to accommodate with targets the earnings required to support market valuations to prevent collapse of stock prices when announcements did not meet estimates. Decisions were distorted to maintain the overvaluations without regard to long-term economic value. M&As and leveraged buyouts (LBO) could not create the profits required to be consistent with overvaluation. Governance failed in its role of preventing the agency costs of management decisions. Theory, evidence, and policy efforts are required to consider the effects of overvaluation of companies on the mechanisms of controlling agency costs.

There is vast literature on corporate governance. A sample of the diverse approaches and methods of research is in Table 4.1.

Incentive compensation

Remuneration contracts between managers and shareholders are constrained by political factors within the organization and in the public sector (Baker, Jensen, and Murphy 1988, 611). The actual contracts differ from those predicted by theory. There are no strong incentives in corporations to structure efficient compensation contracts (Ibid, 614). There is strong non-pecuniary disincentive for a manager in terminating employees, such as loss of esteem by fellow employees, potential

lawsuits, and others. The pecuniary benefits of higher bonuses or promotion could be realized only if there were higher incomes resulting
from the termination. The easily realized non-pecuniary disincentives
in contrast with hard to realize pecuniary incentives discourage efficient compensation contracts from the top compensation committee of
the board of directors throughout the entire organization. Even boards
may be reluctant to terminate CEOs with poor performance. Large organizations tend to become rigid bureaucracies. There are no sound explanations of why competitive labor markets erode the disincentives to
creating efficient compensation contracts.

The separation of ownership by shareholders and management by the
CEO constitutes a critical issue of agency theory (Jensen and Murphy
1990, 226). If shareholders could know the investment opportunities
and actions of CEOs in all possible states of nature, they could design
a contract enforcing decisions by CEOs that maximize shareholder
wealth. In reality, the decisions that shareholders may take and the
investment opportunities are not known at the time of designing such
contracts. Agency theory suggests the use of compensation policy to
create incentives for CEOs to maximize shareholder wealth instead of
their self-interest. These incentives could balance the private and social
costs and benefits of potential measures, leading to sound decisions.

The analysis of Jensen and Murphy (1990) covers more than 2000
CEOs in three samples over five decades. For the average firm in the
sample of 1295 firms in *Forbes*, there is a change of around two cents in
next year's salary and bonus of CEOs for every $1000 change in share-
holder wealth (Jensen and Murphy 1999, table 11, 260). The value of the
CEOs stock options changes by 15 cents per $1000 change in shareholder
wealth. The change in wealth of the CEOs from total pay and stock-
related ownership is $3.25 per $1000 change in shareholder wealth. The
change in total compensation is $8.05 for small firms in the sample and
$1.85 for large firms per every change of $1000 in shareholder wealth.
The results conflict with agency theory that suggests significant payoffs for exceptional performance. Jensen and Murphy hypothesize that
political forces outside and inside the corporation implicitly restrict
large payoffs. These political forces are a form of implicit regulation of
rewards to CEOs. Contrary to uninformed commentary in the press,
there are no major incentives for excellence in performance in public
corporations. This commentary confuses payments of millions of dollars with net incomes of billions of dollars. Another fact is the small and
declining share of CEOs in stocks. The medium stockholdings of CEOs
in the 120 largest firms listed in the New York Stock Exchange (NYSE)

declined from 0.3 percent in 1938 to 0.03 percent in 1984. Another important fact is the lack of penalties for inferior performance.

An important issue with high emotional connotations is the severance contracts popularized with the term "golden parachutes" (Jensen 1988, 39–41). There are advantages and disadvantages in this issue. The managers of the target companies in M&As have invested in human capital specific to their companies over a long period of time. Typically, they lose their jobs within three years of the sale of the company and incur heavy personal losses. A proper incentive is to tie the severance contract to the premium of sale of the stock, creating an incentive for the managers to defend the best interest of shareholders. At the other extreme, generous severance contracts may encourage the managers to negotiate any sale price to receive the severance payment. Designing severance contracts may require focusing on the specific characteristics of the company and the type of management. In some cases, there is confusion of accumulated benefits in stock options realized at the time of severance that have nothing to do with the golden parachute clause. Managers earned the stock options over a long period of service.

In 1970–2005, there was a trebling of the inflation adjusted cash compensation, consisting of salary and bonus, for the CEOs in the largest 500 firms (S&P 500) (Murphy and Zábojník 2007). The average cash compensation increased from $900,000 in 1970 to $3,330,000 in 2005. The cash compensation of the average CEO in 1970 was 28 times that of the average production worker, jumping to 115 times in 2005. There was an increasing trend in the external hiring of CEOs in the largest firms in the United States: from 15 percent in the 1970s and 17 percent in the 1980s to one out of four in the 1990s and close to a third in 2005. In addition, the average number of CEOs hired with prior CEO experience tripled.

These three trends in compensation and source of hiring of CEOs are explained by Murphy and Zábojník (2007) in terms of the increasing importance of general managerial human capital in CEOs relative to human capital that is specific to CEO positions. General managerial capital consists of skills in leading the sophisticated contemporary corporation while managerial capital specific to a firm consists of skills that are valuable only within the firm. Corporations have become more focused on external than on internal constituencies. The modern CEO participates in constant external events in the media and in interactions with capital markets in the issue of equity and debt. During the credit/dollar crisis there has been formidable pressure on CEOs in negotiations with the government and in creating corporate image with shareholders and creditors. The general skills of CEOs are transferable to corporations in other activities; most large corporations and boards increasingly seek these skills in outside hiring. Murphy and Zábojník also propose that recent advances in economics, management science, accounting, and finance have enhanced the management of corporations. The modern CEO has skills in these disciplines that are useful in many corporations. Inside corporate information is now rapidly available in corporate digital files and does not require decades of service in the corporation. Boards will seek outside hiring that can bring the set of skills required of the CEO of the modern corporation. General managerial skills explain the increase in average compensation of CEOs and hiring outside the firms. The general managerial skills allow the CEOs to capture a large part of the increase in marginal product caused by their transferability but the lack of a market for specific managerial skills prevents the capture of the rents originating in this specific human capital. The competition for the most skilled general managers will drive their compensation upward.

This explanation conflicts with work by Bebchuk, Fried and Walker (2002) and Bebchuk and Fried (2003, 2004) introducing an argument that increasing compensation of CEOs occurs by the capture of board members by rent-seeking incumbent CEOs, or the "fat cat" explanation. The introduction of the agency problem by finance economists depends on optimal contracting of CEO compensation to create incentives for maximization of the wealth of shareholders instead of the self-interest of managers. The markets for corporate control, managerial labor, and capital would create the disincentive to mediocre performance by CEOs. In practice, in this view, instead of optimal contracting, CEOs enjoy managerial power that allows them to extract rents in obtaining remuneration benefits from captive boards. In the managerial power approach, CEOs have significant power in nominating board members and setting their remuneration, thus controlling the process of executive compensation by boards. The fear of public outrage resulting from multimillion remuneration packages causes expenses in diverse forms to avoid them that constitute an "outrage" cost of efficiency of public corporations. Boards enter into a public game of using compensation consultants that are effectively hired by the personnel departments controlled by management. There are also hidden compensation schemes, such as loans at low rates, forbearance of loans, and special remuneration to departing managers. Stock option contracts pricing options at the money provide windfall remunerations that may be caused by outside market events unrelated to CEO performance. Optimal contracting alone cannot explain corporate remuneration, which has become part of the agency problem.

There are four objections to the "fat cat" hypothesis by Murphy and Zábojník (2004). First, the boards of directors have become more independent over time relative to 30 years ago (Hall and Murphy 2003, 64). Board independence is also sanctioned in the Sarbanes-Oxley Act (SOX). Independent boards are not subject to capture similar to that of CEO-influenced boards. Second, internally promoted CEOs would have to earn more than those externally hired (Ibid). The premium for externally hired CEOs is about 15.3 percent and has been increasing over time, contradicting the prediction of the "fat cat" hypothesis that incumbent CEOs would be paid more. A study of 94 commercial banks by Vafeas, Waegelein, and Papamichael (2003) shows significant reduction in the number of insiders in executive compensation committees after revisions of the tax codes and disclosure requirements. CEO compensation became more responsive to performance after the reforms. Third, the "fat cat" theory is contradicted by the increasing trend of hiring external CEOs. The appropriation of rents by incumbent CEOs would increase the cost of external hires and the incumbents would not transfer to other companies (Murphy 2002, 854). Fourth, part of the "fat cat" hypothesis is the allegation of "outrage costs" in the form of public outrage at executive pay. Murphy argues that outrage costs are irrefutable and their existence does not negate market forces in determining executive compensation. Camouflaging CEO compensation with stock options was frustrated by the SEC in 1992 (Hall and Murphy 2003, 65). Murphy and Zábojník (2004, 2007) conclude that compensation of CEOs is determined by competitive factors instead of rent-seeking extraction through capture of boards.

Bebchuk and Grinstein (2005) calculate at $92 billion, or 10.3 percent of earnings, the total compensation paid to the top-five executives of public firms in 2001–3. Distortions in compensation agreements could be harmful but it is difficult to separate empirically the various determinants. Bebchuk (2007) advises the introduction of "say on pay," or advisory votes by shareholders on compensation at the annual meeting, which are already practiced in the United Kingdom and Australia. Management has the duty of loyalty, which provides against self-dealing, such as theft, excessive compensation, and issues of securities to the managers and their relatives, diluting existing shareholders (Shleifer and Vishny 1997, 752).

In 1992, corporations in the S&P 500 index gave their employees stock options valued at $11 billion at the time of granting. The value of stock options rose to $119 billion by 2000. The average grant of options by companies in the S&P 500 in 2002 was $141 million, several times higher than $22 million in 1992, of which 4.2 percent was granted to the CEO, 5.3 percent to the top five executives, and 90.5 percent to the other employees (Hall and Murphy 2003). The perceived cost hypothesis may explain why corporations prefer stock options as incentive compensation relative to cash and restricted stock and grant them to both top management and other employees (Murphy 2002; Hall and Murphy 2003). The economic cost of a stock option to the firm is what an outside investor would pay for the option. However, for the firm there is no cash disbursement and accounting charge in granting the option. The firm also earns at the time of exercise a tax deduction for the difference between the stock price and the exercise price. Thus, the perceived cost of the stock option to the company is significantly lower than the economic cost. The result is granting of stock options to too many employees; options with accounting benefits are likely to be preferred relative to plans providing better incentives. The alignment of perceived costs with economic costs, such as by expending stock options, would reduce the number of options granted and restrict it to management as an incentive to improve performance.

Mergers and acquisitions

This section focuses on the issue of whether there is sound governance of the process of M&As, in particular the creation of standards and enforcement of governance. There are numerous stakeholders in M&As. The essence of the problem is whether the governance system protects shareholders from managers and acquirers of public corporations. The first subsection deals with the issue of whether mergers restrict competition. Corporate law is essentially determined by the Chancery Court and the Supreme Court of Delaware. The process evolved on its own, allowing the flexibility for change while protecting the shareholders. Academic research has provided theoretical and empirical analysis of the antitakeover defenses such as classified boards and poison pills.

Bank mergers and competition

There are two types of antitrust policy (Stigler 1955, 176). First, corrective policy is intended to eliminate the barriers to competition that already exist. Second, preventive policy has the intention of preventing the creation of barriers to competition. Antitrust policy is used by a society that desires to use competition in markets. In this view, there is no emphasis on regulation of each and every activity by private or official institutions. Otherwise, antitrust policy would be ubiquitous. Preventive antitrust policy intends to prevent the creation of barriers to competition. Mergers and acquisitions could limit competition.

There is an important issue of whether M&As restrict entry into markets. According to Berger et al. (2004b),the banking industry provides a useful sample because its products are relatively homogeneous. Moreover, banks in the United States operate in segmented markets under different conditions. Expected profits and growth of markets constitute the factors of M&As in early research. Berger et al. use a large sample, including more than 10,000 M&As in over 2700 local markets. The period of observation covers 19 years in which there were almost 4000 actual market entries. The econometric research finds increases in the probability of entry in markets after M&As. The results are robust to the use of different econometric methods, changes in the specification of exogenous variables, and changes in data samples. The key result is that M&As increase subsequent new entry. The reduction in lending to small business caused by M&A consolidation is partly compensated by entrants, what Berger et al. consider to be an external effect of consolidation.

Corporate law

US investors have given trillions of dollars to corporations whose managers have discretion on their fortunes and profits. This power given to people who are not owners of the property has been studied intensely with the rise of the corporate form. The earliest warning of Berle and Means (1932) would suggest investment in bonds instead of equities. However, the returns on equities have surpassed those in bonds and the system of managers of corporations with many shareholders has worked effectively. Rock (1997, 1010) finds this to be the "central mystery" of corporate law. The traditional explanation of corporate law for the system to work rests on three types of arguments, according to Rock (Ibid, 1011):

- *Legal constraints.* The courts enforce legal prohibitions of theft, embezzlement, insider trading, and others. They also enforce more vague legal constraints such as the duty of care and the duty of loyalty. Managers are caught by the courts in violation of these legal constraints, which act as deterrent of misconduct.
- *Institutional structure.* Managers are checked by boards of directors, outside directors, shareholder voting, proxy contests, and derivative suits.

- *Market monitoring.* Managers are also checked by markets in products, labor, capital, and corporate control. Ineffective or corrupt managers can lose their jobs when the companies are restructured or sold.

Rock (1997, 1011) does not find that the checks on managers are very powerful with the exception of competitive markets in cases where they do exist.

The community of the corporate system is relatively small. Rock (1997, 1013) argues that it consists of several thousand senior managers and directors of large, publicly held corporations. There is an additional small group of lawyers, mainly in New York and Wilmington but with some in Chicago and Los Angeles. The court in charge of oversight for the most part, because of Delaware's attractive franchise of corporate form, is the Delaware Chancery Court with judicial review by the Delaware Supreme Court. Highlighting the small legal community, the decision makers responsible have close to only five members. Rock (Ibid, 1014) shows "how a small community imposes formal and informal, legal and nonlegal, sanctions on its members."

The essence of Delaware fiduciary law is that boards have freedom of discretion as long as they follow the right procedural process and act in good faith (Rock 1997, 1015). This can be in marked difference to other countries where protections have a stronger substantive approach. In Delaware, the courts define good faith by means of descriptions of the conduct of manager, director, and lawyer that are fact intensive and saturated with norms. Delaware fiduciary law is characterized by standards that are generated in a narrative process. The stories of this process cannot often be reduced to a rule. Instead, the Delaware courts provide parables of what are good and bad managers and lawyers to define their job descriptions. Rock (Ibid) finds value in thinking "of judges more as preachers than as policemen."

An excellent illustration of the operation of the review function of Delaware courts is provided by Rock in terms of the management buyouts (MBO) of the 1980s. There were 404 MBOs in the value of $162.02 billion during 1981–90. There were only 15 cases in the Delaware courts in that period relating to MBOs even with this amount of deal activity. The MBOs are especially important because they involve the acquisition of the company by the managers from the shareholders, creating opportunities for conflict of interest. An important consideration by Rock (1997, 1095) is that the critical cases involving Macmillan, Fort Howard, and RJR Nabisco were only written in 1988 and 1989, almost a decade after the boom in MBO activity began in 1981. Transactions were rapidly developing, creating pressure on business attorneys to advise their clients in an environment of vaguely defined norms on how the law would develop.

Rock (1997, 1099) argues that "Delaware is a reasonably efficient system of corporate governance." Opinions at this level focus primarily in granting preliminary injunctions. The common thread was that the opinions were critical of the conduct of the defendants. The deep judgments of the conduct of managers consisted of fact intensive narratives of the process by which the companies dealt with bidders and management. They marked the way for future conduct to be examined by courts and to be adhered to by companies facing such situations. These opinions contain narratives on the independence and activism of the special committees, the role of the investment banker adviser, and the search for alternative bids. The Delaware courts shifted the emphasis, in opinions and extrajudicial communication, to influence the conduct and formation of the special committees tasked by the board with evaluating the proposed business transaction (Ibid, 1104). In deciding these cases, the Delaware court used the standard of the "business judgment rule" or alternatively the "entire fairness standard." The courts did not give rules on how MBOs should be conducted, but clear procedural steps arose as best practices which would grant and for process which would gain greater deference to managers from the courts.

A summary of the standard that arises from the written opinions late in the 1990s is provided by Rock (1997, 1062). The Delaware courts recognized the existence of an inherent conflict of interest in MBOs. In those cases, the court has favored a special independent committee to negotiate with management and third parties. Moreover, the special committee has its own independent investment banking and legal advisers. Counsel should ascertain that managers involved in the MBOs do not appoint the members of the special committee and the investment banker adviser. Further procedural safeguards include an effective announcement by the special committee of the existence of a bid by management, ensuring that all material information is available to prospective bidders. The special committee should not improperly favor management over third parties that may enter the bidding. In addition, the special committee should test the market for possible alternative offers but is not required to conduct an English style auction. There is another important norm in the Delaware courts that is relevant to M&As and buyouts developed in the so-called Revlon line of cases. Management can "just say no" to an offer for the corporation if it is contrary to business plans that have been designed to optimize the corporation's long-term business model. Much like all this area of law, exceptions arise too when this situation really occurs.

The value of M&A transactions jumped from $44 billion in 1980 to $247 billion in 1988. Kahan and Rock (2002) argue that a significant share of these transactions were hostile takeovers or defensive transactions. In general, the focus of corporate legal doctrine and scholarship is on the relative power of managers and shareholders in the ultimate decision of selling or keeping the ownership structure of the company unaltered. The poison pill became the centerpiece instrument of defense because of various advantages described by Kahan and Rock. Namely, there are no significant costs in adopting the pill and the conduct of business by the company is not altered. The most important advantage is that it gives the board time to evaluate its options as the pill substantially hinders the short-term ability of an acquirer to takeover a company with a poison pill unless the target board redeems it.

One of the crucial early questions was whether a company could "just say no," using a phrase of the US First Lady of the time, choosing not to redeem the pill indefinitely on the argument that the hostile bid was not high enough. The Delaware Supreme Court provided its opinion on the subject in 1988, permitting Time to proceed with its tender offer for Warner Brothers and maintaining its poison pill. The board of Time was supported in its decision to turn down a conditional offer by Paramount of $200 per share, a premium of 58 percent over Time's pre-offer share price. Kahan and Rock point to the support given by the board's outside directors for the board of Time's decision on the basis of a fairness opinion by the investment banker advising Time. A corporation need not abandon a corporate plan in exchange for short-term shareholder profits unless there is no basis for the corporate strategy. Kahan and Rock argue that the Delaware court prefers bilateral decisions, which are those that are favored by both management and shareholders, because they are more likely to enhance welfare. The "just say no" doctrine was a unilateral doctrine, favored by management. The Delaware court may not be supportive of a "just say no" decision that does not have the support of the outside directors of the board based on the fairness opinion by an investment bank. However, this may have started to shift slightly as one of the central questions post this period was the ability of the shareholders to attain the redemption of the pill by the board.

After a brief interruption in the recession of the early 1990s, M&A activity entered into a phase of even more rapid growth, jumping from 3510 deals in 1995 with value of $356 billion to 10,883 deals in

2000 with value of $1284.8 billion (Kahan and Rock 2002, 10). During
this period, the largest number of takeovers was nominally friendly
in contrast with the hostile bids of the 1980s. There were also significant changes in corporate governance. Outside independent directors
acquired more power than in earlier periods, increasing their share in
corporate boards. Kahan and Rock also contend that outside directors
are more effective, in effect causing the dismissal of CEOs with poor
performance. Moreover, outside directors are more likely to strengthen
shareholders value during tender offers and stock prices increase in
response to their appointment. There are also higher premiums in
MBOs of corporations with boards that have a majority of independent directors. This strengthening of outside directors has increased
the monitoring function of boards. The changes in the composition
and relative influence of outside directors were accompanied by a shift
in compensation of managers by stock options. Stock options are often
seen as the best way to tie the interest of management and the board
with the performance of the company. However, managers gain in takeovers not only by the bidding of stock prices but also by golden parachutes providing severance payments, benefits, early vesting in pension
plans, and acceleration in vesting of unvested options (Kahan and Rock
2002, 14). The equilibrium between these devices is a fine one. While
golden parachutes and other such payments have a legitimate purpose
in maintaining management during the possible takeover transaction
and ensuring continuation of management should it fail, there are also
questions involving self-interest of management in assigning themselves such huge payoffs. Courts often follow the Delaware model of
looking at the process of the implementation of such devices and often
use certain limits communicated via the precedent system. The overall
change in governance on the corporate form has been more in accordance with the bilateral approach of the Delaware courts, benefiting
both management and shareholders.

   The corporation can be viewed as governed by the primacy of the
board or by the primacy of shareholders. Nearly all public corporations
are run by boards of directors. There are two theories considered by Stout
(2003) of why boards manage corporations. The monitoring theory is
more dominant. There are some efficiency explanations for monitoring
by boards in terms of the costs, feasibility, and apathy of decisions by
shareholders that could number in the hundreds of thousands in many
public corporations. The monitoring theory is based on two pillars. It
becomes extremely difficult for shareholders to obtain sufficient information on the business of the corporation to participate in decisions.

Thus, shareholders delegate to better-informed directors the decisions of the corporation. The separation of ownership by shareholders and control of the corporation by managers raises issues of agency costs. Managers, or agents, could pursue their self-interest instead of those of the shareholders, or principals. The directors of the board do not have the conflicts of interest of management. The two pillars of support for monitoring by boards are their knowledge of information relative to shareholders and their lack of conflict of interests relative to managers. The directors in boards monitor, on behalf of shareholders, the conduct of managers.

Boards oversee the performance of professional managers, intervening only in extreme situations. Stout argues that the monitoring model explains why shareholders would hire outside directors to watch and control the conduct of managers. However, there is no explanation in the monitoring model of why shareholders would grant to directors the control of the corporation, including all its assets and output. An important aspect of the limitation of the model is the authority of the board to decide not to distribute cash in the form of dividends. In such a case, the board limits the capacity of shareholders to extract wealth from the corporation.

The mediating theory is the second approach considered by Stout. There are two interesting ways of considering the firm. Executives, shareholders, and directors are not the only actors in corporations and shareholders are not necessarily victims and in fact can exploit companies. Shareholders can exploit other shareholders by obtaining specific concessions for a group in detriment of the majority. Creditors can also be misled by shareholders that take excessive risks not revealed in the creation of the credit contract. Shareholders can also cheat on employees by promising rewards that are not subsequently provided and then firing them.

There are important legal duties owed by officers and directors to the corporation, including the duty of care and the duty of loyalty. The duty of care requires directors to act in good faith, exercising the care of a prudent person and in the reasonable belief that they are promoting the best interests of the corporation. Reasonable diligence requires that directors make decisions based on collecting and analyzing material information. The courts do not rule what should or should not be done but simply state what was done or not in a specific situation and if it constituted due care or not (Knepper and Bailey 2002, 3.01).The duty of loyalty prevents directors from using their positions to make secret or personal profits, giving the corporation the benefit obtained as a result of their official positions (Ibid, 1.05). Directors must be scrupulous in protecting the interests of the corporation and in refraining from injuring the corporation. This duty of loyalty originates in prohibition of self-dealing in a fiduciary relationship (Ibid, 4.01).

The fiduciary duties of directors require that they promote the best interests of the corporation. They are required not to play favoritism among stockholders or classes of stockholders. The fiduciary duties require that directors act in good faith in all cases, in a conscientious way exercising their best judgment. There is a higher standard for directors with specialized knowledge, requiring advocacy within the board of conclusions reached from that knowledge (Ibid, 1.07).

These duties come to play important roles in the context of defending against hostile takeover attempts. Management will often attempt to use defensive devices at such times. However, it should be noted that the main purpose of defensive devices is to increase the capacity of the board to find a better deal by giving the directors more time; it is not to make the corporation immune to takeovers. Perhaps the only true way to make a corporation immune to a takeover under Delaware's jurisprudence is the concentration of voting securities in friendly hands (Ibid, 14.06). Starting in the backdrop of the takeovers of the 1980s, the Delaware courts modified the standard of review by focusing on the duties of directors in approving a takeover in the Unocal line of cases. Takeovers are a special time in the existence of the corporation, because self-interest of managers or the board can clearly clash or mesh with the interest of the corporation. This was an area where previous jurisprudence, first appearing with greenmail cases such as *Cheff v. Mathes* 199 A.2d 548, had stagnated into simply pronouncing certain responses to achieve approval from the court.

In *Unocal v. Mesa Petroleum*, 493 A.2d 946 (Del. 1985) the court unveiled an enhanced scrutiny standard, now commonly known as the Unocal standard. The directors of Unocal had attempted to prevent its acquisition by Mesa Petroleum Corp. by approving an exchange offer of stock held by the public for debt securities but excluding the shares held by Mesa Petroleum Corp, a so-called discriminatory tender offer. The Delaware Supreme Court analyzed the conduct of the directors in excluding the shares of Mesa Petroleum Corp. from the tender offer. The Delaware Supreme Court found that the directors had the "fundamental duty and obligation" to protect the company and its shareholders from possible injury, no matter where it originated. The fundamental aspect of the change in the court's jurisprudence is that the court extended the review of the board's actions in authorizing the action in an enhanced fashion. Consequently, the board now has an initial burden of proof of the existence of a threat to the policy and effectiveness of the corporation. This burden was met my showing good faith and informed decision making. Some threats recognized by the court in this early period included insufficient price, inadequate timing and nature, probable illegality, risk of execution, quality of offered securities, and effects on non-shareholders such as creditors, customers, employees, and possibly the community in general (Knepper and Bailey 2002, 14.06). The second prong of the Unocal test specifies that the defensive measure must be reasonably relative to the threat.

Through much of the 1980s and onto current times this standard evolved substantially, up to where the court follows the current Unocal-Unitrin standard when first evaluating a defensive technique; *Unitrin, Inc. v. American Gen. Corp,* 651 A.2d 1361 (Del. 1995). The new standard adds further clarifications to the second prong of Unocal ensuring that the device is not draconian (meaning it is neither preclusive nor coercive) and that the response falls within a range of reasonableness. As described by Rock, the use of the standard is a fact-intensive pursuit depending heavily on the facts of the previous cases (Rock 1997). However, even the Unocal-Unitrin standard is not the end of the inquiry. Certain situations, such as the board attempting to entrench itself may add the Blasius standard to the second prong of Unocal, which requires a so-far fatal inquiry from the board to show a compelling justification for its action of entrenchment. Other situations can trigger the Revlon moment, when all hopes of corporate effectiveness have failed and all that there is to do is secure the best price for the shareholders, requiring the board to drop its defenses and in some occasions enter into an auction process. *Blasius Indus. v. Atlas Corp.,* 564 A.2d 651 (Del. Ch. 1988); *Paramount Communications, Inc. v. QVC Network, Inc.,* 637 A.2d 34 (Del. 1994); *Paramount Communications, Inc. v. Time, Inc.,* 571 A.2d 1140, 1152 (Del.1989); *Revlon, Inc. v. MacAndrews & Forbes Holdings, Inc.,* 506 A.2d 173 (Del. 1986). It is important to note that directors can implement defenses even if there is no current takeover proposal. In fact, it may very well be in their interest to do so, as the timing of implementation is a factor that the court often looks to in terms of rooting out self-interested behavior of the board. However, there is no duty of directors to implement defenses before takeover attempts.

The objective of Lipton (2002, 1037) in creating the "warrant dividend plan" in September 1982 was "to deal with the takeover abuses that emerged in the 1970s and had become endemic" by the 1980s. Subsequently, the Lipton warrant dividend plan became known as the poison pill. The pill prevents the consummation of a hostile tender offer until the pill's redemption by the board of directors. The proxy fight became the only way for an acquirer to overcome a decision of the target's board to reject and block a bid to take over the target.

The defense of the pill by Lipton (2002, 1039) rests on two arguments. First, managing corporations as if they were being sold continuously has major costs. Second, the academic critique has not produced evidence that the damage of the pill exceeds the costs of continuously managing companies as if they are for sale. The critique of the pill, according to Lipton (Ibid, 1041) borrowed from the efficient markets hypothesis (Fama 1965a,b, 1970, 1991; Samuelson 1965; see an alternative by Shleifer 2000). The argument is that security prices reflect all the available information. If a bidder offered a premium over the current market value of the company, she could manage it more efficiently than current management and the company should be acquired to optimize shareholder wealth. The opposition to the takeover by management could originate in self-preservation instead of sound evaluation of the adequacy of the bid price. Defenses merely help entrenchment of management and directors, preventing shareholders to obtain their best value. The counterargument of the proponents of the pill is that security prices may not reflect accurately the value of a company (Lipton 2002, 1041–2). The costs of continuously managing a company for its sale prevent the long-term optimization of the corporation.

The poison pill aims to make a takeover prohibitively expensive, at least until a friendly board can be voted in to redeem the pill. One of its major advantages is that as long as the charter of the corporation allows the issuance of preferred stock, the board may implement this device without shareholder action. The typical poison pill may have a flip-over, a flip-in component, or both (Knepper and Bailey 2002, 14.06).

The defense begins by the directors approving the issuance rights via dividends to its shareholders and tying it to the common shares. These rights allow the shareholder to purchase stock or other security upon a triggering event. Such a triggering event may be the acquisition of stock by an outsider of above 10–20 percent of the outstanding stock (flip-in) or the actual merger by the outsider of the target corporation (flip-over). The flip-in component thus allows the shareholders to buy the share of the target corporation at a substantial discount, while the flip-over pill allows the shareholders holding the rights to acquire the bidder's stock at a substantial discount. The flip-in discourages the bidder by making the price of acquiring the target corporation more expensive as it dilutes the bidder's ability to acquire shares as target shareholders buy at their discounted price advantage. The flip-over provision only occurs after there is a merger; it works by diluting the value of the bidder's common shares. Consequently, the flip-over provision works well in protecting target shareholders from an unfair coercive second step merger (Cox, Hazen and O'Neal 2002, 23.7; Knepper and Bailey 2002, 14.06). This preferred stock converts into stock after a hostile takeover and requires high dividend payments. The acquirer either purchases the shares at a high price or pays the dividends, in either case, an effective prohibitive price for the acquisition of the company. There are variations of the standard poison pill, such as the poison put. The debt securities of the companies could have a provision by which the holders of the securities can call the bond, recovering their investment, in case of a takeover. There was a broad affirmation of poison pill plans by the Delaware Supreme Court and by the Chancery Court of Delaware *Moran v. Household Int'l, Inc.*, 500 A.2d 1346, 1350 (Del.1985) (Knepper and Bailey 2002, 14.06).

Antitakeover defense

"Director-centric" governance is defended by Lipton and Rowe (2007) as more adequate for the objective of corporation law, which is social prosperity by promoting creation of wealth and jobs with a long-term investment view. The legal framework for this perspective consists of concentrating initiative and decisions in management and the board of directors. There are five critical elements of this type of governance (Ibid, 64): (1) centralization of management in professionals; (2) supervision of managers by competent and mostly independent directors; (3) federal regulation limited to disclosure and fraud; (4) state law recognizing the crucial reliance on the business judgment rule, limiting judicial intervention; (5) restriction of the role of shareholders to extreme events such as mergers and proxy contests. Lipton and Rowe argue vigorously that this model is superior to the proposals of "shareholder-centric" governance.

There are two sides to the use of poison pills and shark repellents, according to Coates (2000, 272). Academics have been, in general, skeptical of the antitakeover defenses, while practicing attorneys advocate them, with judges and legislators generally siding with the case for allowing the defenses. Theoretical arguments claim that defenses increase agency costs by preventing discipline of directors that would occur by takeovers. Event studies claim that stocks of companies decline after adopting defenses. The case for defenses rests on increases in premiums for takeovers of companies that adopted defenses because of the enhanced bargaining for better conditions for shareholders. IPOs have included defenses that are stronger than provided by default law, which typically require yearly election of directors, even with sophisticated investors such as private equity and LBO specialists.

The evidence of two decades of empirical research is analyzed and increased by Coates. The conclusion is that the empirical research has not produced evidence of harmful effects by defenses. However, the research also does not provide evidence supporting the use of defenses by boards or evidence that could be used in litigation and in persuading institutional investors in accepting defenses. In addition, empirical research has not included the shadow pill. There are no effects on the target's takeover vulnerability from not having adopted a pill because the bidder is aware that the target can adopt it after the bid. The various defense strategies interact, clouding studies on bid incidence or bid outcomes.

There is a view by Bebchuk, Coates, and Subramanian (2002a,b) that effective staggered boards (ESB) combined with the pill diminish significantly the probability of successful takeovers and reduce shareholder value. The default law in all states provides that all directors in boards of public companies must face a yearly election. However, most states provide an exception that directors can be grouped in classes with the requirement that a class, typically of four directors, stand for reelection yearly. Thus, this staggered board (SB) system would renew at most four directors per year, or a third of the board, such that acquiring control of the board would require two elections, or two years. In the case of three classes, there would be a yearly election of four directors for terms of three years. In all states, the establishment or dismantling of an SB through amendment of the charter requires approval of both shareholders and the board; the establishment or dismantling of an SB in the bylaws requires approval by either shareholders or the board. The SBs have the same effects if established under the charter or the bylaws, but dismantling an SB through the bylaws is generally much easier (Bebchuk, Coates, and Subramanian 2002a, 894). The ESB is defined when control of the board is required to dismantle the SB. The ESB is characterized by its installation in the charter, removal of directors only for cause and obstacles for shareholders to pack the board through increases in the number of directors and filling vacancies. SBs are designed to provide for stability of the board, since they reduce annual turnover, and its independence, because three-year terms make directors less dependent on management. However, the ESB effectively creates barriers to takeovers.

The safety valve provided by the Delaware courts consists of the ballot box: a bidder or other entity could initiate a proxy contest promising the election of a new board that would redeem the pill (Ibid, 907). The ballot box may not be required if golden parachutes for management are effective with a takeover and the independent board align the interests of shareholders and management, allowing the market for corporate control to function. ESBs can cause a delay in the ballot box of up to two years, which may prove too long for the acquirer. The findings of Bebchuk, Coates, and Subramanian are that ESBs increase from 34 percent to 61 percent the probability that the average target remains independent; lower from 34 percent to 14 percent the probability that the first bidder is successful; and reduce the probability from 32 percent to 25 percent that a white knight or subsequent bidder is successful. They also find that the returns of shareholders of hostile targets declined by 8–10 percent in the second half of the 1990s. The proposal of Bebchuk, Coates, and Subramanian (2002a,b) would prevent target managers from maintaining the pill after losing the first proxy contest against the hostile bidder.

The research of Bebchuk and Cohen (2005) intends to measure the relationship between the value of firms and the incidence of staggered boards. The data includes all companies for which information is available in the volumes of the Investor Responsibility Research Center (IRRC) during 1995–2002. In the year of publication of the books the firms represented more than 90 percent of total capitalization of the US stock market. Tobin's Q as used by Bebchuk and Cohen (2005, 420) is the ratio of the market value of assets to the book value of assets. The market value of assets is equal to book value of assets plus market value of common stock less (book value of common stock plus balance-sheet deferred assets). The industry-adjusted Tobin's Q is the Q of the firm less the median Q in the firm's industry in the year of observation. Bebchuk and Cohen find that controlling for the value of the firm in 1990, the presence of a staggered board in 1990 is associated with significantly lower value during 1995–2002. This negative correlation is not observed for bylaw-based staggered boards relative to charter-based staggered boards.

The data set of Bates, Becher, and Lemmon (2008) consists of 20,335 firm year observations for 3087 unique firms obtained from the books of the IRRC during 1990–2002. They find that the rate of acquisition of targets with classified boards is equivalent to that of targets with a single class of directors. There is no evidence in the employment of target CEOs after completing a bid suggesting greater likelihood that managers of classified targets engage in self-dealing with potential acquirers. The returns of shareholders are equivalent for targets with classified boards as those with a single class of directors. The share of the total surplus to mergers is proportionately higher for targets with classified boards than for those with a single class of directors. The likelihood of a firm becoming a takeover target is reduced by 1 percent with classified boards. Bates, Becher, and Lemmon (2008) do not find empirical support for the proposals to strengthen regulatory or judicial scrutiny of transactions involving classified boards. The dismantling of antitakeover defenses in the form of classified boards may lower the quality of bids for target shareholders. It is uncertain if the elimination of classified boards would improve the bids for target shareholders. There are other factors that determine the quality of governance and shareholders rights in public companies. The independent or indexed consideration of these factors is not an adequate measure of how these firms are exposed to the market for corporate control. Empirical research has not evaluated the benefits of board classification or its relation to firm value. The proposals to abolish board classification are not based on solid evidence and could conceivably damage shareholders.

The problems of establishing empirically the relation between classified boards and firm value and identifying the benefits and costs to shareholders of various forms of corporate governance are common to economic research. Lipton and Rowe (2007, 70) observe

> [t]hat there is no consensus, even among the social scientists, as to what is good and bad about various features of corporate governance. It is inherently foolish to design a corporate law structure based on the "findings" of academics, since their studies are contradictory and their positions change over time.

Lipton and Rowe (Ibid) claim that academic research does not provide good reasons to restructure American corporate governance.

Summary

The distinction between specialized and broad banks was obliterated in the United States by the monetary authorities during the recession after 2007–9. The Glass-Steagall Act is an example of the errors that can result from rushed regulation during hard times, raising also the suspicion of rent-seeking by regulated entities. A system of flexible sound corporate law crafted by the Delaware courts with limited regulation has proved effective for the development of capital markets.

5
Securities Regulation

Introduction

This chapter covers the regulation of securities. The first section focuses on the need for companies to exit segments of activity or even for entire companies to exit in response to technological change. LBOs have provoked significant interest in the law and economics. The approaches of the United States based on rulemaking by the SEC and self-regulatory organizations (SRO) and the light touch of the United Kingdom are contrasted briefly in a separate section. The two following sections consider the regulation of new issues and insider trading. The last remaining sections cover the decision of going public, SOX, and listing of securities. There is a final brief summary.

Exit

Capital markets can play an important role in monitoring and reducing agency costs. The price of stocks reflects the existence of agency costs. Owners can retain investment bankers to price the company as a whole and if sold in segments. There are no agency costs when the owner and manager is the same, as in venture capital and private equity. The process of creative destruction of capitalism of Schumpeter (1942) requires the ability to restructure entire industries and economies to maximize dynamic economic efficiency, or long-term economic growth. Financial institutions provide important checks on distortions such as agency costs.

The essence of capitalism is the process of creation and destruction (Schumpeter 1942). A modern industrial revolution which began in the 1970s has created excess capacity by technology, organizational change, government policy, and globalization (Jensen 1986, 1988, 1991, 1993; Jensen and Meckling 1976; Fama and Jensen 1983a,b). Imperfect information about internal costs and those of competitors do not warn managers of the need to exit in market segments. High-cost producers need to exit the markets. A capital markets exit by M&As is less traumatic than bankruptcy in which valuable segments of corporations may be destroyed (Jensen 1988, 24). The increase in value caused by M&As can derive from increasing efficiency and from wealth transfers.

There are four control forces that can soften the difference between the decisions by managers and what is socially optimal: capital markets, government, markets for products, and factors of production and the system of internal controls of corporations under the responsibility of boards of directors (Jensen 1993). The board is responsible for the entire viability of the firm. It selects, hires, fires, and awards compensation to the CEO. However, boards have taken action too late, when bad performance was evident. CEOs may influence boards in such a way that they create an unfavorable culture, rendering them ineffective. Boards may not be informed adequately by the firm and some members may not be knowledgeable about financial or production issues. There may be more concern in boards about downside issues and adverse publicity than with value maximization. Board members typically have very small or no holdings of shares of the company. Ideally, the CEO should be the only member of management in the board. Excessive size in boards may subject them to easier control by CEOs. Typically, the CEO is the chairman of the board but separation of the two functions may result in better governance for the board.

Venture capital and LBOs provide examples of effective governance (Ibid). In the organization in limited partnerships, investors in the funds delegate the role in managing the corporation to the general partners. The managers and board members hold significant parts of the shares. Board members represent substantial holdings. Boards are relatively small, typically with less than eight members. CEOs rarely chair the boards. The information problem is diminished because active investors become familiar with the entire business during the due diligence in acquisition or investment and bring in their staff. Active investors also link the corporation with capital markets and investors.

An important part of the business of investment banks is advice to clients on the issue of debt and equity. In a way, this is complementary to the advice on restructuring the corporation by M&As. Companies depend on investment banks for the type of securities to issue, the evaluation of the financing available in markets, the timing of placement of securities, and the geographical distribution of the market. Investment banks conduct the underwriting and distribution of the securities.

Corporate takeovers result in major changes with gainers and losers. Restructuring of companies may be required because of technological and organizational changes that affect volumes and prices of products and the profitability of business segments. A dynamic economy requires transfer of resources toward activities that can contribute to higher growth. The restructurings affect various groups of shareholders, creditors, employees, competitors, suppliers, and customers. The closing and opening of plants affect communities in localities and even entire regions. There is significant pressure on legislatures and regulators to influence takeovers.

There is a market for corporate control by competing managers, which can be considered as an extension of the market for managers. Business models change rapidly. For example, the mechanical typewriter lasted decades until replaced by the electric typewriter. The subsequent product, the word processor, lasted only a few years. Segments that generated high profits suddenly cause losses. Managers find hurdles in abandoning older strategies because of the pains of closing or selling entire product lines and divisions. The takeover occurs because new management can change the business model more rapidly and effectively, increasing the profitability of the corporation. Progress requires reallocating resources to more dynamic opportunities. Resistance to change can prevent economic growth. Takeovers are better alternatives for restructuring and exit of business lines than costly bankruptcies.

Leveraged buyouts

LBOs illustrate the benefits and costs of large investors (Shleifer and Vishny 1997, 766). A group of new investors, including incumbent managers, a buyout firm, banks, and holders of public debt, buy the shares of the shareholders of a public company. The acquired company has fewer restraints on compensation, with incumbent managers increasing their stakes in the new company. The buyout firm obtains financing from banks and the issue of debt, such as junk bonds, to acquire the control of the company. There is evidence that LBOs are efficient from high premiums paid for the target company and subsequent higher profits. There is also some evidence of reduction of agency costs. Many of the acquired companies are diversified in segments, some of which may be sold after acquisition. Agency costs may be reduced if the agency problem originated in excessive size and diversification.

There are some arrangements in corporate governance designed to mitigate agency costs (Bolton and Scharfstein 1998, 101). Concentrations in large shareholders and creditors can increase controls on management. In LBOs, management borrows to acquire the company and has enhanced incentives to contain agency costs. The larger stake in the company creates incentives for managers to perform satisfactorily.

Merger activity in the United States was 2 to 3 percent of GDP in the century before the 1980s, when it jumped to a peak of about 10 percent of GDP around 1990 (Holmstrom and Kaplan 2001, 123). Leverage financed the takeovers of the 1980s, instead of the sale of new stock or the use of cash. The investor group in an LBO, frequently associated with incumbent management, takes the company private by purchasing the publicly owned share of a company. Hostile takeovers affected almost one-half of US major public corporations. The interpretation by Holmstrom and Kaplan is that the takeover activity in the 1980s was driven by deregulation in the 1970s, and by the new industrial revolution in IT. Deregulation after the 1980s and during the 1990s was a critical determinant of mergers (Andrade, Mitchell, and Stafford 2001). Change separated actual and potential performance at a time when the incentives in corporations were not designed to optimize shareholder wealth. Simultaneously, capital markets increased in dimension and complexity, with new institutional investors. Takeovers, junk bonds, and LBOs developed in response to the improvements in the performance of corporations together with empowered investors. There were diverse cases: failure of improvements of corporations by capital market actions; elimination of excess capacity; and disciplining of managers through takeovers. In the 1980s, hostile takeovers were more frequent while managers sought political and public support. Successful takeovers and LBOs showed managers, boards, and institutional investors the improvements of restructuring. Takeovers became more peaceful in the 1990s as incentives to managers were aligned with the interests of shareholders.

There are two competing hypotheses of factors determining LBOs (Ambrose and Winters 1992). First, an approach explains LBOs in terms of factors specific to firms, such as management or operating inefficiencies. Second, factors that are common to firms in an industry explain the higher incidence of LBOs. The tax shield afforded by debt could be an important consideration in taking a firm private: higher debt could be tax deductible compared with pure equity subject to tax on dividends. The agency theory of Jensen (1986) predicts that free cash flows that cannot find projects with positive net present value explain LBOs.

Free cash flows must exist in the firms that go private through LBOs to pay for the debt. Free cash flows occur in industries that are not regulated which have low growth prospects and limited research and development (R&D) expenditures. Ambrose and Winters (1992) use a sample of 170 LBOs and 1943 control firms during 1980–7 to test the industry-specific hypothesis. Their nonparametric tests provide only statistically weak support for the industry-specific hypothesis. LBO activity in industries shows low correlation with growth rates and debt capacity. Successful LBOs require debt capacity to raise the funds to take the firm private. However, there is support that free cash flows are required to finance LBOs. They conclude that firm-specific factors may explain LBO activity.[1]

In the presence of free cash flows (Jensen 1988), investors find an opportunity of closing the difference between their assessment of the attainable value of equity by restructuring and the current valuation (Arzac 1992). The model assumes a promotion group consisting of active investors controlling the corporation and management. An example consists of a takeover firm, such as KKR, and management. Outside investors include limited partners of LBO equity funds and lenders. The promoters engage in the LBO if they expect to obtain significant gains from the use of cash flows to generate higher value than the buyout price. The equity participation provides the gains to the promoters, being an increasing function of the value assessed by other investors of the future cash flows. Arzac (1992, 17) proposes a credible signal, unambiguously showing the commitment of the promoters in generating and distributing free cash flows to investors. The interest payment on the debt and the potential loss in case of default provides the signal of the cash flows resulting from the LBO, stimulating the valuation of equity desired by the promoters.

The model of Arzac consists of two periods. At date 0, the promoters plan to acquire the firm for a price K, with own resources of W, with $W < K$, and assuming that they cannot obtain the difference $K - W$ by borrowing on their own. Debt or sale of equity to outside investors generates the difference $K - W$. The firm generates free cash flows of c_1 at date 1 and c_2, derived from liquidation or going public, at date 2. Assuming that expectations of investors about future valuation are equal to those of promoters, the post-acquisition value of the firm with return r is (Arzac 1992, 17):

$$V = \frac{c_1}{(1+r)} + \frac{c_2}{(1+r)^2} \tag{5.1}$$

A positive net present value of the buyout, $V - K > 0$, requires that promoters generate cash flows above what potential buyers or management if not part of the promotion group would generate. The model can be extended by assuming different expectations by investors and the promoters (Ibid, 18–9). The firm can be acquired only by promoters providing a credible signal of future disposition of free cash flows.

The promoters finance the LBO by borrowing an amount D, keeping a fraction of equity α, and selling a fraction of equity $1 - \alpha$. The promoters choose D and α in maximizing the present value of their share in equity. The expression for the value of equity is (Arzac, 18):

$$S(D) = V - D \tag{5.2}$$

The promoters maximize $\alpha S(D)$ with respect to α and D, α in [0,1], with the budget constraint given by

$$W + D + (1 - \alpha)S(D) = K \tag{5.3}$$

There is no unique solution. Promoters keep the net present value of the buyout, irrespective of the chosen financial structure, paying bondholders and other investors the return r. The model can be used to analyze strip financing, in which investors must buy a mix of debt and equity securities, and equity kickers, in which lenders receive equity claims to compensate for below market interest rates.

There was a roundtrip of corporate America: the conglomerates created by unrelated takeovers in the 1960s were followed by divestiture of divisions, LBOs, and specialized takeovers in the 1980s (Shleifer and Vishny 1991). The two major theoretical interpretations of this roundtrip reveal a significant role of antitrust policy. First, the efficiency theory postulates that takeovers of related companies were sound policy of corporations, always moving toward efficiency. The conditions that dictated conglomerates in the 1960s changed with more competitive markets and the oil shock in the 1980s, leading to undoing conglomerates through the capital markets. Williamson (1975) generalized Chandler (1962) with the M-form of corporate organization, consisting of multidivisional structure with a central office allocating investment resources to the divisions (Shleifer and Vishny 1991). The central office would have better capacity than the market in identifying growth opportunities, compensating the inferiority in knowledge about the business of the divisions. Capital was reallocated by the central office from divisions facing low growth, thus generating cash, to the more dynamic divisions, with promising investment projects (Shleifer and Vishny 1990, 74). The central office could allocate capital among divisions more efficiently than banks and markets for bonds and equities. The environment changed in the 1980s with competition and the oil shock requiring management that the central offices of conglomerates could not deliver. The response of the market was the breaking up of conglomerates, resulting in allocation of assets to specialized corporate structures that had management delivering enhanced results.

Second, the alternative interpretation postulates that the conglomerate form, with unrelated diversification, was a mistake from the beginning (Shleifer and Vishny 1991). The United States took a detour in the road to attaining efficiency. In this view, the central office was not capable of dealing with unrelated diversification, failing to provide effective management of R&D and divisions requiring intensive investment (see Hall 1990 on R&D). In fact, Shleifer and Vishny (1990, 746) quote an estimate that 60 percent of the acquisitions of unrelated companies by conglomerates during 1970–82 were divested by 1989. Conglomeration in the 1960s ignored the central thesis of Adam Smith that specialization increases productivity (Shleifer and Vishny 1990, 746). Centralized managers could not allocate resources and manage corporations as effectively as specialized experts in the divisions. There were also agency problems of the division managers, entrenching in their positions by lobbying for their own business, lacking incentives to channel their resources to other divisions of the conglomerate. Managers in central offices were not exposed to the discipline of markets for capital control and managerial talent as would be the case of specialized companies. Divisions of conglomerate became uncompetitive with low earnings and high rates of divestiture.

Objections to takeovers in the 1980s focused on their effects on competition, employment, and R&D (Shleifer and Vishny 1990,747–8). Mergers within the same industry could create market power that would increase prices to consumers. Shleifer and Vishny (1990, 747) find that the effects of the takeovers of the 1980s on competition were not important. Mergers could cause wage reductions, transferring wealth from employees to shareholders, and layoffs. Shleifer and Vishny (Ibid) do not find significant effects of layoffs in the takeovers of the 1980s; most of the layoffs were concentrated in white collar workers in headquarters and other corporate staff who had easier adjustment (Bhagat, Shleifer, and Vishny 1990, 2). There is no evidence of significant reduction in investment except in some highly leveraged acquisitions. Most targets of takeovers are companies without significant expenditures in R&D.

There is a revealing relation of the theories to antitrust policy (Shleifer and Vishny 1990, 1991). Unrelated diversification was pursued by management in promoting personal objectives of survival and growth of their corporations. Instead of returning cash to shareholders, firms engaged in unrelated diversification because of the strong antitrust policy of the 1960s that made related acquisitions costly or nearly impossible. The lower posture of antitrust policy in the 1980s permitted the undoing of the diversification of the 1960s, permitting a return to specialized related acquisitions as it was the case in the 1920s and 1940s. Policy imposed a wedge in the efficiency of companies. Antitrust policy can entrench inept management in companies (Shleifer and Vishny 1990, 748). Agency problems developed in managerial capitalism in the United States because of the lack of monitoring that impeded the alignment of incentives of managers and shareholders. Financial regulation in the United States since the mid-1930s prevented the monitoring function by prohibiting cross-ownership between financial and industrial companies (Kaufman and Englander 1993). The LBO firm obtained funds from various investors, in particular pension funds, to discipline companies plagued by managerial agency problems. The structure of the company consisted of the general partners, limited partners who contributed funds and managers with equity shares. This structured aligned incentives of management and stakeholders.

If LBOs are motivated by the objective of realigning incentives for efficient management of the target firms, they are more likely to create instead of redistribute wealth. If LBOs are deterred by high financial distress costs, they are more viable and less threatening to economic stability. Opler and Titman (1993) tests these two characteristics by comparison of firms that undertook LBOs with those that did not with panel data for more than 2500 companies during 1959–87, including 180 firms that undertook LBOs during 1980–9. They conclude that free cash flows problems and potential financial distress costs are important factors explaining why firms engage in LBOs. There is higher likelihood that firms with low Tobin's Q and high cash flows will undertake LBOs, which is consistent with the free cash flow hypothesis. Firms engaging in LBOs have low R&D expenses and are not likely to be engaged in manufacturing of machines and equipment, which is consistent with the financial distress cost hypothesis. Tax advantages are the deciding motivation because LBO firms have more debt than what is required to eliminate taxes.

In standard price theory, if the supply of a commodity grows faster than demand, price will decline and output may contract. Miller (1991,

486) applies this basic principle to the junk bond market of the late 1980s. Overestimation by takeover promoters of the public's desire for junk bonds may result in higher yields that would reduce the profits of LBOs. The pace of leveraging would decline or maybe even contract. This endogenous mechanism was apparent in early 1989. The subsequent indictment of investment bankers and market makers in junk bonds caused the fire sale of inventories of junk bonds by S&Ls together with tightening regulations on leveraged lending by commercial banks. The result of the subsequent events was sharp contraction of the liquidity of high-yield bonds. Firms with high leverage replaced debt with equity.

The volume of LBOs in the United States rose from approximately $1 billion in 1980, peaked at $60 billion in 1988, and fell to $4 billion in 1990 (Kaplan and Stein 1993, 313). A sample of 124 MBOs in the 1980s provides the following behavior. The ratio of the buyout price to cash flow increased but not much more than for the markets or industries as a whole. Prices of junk-bond financed deals were especially high. The increase in prices was associated with transactions in riskier industries with relatively higher leverage ratios. The share of banks in deals declined toward the end of the decade together with acceleration of required principal repayments; the ratios of cash flows to total debt declined. Private subordinated debt was replaced by junk-bond debt; strip financing, or equity stakes of subordinated debt holders, also declined. Management, investment bankers, and promoters received more upfront money in the later deals. This evidence is consistent with a version of the overheated buyout market hypothesis. In this version, the availability of finance in the junk bond market in the second half of the 1980s increased demand for deals that were priced aggressively with higher risk of financial distress. However, Kaplan and Stein argue that there is no definitive proof of the overheated market hypothesis because of alternative arguments more consistent with rational investor behavior. For example, the liquidity provided by the junk bond market may have been created by increasing liquidity in the market for asset sales, reducing the potential for costly distress.

During 1976–90, Jensen (1991, 15) estimates $1.8 trillion of corporate control transactions, consisting of mergers, tender offers, divestitures and LBOS, creating $650 billion in value for the shareholders of selling firms. There were additional gains in the form of value for the buyers and in improvements of efficiency by the restructured firms. The losses to bondholders, banks, and other creditors financing the deals were at most $50 billion and likely around $25 billion. In the view of Jensen (1991, 21), the main objective of the corporation is to maximize its long-term value. The value-maximizing rule guides the tradeoffs of use of resources faced by the corporation over time. The inclusion of the effects of uncertainty sets the foundation of modern capital theory. Interference by Congress, courts, and regulatory agencies with the fundamental rule of the corporation undermines the source of creation of value that increases social standards of living. The interests of all stakeholders in the corporation, including employees, creditors, suppliers, taxpayers, and so on, are promoted jointly by the value-maximizing rule. Kaplan (1989) estimates yearly operating earnings of buyouts of 42 percent from the first year before the transaction to the third year after the transaction and of 25 percent after adjusting for cyclical trends. Nonvalue maximizing behavior by management is observed in the modern corporation because of problems of internal control (Shleifer and Vishny 1988).

There were two difficulties with the LBO market in the late 1980s according to Jensen (1991, 26). First, there was a contracting failure, which the market could have solved on its own. The problem originated in a misalignment of incentives of the promoters of the deals and the investors and creditors that they bring to the highly leveraged transactions (HLT). The LBO structure provides for effective monitoring of the business unit without the problem of free cash flows. The uploading of payments to the dealmakers may result in HLTs that do not have worth above price. Second, regulatory shocks at the federal and state levels, such as credit tightening, the breakup of the junk bond market, and obstacles to takeovers, prevented the refinancing of HLTs. Regulation prevented the private solution of problems, forcing a company into bankruptcy. Many of these shocks resulted from the collapse of real estate financing but affected the LBO markets at the time in which refinancing was required as an optimal solution.

Rules and principles

Congress passed the Securities Act of 1933 and the Securities Exchange Act of 1934. In the exegesis of the Securities and Exchange Commission (SEC 2006), the intention of Congress was to restore confidence by investors in the stock market by means of "more structure and government oversight." In this view, the securities laws are based on two common sense principles. First, the issuing companies must inform the public about the securities, their business, and the risks. Second, the distributors and traders of securities—brokers, dealers, and exchanges—have to give fair and honest treatment to investors, placing the interests of investors above everything. In 1934, Congress established the SEC with the objective of enforcing the new laws, promoting market stability and protecting investors.

The objective of the Division of Market Regulation of the SEC (2006) is to establish and maintain standards "for fair, orderly and efficient markets." Its main instrument to attain this objective is the regulation of broker-dealer firms, SROs, such as stock exchanges and clearing agencies, and other market participants. The definition of an SRO by the SEC is as follows:

> A self-regulatory organization is a member organization that creates and enforces rules for its members based on the federal securities laws. SROs, which are overseen by the SEC, are the front line in regulating broker-dealers.

The SEC (operates by making rules. Rulemaking is the instrument for implementing legislation passed by Congress and signed into law by the President. The framework of oversight of the SEC consists of the Securities Act of 1933, the Securities Exchange Act of 1934, and the Investment Company Act of 1940. The statutes are quite broad in nature, consisting of basic principles and objectives. The evolution of securities markets requires rules by the SEC "to maintain fair and orderly markets and to protect investors by altering regulations or creating new ones." The process of rulemaking may start with a specific proposal or with a concept release in which the SEC requests views of the public on a given issue. The SEC then elaborates a rule proposal for the consideration of the Commission. After approval of the proposal by the Commission, the SEC presents it to the public for a period of 30–60 days for review and comment. The final rule takes the replies by the public as input into consideration for the final draft. The final draft is presented to the Commission; if adopted it becomes part of the official rules governing the securities markets. A major rule may require congressional review and veto consideration before it becomes effective.

The approach of the United Kingdom is a unitary authority of regulation, the Financial Services Authority (FSA). According to the Director of Enforcement of the FSA, Margaret Cole (2007, 266), the London philosophy consists of a "light touch." This flexible approach has permitted London to become a "leading center for mobile capital." The FSA does not consider itself to be a regulator driven by high-profile enforcement. The leading aspect of regulation is the use of supervision and relations with the regulated firms. It has implemented a deliberate move to principles-based regulation. The FSA (2009Turner) has made an extensive proposal for intrusive and systemic regulation, which is considered with other proposals in Chapter 6 (see Finger 2009Apr).

The philosophy of the FSA could be criticized, according to Cole (2007, 267), in contrast with US regulation. Cole argues that there is no evidence of high-profile prosecution of violation of securities laws in the United Kingdom. On the contrary, the approach consists of selective messages and "allows some illicit activity to go unpunished" (Cole 2007, 267). However, the FSA claims that it has created an innovative and extremely effective system.

The FSA is independent of the UK government (Ibid). Its origin is in the Labor administration taking office in 1997 and it was created after giving independence to the BOE in the conduct of monetary policy. The FSA was the successor organization of ten predecessor UK regulators. It is now the only regulator of financial services in the United Kingdom. The funding of the FSA originates in fees paid by large and small firms that it regulates. Its responsibility of supervision encompasses wholesale and retail markets, equities and derivatives trading, banking, and insurance. It is also the listing authority of securities in the United Kingdom. The regulation of mortgages and insurance has been recently added to the FSA.

Regulation of new issues

The Securities Act of 1933, also known as the Truth-in-Securities law, intends to prevent the exploitation of buyers of securities with limited information by sellers with better information (Jarrell 1981, 613). Stigler (1964, 117) argues that "it is doubtful whether any other type of public regulation of economic activity has been so widely admired as the regulation of the securities markets by the Securities and Exchange Commission." The Securities Act of 1933 provided for the registration with the SEC of new issues of securities with various types of material information, including things such as corporate charter provisions, the capital structure of the company, the company's business, and the objective of the funds to be raised by the new issue. The issuer must publish a prospectus with the information and make it available to potential investors. Individual state "blue sky" laws regulating securities were passed in all states by 1933 except Nevada. These laws were typically more "paternalistic" in that they provided for qualitative standards for registration (Jarrell 1981, 616). However, these laws were not as comprehensive as the

Securities Act of 1933 and in the key states for securities of New York, Delaware, and Pennsylvania amounted only to registration of dealers and taxation of their operations (Simon 1989, 297).

In the last quarter of 1929, the market portfolio lost almost one-half of its value, losing 48 percent in 1930 and 59 percent in 1931 (Jarrell 1981, 619). The aggregate cost of new issues of equities during 1928–30 was $11.6 billion but in 1932 the value of these securities was only $3.6 billion. The opportunity loss relative to risk-free investment in government bonds is calculated by Jarrell (Ibid) as $9.2 billion. The per voter loss to the 38.6 million voters in the 1932 election was $200 compared with the average earning in manufacturing by a typical worker of $900 per year. Sale of war bonds during World War I was followed by increasing participation of small, new investors in the 1920s who suffered high losses. New Deal reforms promised in the presidential campaign of Roosevelt focused on regulation to prevent losses resulting from unethical practices by sellers of securities within a broad plan to recover the economy.

The analysis of the Securities Act of 1933 poses a tough counterfactual of whether there were benefits from the provisions of the act that exceeded their costs or if investors, issuers, and the public in general would have been better-off without the Securities Act. The approach by Stigler (1964, 120) is to measure the values of all new issues exceeding $2.5 million during 1923–8 comparing the offering prices with the price after five years of seasoning and measuring the value of all issues exceeding $5 million during 1949–55 and comparing the offering prices with the value after five years of seasoning. Stigler measured stock prices relative to the market average to avoid confusion of comparing absolute differences of the two periods in terms of fortunes of investors. He divided the ratio of the market prices for a span of time in a period, p_t/p_0, by the ratio of the market average in the same period. This was one of the first analyses of the economic effects of the Securities Act of 1933. The conclusion of Stigler (1964, 121) is that investors in the 1950s were not better off than in the 1920s, especially if they held the securities for one or two years.

The sample of Jarrell (1981, 627) consists of all new issues of common stock exceeding $200 million issued by manufacturing and railroad companies during 1926–39. Jarrell tests two hypotheses. First, the Securities Act of 1933 is based on the hypothesis that new issues before 1933 were characterized by insufficient disclosure and excessively high costs of promotion. The new act should have resulted in higher returns relative to the market. Second, the alternative hypothesis is that

issuers and underwriters of securities have incentives to disclose efficient quantity and quality of information. Otherwise, investors would
prefer alternative investment opportunities, refusing to absorb the costs
of ignorance and fraud. The existing underwriting industry had comparative advantage in assessing the value of new issues.

The basic equation for calculating returns used by Jarrell (1981, 637)
is obtained from the capital asset pricing model (CAPM):

$$R_{st} - R_{Ft} = \alpha_s + \beta_s(R_{Mt} - R_{Ft}) - \beta_{s-1}(R_{Mt-1} - R_{Ft-1}) + \varepsilon_t \qquad (5.4)$$

where R_{st} is the return to stock s at time t, R_{Ft} is the risk-free return at
time t, R_{Mt} is the return to the market portfolio M at time t, ε_t is the
random disturbance, and α and β parameters. The estimation of this
regression for the first five years after issue of a new security provides a
test for average abnormal returns. If there was overpricing of securities
by investors, the estimated α would be negative for a significantly large
number of securities. The regression also provides an estimate of abnormal performance for any period of seasoning of a security. At time t,
the measurement of abnormal performance for security s is merely the
sum of the monthly mean abnormal return in the form of the estimated
α_s plus the residual ε_t. There is a test of overpricing because of insufficient disclosure and promotional costs in the cross-sectional averages
of abnormal performance provided by the sum of the estimated α_s and
the residual ε_t. Jarrell provides tests for the period before and after the
Securities Act of 1933. There are two major results. First, in the pre-
SEC the abnormal return is negative in the first year of seasoning but
becomes significantly positive over the entire five-year period of seasoning. Second, the abnormal return for the five-year seasoning period
is higher for new issues before the SEC than for new issues after creation
of the SEC. An additional result is the finding of lower systematic and
unsystematic risk in registered securities relative to unregistered securities, which was also found by Stigler (1964). The premium for default
and risk of bonds declined in the post-SEC regulation relative to the
earlier period.

Government intervention in markets in which sellers have better
information than buyers can be justified in terms of two conditions
(Simon 1989, 296). First, sellers have incentives in providing inferior
information when they provide both the good and information on its
quality, which is the case of newly issued securities. However, it is difficult to find reasons why the government would have economies of
scale or externalities in providing better information relative to firms.

Simon (1989, 297–8) argues that information on quality was provided by the circulars of brokers and the listing requirements of the NYSE that was equivalent to what the Securities Act of 1933 mandated, which was described earlier by Berle and Means (1932). Second, information could be considered as a public good in which case the market may not produce sufficient quantities for the social needs. The Securities Act of 1933 provided for both seasoned and unseasoned issues. Seasoned issues are those in which there is a new issue of an already existing stock. Unseasoned issues are those first issued by a firm or IPOs. There are histories of seasoned issues that permit better monitoring, which is not necessarily the case of unseasoned issues. Moreover, there were stock exchanges that did not have the listing requirements of the NYSE.

The studies of Stigler (1964) and Jarrell (1981) did not find significant difference in abnormal returns before and after the SEC. Simon (1989) argues that the dispersion of returns is a more adequate measurement of the risk in securities and expands the analysis beyond the single-factor market index of the CAPM to the multiple-factor arbitrate pricing theory (APT) of Ross (1976). The empirical model is as follows (Simon 1989, 302–3):

$$R_{st} - R_{Ft} = \alpha_s + \beta_s (R_{Mt} - R_{Ft}) + \sum_{j}^{4} \gamma_{js} D_{jt} + \delta_s [RIND_{st} - R_{Mt} - R_{Ft}]$$
$$+ \theta_s UVAR_t + \varphi_s [CYCLE_t^* (R_{MT} - R_{Ft})] + \varepsilon_{st} \tag{5.5}$$

where the variables are the same as in equation (5.4), the Greek letters are parameters, ε_{st} is the disturbance, Ds are dummies designed to capture time-specific abnormal returns, $RIND$ is an equally weighted portfolio of firms in the same industry, $UVAR$ captures the unanticipated component of the market variance estimated by an ARIMA (1,0,1) process, and $CYCLE$ captures business cycles by the detrend value of the index of industrial production. Two samples are tested for the pre-SEC period 1926–33 and for the post-SEC period 1934–9 for seasoned and unseasoned securities listed in the NYSE and in other exchanges. The approach of Simon (1989) is to analyze the effects of the Securities Act of 1933 in securities that had the highest information costs, that is, in differences between seasoned and unseasoned IPO issues and between NYSE-listed securities and exchanges not providing quality information. The normal risk-adjusted returns in seasoned and unseasoned securities listed in the NYSE did not differ after the SEC relative to those before the SEC. Returns in IPOs listed in exchanges other than the NYSE were highly overpriced. The dispersion of returns for all securities, seasoned and unseasoned in the NYSE or other exchanges was significantly lower after the SEC.

None of the studies on the Securities Act of 1933 calculate the costs and benefits of regulation, which presents almost insurmountable technical and data barriers. There are high costs of complying with the SEC over several decades. Simon (1989) mentions the benefit of development of the over the counter (OTC) market for securities, allowing the raising of capital for small companies. It is not known if the requirements introduced by securities regulation provided benefits that exceeded their costs to conclude if the regulation was superior to other forms by which the market could have provided quality information. The still open issue is if government regulation of securities provided enhanced information at a lower cost than privately provided information; that is, if the SEC provided a more efficient system than the one it replaced. Mahoney (1997) argues that exchanges are more likely to be superior regulators relative to the government.

There was an effort to pursue socially useful goals in the Securities Act of 1933 (Mahoney 2001). It provided for mandatory disclosure of the fees and stakes in companies of promoters and underwriters of new issues, correcting abuse that occurred in England and the United States since the mid-1800s. The syndicate system developed in the United States several decades before 1916 consisted at the top of the originating or issuing investment bank, which performed the functions of the current underwriting manager (1990, 4). The manager advises the issuer, conducts due diligence of the company, and negotiates the terms of the deal. The compensation of the underwriters consisted of the discount in purchasing from the issuer. A fixed price for purchases by investors was fixed by the originating investment bank that consulted with the issuer. The spread between the price received by the issuer and the price paid by the investors was the compensation of the underwriters. The originating investment bank received from the syndicate the largest part of the compensation and chose the other underwriters and distributors. There were a few originating investment houses with strong political influence. Mahoney (2001, 13) finds significant deterioration in the concentration of business in the top five investment houses, declining from 37 percent in 1925 to 12.9 percent in 1929. The war effort included the sale and distribution of government securities through a new and growing retail system. In the 1920s, this system welded into integrated originating and distributing investment houses.

The integrated investment bank challenged the market power of the politically more powerful wholesale originating investment houses.

Insider trading

Insider trading occurs when a party to a trade has possession of material nonpublic information (Bainbridge 2000, 773). The courts created the two rules of disclose or abstain and the theory of misappropriation under Section 10(b) of the Securities Exchange Act of 1934 and Rule 10b-5. The SEC adopted rule 14e-3 proscribing insider trading using information on tender offers under its rulemaking authority under Section 14(e) of the Securities Exchange Act of 1934. In 1969, *SEC v Texas Gulf Sulphur Co.* "rested on a policy of equality of access to information" (Bainbridge 2000, 773). The party in possession of information was required to disclose it before trading or else abstain from trading. In 1989, the US Supreme Court, in *Chiarella v. United States* and *Dirks v. SEC*, "made clear that liability could be imposed only if the defendant was subject to a duty to disclose prior to trading" (Ibid, 773–4). The mere possession of information by an insider trader was insufficient for liability. The duty to disclose occurs when the insider trader breaches a pre-existing "fiduciary duty owed to the person with whom the trade was made" (Ibid, 774). The misappropriation theory rests on whether the insider trader violates a fiduciary duty to the source of the information (Ibid, 776). This theory was validated by the Supreme Court in 1996 in *U.S. v. O'Hagan*.

There has been active debate among law and economics scholars on the merits of insider trading regulation. The contributions can be summarized in terms of four categories used in surveys of vast literature (Bainbridge 2000; Beny 2007; Manne 2005, 1966).

First, *market efficiency*: The initial contribution was made by Manne (1966) directing the debate to the effects of insider trading on market efficiency. Manne (2005) argues that Manne (1966) contributed two arguments on market efficiency: (1) insider trading did not cause major damage to long-term investors and (2) improved significantly the efficiency of pricing in stock markets (Carlton and Fischel 1983). A critique of this argument is in terms of the "insider trading tax," consisting of widening bid-ask spreads resulting from systematic insider trading in markets. If traders lose frequently to insider traders, they will increase the bid-ask spreads to compensate their losses. Systematic gains by insiders drive out outsiders that invest in gathering and analyzing information, such as professional traders, reducing the competitiveness in the market (Beny 2007, 250). Markets with high bid-ask spreads reflect lower liquidity with fewer trades in lower volume. Demsetz (1986) argues that controlling shareholders may use inside information to compensate their risks for not being diversified by holding ownership concentrations in the company. Markets become more efficient if security prices move in markets to reflect all the information on the company, improving the intermediation function of finance. There are gains to both the companies and society from improved market efficiency via the enhanced allocation of resources and improved functions of financial institutions. The initial trading by parties having material nonpublic information is followed by other market participants or what is called derivate trading, which works slowly, diminishing the adjustment to the fair price caused by insider trading (Bainbridge 2000, 779–80). The problem rests in the asymmetry of information because not all relevant material information has to be disclosed to maintain an incentive and protect companies in making innovative investments. Beny (2007, 248–9) finds three counterarguments of proponents of insider trading regulation: (1) managers may delay disclosure of information to maximize their rents from insider trading; (2) outsiders may not detect the trading of insiders because it is disguised in multiple ways; and (3) the additional information of insider trading over normal disclosure may not be significant. The defense of regulation is based on the general argument that traditional disclosure may be relatively cheap (Beny 2007, 249).

Second, *agency costs*: Manne (1966) proposed the use of insider trading by firm entrepreneurs, who are those contributing to dynamic growth of the firm, as a form of realigning the incentives of management and shareholders. This proposal was subsequently reformulated by Manne (2005). It is difficult in practice to design compensation schemes by insider trading (Bainbridge 2000, 781–2; Beny 2007, 244–5): insider trading may not capture the remuneration corresponding to the contribution to the insider; it may be difficult to exclude others who do not make the contribution from gaining by insider trading; insiders may trade on adverse news; managers may take excessive risk in an effort to maximize their rents from insider trading; and the information is state contingent, creating probable outcomes that are inferior to remuneration fixed ex ante.

Third, *political economy*: The public choice argument is that insider trading rules are sold by regulators to those benefitting from the regulation (Bainbridge 2000, 783–5). The motivation for the sellers is to augment the agencies under their responsibility. The buyers would be professional traders who would systematically lose to insiders. The view that trading profits would be fairly distributed among investors by banning insider trading is naïve. Information specialists or professional traders compete with insiders for profits and can organize, in a private interest model, much more effectively than insiders (Haddock and Macey 1987, 338). Insiders have higher stakes than outside investors and can also organize to influence regulation.

Fourth, *property rights*: Bainbridge (2000, 791–4) surveys vast literature and court decisions and his own contribution. The conclusion is that the property rights should be assigned to the corporation, in particular under the theory of misappropriation.

The analysis of the law and economics literature leads Beny (2006, 262) to test three hypothesis; stringent insider trading laws result in (1) less concentrated equity ownership, (2) more informative stock prices, and (3) more liquid stock markets. The economic and stock market data are from a cross-section of 33 countries. The empirical results confirm an association but do not prove causality that stricter insider trading laws increase stock market liquidity and price accuracy while reducing concentration of equity ownership. There appear to be external economies of insider trading laws that promote higher efficiency in the allocation of capital to productive activities through the financial system. In Congressional testimony, Beny (2006) concludes that these empirical results provide evidence on the soundness of regulation of insider trading but must be followed by intensive additional research.

The first great merger wave during 1897–1903 provides a meaningful sample because there was concentration of ownership but no insider trading prohibitions (Banerjee and Eckard 2001). Mergers in that period occurred by the creation of a shell company, called a trust, and the exchange of stock of several companies in the same industrial or mining segment into the trust. There was a leading investment bank of a syndicate that brought in other investments and carried the underwriting of stock. Investment banks received significant stakes in the trust and participating companies and their representatives in the boards had management functions. Banerjee and Eckard (2001, 1331) identify various potential insider traders possessing material information: investment bankers, trust promoters, and original owners and officers of participating companies. Reports of the time indicate significant insider trading. The sample consists of 56 participant firms of which 19 disclosed information when the merger was done, or *fait-acompli* disclosure, and 37 that disclosed in preannouncements, or prospective disclosure. There are 41 trusts in 26 industries in the sample; the sample has one out of five industries traded at the time.

The study of Banerjee and Eckard (2001) uses a standard model in event studies:

$$AR_{it} = R_{it} - (a_i - b_i R_{mt}) \qquad (5.6)$$

where AR_{it} represents abnormal returns, t time in weeks, i the stock, R_{it} returns, a and b are constants, and R_{mt} is the return of the market, in their sample the Dow Jones index of that period. Because efficiency is not established for the period, they also use a model that does not require a market index:

$$AR_{it} = R_{it} - \mu_i \qquad (5.7)$$

where μ_i is the mean return in the sample period. The runup is the sum of the abnormal returns in the eight weeks preceding the event; the event gain is the sum of abnormal returns around the event; and postevent drift is the sum of abnormal returns in the three weeks following the event. Premium is defined as the sum of runup and event gain and the runup index is the percentage runup to premium ratio. The runup index for the entire sample of 56 firms is 75 percent. A subsample of 37 firms corresponding to the modern-day disclosure standards has a runup index of slightly over 50 percent, which is comparable to that measured in modern insider trading studies. Merger announcements have impact on stock prices even in the presence of trading by insiders before the public knows all the information. About one-half of the gain in price occurs on the announcement of a prospective merger. Gains from insider trading are higher for firms with more disclosure of information; enhanced transparency attracts outsider trading. In *fait-acompli* disclosure, the runup index exceeds 100 percent with insiders capturing all of the gains before announcement to the public. The results of Banerjee and Eckard (2001) suggest that outsiders may have gained very little from insider trading regulation in which case the social benefits may have been inferior to the costs.

The comprehensive world survey by Bhattacharya and Daouk (2002) finds that the United States passed a law with insider trading provisions in 1934 but most of the rest of the world did not implement and prosecute insider trading until the 1990s. US law was the only law providing insider trading until the establishment of this law by France in 1967. The median year of establishment of insider trading laws in developed countries is by 1989 whereas the median year in emerging markets is 1992. By 1998, 100 percent of developed countries had insider trading laws but only 80 percent of emerging markets. Before 1990, 55 percent of developed countries had insider trading laws compared with 39 percent for emerging markets. The first case of indictment of insider trade was in the United States in 1961 but only nine countries had indicted insider trading before 1990 (Bhattacharya and Daouk 2002, 88–9). The median year for prosecution in developed and emerging markets is the same, 1994, but only 25 percent of emerging markets prosecuted by 1998 compared with 82 percent of developed countries (Ibid).

Using the world sample and four approaches, Bhattacharya and Daouk (2002, 88–9) find that the establishment of the insider trading law does not affect the cost of equity as much as the first enforcement. They caution the interpretation of these results because of two problems. First, there is an endogenous effect because countries could enforce the laws when the cost of equity becomes very high. Second, although there is an economically and significant association between enforcement and reduction of the cost of equity, they are reluctant to conclude in favor of causality because enforcement is also associated with an improvement in country credit ratings. The attractiveness of the national stock market to outside investors may be correlated with the reduction in the cost of equity and the improvement in country credit ratings.[2]

The decision of going public

The traditional analysis of the decision of a firm going public considers it as a normal stage in the development of a company (Pagano, Panetta, and Zingales 1998). The decision to go public can be analyzed in terms of a tradeoff of costs and benefits (Zingales, 1995, 425). The costs include registration, underwriting, IPO underpricing, annual disclosure, and the agency problems analyzed by Jensen and Meckling (1976). The benefits include diversification, higher access to funds by equity financing, lower costs of capital, enhanced liquidity of stock, and outside monitoring. Zingales (1995) argues that corporate control is an important determinant. The decision of going public originates in value maximization by the initial owner who can change the proportion of cash flow rights and control rights while bargaining with a potential buyer.

The decision of going public is analyzed by Pagano, Panetta, and Zingales (1998) in terms of ex ante, or before listing factors, and ex post, or after listing factors. The ex ante analysis measures the probability of listing in terms of firm size, capital expenditures, growth, profitability, leverage, market-to-book ratio, cost of funds, and concentration. The sample of Pagano, Panetta, and Zingales (1998, 33) contains

40 new listings of independent companies and 29 carve-outs for a total of 69 companies in Italy in 1982–92; there are 19,817 firm years in the sample. An important aspect of the sample is that it allows for comparison of financial information in the years before and after the IPOs, allowing also for comparison of firms that listed with similar ones that did not list. The two most important ex ante determinants are size, increasing the sample average probability of going public by 40 percent, and market-to-book ratio, increasing the sample average probability of going public by 25 percent. An important finding is that companies go public to stabilize their balance sheets following a period of high growth instead of with the objective of financing future growth and investment. Companies obtain more credit at lower rates after IPOs. In the sample of Pagano, Panetta, and Zingales (1998) there is significantly high turnover in the control of firms even when the controlling group maintains significant block of ownership after the IPO. This finding is consistent with the argument of Zingales (1995) that companies go public with the objective of maximizing the proceeds of the incumbent in selling the company.

Private benefits of control consist of value in a firm that is appropriated by the "party in control" without sharing it with the remaining shareholders (Dyck and Zingales 2004, 541). There are many theoretical forms in which private benefits might be appropriated by the controlling party in a firm. There is psychic value or pleasure in commanding a corporation, but it does not explain high premiums paid for its acquisition. There are also the perquisites in the Jensen and Meckling (1976) theory of the firm but they may not be the most important private benefits of control. There are also differences in transfer prices of corporate control that may not even be solved by appeal to evaluation by finance economists. Another possibility is that a manager in a firm may discover a new way to add value and use a personal investment vehicle for its exploitation. There are costs of control resulting from the lack of diversification by the owner of a controlling share. Fraud can also occur as the controlling party expropriates value from minority shareholders, such as by creating a shell company to "tunnel" wealth of the firm to the controlling party. Dyck and Zingales (2004, 541) argue that private benefits of control may not be inefficient in capturing some of the created value for the firm. In the case of a manager creating value by an innovation, it may be efficient for the company that the manager exploits the opportunity through her own vehicle. Even in the case of some inefficiency, there may be social benefit in enhancing takeovers (Grossman and Hart 1980 as cited by Dyck and Zingales 2004).

The model of Barclay and Holderness (1989) is used by Dyck and Zingales (2004) to measure private benefits by means of the following equation:

$$B = \lambda B_b + (1 - \lambda)B_s - \alpha(1 - \lambda)(Y_b - Y_s) \qquad (5.8)$$

where B is the private benefits of control, λ, in the interval [0,1], is the bargaining power of the controlling party or percentage of the private benefits of control that it can obtain in selling, $B_{b,s}$ capture the private benefits extracted by the buyer b (seller s), and $Y_{b,s}$ are the security benefits created by the buyer b (seller s). The market for cash flow rights sold to dispersed shareholders is likely competitive but this is not the case of the market for corporate control (Zingales 1995; Pagano, Panetta, and Zingales 1998, 41). If the market is perfectly competitive, λ is unity and B equals B_b; the control premium measures the benefits enjoyed by the buyer of control. If the market is not perfectly competitive and $Y_b = Y_s$, B still measures the private benefit of control, representing a weighted average of the private benefits of the seller and buyer. Dyck and Zingales (2004, 552) obtain an estimate of λ of 0.655, inside the [0,1] interval.

The sample used by Dyck and Zingales (2004) consists of 393 observations from 39 countries during 1990–2000. The average private benefit of control is 14 percent, ranging from −4 percent for Japan to 65 percent for Brazil. They conclude that their estimates are consistent with previous ones, showing that private controls are "a very real phenomenon that can be consistently measured" (Dyck and Zingales 2004, 589). In the sample of 39 countries, large private benefits of control are associated with more concentrated ownership, privatization more likely through public offerings, and less developed capital markets. The findings are consistent with research on corporate finance on the need of protecting outside investors from expropriation by insiders. There is positive association between lower level of private benefits of control and enhanced law enforcement, product market competition, diffusion of the press, and tax compliance. Tax enforcement emerges as potentially important in reducing private benefits of control, leading to financial development.

There is a test by Gompers and Lerner (1999) of the "naïve investor hypothesis" analyzed by (Kroszner and Rajan 1994) by which the underwriter may mislead investors about the quality of the issues in which they have a conflict of interest through lending. The alternative rational discounting hypothesis postulates that investors perceive the conflict of interest, discounting the price of the security. There would not be long-term adverse performance effects of securities underwritten by investment banks that have an investment in the firm through an affiliated venture capital fund. The sample of Gompers and Lerner (1999) consists of 885 IPOs during 1972–92. A venture fund affiliated with an investment bank was part of 386 of the IPOs and in 127 of these there was an earlier venture investment in the company by a lead or co-lead underwriter. IPOs are especially useful in testing the potential conflicts of interest of underwriters that led to the Glass-Steagall Act. There is information of whether the underwriter has an equity position in the listing firm and a precise quantitative measurement. Gompers and Lerner conclude that the conflicts of interest appear to be discounted by the market. There is no inferior performance by IPOs underwritten by an investment bank that is also a venture investor. The reputation of the investment bank tends to reduce the required discount. Firms with lower asymmetric information are preferred by investment banks for investment and underwriting. With more precise information about the potential conflict of interest of underwriting and investment in the same firm, Gompers and Lerner conclude that the evidence provides support for rejecting the naïve investor hypothesis in favor of the rational discounting hypothesis. Markets are capable of adequately anticipating conflicts of interest and price securities efficiently.[3]

Sarbanes-Oxley

Accounting restatements by US public companies rose from 49 during 1992–6 to a two-year average of 97 during 1997–8 and to cumulative 850 during 1999–2002 (Coates 2007, 93). Jensen (2005) argues that earnings management occurs when managers attempt to justify excessively high market valuations, as it was the case at the turn of the millennium. There was a wave of frauds in companies with very high valuation, such as Enron (Healy and Palepu 2003; Lev 2003). The period leading to SOX was characterized by tightening liquidity as reflected in increasing bid-ask spreads and a rise in class action lawsuits; auditing firms were sued by shareholders and investigated and sued for fraud by the SEC (Coates 2007, 93–4). There are problems of agency and collective actions in private enforcement of fraud in companies that have numerous disperse shareholders. Management can use company funds to settle the lawsuits with resulting harms to shareholders. There are funding and information constraints for enforcement by the SEC (Ibid, 95). Protection against fraud is provided by gatekeepers (Coffee 2006), which are informed private actors such as auditors, mandated by law in public companies since 1934. However, auditors failed before SOX in detecting and reporting improper accounting. SOX created significant costs that would be compensated by long-term benefits. The risks of losses from fraud and theft would decline and other benefits would be derived from transparency, accountability, and more reliable financial reporting. The cost of capital would decline for public companies, fostering resource allocation and growth.

The structure of SOX as it originally entered in force is in Table 5.1. There are 11 titles in SOX. The objective of the law is to generate rules of conduct for the principal participants in publicly issued securities. Title I is directed to the auditing and accounting profession. It creates the Public Company Accounting Oversight Board (PCAOB) as a nonprofit institution, entirely separate from the federal government. The PCAOB regulates the profession of public accounting firms to enforce compliance with SOX. Public accounting firms involved in financial reports of issuers are required to register with the PCAOB, which will determine standards, conduct inspection, investigations, disciplinary processes, issue rules, and take actions designed to promote high professional standards.

Title III introduces important measures of corporate responsibility. An important complaint that led to SOX was that management anticipated and/or fabricated earnings with the objective of receiving bonuses and higher compensation. Sec. 301 created the corporate independent audit committee. Criteria have been introduced to ensure the independence of the members. The role of the audit committee is to directly hire the public auditors and to communicate with them. There is the recommendation that one member should be a financial expert with knowledge of Generally Accepted Accounting Principles (GAAP) and interpretation of financial statements. SOX enhanced corporate responsibility of financial reports by senior management signing financial reports. In addition, it made signing officers accountable for establishing and maintaining internal controls, disclosing to auditors, and the public deficiencies and fraud. SOX provided for the forfeiture of bonuses and profits from sale of corporate stock during the 12-month period following a financial report that is subsequently restated. It prohibited insider trading during pension fund blackout periods.

The disclosure requirements of financial reports are provided in Title IV. A critical provision is the disclosure of all off-balance sheet activities with unconsolidated persons or entities. In particular, this covers the special purpose entities (SPE) that surfaced during the Enron events. SOX prohibits the loans of corporations to executives. It requires a corporate code of ethics for senior financial officers.

Table 5.1   Structure of SOX

Established PCAOB 15 USC 7211 Title I
- Nonprofit corporation under the District of Columbia Nonprofit Corporation Act
- Not "an agency of establishment of the United States Government" Sec. 101(b)
- Duties of the PCAOB, Sec. 101(c):
  - "Register public accounting firms that prepare audit reports for issuers"
  - Determine standards of "auditing, quality control, ethics, independence and other standards relating to the preparation of audit report for issuers"
  - "Conduct inspections of registered public accounting firms"
  - "Conduct investigations and disciplinary proceedings" of registered public accounting firms and associated persons
  - Promote high professional standards by registered public accounting firms and associated persons
  - Mandatory registration of public accounting firms that prepare, issue, or participate in the preparation of any audit report to any issuer
  - Enforce compliance with SOX

Auditor Independence Title II
- Auditor reporting to audit committees, including communications with management
- Prohibited activities such as services to management
- Rotation of lead auditor after five consecutive years

Corporate Responsibility Title III
- Creation of corporate independent audit committee, Sec. 301, by amending 15 USC 78f Sec.10A
- Objective: prevent management to mislead and influence public auditors
- Composition: entirely independent membership
- Role: hire the public auditor and communicate with it
- Complaints: procedures to receive complaints of the public and anonymous complaints by employees
- Recommendation: one member should be a financial expert with knowledge of GAAP and financial statements
- Corporate responsibility for financial reports I: signing officers must certify reviewing the reports, that they do not have material misrepresentations and omissions and that they are complete
- Corporate responsibility for financial reports II: signing officers must certify their responsibility for internal controls, that such controls are adequate to ensure disclosure of all material information, that they have evaluated the effectiveness of the controls, that they have disclosed to the auditors and audit committee any deficiencies in the controls and frauds, and that all changes in the controls are disclosed
- Forfeiture of bonuses and compensation: the CEO and CFO forfeit bonuses and profits received in the 12-month period after filing of a report that requires restatement

---

Continued

Table 5.1   Continued

- Prohibition of insider trading during pension fund blackouts periods
  Rules of professional conduct for attorneys: attorneys appearing before the
  SEC must report material violations of securities law, breach of fiduciary law
  or similar violation to the chief legal counsel or the CEO. If the counsel or
  CEO does not respond to the evidence, the attorney must report to the audit
  committee, another committee of the board of directors composed solely of
  independent directors or to the board of directors Sec. 307

Financial Disclosures Title IV
- Disclosure of all off-balance sheet transactions, arrangements, obligations,
  and other relationships with unconsolidated persons or entities
- Prohibition of personal loans to executives
- Disclosure of transactions of management and shareholders
- Assessment of internal controls by management
- Corporate code of ethics for senior financial officers
- Disclosure of financial expert in audit committee

Conflicts of Interests of Analysts Title V
- Objective: increase public confidence in analyst reports
- Rules of conflicts of interest by analysts
- Public disclosure of conflicts of interests by analysts

Accountability of Corporate and Criminal Fraud Title VIII
- Stiff penalties

Enhancement of White Collar Crime Penalty Title IX
- Stiff penalties

Corporate Tax Returns Title X
- Signature of corporate returns by the CEO

Corporate Fraud Accountability Title XI
- Increased criminal penalties

Source: http://www.sec.gov/about/laws/soa2002.pdf

There were complaints about information by stock analysts after the end of the high-tech boom and during the restatements of balance sheets and the wider corporate scandals. SOX intends to improve the confidence of the public in the reports of analysts. It requires the public disclosure of potential conflicts of interests that analysts may have in their reports on stocks. Several titles of SOX provide enhanced penalties for violations and fraud.

A control system is the set of processes, practice, and technology that a public company implements to provide "reasonable assurance" in recording and authorizing transactions required for compliant financial reports. Internal control systems should detect and prevent fraud, theft, and deception. Courts have interpreted "reasonable assurance" as controls that are justified by costs, considering the size of the firm and the nature of its operations (Coates 2007, 101).

Corporate officers and independent directors in the independent audit committee do not hold large amounts of shares in the public company and, thus, may have an incentive to spend under SOX. The PCAOB could issue rules and take enforcement measures designed to reduce overspending (Ibid, 104).

There are significant benefits of SOX found in a survey of the literature by Coates (2007, 107). In general, the benefits are derived from more reliable financial statements. As in all empirical economics, it is hard to determine if the benefits originated in SOX or in other factors. There are several conclusions on the costs: they are large, difficult to estimate, have a fixed component that is proportionately onerous for small companies and decline over time. There are no precise measurements of the benefits net of costs.

SOX could be the "final act in regulation of corporate disclosure," according to Carney (2006, 141). There is a critical issue if the costs of regulation have become sufficiently high to drive honest small and foreign companies from public registration. Carney (Ibid) argues that the costs of entirely eliminating fraud could be more expensive than allowing some fraud to exist. Fraud should be prevented until the marginal cost of prevention is about equal to the returns from prevention. There is a social loss if the cost of prevention exceeds the returns. The main cost increase from SOX originates in Section 404 that is strictly confined to financial statements. The remaining aspects of corporate disclosure are left unchanged, according to Carney (2006, 142). Most of the controls in SOX already existed and did not prevent episodes such as Enron and WorldCom. Concerted action by employees can defeat such controls. Section 404 is merely due diligence instead of protection against fraud. The impact of SOX is to impose procedures that would not be selected otherwise.

Section 404 is creating a cottage industry of consultants. The implementation of internal controls involves management at all levels that contract outside consultants (Carney 2006, 145). CEOs head teams to operate these controls. Another structure of bureaucracy is being created in companies around a compliance officer. Auditing committees may retain counsel. SOX compliance also absorbs time of the CFO. The opportunity cost of compliance could be extremely high as the company abandons the focus on business development in favor of avoiding the penalties imposed by SOX. Risk aversion could have highly detrimental effects on the corporate culture of the United States, currently leading ahead of Europe and Japan in innovation. A culture of risk aversion could jeopardize the future growth of the US economy.

Some of the costs of complying with SOX will not be reported in the income statement (Ibid, 147). These are the opportunity costs of complying with executive certification of financial statements, Section 302, and the certification of internal controls, Section 404. There are multiple direct costs of specialized staff required for compliance with these items. The available surveys of increases in costs caused by compliance with SOX show higher costs for every new survey (Ibid, 148). Most of these surveys are for larger companies. It is difficult to find accurate estimates for smaller companies. According to Carney (2006, 151), there are about 16,000 companies requiring compliance with SOX. Assuming a conservative estimate of $500,000 per company, the costs of complying with SOX are at least $8 billion per year. The estimates of losses of investors in Enron and WorldCom are about $100 billion. These were highly unusual losses and it is fair to argue that a part would not have been prevented by SOX. Carney (Ibid) estimates the present value of the costs of compliance at $266 billion, using a 3 percent per year discount rate and assuming that the costs are as certain as death and taxes. He refers to a study of the loss of $1.4 trillion in market value from the most significant rule-making events. There is evidence mentioned by Carney (2006, 152–3) of regulatory arbitrage with companies choosing other markets where to issue their stock.

There are multiple advantages for a company to become private (Ibid, 154–5). The private structure avoids numerous costs of public registration, including costs of litigation, insurance of higher directors and officers (D&O), and higher legal and accounting fees. In addition, an LBO provides the opportunity to sell large holdings that would obtain lower prices in thin markets. The total disclosed buyout transactions increased from $23.1 billion in 2001 to $136.5 billion in 2004. However, there are many factors determining LBOs that cannot be separated from the motivation of higher costs of compliance under SOX.

The analysis of research literature and data by Romano (2005, 1529) is used to support the view that SOX will not improve corporate governance or performance. The emphasis of SOX on independent directors and independent audit committees is based on the presumption that independent directors receive fees as compensation instead of bonuses based on performance. Thus, independent directors will not feel tempted to falsify financial reporting. There is no empirical evidence in the research literature surveyed by Romano (2005, 1529–33) in support of the proposition that independent directors and audit committees improve corporate performance. Congress did not match the problem of the corporate scandals with a solution.

Another measure of SOX is the banning in public corporations of purchasing nonaudit services from their auditors. The rationale for this measure is that management could possibly bribe the audit firms into misstatements by purchasing of nonaudit fees. Empirical research finds no relation of audit quality and the purchase of nonaudit services from the auditors. Romano (2005, 1536) concludes that "SOX's prohibition of the purchase of nonaudit services from an auditor is an exercise in legislating away a nonproblem." The result of no relation between audit quality and purchase of nonaudit services is the conclusion of the majority of scholarly research and the unanimous conclusion of the studies using the most advanced techniques. Moreover, the Panel on Audit Effectiveness does not find even one instance of compromise of an audit because of the purchasing of nonaudit services from the auditor by the audited company (Romano 2005, 1537).

SOX prohibits corporations, by Section 402(a), of extending loans to executive officers or directors. Corporate loans surfaced during the scandals of Enron, WorldCom, Tyco International, and Adelphia Communications. The objective of the prohibition is to avoid the repetition of similar cases. Romano (2005, 1538–9) finds that the effectiveness of the measure is dubious. Attempts to restrict the compensation of corporate executives typically result in different forms to maintain the compensation required to retain desired talent. Moreover, Romano (2005, 1538–9) argues that SOX conflicts with the state law approach. Most of the loans are used to facilitate the conversion of stock ownership provided in remuneration packages. Thus, the loans merely serve to align the interests of shareholders and managers. In this sense, Romano (2005, 1539) argues that the prohibition "is self-evidently a public policy error." The issues have been settled for decades by means of state laws.

Listing

There are three broad motives for a company to cross-list in a foreign market (Pagano, Roell, and Zechner 2002, 2653–60). First, there are financial incentives. Cross-listing may increase access to equity-funded capital for investment. Deeper and more liquid stock markets abroad may provide that capital, which may also be the source for sales of shares by controlling stockholders. A large stock market may increase the base of shareholders, providing higher turnover. There could be higher expertise in a foreign market, such as analysts covering high-tech industries in the United States. Stricter regulatory standards can enhance disclosure and governance, attracting minority shareholders. A foreign market may have lower spreads and brokerage fees and high volume, deepening liquidity of the stocks. A final financial incentive is lower relative mispricing, that is, more efficient markets. Second, companies also cross-list in foreign exchanges in an effort to improve capital and product reputation because the company's overseas market is closer to the exchange of cross-listing choice. Higher potential growth in the foreign market of cross-listing may strengthen the market for the company's output. Third, lower listing and disclosure costs may encourage companies to cross-list in foreign markets.

Empirical analysis by Pagano, Roell, and Zechner (2002) shows that the geography of cross-listing, or where companies cross-list, is influenced by language and proximity; for example, the natural cross-listing for German companies is Austria and for US companies the United Kingdom. Pagano, Roell, and Zechner analyze a sample of exchanges in nine European countries and the United States during 1986–97. The number of European listings in the United States increased sharply from 53 to 207 while US listings in Europe declined significantly from 284 to 309.

The microeconomic analysis of the listing decision of European companies by Pagano, Roell, and Zechner is based on a sample of 2332 companies with median assets of $350 million, of which 111 companies had cross-listed before 1986 and 141 cross-listed during 1987–97 (Pagano, Roell, and Zechner 2002, 2670). Companies that cross-list are significantly larger than the ones listing only in domestic markets. There is evidence of economies of scale, with fixed costs resulting in benefits increasing with size of the company. The growth rates of cross-listing companies is higher than those of the companies in the control sample by 4–6 percent in the three years preceding cross-listing, peaking at around the time of cross-listing but the growth differential is not maintained over the long term. The high growth rates are consistent with the need to raise capital for growth. The proportionate share of foreign sales in total sales is significantly larger for companies that cross-list and especially after the date of cross-listing, suggesting that cross-listing is more actively sought by companies with strategies of expansion in foreign markets. There is some weaker evidence suggesting cross-listing by intensive-R&D firms. High volume and turnover in the domestic market characterizes cross-listing companies, suggesting that they are large companies in their local markets. There is no significant difference in the return on assets (ROA) of cross-listing companies relative to those that do not cross-list. European companies that cross-list in the United States tend to have relatively higher R&D expenditures than those in the control sample and a higher long-term growth rate.

Pagano, Roell, and Zechner (2002, 2677) examine this prediction with a proportional Cox (1972, 189, equation 9) hazard model:

$$h(t|x_{jk}) = h_{ok}(t) \exp(\beta'_k x_{jk}) \tag{5.9}$$

in which $h_{ok}(t)$ is the base line event for the kth event, x_{jk} is a column vector of independent variables for the kth event, and β'_k is a row vector of parameters. Dividing both sides of this expression by the base line event and taking natural logarithms yields a linear relation. The variables that most influence the decision to list abroad are the proportion of sales abroad and the size of the company as the log of total assets. The increase of the proportion of sales abroad by one standard deviation, 26.8, increases the relative probability of a first cross-listing by 84 percent in a ten-year period, from 2.9 percent to 5.3 percent. This result is consistent with the reputation argument that listing abroad is a form of exploiting the presence in foreign output markets. Size is also consistent with the presence of large fixed costs and economies of scale. The results are also consistent with the proposition that companies cross-list after a jump in growth and investment. The significant high-tech effect suggests that companies cross-list in search of better-informed analysts and markets about their products. Another empirical result is that companies recently privatized tend to cross-list in Europe or the United States. Companies that cross-list in the United States are motivated by financing rapid expansion with new equity issues. Those cross-listing in Europe seek increases in debt capacity and do not experience subsequent rapid growth.

Listing decisions of global IPOs, defined as a company going public in a market other than its domestic market, are highly sensitive to the costs and benefits of listing in different markets (Zingales 2007). The share of the US capital markets in global IPOs declined from 48 percent in the late 1990s to 6 percent in 2005. US companies began to choose London for IPOs. Zingales finds that this trend is not determined by segment decisions, such as the choice of the United States by high-tech IPOs, or geographical considerations, such as the choice of local regional exchanges by Asian and Indian companies. In 2000, one of every two dollars raised by global IPOs was raised in the United States, declining to one of every 20 dollars in 2005. During 2000–5, the percentage of IPOs listed in the United States declined from 37 percent to 10 percent. London exchanges were the beneficiary of the exodus of global IPOs from the United States. Global IPOs are still marketed in the United States but under rule 144a through which they avoid disclosure and compliance costs of public offerings.

There are estimates of the compliance costs and benefits of listing in US markets after SOX, provided by Zingales (2007) on the basis of law firm calculations and academic research. The estimated direct costs of compliance for an S&P small-cap firm, with average equity capitalization of $750 million, are about $1 million per year, with additional indirect costs of productivity loss of $1.1 million, for total compliance costs of $2.1 million per year. The reduced costs of capital from enhanced transparency and governance amount to $6.75 per million. Even in the case of a small-cap firm the listing benefits exceed the costs. This is the case for companies with market capitalization of $230 million. The typical company not listing in the United States had a capitalization of $387 million, making listing benefits exceed costs. Compliance costs do not explain the exodus of global IPOs unless the benefits have declined significantly. The value of class action settlements increased from $150 million in 1997 to $9.7 billion in 2005. In addition, the value of the biggest awards increased after the corporate scandals. Litigation by the New York Attorney General and lawsuits against directors also increased costs. Perhaps the marketing in the United States through rule 144a of global IPOs that do not list in the United States may be explained by the desire to avoid legal liability. An important effect of the loss of listing by the United States, emphasized by Zingales, is the loss of revenue and jobs because of foregone underwriting, trading, and work of analysts. The solution is better consideration of the tradeoff of the costs and benefits resulting from regulation. Zingales proposes a Regulation Oversight Board to calculate the costs of compliance, benefits, and the potential deadweight cost. The objective would be to make US regulation more cost effective.

Comprehensive and intensive empirical research by Doidge, Karolyi, and Stulz (2007Jul) disputes the description, analysis, and empirical measurement of loss of competitiveness in finance of the United States relative to the United Kingdom. There were 2978 foreign listings in the world in 1998. The LSE main market had 466 foreign listings and an additional 21 in the Alternative Investment Market (AIM), representing 16 percent of the total. The three major stock exchanges in New York (NYEs), AMEX, NYSE, and NASDAQ had 894, equal to 30 percent of the total. The two markets in London, the main LSE, and AIM, increased their share of world foreign listings to 19 percent in 2005, primarily because of an increase of 220 listings in AIM. In 2005, the NYEs maintained a 30 percent share of the market, 884 listings of a total 2924 in the world. A closer look at the data shows that the LSE main market experienced a decline in foreign listings from 466 in 1998 to 334 in 2005 simultaneously with an increase from 4 to 220 in AIM (Doidge, Karolyi, and Stulz 2007Jul, 6–7). There was a surge of listings in the LSE main market and in the NYEs in the 1990s but declines in both the United States and the United Kingdom after 2000 with decrease in the number of listings and increasing voluntary delisting. There is no evidence that the NYEs lost to the LSE main market with the difference accounted by growth in the AIM of the LSE.

Doidge, Karolyi, and Stulz (2007Jul) construct a comprehensive data set with information on the listing decisions of firms, characteristics of firms, and of the home country of firms during 1990–2005. They argue that if there had been a loss in competitiveness by New York (NY), firms that would have listed in the NYEs in the 1990s would not have listed after 2002. Thus, firm characteristics are important in analyzing cross-listing. The firms that list in the main LSE and the NYEs are large, with median total assets between $600 and $700 million; they are rapidly growing with growth of two-year annualized sales of 14 percent; leverage is moderate, being below 20 percent of total assets; and ownership is concentrated. The firms that list under Rule 144a and OTC in the United States and through AIM in the United Kingdom have median size of only $11.5 million and median leverage of zero percent of assets. None of the firms listing in the NYSE, 5.5 percent of those listing in NASDAQ and only 11 percent of those listing in AMEX had median size of less than $11.5 million. The analysis of firm characteristics leads Doidge, Karolyi, and Stulz (2007Jul, 20) to conclude that the firms listing in the NYSEs and the LSE main market are not very different. There is significant difference between the firms attracted to listings in the NYEs and the LSE main market and those attracted to Rule 144a and OTC markets in NY and AIM in London. There is no difference in these firm characteristics during 1990–2001 and after SOX during 2002–5.

If there was a decline in competitiveness of NYEs relative to the LSE main market, firms would make decisions after SOX differently than during 1990–2001. Doidge, Karolyi, and Stulz (2007Jul, 20) examine this prediction with a competitive Cox (1972, 189, equation 9) hazard model of general type:

$$h(t|\mathbf{x}_{jk}) = h_{ok}(t)\exp(\beta'_k \mathbf{x}_{jk}) \qquad (5.10)$$

in which $h_{ok}(t)$ is the base line event for the kth event, x_{jk} is a column vector of independent variables for the kth event, and β'_k is a row vector of parameters. Dividing both sides of this expression by the base line event and taking natural logarithms yields a linear relation. Doidge, Karolyi, and Stulz (2007Jul) report findings that large firms with positive sales growth in industries where Tobin's Q ratios are high and originating in countries with better protection of rights of minority shareholders are more likely to cross-list in the NY and London markets.

Firms with concentrated ownership may not be able to extract the same private benefits by listing in the NYEs. The higher value for cross-listing in the United States by those firms should originate in enhanced opportunities for growth that could not have been exploited without cross-listing together with declining fraction of cash flows expropriated by insiders (Doidge, Karolyi, and Stulz 2007Jul, 30). Had there been a decline in the benefits of listing in the NYSEs, there would be a declining premium to listing in NY or at least relatively to listing in London. The research strategy is to measure regressions of Tobin's Q on control variables of characteristics of firms and country factors yearly during 1990–2005. Using various approaches, Doidge, Karolyi, and Stulz conclude that there is a premium for listing in NYEs but not for listing in London. The premium for listing in NYEs exists yearly and is permanent in event time. There is no evidence of decline of the premium after 2001, even for firms originating in countries with good protection of minority investors. Doidge, Karolyi, and Stulz find that there is a benefit of enhanced governance in listing in US exchanges that is not available by listing in London or exchanges outside of the United States.

There are two hypotheses on home bias considered by Sarkissian and Schill (2004, 774–5). First, the home bias solution hypothesis postulates that foreign listing overcomes the preference of investors for proximity. High diversification gains and familiarity barriers motivate foreign listings by firms. Empirically, there should be more cross-listing activity between countries separated by large geographical distance, no economic relations, no cultural links, different industrial activities, and greater gains from diversification. Second, the home bias reflection hypothesis postulates that preference for proximity of investors constrains foreign listing. Small diversification gains and low familiarity barriers encourage foreign listing by firms. Empirically, there should be more cross-listings between countries with short geographical distance, broad economic relations, cultural links, similar industrial activities, and few diversification gains. The data set of Sarkissian and Schill (2004, 777) consists of 2251 listings from 44 home countries on 25 host markets. The number of listings in the United States is 659 and 406 in the United Kingdom, which they believe approximates the universe of world foreign listing. The number of overseas listings in the 1990s were 1146, or 51 percent, and 77 listings traded since the 1950s. Sarkissian and Schill conclude that there are important roles in the choice of host market selection for cross-listings between countries by short geographic distance, economic similarity, culture, and industrial proximity. Proximity bias is especially important for markets outside the G5 group of industrialized countries and for small firms with products that are not traded. Diversification gains do not appear to be important in selecting the host market for cross-listing. Larger market capitalization and lax taxation are important. There is a dominant role for cross-country familiarity. The results are consistent with the home bias reflection hypothesis.

There are costs and benefits of SOX (Piotroski and Srinivassan 2008). SOX increased the expected costs of regulation, listing, reporting, and litigation, which may deter companies from cross-listing in US exchanges. The application of the legal bonding theory of Coffee (1999, 2002) and Stulz (1999) would possibly predict expected benefits from enhanced legal and regulatory requirements of SOX that would attract listings of firms from countries with weaker institutions. The empirical analysis of costs and benefits of SOX finds typical hurdles of economic samples. Piotroski and Srinivassan develop an exchange choice model to analyze the relative attractiveness of listing in the NYSE and NASDAK relative to the LSE main market and AIM. The empirical model measures the probability of listing in the NYSE or NASDAK and the probability of listing in the LSE main or AIM. The explanatory variables tend to assess the factors that determine the decision of a firm to list in the NY and London exchanges: characteristics of the home country, attributes of the exchanges, and characteristics of the firms. The sample consists of foreign firms listing in the NYSE, NASDAQ, and LSE between June 1, 1995, when AIM started at the LSE, and June 30, 2006, with subsamples for the periods before and after SOX.

The strategy of Piotroski and Srinivassan (2008) is to determine if the LSE attracted foreign firms during the post-SOX period that would have listed in US exchanges before SOX. Piotroski and Srinivassan conclude that there were no effects of SOX on large firms eligible to list in the NYSE and NASDAQ in choosing between the two jurisdictions. The costs of SOX are relatively lower for large firms, in particular for those originating in countries with strong institutions. Declines in US listings were caused by changes in attributes of foreign firms interested in cross-listing. The impact of SOX is confirmed by lower probability of listing in NY relative to London for smaller firms choosing between NASDAQ and the AIM of the LSE. Firms seeking listing at the AIM of the LSE were characterized by smaller size, lower profitability, and less likelihood of using a higher quality auditor than those listing at NASDAQ. These lower quality firms account for about $36.5 billion of market capitalization. In this analysis, the cost of SOX could be considered as the exclusion of these firms in the left tail of the distribution of potential foreign firms that could list in the United States. Foreign firms that cannot meet the standards of SOX choose London over NY for cross-listing, which is consistent with the legal bonding benefit of listing in the United States.

The difficulty of separating effects of SOX from other contemporaneous events is circumvented by Litvak (2007a,b) by using a sample for three dozen countries with three differentiated groups of companies: (1) the treatment group subject to SOX, companies listed on levels 2 or 3 (Level 23); (2) a control group including firms not subject to SOX but sensitive to stricter US business regulation listed on levels 1 and 4 (Level 14); and (3) another control group of firms that are not subject to SOX and US regulation (non-cross-listed companies). Litvak (2007a) compares stock price reactions of the three groups to SOX. Pairs of Level 23 companies matched to a non-cross-listed company from the same country, industry, and size had significant negative returns around events suggesting adoption of SOX and its full application to foreign issuers and significant positive returns around events suggesting failure in approval of SOX. There was similar but much weaker behavior by Level 14 companies and statistically significant difference between Level 23 and Level 14 companies. The results are consistent with adverse expectations from SOX in pricing of cross-listed stocks in the United States. Latvik finds that measures of premiums, Tobin's Q, and market-to-book ratios of Level 23 companies significantly declined relative to Level 14 companies in 2002; the same significant decline is observed relative to non-cross-listed companies. The results are consistent with a decline in the premium of being subject to SOX.

Cross-listing in US exchanges is easier than delisting and deregistering. There are two broad reasons why a company should delist from a US exchange and subsequently deregister from the SEC (Marosi and Massoud 2008). First, there are reasons to escape regulation and SOX and governance issues, such as the different incentives to delist and deregister for controlling shareholders and other holders of claims. Second, there are economic reasons in the form of the costs and benefits of cross-listing. The sample used by Marosi and Massoud consists of the universe of foreign firms that delisted from major US exchanges and subsequently deregistered from the SEC during 1990–2006. Most foreign listings of companies in the US consisted of issues of American Depository Receipts (ADR) managed by a US bank; ADRs are described by Miller (1999, 105–8). In 2006, a record volume of trading of ADRs in US exchanges reached 52.6 billion for corresponding value of $1.5 trillion. During 2001–6, exchange-listed ADRs in the United States declined from 610 to 478 while the world number of exchange listed firms outside the United States increased from 27,110 to 34,630 (Marosi and Massoud 2008). Only 22 foreign firms deregistered during 1990–2001. The results of logistic regressions with the sample show that a combination of regulatory/governance and economic factors determined the decision to delist and then deregister. The adoption of SOX had a positive impact on the probability that a foreign firm would withdraw from the US financial market, especially for small foreign firms with low trading volume. The result is consistent with the costs of US registration exceeding the benefits. The SEC relaxed the requirements of deregistration from less than 300 individual shareholders to a percentage of world trading volume in the stock, effective from June 2007 (Ibid).

The SEC softened the requirements for deregistration by foreign private issuers (FPI) on March 1, 2007, effective from June 4, 2007, by means of Rule 12h-6 (Fernandes, Lel, and Miller 2008). FPIs are not required after deregistration to file reports under the Securities and Exchange Act of 1934, including provisions by SOX. There are three main provisions in Rule 12h-6 (Ibid, 10). First, FPIs may deregister if the average daily trading volume (ADTV) in the United States has been no greater than 5 percent of the ADTV in the world of the same class of securities in the prior 12-month period. Second, Rule 12h-6 permits permanent deregistration and required reporting instead of suspension. Third, Rule 12h-6 allows deregistration if there are less than 300 US record holders, simplifying the counting of record holders to those in the United States and the FPI's country of incorporation. Fernandes, Lel, and Miller use a comprehensive sample of 638 registered foreign issuers in the United States from 36 countries to test the effects of the new deregistration rules. During 1990–2001, there were on average only two FPIs engaged in deregistration. During the SOX period (2002–6), the average number per year increased to 15. The highest number of deregistration occurred in 2006 with 33. In the eight months from March to December 2007, deregistration of FPIs jumped to the highest level of 80 (Ibid). There was negative market reaction to Rule 12h-6 for firms located in countries with poor disclosure requirements and civil law legal origin. However, there was not significant market reaction for firms originating in countries with strong protection of investors. Fernandes, Lel, and Miller conclude that shareholders place strong value on US disclosure protection when foreign issuers originate in countries with weak disclosure requirements and investor protection. In general, the results with the exogenous shock of Rule 12h-6 support the view that there are significant economic benefits of US regulation and laws of disclosure and investor protection, in particular for cross-listed firms.

The effects of SOX on costs may encourage some firms to go private, especially for firms where SOX benefits are small and with small benefits even before SOX. Engel, Hayes, and Wang (2007) use a sample of firms going private shortly before and after SOX. They find a modest but significant increase in the quarterly frequency of firms going private. There is positive association of abnormal returns related to the adoption of SOX with firm size and share turnover. Smaller firms had higher returns of announcing the decision of going private in the period after SOX relative to the period before SOX with sharper effects for firms with high inside ownership. The benefits of being public before SOX are likely to be more limited in the case of smaller firms. The shares of large insiders were relatively illiquid before SOX and the intention of the Act to make them less liquid reduced benefits from being public.

A firm goes "dark" when it deregisters from the SEC after it has less than 300 registered shareholders of record or less than 500 if total assets are less than $10 million after three reporting years, avoiding the costs of disclosure, but continuing to trade OTC. Dark firms do not go private, continuing to trade OTC without reporting under the SEC. Leuz, Triantis, and Wang (2008) consider an alternative hypothesis for going dark. The "cost savings" hypothesis explains the decision of going dark by the onerous costs of reporting. This hypothesis includes factors such as financial distress, higher costs of complying with SOX, and diminishing growth prospects that reduce the need for external finance. Management of going dark firms finds that the benefits of SEC registration are lower than the costs. The "private benefits" hypothesis explains the decision of going dark by the promotion of benefits of insiders instead of the pursuit of higher value for shareholders. Controlling insiders could force the company dark to derive private benefits outside SEC reporting such as perk consumption, favorable-term loans, generous compensation, investment of free cash flows in self-interest projects, and deals with other companies with relations to insiders. Firms may differ by the influence of factors of both hypotheses that determine the decision of going dark. The sample of Leuz, Triantis, and Wang consists of 484 companies that went dark during 1998–2004 with a control sample of 2061 firms that qualified but did not go dark.

Firms that go dark relative to those that could but did not choose to go dark are smaller in size; have weaker recent performance in the stock market; exhibit higher leverage; have higher distress, facing lower opportunities for growth; and suffered declining interest in capital markets (Leuz, Triantis, and Wang 2008). Going dark for these firms may save more in costs than the benefits of registration, supporting the announcements by management of the intention to maximize shareholder value. However, firms that go dark have weaker quality of accounting, free cash flow problems, poor governance, and weak outside monitoring. Consistent with both the cost saving and private benefits hypotheses, going dark firms suffer adverse market reactions. Stronger firms go private instead of dark. SOX increased reporting costs on firms with agency problems, probably encouraging going dark decisions, although Leuz, Triantis, and Wang advise caution on the strength of this result.[4]

Summary

A flexible exit market for business is apparently superior to more costly bankruptcy. Diversified conglomerates were partly caused by antitrust enforcement policies. The flexibility of LBOs reversed the inefficiency of conglomerates. There are valid arguments for the benefits of principles over rules in financial regulation. Research on the regulation of new issues has not uncovered benefits that were not already provided pre-regulation by exchanges and agents such as underwriters. The law and economics literature on insider trading has not resolved the doubts on the need for regulation. Research on the decision on going public has identified determinants such as geography, product proximity, bonding, and reputation. SOX is still the subject of significant debate, an important part of which is concentrated in cross-listing.

6
The Credit/Dollar Crisis and Recession Regulation

Introduction

The global recession is causing output contraction and unemployment in advanced countries, sharp reduction of growth in emerging and developing countries, and contraction of world trade in goods and services. The impact on output and employment is minute compared with the Great Depression of the 1930s. There is a section reviewing the literature on the Great Depression because of the significant rise of regulation and the constant reference to current events and policies. The origins of the credit crisis are critical in evaluating regulatory proposals. Monetary and fiscal policies in the current crisis are more aggressive than even during the Great Depression. The regulatory agenda is highly ambitious.

The global recession

The forecast of the IMF (2009WEOApr) is for world output declining by 1.3 percent in 2009, bouncing by 1.9 percent in 2010 after growing by 5.2 percent in 2007, and 3.2 percent in 2008. Output in advanced countries is forecast to decline by 3.8 percent in 2009, growing by 0 percent in 2010. US output would decline by 2.8 percent in 2009, growing by 0 percent in 2010. The volume of world trade of goods and services is forecast to decline by 11 percent in 2009, bouncing by 0.6 percent in 2010 after growing by 7.2 percent in 2007 and by 3.3 percent in 2008. Recession in the form of contraction of output or sharp reduction in the rate of growth affects the entire world.

The Great Depression

There is frequent mention of the Great Depression in analysis and policy for the credit/dollar crisis (Romer 2009Mar9, 2009Mar31). Significant part of the regulatory framework of the United States was created in the 1930s. The objective of this section is to provide a comprehensive review of the vast literature on the Great Depression. Various subsections below consider the major areas of inquiry: the monetary views, the debt deflation theories, the approach of frictions in financial markets, the role of the gold standard, the nonmonetary factors, wages and employment, and the growth-theory framework.

Banks and money

One of the most important and debated counterfactuals in history is that posed by Friedman and Schwartz (1963); that the Great Depression in the United States was caused by contraction of the money stock that could have been avoided if the Fed had engaged in LOLR policy in response to the banking panic of the 1930s. The panics resulted in an increase in the currency/deposit and reserve/deposit ratios that decreased the money stock, causing a decline in nominal income. Friedman (2005) argues that the decline by one third of the money stock during 1929–33 is what differentiates the "Great Contraction" of the 1930s from two similar episodes of rapid growth, consumption, and technological change: Japan in the 1990s and the collapse of the high-tech market after 2000 in the United States. McCallum (1990) constructed a model showing with simulations that Friedman's rule with feedback would have prevented the sharp decline in nominal income in the United States during 1929–33. The proposal of Friedman (1960) of a central bank rule of constant increase of the money stock of 3 to 5 percent in the environment of 1960, instead of fine tuning by central banks, would prevent adverse economic events that threaten the social fabric periodically (see Friedman 1967 for the relation to Henry Simons). Bordo, Choudhri, and Schwartz (1995) use a more general form of the model of McCallum (1990) to also analyze the Friedman and Schwartz (1963) counterfactual in case the Friedman (1960) rule of constant rate of increase of money had been followed.

In the first strong form of the Friedman (1960) rule used by Bordo, Choudhri, and Schwartz (1995, 485), the Fed can maintain the constant growth rate of money every quarter by rapidly compensating variations in the money multiplier with changes in high-powered or base money. In the second weaker form, the Fed observes the money multiplier with a lag of one quarter, maintaining the constant rate of growth of money conditional on information on the past quarter. Bordo, Choudhri, and Schwartz (1995, 491) simplify the basic model by considering only three variables, output, the price level, and money, and add the interest rate and the ratio of suspended to total deposits to capture the effect of banking panics. Using the model estimated for 1921–41, the maintenance of the average yearly rate of 2.95 percent of growth of the money stock would have avoided the Great Depression. The cumulative decline of output during 1929–33 was 36.2 percent at a yearly rate of decline of 12.1 percent, much higher than the simulated cumulative change of −21.6 percent to −11.1 percent, corresponding to yearly change of −6.6 percent to −3.3 percent, similar to other recessions in the nineteenth and twentieth centuries.

The simulations of the 1930s could be subject to the Lucas (1976) critique that the Great Depression could have caused a strong regime change, altering the reduced equations parameters. Based on Chow tests for differences in the coefficients, Bordo, Choudhri, and Schwartz (1995, 501) argue that there would not have been shifts in the output and price relations if the Fed had implemented a constant money growth rate to avoid the Depression. They reestimated the model for the 1920s pre-Depression and for 1930–40, calculating reduced-form shocks for the entire period. The behavior of money, prices, and output was simulated using the output and price equations with the pre-Depression data. The simulation results reveal no significant contraction during 1929–33 under both the strong and weak forms of the rule of constant growth of money. Bordo, Choudhri, and Schwartz conclude that the output and price relations of the 1920s would have been preserved by the policy of constant growth of money.

A general equilibrium dynamic (GED) model is estimated by Christiano, Motto, and Rostagno (2003) to probe the Friedman and Schwartz (1963) counterfactual of monetary policy during the Great Depression. Their model finds that a liquidity preference shock, in the form of a shift to currency away from demand deposits and similar liabilities, best explains the contraction during 1929–33, which could have been softened by monetary policy reacting to the liquidity preference shocks. They identify a specific monetary rule that could have reduced the impact of the Depression. The model also captures an increase in market power of workers as the main cause of the slow recovery from the Depression in the second half of the 1930s. Bordo (2003, 1200) argues that the liquidity preference shocks are similar to the increase in the currency/deposit and reserve/deposit ratios observed by Friedman and Schwartz (1963). An important novelty in the Christiano, Motto, and Rostagno (2003) model is the introduction of financial frictions such as by Bernanke, Gertler, and Gilchrist (1999) through the effects of deflation proposed by Fisher (1933) and Bernanke (1983b).

Debt deflation theories

The debt deflation theory of Fisher (1933, 341) argues that the key factors of depressions are excessive debt followed soon by deflation. Speculation and excessive investment would not have serious adverse effects unless financed with debt. Excessive indebtedness is followed by debt liquidation in the form of distressed selling, which contracts bank deposits as loans are repaid, lowering velocity and causing a decline in prices. The next step is an even greater decline in the net worth of businesses, causing failure of their creditor banks. The resulting decline of profits causes contraction of output, commerce, and employment, which increase pessimism or loss of confidence, provoking hoarding that lowers velocity further. Fisher (1933, 342) argues that this sequence causes "complicated disturbances in the rates of interest, in particular, a fall in the nominal, or money, rates and a rise in the real, or commodity, rates of interest."

The contribution of Bernanke (1983b) departs from the assumption that financial markets are incomplete to explain the fracture of financial intermediation in the Great Depression. There are important information services of financial institutions in market making and gathering of information. The cost of financial intermediation (CCI) consists of costs of transferring funds from saving and lending agents to sound borrowers. CCI consists of costs to financial intermediaries of screening, monitoring, and accounting together with the anticipated loss caused by unsound debtors. Bernanke argues that the banking panics of 1930–3 undermined the effective delivery of intermediation services of banking, raising the CCI. Banks shifted their assets to those that could be easily converted into cash. The resulting credit squeeze affected households, farmers, and small firms that experienced significant difficulty in finding credit. Low nominal rates of interest observed in the 1930s obscure the lack of credit because they were paid by few debtors while large numbers of potentially sound debtors could not find credit. The problem was accentuated by the collapse or even disappearance of collateral that debtors could use to obtain credit. The credit squeeze affected aggregate demand, converting the severe but not uncommon contraction of 1929–30 into the Great Depression. The unit banking system of the United States with the dismantling of the suspension of convertibility through clearing unions caused by the introduction of the FRS was more likely to result in banking panics, which did not occur as severely in other countries.

The test of the relation of deflation and depression of Atkeson and Kehoe (2004) uses panel data for 17 countries over more than 100 years. The joint occurrence of deflation and depression was concentrated in the Great Depression when eight countries in the sample suffered deflation and depression while the remaining eight had deflation without depression. Five-year periods excluding the Great Depression of 1929–34 exhibit the joint occurrence of deflation and depression in only eight cases. There are 65 cases of deflation without depression and 21 in which depression occurred without deflation. The 65 of 73 cases of deflation occurred without depression and in eight of 29 cases of depression there was no deflation. Atkeson and Kehoe (2004, 101) point to the remarkable observation that there was no depression in 90 percent of the cases of deflation. Japan's lost decade in the 1990s is explained by the acceleration of the growth rate after World War II and its decline together with inflation after 1960. Atkeson and Kehoe observe that the average rate of growth of Japan of 1.41 percent per year was not "dismal" in comparison with that in the same period of countries such as Italy, 1.61 percent, and France, 1.84 percent. Without using controls, they conclude that the data do not provide an association of deflation and depression.

Financial market frictions

Reviewing vast literature, Calomiris (1993) concludes that cross-sectional evidence supports the time series interpretation of Bernanke (1983b), or what he identifies as the "finance view." There were high costs of external finance during the Great Depression, which were substantially high for small and growing companies. The declining creditworthiness of firms and the reduction in bank debt to firm insiders were important determinants of the high finance costs.

The distress of firm balance sheets, in the view of Bernanke (1983b), caused distress of bank balance sheets. The combined effect was a reduction not only of the number of qualified borrowers because of firm distress but also of the availability of loans to qualified borrowers because of the distress of banks, further contracting the economy. Calomiris and Mason (2003) analyze two criticisms of the effects of bank distress on output. First, they consider a "loan demand critique," which is the typical economic problem of identifying pure loan supply effects. The decline in loan volume may have been caused entirely or partly by anticipation and actual output decline that caused a decrease in loan demand. Second, they also consider the "quality of money" critique of Rockoff (1993) by which another explanatory variable with similar spikes in the sample period of Bernanke (1983b) can reduce the explanatory power of Bernanke's measurements. The approach of Calomiris and Mason (2003) is to use state and county data in identifying loan supply shocks and then relate them to subsequent growth of income. They use three loan supply instruments in 1929 that are independent of loan demand and economic activity—bank size, bank capital, and foreclosures—to derive bank conditions in 1929 that determine bank loan supply during 1930–2. A chain of causality could exist from the instruments to economic activity through the effects of bank distress on bank loan supply during 1930–2. Calomiris and Mason find that a substantial part of the variation in growth of state income during the Great Depression is explained by the supply of bank credit. There is a similar result for county-level econometric analysis using building permits as a proxy of income growth.

A banking panic is defined by Calomiris and Gorton (1991) as sudden withdrawals of cash by depositors in all or a substantial number of banks, characterized by suspension of convertibility of bank debts into cash or in the United States by clearing house loan certificates. The worst loss of depositors before the 1930s was 2.1 cents per dollar and the worst percentage of banks failing was 1.3 percent in the panic of 1893; during the Great Depression 26 to 16 percent of national banks in the United States failed (depending on the type of measurement) and deposit losses reached almost 5 percent (Calomiris and Gorton 1991, 100).

There are two theories of banking panics considered by Calomiris and Gorton (1991). First, the theory of random withdrawal explains historical banking panics by the Diamond and Dybvig (1983) model refined to consider sequential withdrawal of deposits in the pyramid of reserve city banks and New York City reserve banks after a seasonal agricultural shock. The original random withdrawal theory leading to the creation of the FRS proposed the injection of bank reserves by the central bank to correct temporary increases in the currency/deposit ratio. Diamond and Dybvig consider policy solutions in the form of government-insured deposits. Calomiris and Gorton (1991) argue on the basis of survey of literature that the existence of banking panics in the Diamond and Dybvig framework requires the assumption of incomplete markets for assets and sequential deposit withdrawal. The application of the random-withdrawal theory to historical banking panics in the United States rests on the system of unit banks and the system of reserves city banks ultimately depending on the New York City reserve banks.

Second, Calomiris and Gorton (1991) propose an alternative asymmetric information view with emphasis on market structure. It is not possible for bank depositors to value without high costs the assets of individual banks. The arrival of nonbank-specific information, such as macroeconomic events, raises doubts about the quality of assets of all banks. Because of asymmetry of information, or the impossibility of monitoring asset quality, depositors convert deposits into cash at many or all banks. The function of banks in the asymmetric information view is not providing insurance but instead provide the means of payment and the creation of nonmarketable loans. There is asymmetry of information between depositors and banks in valuing bank management and asset portfolios. Sequential service constraints and panics are forms by which depositors monitor banks. The unit banking system is more prone to banking panics. Self-regulation of banks in a national system of multiple branches across all states together with appropriate government rules and institutions would be effective in preventing banking panics.

Calomiris and Gorton (1991) are careful in warning about extending results from the historical banking panics to subsequent periods because of technological change in finance and the impossibility of evaluating what banking structure would have been without regulation. They find that the impact of real events on banking panics can be traced to earlier research, including that by Friedman and Schwartz (1963). The random withdrawal view attributes banking panics and their effects on economic activity to a natural propensity of banks to suffer illiquidity shocks, justifying government intervention as LOLR and insurer of deposits. The asymmetric information view attributes banking panics to an external shock in which depositors cannot monitor the management and value of bank portfolios, leading to self-regulation strengthened by different government rules.

In June 1932, 49 banks failed in Illinois, of which 40 in Chicago and 26 in the week of June 20–7; there were no similar events regionally or at the national level. Calomiris and Mason (2003) use the unusual sample of Chicago in June 1932 to test the applicability of the random withdrawal and asymmetric information views. There were specific triggers of the panic in Chicago in the form of declines of stock prices of public utilities, a high-profile case of bank fraud by a developer owning a chain of banks, and revenue contraction for the city of Chicago. Calomiris and Mason (2003, 869) consider a strong null hypothesis of the random withdrawal view predicting that banks failing during the panic were as sound as surviving banks. The fact that banks that failed were weaker than those that survived leads to the rejection of the strong random withdrawal null hypothesis.

However, there could still be high social costs if a large solvent bank failed because of depositor confusion about its soundness. The weak null hypothesis consists of the economic cost of an important random withdrawal failure. The analysis and historical evidence of Calomiris and Mason (2003) show that the characteristics of failing banks were evident before the panic and anticipated by bank stock prices, probabilities of failures, evaluations of examiners, debt structure, and interest paid. Banks that failed ranked among the worst when the panic occurred. There was not contagion in the Chicago banking panic but rather common asset shocks that caused the failure of the weakest banks. There is no evidence that asymmetric information provoked the failure of solvent banks. Calomiris and Mason argue that the perception that bank failures during the Great Depression were caused by contagion, causing failure of even solvent banks, motivated deposit insurance and government intervention in banking markets. The panic of Chicago is one of multiple panics located in different regions at different times. General conclusions require analysis of these localized banking panics.

Approximately 40 percent of commercial banks in the United States, 9440, of which 79 percent state banks and 21 percent national banks, were suspended during 1929–33 (Mitchener 2005, 156). There was an uneven pattern of suspensions, with some counties losing all their commercial state banks and others without suffering suspensions. The average yearly rate of suspension for banks with state charters was 9.5 percent during 1929–33. The highest average annual suspension rate, 12.4 percent, occurred in counties in the Midwest and the lowest, 4 percent, in the Northeast. Using proper controls for county characteristics and differential impact of the Great Depression, the econometric tests of Mitchener suggest an important role for supervisory and regulatory practices in explaining county suspension rates of state-chartered banks. Stricter capital requirements were associated with lower suspension rates for state-chartered commercial banks; laws restricting branching and higher reserve requirements were associated with greater instability of banks.

Although the US experience during the Great Depression was characterized by banking instability, Grossman (1994) argues that Britain, Canada, and ten other countries exhibited "exceptional stability" during the Great Depression. There are three competing explanations for this stability. First, banking structures characterized by large, highly concentrated banks with major branch networks in contrast were less prone to instability than the US system of unit branch banking. Second, macroeconomic policy, in particular flexibility of the exchange rate in contrast with rigidity in the gold standard, affected banking stability; exchange rate flexibility permitted more accommodating monetary policy and avoidance of a run on domestic financial institutions. Third, LOLR policies by the central bank may have prevented banking instability. Grossman tests the effect of these three explanatory variables on banking stability in 25 countries in Europe and North America. The econometric tests of Grossman suggest that exchange rate flexibility was significantly associated with banking stability but not as robustly with bank structure while there is little evidence of association with the LOLR function. The three countries that suspended the gold standard or imposed exchange controls before the collapse of the Creditanstalt in Austria in May 1931 did not suffer banking crises. Half of the countries that suspended the gold standard in the second half of 1931 suffered crises while the other half did not. Seven of the nine countries delaying suspension until 1932 or later suffered banking crises (Grossman 1994, 665). Sustained overvaluation of the exchange rate by adherence to the gold standard resulted in subsequent capital flight and disruption of the domestic financial sector.

The banking view of the Great Depression proposes that shocks of deflation caused bank failures, reducing the efficiency of financial intermediation, ultimately contracting lending and output (Cole and Ohanian 2000). The general equilibrium model of Cole and Ohanian finds a banking shock of small magnitude and also small elasticity of aggregate output in response to a bank shock. There are also contradictions with actual behavior in three predictions of the banking shock view. First, the prediction of this view that the state with worst banking events would have sharper decline of economic activity is different from actual behavior of no systematic relationship of economic activity and number of bank closings. Second, firms lowered retained earnings during the Great Depression in contrast with the prediction of the banking view of increases in retained earnings. Third, the ratio of bank deposits to output increased substantially during the Great Depression in contrast with the prediction of decline by the banking view.

The gold standard

There is an unusual sample of exchange rate regimes during the Great Depression by Choudhri and Kochin (1980) to test the international transmission of business cycles. Spain maintained a flexible exchange rate regime before and during the Great Depression while significant part of the world adhered to the fixed exchange rates of the gold standard. A group of other European countries (the gold countries)—the Netherlands, Belgium, Italy, and Poland—maintained the gold standard during the Great Depression. Finally, the Scandinavian countries—Denmark, Finland, and Norway—entered the Great Depression under the gold standard but suspended it following the United Kingdom in September 1931. Spain devalued the most followed by the Scandinavian countries while the gold countries fixed the exchange rate. Correspondingly, the money supply increased in Spain and more mildly in the Scandinavian countries while contracting in the gold countries. The share of Spain's exports in manufactures was 8 percent, higher than 5.4 percent in Poland, somewhat lower than 12 percent in Italy but lower than 23.6 percent in Belgium and 21.2 percent in the Netherlands. There is a similar pattern in manufacturing per person. Thus, the argument that Spain was a small agricultural country does not invalidate the comparison with behavior in more industrialized "small" countries. Choudhri and Kochin compared the experience of the countries in their sample with that of the United States. There was substantial decline in prices and output in all the gold countries during 1928–32 similar to that in the United States in contrast with production and prices in Spain not very different from the levels in 1928 (Choudhri and Kochin 1980, 569).

The regressions of Choudhri and Kochin for the countries in the sample are of the following form:

$$X_i = \alpha_i + \beta_i(XUS_i) \qquad (6.1)$$

where X_i are the natural logs of industrial production or the wholesale price level for the small countries in the sample and XUS_i the natural logs of industrial production or the wholesale price level in the United States. The results show no significant association of industrial production and the level of wholesale prices of Spain with those of the United States but significant association for all four gold countries. The results are similar for the Scandinavian countries with negligible association with US output for Denmark and Norway and small for Finland in comparison with the gold countries. There is similar experience in the case of Brazil (Peláez 1968a,b, 1972).

A synthesis of sorts of research on the Great Depression combines the policy errors in the United States, Germany, and France with their worldwide amplification by an unstable international monetary and financial system (Eichengreen 2004). Worldwide output contraction is explained by banking crises and the breakdown of the gold/exchange standard. The return to gold by Britain in 1925 and de facto by France in 1926 recreated the international gold standard (Eichengreen 1992). There were factors increasing the vulnerability of the system. Foreign exchange reserves as a share in international reserves increased by 50 percent during 1913–28. A run out of the dollar or sterling could exert significant pressure on the balance of payments of the United States and Britain, which were the main currency reserve countries, creating a deflationary run on gold (Ibid). The rules of the gold standard were abandoned sporadically, eroding the confidence on the system. The scope for international financial cooperation declined. Tightening monetary policy in the United States in 1928 reduced foreign lending, leading to tight monetary policy in other countries. The movement of gold and financial capital to the United States and France forced central banks in other countries to increase discount rates (Ibid, 221). While money declined by 2 percent in the United States and Canada during 1927–8 and 4 percent during 1928–9, it declined by 5 percent in Europe and Latin America during 1927–8 and another 5 percent during 1928–9. The fragility of the international system was affected by the reliance on foreign borrowing without an adjustment in relative competitiveness. Deflation in the United States was transmitted to other countries through the fixed rates of the gold standard. The gold standard also frustrated LOLR functions of central banks to ameliorate banking distress (Ibid, 229).

Recovery is explained by the liberal monetary policies resulting from the suspension of the gold standard together with the return to stability in banking and finance. Eichengreen (2004) argues that banking crises had a more profound effect in the United States but the breakdown of the gold standard was more critical in other countries. The timing and extent of recovery are associated with depreciation (Eichengreen 1992, 232). Fear of inflation while deflation was the problem delayed recovery with few countries implementing systematic liberal monetary policy. Other references on the gold standard and the Great Depression are Temin (1993), Eichengreen and Temin (1997, 2003), and Ferguson and Temin (2001).

The role of budget deficits in eroding confidence on the currencies of gold standard countries is proposed by James (1992) as a key mechanism of transmission of the Great Depression. Budget deficits threatened the endurance of the gold standard not only because of the fear of the return to hyperinflation but also because of the possibility of difficulty in funding public deficits. The problem was not an increase in capital flows, which were actually lower than before the war, but an increase in the volatility of the flows because of confidence crises triggered by public deficits. James (1992, 608) calculates extremely high increases in public deficits as percent of GNP in the beginning of the Depression: −2.2 in 1930 for Austria, growing to −3.1 in 1931, −0.9 in 1931 for France, growing to −4.5 in 1934, −2.1 in Germany in 1930, −3.6 in Hungary in 1930, −3.4 in Italy in 1930, growing to −8.7 in 1933, −0.5 in the United Kingdom in 1930 and −3.2 in the United States in 1931, growing to −4.0 in 1934. The interpretation of the size of the public deficit that could be financed in the short-term eroded the confidence on the center of world financial markets in London, New York, and Paris, frustrating the possibility of international coordination in resolving the crisis.

The German banking crisis of 1931 is interpreted by Schnabel (2004) as resulting from moral hazard in unsound lending generated by politics and the too-big-to-fail doctrine of the Reichsbank to the large branch banks instead of merely a macroeconomic shock. The characterization of the Reichsbank as concerned with strengthening the currency instead of assisting the banking system is contradicted by the evidence of major short-term foreign liabilities of banks. The incentive of the Reischsbank in preventing bank withdrawals originated in the interest of protecting the gold standard. Faced with the responsibility of preventing hot money outflows, the Reischsbank could not commit credibly to simultaneously protecting the gold standard and supporting domestic banks.

During 1927–9, Brazil accumulated £30 million of foreign exchange of which £20 million were deposited at its stabilization fund (Peláez 1968b, 43–4). After the decline in coffee prices and the first impact of the Great Depression in Brazil a hot money movement wiped out foreign exchange reserves. In addition, capital inflows stopped entirely. The deterioration of the terms of trade further complicated matters, as the value of exports in foreign currency declined abruptly. Because of this exchange crisis, the service of the foreign debt of Brazil became impossible. In August 1931, the federal government was forced to cancel the payment of principal on certain foreign loans. The balance of trade in 1931 was expected to yield £20 million whereas the service of the foreign debt alone amounted to £22.6 million. Part of the solution given to these problems was typical of the 1930s. In September 1931, the government of Brazil required that all foreign transactions were to be conducted through the Bank of Brazil. This monopoly of foreign exchange was exercised by the Bank of Brazil for the following three years. Export permits were granted only after the exchange derived from sales abroad was officially sold to the Bank, which in turn allocated it in accordance with the needs of the economy. An active black market in foreign exchange developed. Brazil was in the first group of countries that abandoned early the gold standard, in 1931, and suffered comparatively less from the Great Depression. The Brazilian federal government, advised by the BOE, increased taxes and reduced expenditures in 1931 to compensate a decline in custom receipts (Peláez 1968b, 40). Expenditures caused by a revolution in 1932 in the state of São Paulo and a drought in the northeast explain the deficit. During 1932–6, the federal government engaged in strong efforts to stabilize the budget. Apart from the deliberate efforts to balance the budget during the 1930s, the recovery in economic activity itself may have induced a large part of the reduction of the deficit (Ibid, 41). Brazil's experience is similar to that of the United States in that fiscal policy did not promote recovery from the Great Depression.

Nonmonetary factors

A five-variable VAR approach is used by Raynold, McMillin, and Beard (1991) to analyze the role of fiscal policy during the Great Depression. The five variables are output, the price level, the interest rate, the money supply, and government expenditures. They find significant but small effects of government spending on production and nonsignificant effects on prices. The impact of government spending on output was of smaller magnitude in the Roosevelt administration than in the preceding Hoover administration. There is no information suggesting that government spending was used during the Roosevelt administration to reverse the impact of the Depression on economic activity. Vernon (1994) argues that fiscal policies were important in the recovery of the US economy to full employment after 1940 and during World War II.

Real GNP in the United States during 1929–33 declined 35 percent, increasing by 33 percent during 1933–7, declining again by 5 percent in 1938 and rising by 49 percent during 1938–42, according to Romer (1992, 760). The effects of monetary and fiscal policy are simulated by Romer (1992, 761) by means of the following equation:

$$\Delta y_t = \beta_m m_{t-1} + \beta_f f_{t-1} + \varepsilon_t \tag{6.2}$$

This equation expresses the deviations in output from normal, y, by the deviations of the change of money from normal, m, and the deviations of the fiscal change from normal, f, where β_m is the multiplier of monetary policy, β_f the multiplier of fiscal change, and ε a residual. The trends of normal output and money are obtained from data during 1923–7 and the fiscal change is captured by the change in the ratio of the real federal surplus to GNP. Romer (1992, 763) estimates the multipliers in two years, 1921 and 1938, when presumably the residual ε was small and changes in monetary and fiscal policy were independent of the change in output. The results are unaltered by using monetary and fiscal multipliers of large econometric models in the postwar period. US recovery from the Great Depression was promoted by the unsterilized inflow of gold after 1933 that lowered real interest rates, stimulating consumption and investment expenditures through the conventional mechanism of transmission of monetary shocks to the real sector. There was a negligible effect of fiscal policy.

The framework of interpretation of the Great Depression by Romer (1990, 1992, 1993) considers the factors of the initial decline of economic activity in 1929, the factors of deepening contraction in 1930 and the impulse of recovery after 1937. The peak of seasonally adjusted industrial production was in July 1929, with a cumulative decline by 3 percent in July–October 1929 (Romer 1993, 26). Hamilton (1987) documents a move to tighter monetary policy by the Fed in late 1928 primarily because of the overvaluation of the stock market, as observed by Friedman and Schwartz (1963), and to a lesser extent by the outflow of gold. The mild recession starting in the summer of 1929 worsened significantly after the stock market crash of September 1929, which was followed by a decline in industrial production of 10 percent in October–December 1929; industrial production declined by 37 percent from the peak in July 1929 to December 1930, much sharper than in other countries (Romer 1993, 29). Temin (1976, 1989) identified sharp decline of consumption in the United States in 1930 in contrast with relative stability during interwar recessions. White (1990) argues that qualitative information suggests a stock market bubble in 1929. In reconstruction of the decomposition of contributing factors to GNP in the recessions in the first four decades of the twentieth century, Romer (1993, 30) finds that the decline of consumption explains 46 percent of the change of -9.3 percent in GNP in 1930, with the decline of investment explaining 38 percent. She argues that nominal and real interest rates initially declined in the fourth quarter of 1929 and the first quarter of 1930, rising in the second quarter of 1930, but in magnitudes that cannot explain the substantial reduction in economic activity.

Aggregate investment in the business cycle is unstable because of the optimal reaction of investors to events that are resolved over time, in the view of Bernanke (1983a). The current rate of investment may be retarded by uncertainty, increasing the value of waiting for new information. Romer (1992) extends the uncertainty framework of Bernanke (1983a) from effects on investment to effects on consumption. She argues that the significant variability of stock prices in the Depression after the crash of 1929 created uncertainty in consumers who postponed buying irreversible durable goods. There was value in the satisfaction of consuming the goods immediately. Consumers had doubts as to the quality of the goods to purchase because of the uncertainty of future income generated by stock market volatility, creating value in postponing the decision when higher quality goods could be acquired. The equation used by Romer (1992, 608) is

$$y_{it} = \alpha_i + \beta_{1i}y_{it-1} + \beta_{2i}y_{t-1} + \beta_{3i}V_t + \beta_{4i}W_t \tag{6.3}$$

This equation expresses the percentage change in a category of commodity output, y_{it}, in terms of its lagged value, y_{it-1}, the lagged value of total commodity output, y_{t-1}, a measure of the variability of the stock market, V_t, and the change in the level of real stock prices, W_t. Romer estimated this equation for 1891–1928, excluding the period of World War I and the immediately following years. The coefficient of stock market variability is significant, economically substantial, and of the correct negative sign. Romer interprets the results as consistent with the uncertainty hypothesis, exhibiting contraction of the production of consumer durable goods in response to large changes in stock prices. The model explains the substantial decline in consumer spending in 1930. Irreversible purchase of consumer goods declined substantially after the crash of 1929 while there was much lower reduction of consumption of reversible perishable goods.

From April 1931 to July 1932, industrial production in the United States declined by 43 percent, falling in July 1932 to less than one half of the peak value of the index in July 1929 while the rate of unemployment reached 24 percent and the producer price index declined by 40 percent (Romer 1993, 32). The failure of the Fed to arrest the banking panic after 1930 contributed to deepening recession. Congressional pressure forced the Fed to ease monetary policy in the spring of 1932 with industrial output growing by 12 percent in July–November 1932. The Fed abandoned the policy when Congress adjourned in 1933. Another banking panic threw the economy into contraction again. Recovery began only in April 1933 (Romer 1993, 34).

The macroeconomic indicators of the Great Depression analyzed by Romer (1999, 168) contain a puzzle in the form of significantly high deviations of GNP from trend ranging from −25.9 percent in 1940 to −47.3 percent in 1933, continuing high rates of unemployment ranging from 14.6 percent in 1940 to 25.2 percent in 1933, coexisting with high percentage inflation rates: 8.6 in 1934, 2.4 in 1936, 4.7 in 1937, 2.3 in 1940, and 6.0 percent in 1941. An important factor of inflation found by Romer (1999) is the high growth rates in the upswing after the Great Depression: 37.5 percent growth in four years 1934–7, for a yearly average of 8.3 percent, and 34.6 percent during 1939–40, for a yearly average rate of 10.4 percent. Romer (1999, 178) estimates the following equation with data for 1880–1932, excluding some years around World War I and using instruments:

$$\pi_t = 0.20(y_t - y_t^*) + 0.58\Delta y_t + 0.15\pi_{t-1} - 3.40 + 0.06t \qquad (6.4)$$

This equation expresses the current rate of inflation, π_t, in terms of the percentage deviation of output, y_t, from trend, y_t^*, the growth rate of real output, Δy_t, the past rate of inflation, π_{t-1}, and trend, t. The coefficients are also significant except for that of the past rate of inflation. The coefficient of the growth rate of output is significant and more substantial than that of the deviation from trend. A one percentage point increase in the rate of growth of real output increases the rate of inflation by almost six tenths of one percentage point (Romer 1993, 178).

However, the inclusion of the pull on inflation by fast growth of real output, while consistent with similar experience in other prewar recessions characterized by inflation and fast recovery, does not explain the high rates of inflation in the 1930s. In particular, it does not explain the rate of inflation during 1934–7. Romer broadens the analysis by considering the combined effects of the National Industrial Recovery Act (NIRA), favoring minimum wages and collusive agreements, and the Agricultural Adjustment Act (AAA) in frustrating the mechanism of autonomous adjustment of the deviation of output from trend by preventing increases in real balances through nominal wage and cost declines. The consideration of these additional factors provides more satisfactory explanation of inflation in the upswing following the Great Depression. In spite of the high growth rates, the economy did not return to trend output until 1942.

Wages and employment

The more accepted interpretation of the Great Depression proposes what Bernanke and Carey (1996, 854) call a solution to the "aggregate demand puzzle," explaining the simultaneous decline in aggregate demand in many countries in the early 1930s by a mostly unplanned contraction of aggregate demand transmitted worldwide by the gold standard. They argue that there is still a need to solve the "aggregate supply puzzle," consisting of an explanation of the association of aggregate nominal demand worldwide and continuing declines in real output and employment. Bernanke and Carey augment the sticky wage equations of Eichengreen and Sachs (1985, 1986) by the following system:

$$q_t = -\alpha_w w_t + \alpha_p p_t + \delta q_{t-1} + X_t \beta + \varepsilon_t^q \tag{6.5}$$

This equation is an extension of the simpler output supply equation used by Eichengreen and Sachs (1985): $q_t = -\alpha(w^* - p_t)$, expressing output q in terms of the exogenously determined wage rate, w, and the price level, p. Bernanke and Carey separate the wage and price effects to test for their equality that would confirm the impact of wages on output independently of prices, add lagged output q_{t-1} and a set of shift instrumental variables X_t with parameter set β and ε_t^q is the error term. The second equation in the system of Bernanke and Carey is a more broadly specified wage equation compared with the exogenous wage equation of Eichengreen and Sachs (1985):

$$w_t = \lambda_p p_t + \lambda_w w_{t-1} - \gamma u_t - \theta(\Delta u) + \varepsilon_t^u \tag{6.6}$$

The first term in the equation, $\lambda_p p_t$, is a measurement of the degree of response of nominal wages to current price movements, and the second term, $\lambda_w w_{t-1}$, captures nominal inertia from the lagged nominal wage. The equation also allows the effect of the rate of unemployment, u, and its change, Δu, on the desired wage level. Bernanke and Carey (1996, 876) obtain the following aggregate supply equation by substituting the wage adjustment equation (6.6) into the output supply equation (6.5):

$$q_t = \alpha(1 - \lambda_p)p_t - \alpha \lambda_w w_{t-1} + \alpha \gamma u_t + \delta_{t-1} + X_t \beta + (\varepsilon_t^q - \alpha \varepsilon_t^w) \tag{6.7}$$

The sample of Bernanke and Carey consists of data for 22 countries some of which retained and other suspended the gold standard during 1931–6. They estimate the three equations separately, with the broader result consisting of the aggregate supply equation (6.7). Their findings measure a strong inverse relationship between output and real wages, across countries and over time. The countries that left the gold standard earlier had high output and low real wages while those that remained in the gold standard had low output and high real wages. The evidence suggests that sticky nominal wages were the cause of monetary non-neutrality. The coefficients of wages and prices were not significantly different, suggesting that nonwage price channels were not important. There is evidence of significant effects of lagged wages.

The simulation model of Bordo, Erceg, and Evans (2000) quantifies the effects of wage stickiness on the magnitude and persistence of the Great Depression. It departs from the assumptions that wage contracts are staggered and overlapping, such that the wage level responds slowly to employment, and the effects of money on prices are unanticipated. The baseline model suggests that 70 percent of the decline in economic activity by the trough of the Depression in 1933 is explained by monetary shocks. The good performance of the model from 1929 to early 1932 is consistent with the sticky wage hypothesis. From the third quarter of 1929 to the first quarter of 1932 real wages increased at the yearly rate of 4.3 percent, more than twice the rate of 1.6 percent during 1920–9 (Bordo, Erceg, and Evans 2000, 1499). By the trough of 1933, labor hours in the United States declined by 35 percent relative to the period before the Depression.

However, the model of Bordo, Erceg, and Evans (2000) predicts stabilization of economic activity after 1932 while output continued to decline. The United States abandoned the gold standard in April 1933, clearing the way for monetization that would have caused stimulating decline in real wages. The NIRA approved by Congress in June 1933 prevented more robust recovery of the US economy by mandating increases in nominal wages for all industrial activities together with caps on labor hours. Increases in money during 1933–5 probably compensated for some of the adverse effects of the increases in nominal wages by NIRA but monetization was insufficient to move the US economy out of the Depression. Bordo, Erceg, and Evans conclude that if wages were legislated by NIRA above the marginal product of labor, monetization was incapable of igniting the recovery of the economy. Nonmonetary government policy flattened the path of recovery of the US from the Great Depression.

The rate of unemployment of the US increased from 3.2 percent in 1929 to 22.9 percent or 23.6 percent in 1932, according to two different estimates, while real wages increased by 16.4 percent (Margo 1993, 43). By 1940, the rate of unemployment was 17.2 percent or 9.5 percent, according to different estimates, while real wages increased by 44 percent (Margo 1993, 43). Using disaggregated data, Margo (1991) finds that the unemployed of the 1930s were mostly workers earning low wages who remained unemployment for long periods. Many of the unemployed were absorbed in sustained worker relief under the Works

Progress Administration (WPA) or similar federal or state relief agencies, which afforded more stable jobs than in the private sector. Margo argues that increases in aggregate demand could have reduced long-term unemployment outside the worker relief programs. This explains why the 1930s were characterized by increasing real wages for those employed, long period of unemployment, and high aggregate rates of unemployment. It also explains why unemployment was only reduced with the huge labor demands of the war economy.

Growth theory and the New Deal

There are two requirements for an explanation of the severity of the Great Depression by high real wage rates, according to Cole and Ohanian (2000, 189). First, real wages must have been significantly above trend in the 1930s and much higher than in the comparable recession with deflation during 1921–2. Second, there must have been a labor market failure because of the otherwise competitive pressure for lower wages. Cole and Ohanian find that the wage data are not complete, showing significant wage declines by 28 percent in agriculture below trend in both periods and moderate increases in manufacturing above trend by 5 percent during 1930–3 and 1 percent during 1921–2. The predicted path of their two-sector general equilibrium model is significantly less severe than the actual experience in the US Great Depression. The benchmark model shows that the wage increase in manufacturing explains a decline in output of 3 percent by the trough of the Great Depression compared with an actual decline of 38 percent. In addition, increases in wages coincide with declining output only in 1931.

An important current of thought applies growth theory to the analysis of depressions (Kehoe and Prescott 2001; Prescott 1999, 2002; Cole and Ohanian 1999, 2001). Output per working age person is depicted by the trend and deviation from the trend (Kehoe and Prescott 2001, 11). The economy experiences a boom if output is significantly above trend and a depression when it is significantly below trend. The concept of trend is obtained from the aggregate production function as the trend growth of output per person of working age in a given country without changes in the productivity or input factors. Kehoe and Prescott (2001, 13) define a depression as a decline of detrended output per working-age person of at least 15 percent in the first ten years of the depression.

During 1929–33, the United States experienced a decline of employment by 25 percent and of output by 30 percent (Cole and Ohanian 1999, 3). In 1939, employment and output remained substantially below their levels in 1929. The severity of the Great Depression is shown by real per capita output remaining 11 percent below the 1929 level while real per capita output typically increases by 31 percent in a ten-year period. Cole and Ohanian use growth theory to explain the sharp decline of economic activity during 1929–33 and the inadequate recovery during 1934–9. Real shocks in technology, fiscal policy, and trade appear to have contributed to the decline during 1929–33 but predict strong recovery after 1934 that did not occur. Cole and Ohanian use the model of Lucas and Rapping (1969) (see Lucas and Rapping 1972 and Rees 1970) to analyze monetary shocks, finding that monetary shocks predict not only reduction of output in the early 1930s but also return of output and employment to trend by the mid-1930s. Financial intermediation shocks, such as banking panics, and inflexible wages, also cannot predict the weak recovery after 1934. Cole and Ohanian (1999) conclude that another type of shock should explain the puzzle of economic activity in the United States significantly below trend a decade after the beginning of the Great Depression.

The 1930s were characterized by significant decline in employment. Cole and Ohanion (1999) find that total hours worked, reflecting changes in employment and in hours per worker, fell by more than total employment, with a trough only in 1934, remaining 29 percent in 1939 below the 1929 level. Private hours, excluding hours by government workers, fell more sharply than total hours because there were no losses in government hours; by 1939, private hours fell 25 percent relative to the level in 1929. The labor data suggest that the economy declined to a lower path level than the one prevailing in 1929. The data on the continuation of the Depression provided by Cole and Ohanian (1999, 2001 table 1, 67) are deflated by the adult population (over 16 years of age) and adjusted for trend relative to 1929. In 1939, the real variables of output and employment were significantly below trend: −26.8 percent for GNP, −25.4 for consumption, −51 percent for investment, and −25.6 percent for hours worked. In contrast, total factor productivity was 3.1 percent above trend and real wages 21.8 percent above trend. There is no international shock because most countries recovered toward trend after the trough of the Great Depression. Financial, banking, monetary, productivity, and real shocks do not explain the failure of the US economy to return to full employment. Cole and Ohanion (2001) find that the data are puzzling: weak recovery with rapid growth of productivity, high real wages during weak economic activity, and low labor input coexisting with high wages and weak consumption. Competition would have resulted in higher consumption and utilization of labor with a lower real wage. The answer is in the shock of New Deal policies to the labor market.

There are three phases in the New Deal identified by Cole and Ohanian. First, the NIRA during 1933–35 linked collusion by firms with rents by labor by the suspension of antitrust law enforcement if the industry accepted collective bargaining and immediately increased wages. Second, the Supreme Court declared the NIRA unconstitutional in 1935; the National Labor Relations Act (NLRA) in 1935 and the ruling of constitutionality by the Supreme Court in 1937 strengthened collective bargaining, union representation, and strikes, together with bland enforcement of antitrust prosecution by the Department of Justice. Third, toward the end of the 1930s Roosevelt became disillusioned with the recovery of the economy by high prices and wages and the war eliminated the distortion linking firm collusion with labor bargaining power.

An adviser of Roosevelt, according to Cole and Ohanian, suggested a return to the policy of World War I of relaxing antitrust law enforcement to increase cooperation among firms, raising wages and output; such policies would promote growth similar to that during World War I. Cole and Ohanion measure the performance of the balanced growth paths of a cartel model similar to the phases of the New Deal and a perfectly competitive model. The combination of cartels with significant labor bargaining power depresses aggregate output and employment, explaining significant parts of the failure of the United States in fully recovering in the 1930s. The cartel model predicts output in 1939 that is 14 percent below the competitive balanced growth path and labor input 11 percent below the competitive balanced growth path, explaining 50 to 60 percent of the depression of output and labor input after 1933. The model also provides an explanation for the return to recession during 1937–8 and the movement toward full employment during World War II when the policies were relaxed.

Origins of the credit crisis

Bank fragility, in the models of Diamond and Rajan (2000, 2001a,b) and Diamond and Dybvig (1983) analyzed in Chapter 2 in relation to the credit/dollar crisis, originates in the transformation function of illiquid assets into liquid demand deposits. Diamond and Dybvig (1983, 418) analyze similar transformation in a firm with illiquid technology that issues short-term bonds as part of its capital structure. The viability of this strategy depends on the rollover of the bonds by creditors. If one creditor believed that others would not roll over their bond holdings, her best response would be not to roll over her own. Diamond and Dybvig (1983, 418) argue that "such liquidity crises are similar to bank runs." Financial intermediation has evolved into a structure in which illiquid assets—residences, receivables, cars, appliances, student expenses, consumer expenditures, and nearly every consumption and investment need—are converted into ABS that are financed in short-term SRPs. There is fragility in the securitization of financial assets that is similar to the uninsured demand deposit contract without an option of suspending convertibility.

Consider the Diamond and Dybvig analysis. There are three periods, $T = 0, 1, 2$, with investment of -1 at $T = 0$. The yield of the productive technology is $R > 1$, which is realized only at $T = 2$. The technology provides either 0 or 1 at $T = 1$. If nothing is consumed at T = 1, the technology provides R at $T = 2$; if 1 is consumed at $T = 1$, the technology provides 0. There are two types of agents. Type 1 agents consume $c_1^1 = 1$ at $T = 1$ and type 2 agents wait until $T = 2$ to consume $c_2^2 = R$, where the superscript denotes types 1 and 2 agents and the subscript the time periods 1 and 2. The demand deposit contract provides insurance against being a type 1 agent by allowing consumption at $T = 1$. Let r_1 be the fixed claim received by a type 1 agent at $T = 1$ after making an investment of 1 at $T = 0$. There is a "good" equilibrium in the Diamond and Dybvig model when the payment per dollar of deposit at $T = 1$, r_1, is equal to the optimal consumption of a type 1 agent, c_1^{1*}, or $r_1 = c_1^{1*}$. Optimal risk-sharing is attained in this pure strategy Nash equilibrium with type 1 agents withdrawing at $T = 1$ and type 2 agents waiting for $T = 2$. There is another adverse equilibrium, a bank run, when all agents attempt to withdraw at $T = 1$. The anticipation of this possibility results in withdrawal by all agents at $T = 1$. The model assumes sequential withdrawal of deposits. Because of the illiquidity of bank assets, the face value of deposits exceeds the liquidation value of assets.

The popular analysis of the credit/dollar crisis has emphasized the trigger of subprime mortgages with the separation of the careless originator and the final investor by the intermediation of financial institutions seeking abnormal profits. Goodhart (2008) provides comprehensive analysis of the actual probable causes of the credit/dollar crisis, carefully concluding that definitive analysis will require more information. An important cause is the underpricing of risk observed by the BIS, the IMF, and most central banks before the beginning of the crisis around mid-2007 (Goodhart 2008, 331):

> This was characterized by very low risk spreads, with differentials between risky assets and safe assets, having declined to historically low levels. Volatility was unusually low. Leverage was high, as financial institutions sought to add to yield, in the face of very low interest

rates. In part, this under-pricing of risk had resulted from the long period of extraordinarily low nominal, and very low real interest rates that had continued from the ending of the Tech bubble in 2001, until central banks generally began to raise interest rates again in 2005.

The consequences of lowering interest rates on increasing financial risk and a credit crisis were remarkably anticipated by Rajan (2005).

The strong dollar of the 1990s caused a current account deficit (CAD) of 4.3 percent by 2000 (Peláez and Peláez 2007, 20) that Bernanke (2005) interprets as a savings glut in the world which lowered interest rates. Fear of deflation because of the experience during the Great Depression and the interpretation of the lost decade in Japan (Bernanke 2002) led the Fed to lower interest rates toward zero during 2003–4 (Peláez and Peláez 2005, 2007, 2008a,b,c). Income is a flow, Y, obtained from a stock of wealth, W, by a rate of interest, r (Friedman 1957):

$$Y = rW \text{ or} \tag{6.8}$$
$$W = \frac{Y}{r} \tag{6.9}$$

As the rates collapsed toward zero, $r \to 0$, agents believed that wealth would grow without bound, $W \to \infty$. The low interest rates created the impression that assets such as residences would increase in value forever resulting in imprudent decisions by borrowers and lenders.

The essential calculus of risk and return in financial decisions and productive investment was distorted. The first lowering of interest rates toward zero propagated through the financial structure of securitization, causing mispricing of risk, low volatility, and high leverage. The prolonged and substantial subsidy of housing in the United States, estimated at $221 billion per year (Jaffee and Quigley 2007), and the entry of Fannie Mae and Freddie Mac in subprime and Alt-A mortgages (Pinto 2008) were key contributors to the erosion of the calculus of risk and the magnitude, propagation, and duration of the recession.

Econometric research finds that the low interest rates by the Fed during 2003–4 caused a real estate boom, replicated in countries such as Spain that also lowered interest rates significantly (Taylor 2007). The timing of entry of Fannie Mae and Freddie Mac in subprime and Alt-A mortgages coincided with the acceleration of that market from $395 billion in 2003 to $715 billion in 2004, reaching $1005 billion in 2005 (Calomiris 2008, 2009Feb). In addition, the GSE remained in the market after the interruption in the rise of house prices in 2006. The combined holdings or guarantees of subprime and Alt-A mortgages of Fannie Mae and Freddie Mac reached $1.6 trillion, accounting for one half of the total outside the FHA (Pinto 2008). The other possible causes of the credit/dollar crisis could have been the new financial structure, inadequate risk management, lack of regulation of derivatives, mortgage origination, systemic risk, and others. The use of Fannie Mae and Freddie Mac to broaden house ownership together with the elimination of the 30-year Treasury bond may have contributed more to real estate exuberance than the separation of mortgage origination and short-term financing of MBS in SRPs. None of these probable causes could have created the severe credit/dollar crisis without interest rates close to zero processing through the large yearly US housing subsidy. In elementary price theory subsidies cause overproduction.

The origin of the credit/dollar crisis is interpreted as (Markowitz 2009, 25)

> [a] basic cause of the current financial crisis was the mandate by the US Congress for the Federal National Mortgage Association (Fannie Mae) to vastly increase its support of low-income housing. This mandate required a lowering of lending standards. These lower standards encouraged people with relatively high incomes to buy more expensive houses than they otherwise would have or to buy speculative second homes with the option of walking away from them if house prices fell.

In this view, part of the policy solution would consist of an end by Congress of pressure on Fannie Mae to buy mortgages with inadequate borrowing standards and acquire mortgages with sound credit standards, down payment, and documentation (Ibid).

Finance facilitates the implementation of projects with technical innovations that drive economic growth and prosperity. The consequences of restricting financial innovation could be quite harmful (Merton and Bodie 2005, 18):

> If financial innovation is stifled for fear that it will reduce the effectiveness of short-run monetary and fiscal policies, the consequences could be a much slower pace of technological progress. Furthermore, long-run policies that focus on domestic saving and capital formation as key determinants of economic growth do not appear to be effective. Policies designed to stimulate innovation in the financial

system would thus appear to be more important for long-term economic development.

Design of policies to recover credit and the real economy in the credit/dollar crisis should be forward looking, preserving innovation channels, and allowing institutions to correct frictions.

Spirals of innovation in products and markets have been accompanied by academic breakthroughs (Black and Scholes 1973; Merton 1973, 1998) and risk-management tools (Finger 2009Apr).

The lowering of interest rates is the prime suspect of the necessary condition for the credit crisis. This is not a criticism of the intentions of central banking but rather of the almost impossible task of lowering and increasing interest rates without more precise knowledge of the future and of the impact of policy instruments on the financial and real sectors of the economy. It is simplistic to argue that markets failed when government also failed. The focus of policy should be in balancing regulation with market allocation. The origin, duration, and depth of the credit crisis can be explained in terms of government policy (Taylor 2008Nov, 2007, 2009, 2009Feb; Taylor and Williams 2009; Calomiris 2008, 2009Feb). According to this view, the origin of the crisis is explained by the departure from the monetary policy of central banks during the two decades of the "great moderation" (Rogoff 2006) when there was growth with low inflation characterized by low volatility. The Fed lowered interest rates too fast confusing a counterparty risk problem with a liquidity problem. The widening spread of the three month Libor and the three-month overnight index swap (OIS) and evidence from the spread of unsecured versus secured loans among banks shows the widening risk component in counterparty transactions (Taylor 2008Nov). The liquidity facilities of central banks and lower fed funds rates fueled a carry trade with positions shorting the dollar and simultaneously going long in oil futures and other commodities. The carry trade in oil futures was observed in daily transactions of those following the markets (Peláez and Peláez 2008c, 74). The realization of the global recession caused collapsing futures prices of oil and other commodities. The emphasis on interpreting the credit/dollar crisis as originating in undisciplined financial institutions contrasts with evident regulatory policy impulses originating, prolonging, and deepening the crisis.

The hand-collected sample of 3912 tranches of collateralized loan obligations (CLO) by Benmelech and Dlugosz (2008) reveals the quality mismatch between the AAA rating of 70.7 percent of the amount issued of CDOs, corresponding to 79.2 percent of the dollar value, with the fact that 85 percent of the collateral pools have a weighted average rating (WAR) of B, 8 percent a WAR of BB and information is missing for 7 percent. With a sample covering about 60 percent of outstanding CLOs, Benmelech, Dlugosz, and Ivashina (2009) do not find support for the view that corporate loans included in CLOs are inferior in quality relative to nonsecuritized loans. Loans arranged by the CLO underwriter do not perform as well as other loans in the CLO portfolio. The statistical default models of subprime are shown by Rajan, Seru, and Vig (2008) to be open to the Lucas (1976) critique. These models were fit during periods of low securitization. As securitization increased lenders began to rely on less than full information, such as FICO scores and LTV ratios, instead of more costly information on the specific characteristics of borrowers. The models underpredicted the decline in value of AAA subprime tranches.

The financial structure has changed significantly through increasing securitization financed with SRPs in transactions among financial intermediaries. Investment banks increased the share of overnight SRPs in financing their balance sheets (Brunnermeier 2009, 80). Rajan (2005, 314) provides an early warning that "banks are moving on to more illiquid transactions. Competition forces them to flirt continuously with the limits of illiquidity." This view finds significant contribution of this new financial structure (Mishkin 2006; Rajan and Zingales 2003; Shiller 2002) in lowering transaction costs, widening and deepening financial capital with enhanced risk-sharing. Rajan (2005) analyzes the new risks of illiquidity originating in tail risks that can weaken bank balance sheets. SIVs disguised off-balance sheet tail risks manifested in the perception of counterparty risk in financing with SRPs structured products that have become illiquid. Banks provided guarantees or "liquidity backstops" (Brunnermeier 2009, 80) to the SRPs of their SIVs; in case of failure to refinance the SRPs a bank credit line would repurchase the securities from the counterparty. Rajan (2005, 318) warned of "probability of a catastrophic meltdown." Credit risk transfer through securitization and derivatives did not eliminate risks in banks because they kept significant default risk. The holding of structured products in off-balance sheet vehicles arbitraged regulatory capital and the assets issued by these vehicles received a higher rating than the securities in the pool (Brunnermeier 2009, 81).

Low, riskless interest rates motivated a hunt for high returns in a variety of financial segments, from hedge funds to emerging markets (Rajan

2005, 339–41). Lowering central bank policy rates eroded the discipline of sound risk/return decisions with a bias toward taking excessive risk.

Brunnermeier (2009, 82) provides revealing description and the reasons for the growth of subprime lending:

> Mortgage brokers offered teaser rates, no-documentation mortgages, piggyback mortgages (a combination of two mortgages that eliminates the need for a down payment, and NINJA ("no income, no job or assets") loans. All these mortgages were granted under the premise that background checks are unnecessary because house prices could only rise, and a borrower could thus always refinance a loan using the increased value of the house. This combination of cheap credit and low lending standards resulted in the housing frenzy that laid the foundations for the crisis.

The generalized perception of house prices increasing forever was created by the lowering of the fed funds rate to 1 percent during 2003–4 with the announced intention to lower it to zero for how long was necessary to eliminate the risk of deflation. Fannie Mae and Freddie Mac provided the guarantee and market of nonprime mortgages by the full faith and credit of the United States.

There should be an amplifying mechanism explaining how a loss of subprime mortgages of several hundred billion dollars caused a loss in equity markets of $8 trillion in October 2007–8 (Brunnermeier 2009). Liquidity is divided for analysis into *market liquidity* consisting of the transfer of the asset with all its cash flow and *funding liquidity* consisting of a financial contract based on a cash flow created by an asset or trading strategy (Ibid, 92). The amplifying mechanism rests on the interaction of market and funding liquidity (Brunnermeier and Pedersen 2009). In simplified form, assume that there is an initial decline in market value of assets of traders financed with short-term debt caused by divergence of transaction price and fundamental value, triggering higher haircuts or margins in short-term contracts such as SRPs, or compressed funding liquidity that reduce capital of traders and force lower positions. Market liquidity is compressed by losses resulting from fire-sales of assets as transaction prices diverge further from fundamental values, causing higher haircuts or margins that in turn lead to new sales as traders reduce positions because of the loss of capital. In the model of Brunnermeier and Pedersen (2009) many securities with high margin requirements are simultaneously affected by liquidity crises causing common liquidity effects and flight to quality. Margins are destabilizing, resulting in liquidity dry-ups and margin spirals, or widening haircuts and margins. Kashyap, Rajan, and Stein (2008, 2) agree that in the crisis "funding problems led to fire sales and depressed prices."

Monetary and fiscal policy

According to Pittman and Ivry (2009), by March 2009 "the US government and the Federal Reserve have spent, lent or committed $12.8 trillion, an amount that approaches the value of everything produced in the country last year." The amount committed sums to $12.8 trillion and the amount disbursed or lent to $4.2 trillion. The analysis of the commitments, disbursements, and loans can be broken into components: monetary policy by the Fed and programs by Treasury, FDIC, and homeownership. The individual components are discussed in turn.

The management of the balance sheet has become the instrument of Fed policy (Bernanke 2009Apr3, 2009 Feb10, 2009Jan 13; FOMC 2009Jan; FSOB 2009Jan). The policy of the Fed is moving closer to "quantitative easing." When policy rates, such as the fed funds rate, are at or near zero, the central bank can expand the balance sheet injecting reserves by the purchase of government securities, disregarding the policy rates and focusing on the quantity of reserves (Bernanke and Reinhart 2004AER, 87). This policy is sometimes called "quantitative easing." The injection of reserves by quantitative easing could lead to rebalancing of portfolios by investors, increasing prices of alternative long-term securities (Bernanke and Reinhart 2004AER, 88). The resulting reduction in long-term interest rates could stimulate investment and economic recovery. An alternative interpretation is that the maintenance of reserve levels higher than needed for the zero interest rates could generate expectations that the central bank is prepared to maintain quantitative easing until economic conditions improve. Another effect could occur through expectations of lower taxation as the public debt burden shifts from holdings by the public to the central bank. Policies of zero interest rates face tough operational and communications challenges. Bernanke and Reinhart (2004AER, 90) conclude that "policymakers are well advised to act preemptively and aggressively to avoid facing the complications raised by the zero lower bounds." Empirical evidence finds optimism for the communication of policy by the Fed and some evidence for lowering yields in Japan as a result of quantitative easing (Bernanke, Reinhart, and Sack 2004BPEA). There is ample research on quantitative easing in Japan (Hori and Shimizutani 2005; Kurihara 2006; Maeda et al. 2005; Suda 2003; Ugai 2006).

Fed policy initially focused on providing liquidity in the LOLR function. When various sectors of the credit market experienced liquidity squeezes the Fed acted by creating 11 directed credit facilities targeting short-term credit to depository institutions (TAF), overnight loans to primary dealers (PDCF), lending of Treasury securities to primary dealers (TLSF), financing purchasing of asset backed commercial paper from money market mutual funds (AMLF), loans to acquire ABCP from primary dealers (CPFF), loans for purchasing ABCP and money market instruments (MMIFF), loans for purchasing ABS originating in consumer loans and small business (TALF), purchase of MBS and Treasury securities, dollar swaps with foreign central banks, assistance to the acquisition of Bear Stearns, and assistance to AIG.[1]

Table 6.1 provides a simplified version of the Fed balance sheet available weekly. The Fed generated resources for the directed credit facilities by reducing its portfolio of securities, increasing bank reserves, and the Treasury supplemental account. This is shown in Table 6.1 by a decrease of treasury securities in the balance sheet of the Fed from $713.4 billion in February 2008 to $524.1 billion in February 2009. Sales and redemptions of treasuries were intended to maintain the fed funds rates near target levels (FOMC 2009Jan, 13). Another important source of resources for the

Table 6.1 Federal Reserve System simplified balance sheet

	Billions of dollars and percent		
	Feb 13, 2008	Feb 11, 2009	Percent change
Assets	855.1	1844.9	115.7
Securities and loans	801.4	1079.1	34.7
Treasury securities	713.4	524.1	−26.5
Central Bank swaps	n.a.	390.9	—
Holding commercial paper	n.a.	251.2	—
Other	53.7	123.7	—
Liabilities and capital	855.1	1844.9	115.7
Net FRS notes	778.9	856.0	9.9
Deposits	23.4	862.3	36.9*
Depository institutions	18.0	600.1	33.3*
Treasury supplementary	n.a.	199.9	—
Capital	37.8	41.4	9.5
Other	38.4	85.2	121.8

Note: *Multiples

Source: Bernanke (2009Feb10, 2009Jan13, 2009Feb24, 2009Mar3), FRBO http://www.federalreserve.gov/releases/h41/

Fed was the increase in idle reserves of banks from $18 billion in February 2008 to $600.1 billion in February 2009. The increase in idle reserves partly originated in the lack of sound lending opportunities and toward the end of 2008 by the rise in demand deposits with the worsening credit crisis (FOMC 2009Jan, 30). However, the Fed motivated the increase by paying interest on required and excess reserve balances with a decision on October 8, 2008 to anticipate the Financial Services Regulatory Relief Act of 2006, which provided for interest payments as of October 1, 2011 (FOMC 2009Jan, 4). The Fed intended to maintain the fed funds rate at target levels by paying interest on excess and required reserve balances.

The supplementary Treasury account (Treasury 2008Sep17) of $199.9 billion also contributed to funding the Fed (Hamilton 2008). The supplementary Treasury account consists of the issue of Treasury bills by Treasury with proceeds deposited in an account of the FRS, resulting in draining of bank reserve balances (FOMC 2009Jan, 28). This account peaked at $559 billion in 2008, declining to $259 billion by year end. The combined resources allowed the Fed to increase its balance sheet by 115.7 percent, from $855.1 billion in February 2008 to $1844.9 billion in February 2009 as shown in Table 6.1.

Treasury programs disbursed and lent $1.8 trillion with pledges reaching $2.7 trillion. The Troubled Asset Relief Program (TARP) was created by the Emergency Economic Stabilization Act of 2008, receiving pledges of $700 billion with loans for capital of financial institutions and automobile manufacturers of $599 billion. There are evaluations of the TARP by the Financial Stability Oversight Board (FSOB 2009), the Congressional Oversight Panel (COP 2009), and Duff & Phelps (2009). On February 10, 2009, Treasury Secretary Timothy Geithner (2009Feb10) announced the replacement of the TARP with the Financial Stability Plan (FSP) (Treasury 2009Feb10, 2009Feb25). The FSP consists of comprehensive stress tests for major banks (FRBO 2009Apr24), increased balance sheet transparency and disclosure, capital assistance program (CAP), public-private investment fund of $500 billion to $1 trillion to remove illiquid financial assets, increase of the TALF to $1 trillion, agenda of transparency and affordable housing, and foreclosure prevention (Treasury 2009Feb10). In March 2009, Treasury announced the creation of the Public-Private Investment Program (PPIP) (Treasury 2009Mar30). The objective of the PPIP is to remove legacy loans and legacy assets from the balance sheets of banks. Legacy loans are loans with uncertain future performance and legacy securities do not have liquidity and, thus, a ready market. Legacy loans and securities in the balance sheets prevent banks from raising additional capital because of the fear of potential investors of further write downs. Banks could restrict lending because of the uncertainty of the performance of legacy loans and securities, which could result in reduction of capital. The PPIP begins with $500 billion that can expand to $1 trillion.

The two fiscal stimulus packages, $168 billion in 2008 and $787 billion during 2009–10 (Obama 2009Jan8), add to $955 billion (Pittman and Ivry 2009). There are two other significant pledged items in Treasury, a line of credit for the FDIC of $500 billion and support for Fannie and Freddie of $400 billion.

The pledged resources of the FDIC total $2.0 trillion, of which only $357 billion are disbursed or lent. The largest pledged item is liquidity guarantee, $1.4 trillion. This consists mainly of guarantees of transactions deposits and unsecured debt of financial institutions (FDIC 2008Nov 26, 2009Jan12). There is also the guarantee of $500 billion of debt of vehicles created to acquire legacy loans of the PPIP. The leverage of the legacy securities would be provided by the Fed.

The Housing and Economic Recovery Act of 2008 (Geithner 2009Feb18; HUD 2008Jul30, 2009Feb; Treasury 2009Feb18, 2009Mar4) provides through the Federal Housing Administration (FHA), as of October 1, 2008, government insurance to lenders who voluntarily reduce the value of mortgages to at least 90 percent of the current value of the property. The objective was to support about 400,000 homeowners at risk affordable mortgage rates to avoid foreclosure; the HOPE programs for homeowners of HUD has used or pledged resources of $300 billion.

Government ownership and control of banks

There are two views on government ownership of banks (La Porta et al. 2002a, 265–6). First, according to the development view, in a situation where markets are not conducive to economic growth and development, the government should create government owned and controlled banks and companies in strategic sectors to aggressively allocate resources toward rapid economic growth. Second, the alternative or political view argues that the motivation for acquisition or creation of government banks and companies is to provide employment, subsidies, and other benefits to allies that can in turn provide to the politicians' votes, contributions, and bribes. In developing countries without well-defined property rights and incipient financial systems, the political view finds a better environment because of the lack of competition for funds between the government and the private sector. In fact, the private sector that is allowed to exist is closely tied politically to the public sector, as shown in China. In many cases, the private sector has complex links with the government, as in

Korea. In other cases, the creation of state-owned companies has coexisted with subsidies to the private sector, as in Brazil.

There is a wide range of participation by the government in banking and strategic activities (Ibid, 266–7). The government can directly subsidize private entities or use regulation and moral suasion to direct them toward certain interests or activities. In many countries, regulatory authorities have used regulation and moral suasion to force bank loans toward desired companies and projects. Bank ownership has significant advantage in that the government can directly allocate the funds, and thus control of resources, to desired companies and projects. The government can capture deposits and allocate them to desired projects through direct ownership of banks. The development view proposes that in this way the government can ameliorate market failures, channeling resources in such a way as to promote long-term growth and development. The political view proposes that the government simply finances politically desirable but inefficient projects that would not be otherwise financed. Both theories coincide in the proposition that there is financing of projects that would not be otherwise financed: the political theory argues that those projects are not socially desirable while the development theory argues the contrary.

The two theories predict that government ownership of banks will be more prevalent in developing countries, in countries with incipient financial markets, and in those with weak institutions (Ibid, 267). The development theory predicts that countries with state ownership of banks will benefit in the form of financial and economic development, capital accumulation, and growth of productivity. The political view argues that the state ownership of banks will crowd out financing of the private sector. The projects financed by state banks are likely to be inefficient, having adverse effects on productivity growth. The behavior of financial development and productivity growth should permit discriminating between the two theories.

La Porta et al. use data from 92 countries. On the average, the government owned 59 percent of the equity of the ten largest banks in 1970 and 42 percent in 1995. State ownership of banks is very common in poorer countries and in those with weak protection of property rights, strong state intervention in the economy, and incipient financial sectors. The ownership of banks by the state was followed by slower pace of development of the financial sector and lower productivity and economic growth. These results support the political view of state ownership of banks. The analysis of the monumental worldwide sample of Barth, Caprio, and Levine (2006) supports the results of La Porta et al. (2002a).

Bank de facto nationalization with the government as a major share-holder could result in distortions similar to those of related lending ana-lyzed in the literature. The government could influence direction of credit to projects with potentially high rate of default because of political inter-ests. The information view on related lending argues that ownership and representation of real sector interests in the board of banks improve their information and thus efficiency in the allocation of loans (Gerschenkron 1962; Stiglitz and Weiss 1981). The alternative or looting (Johnson et al. 2000) view argues that real-sector owners or representatives in banks merely capture resources from depositors and minority shareholders by lending to themselves. Related lending is attractive to the borrower but could bankrupt the lender, socializing the losses (La Porta et al. 2003). Related lending could be considered an eventual form of nationalization. With a new sample of Mexico, La Porta et al. find that related borrow-ers are more likely to default by 33 to 35 percent than unrelated ones. Default rates on loans to related persons and privately held companies related to the bank is 77.4 percent compared with 31.2 percent for unre-lated borrowers. The rate of recovery of defaulted loans to related bor-rowers is $0.30 lower than for other borrowers. Maurer and Haber (2005, 2007) analyze related lending in terms of two hypotheses. First, the rule of law and effective property rights may create barriers to looting. Second, sound corporate governance may lower the costs of monitoring bank directors. In the analysis of Mexico by Maurer and Haber (2007) the incentives and monitoring costs of bank directors by minority sharehold-ers and depositors can influence the outcome of related lending.

Regulation

Citation analysis can be useful in understanding the legal system and in attempts to improve its performance (Posner 2000). One of the most cited legal scholars, actually ranked first by Shapiro (2000), observes the regulatory environment of the credit/dollar crisis as (Posner 2009)

> [a] natural response is to tighten up regulation. In the case of commer-cial banks, this would not require new legislation. The bank regulators have virtually plenary control over banks: thus the crack "what does a bank say when a regulator tells it to jump?" Answer: "How high?"

The regulatory proposals listed in Table 6.2 mirror the actions of the central banks and finance ministries in pursuing ways of steering the financial sector of problems as they surfaced during the credit/dollar

Table 6.2 Regulation proposals

Systemic regulation
- The United States proposes the creation of a single, independent regulator of systemic risk and critical payment and settlement systems (US Treasury 2009RRProposal, 2009Frame; Geithner 2009Mar25, 2009Mar26)
- The G30 (2009) proposes a proper dose of supervisory oversight of systemically important financial institutions
- The FSA (2009Turner) focuses on regulation preventing and responding to systemic crises

Large and Complex Systemic Financial Institutions
- The US Treasury is proposing higher capital standard and stricter risk management for systemically important firms (US Treasury 2009RRProposal, 2009Frame; Geithner 2009Mar25, 2009Mar26)
- The US Treasury is proposing stronger resolution authority for protection against failure of large and complex systemic institutions and the funding of the resolution insurance by the institutions (US Treasury 2009RRProposal, 2009Frame; Geithner 2009Mar25, 2009Mar26)

Procyclicality
- The FSF (2009Procy) followed a framework (BIS 2009Sep1) to provide recommendations on procyclicality in the bank capital framework (FSF-BCBS 2009BankProc), provisioning (FSF 2009Prov) and valuation and leverage (FSF-CGFS 2009Val). The FSA (2009Turner) endorses procyclicality
- BCBS should revise the capital framework to create capital buffers in upswings that can be used in downswings, reduce the cyclicality of VaR measures of risk and contain increasing banking leverage with a simple measure not based on risk that creates a leverage floor under Basel II (FSF 2009Procy). The FSA (2009Turner) proposes capital buffers
- Statement by the Financial Accounting Standards Board (FASB) and the International Accounting Standards Board (IASB) reiterating the use of judgment in determining incurred loan losses; urgent technical study by FASB and IASB on alternative approaches in reforming incurred loss model; BCBS review of Basel II of disclosure of loan loss provisioning and disincentives to adequate loan loss provisions (FSF 2009Procy)
- Macroprudential assessment of the relationship of valuation and leverage; regulators should have clear and complete depiction of aggregate leverage and liquidity with tools required to engage in necessary enhanced surveillance (FSF 2009Procy)

Cross-border cooperation on crisis management
- The objective of financial crisis management is preventing adverse effects on the real economy resulting from domestic or international financial instability (FSF 2009Coop)
- Authorities should consider the future tax effects of their actions, maintaining incentives for prudent risk-taking by financial institutions, promoting solutions by the private sector and only by the public sector when indispensable and ensuring competition in international finance in accordance with the Basel Capital Accord (FSF 2009Coop)

Continued

Table 6.2 Continued

- Focus on coordinated actions on specific firms that may have systemic implications in various jurisdictions (FSF 2009Coop)
- Enhance cooperation, information sharing, tools, prevention systems, colleges of supervisors, and so on (FSF 2009Coop)
- The FSA (2009Turner) proposes international cooperation through an international college of supervisors

Capital requirements: Pillar I of Basel II
- BCBS (2009Jan; Wellink 2009Mar) distributed consultative package on proposals to change capital requirements in trading book exposure; introduce incremental risk capital charge for unsecuritized credit products; apply banking book charges to securitized products; stressed VaR on one-year window of significant losses; higher capital charges for CDOs involving re-securitization (ABS CDOs); increase capital requirements for liquidity guarantees to ABCP SIVs; analysis of credit ratings by external agencies (FSF 2009Enh, 2009UpEnh); economic capital is analyzed by BCBS (2009Econ)

Liquidity risk management
- BCBS (2008Sep) provides 17 principles of sound liquidity risk management
- Fundamental principle: banks must have robust liquidity risk management process with pools of quality liquid assets as cushion against impairment of funding sources; supervisors must assess the process, taking prompt action in case of deficiencies that pose risks to deposits and the financial system
- Three principles cover the governance of liquidity risk management departing from appropriate liquidity tolerance criteria involving senior management in strategy, policies, and practices
- Eight principles cover the management and measurement of liquidity risk
- One principle provides for timely and material disclosure to the public to inform market participants on the adequacy of liquidity risk management and soundness of liquidity position
- Four principles of supervisory oversight provide for regular, comprehensive assessment of resilience to liquidity stress and appropriate measures

Risk management oversight by supervisors: Pillar 2 of Basel II
- BCBS (2009Jan) strengthened risk management oversight through Pillar 2 of Basel II (BCBS 2004)
- Banks need to consider the interrelation of credit risk with a variety of other risks that created problems: concentration, market, liquidity, legal, counterparty, and reputational
- Supervisors must enhance risk management throughout the entire firm
- Supervisors must improve stress testing at banks

Effective deposit insurance systems
- Requires sound financial institutions, macro prudential regulation and supervision, LOLR, legal institutions, and disclosure such as by Pillar 3 of Basel II (BCBS 2009Ins); costs may have to be shared with the state
- The objectives of the BCBS (2009Ins) core principles for effective deposit insurance systems are the maintenance of financial stability and avoiding moral hazard

Continued

Table 6.2   Continued

- Deposit insurer must have sound governance, clear mandate, required powers, coordination with the safety net, and cross-borders insurers and safety net (BCBS 2009Ins)
- Membership should be mandatory for all deposit-taking institutions, coverage clearly defined to cover the large majority of depositors and transitions carefully managed (BCBS 2009Ins)
- Funding should be adequately provided, access to funds effective and rapid; the insurer must resolve failed institutions effectively and in time (BCBS 2009Ins)
- The FSA (2009Turner) proposes retail insurance for most depositors and resolution powers

Regulation of capital pools
- The US Treasury is proposing registration of all hedge funds above a certain size, investor, and counterparty disclosure, information required to evaluate threats to financial stability and sharing reports with systemic regulator (US Treasury 2009RRProposal, 2009Frame; Geithner 2009Mar25, 2009Mar26)
- The G30 (2009) working group proposes registration of capital pools, such as hedge funds and private equity, with a proper prudential regulator.
- The G30 (2009) proposes that capital pools disclose to the regulator and the public size, investment strategy, borrowing, and performance
- The regulator of capital pools should have the authority to determine proper standards for capital, liquidity, and risk management (G30 2009)
- The FSA (2009Turner) proposes to obtain more information on hedge, applying prudential regulation if they pose systemic risks

Principles for sound compensation practices
- The FSF (2009Comp) finds that external regulatory measures would be more effective in aligning competition and prudent risk-taking than competition
- The objective of the FSF (2009Comp) is to provide for effective compensation governance, aligning compensation with prudent risk-taking and involving oversight by supervisors and stakeholders
- Effective compensation governance under the principles of the FSF (2009Comp) requires involvement of independent directors, with knowledge of both compensation and risk management, on all compensation practices and oversight of policy and practice
- Compensation must be aligned with prudent risk-taking, symmetric with overall firm performance, realized over long periods and consist of proper mix of cash, equity, and other forms with regard to aligning risk (FSF 2009Comp)
- Aligning compensation and prudent risk-taking requires involvement of supervisory oversight and engagement of stakeholders (FSF 2009Comp)

OTC derivatives
- The US Treasury is proposing regulation of CDS and OTC derivatives under a strict regulatory and supervisory regime, clearing through designated central counterparties (see Duffie and Zhu 2009 for analysis), strict eligibility requirements for all market participants and robust standards for nonstandardized derivatives (US Treasury 2009RRProposal, 2009Frame; Geithner 2009Mar25, 2009Mar26)

Continued

Table 6.2 Continued

- The Seniors Supervisors Group (2009Mar) reported to the FSF on the infrastructure of OTC derivatives clearing because of eight credit events in the second half of 2008. The auction system of net settling in cash introduced in 2005 by the International Swaps and Derivatives Association (ISDA) allowed timely settlement of CDS contracts. The ISDA is publishing a protocol that will provide market participants forms to amend existing CDS trade in using the auction system

Fannie Mae and Freddie Mac
- The G30 (2009) proposes separation of the functions of government guarantee of housing finance from the operations in intermediating risk in private sector mortgage finance, selling the retained portfolio to private entities; government participation in housing finance should be, if desirable, through an entity wholly owned by the government

Money market funds
- The US Treasury proposes strong conditions for reduction of withdrawal risks by money market funds (US Treasury 2009RRProposal, 2009Frame; Geithner 2009Mar25, 2009Mar26)

---

crisis. The ad hoc measures have become regulatory proposals. There were no observable problems originating in hedge funds and private equity in the credit/dollar crisis but tight regulation is proposed.

Summary

The analysis of the New Deal with growth theory creates concern on the possible combination of increases in minimum wages with proposed laws to broaden union membership. The monetary and fiscal stimulus exceeds by far any conceived during the Great Depression, raising major doubts on the theory and policy. The decline in output forecast by the IMF for the United States is -2.8 percent compared with a cumulative decline of 25.7 percent during 1930–3. Systemic regulation is addressed by the function of LOLR. The Fed has used every LOLR tool that was known and almost every other that could be imagined. In fact, the regulatory agenda appears to pursue the facilities that the Fed and Treasury created ad hoc as new problems surfaced. There is no theory and discernible effects of recovery from the credit/dollar crisis from the tools used by the Fed/Treasury. There is an articulate explanation of the origin of the credit/dollar crisis in the reduction of interest rates to nearly zero during 2003–4 combined with the housing subsidy and the lax credit standards of Fannie Mae and Freddie Mac. The regulatory agenda requires solid foundations in the experience with the credit/dollar crisis and a balanced approach of private and public roles.

Conclusion

There are two main views on the origin of the credit/dollar crisis and the new measures for regulatory reform. The first view is based on the public interest or official regulatory view proposing tight regulation to avoid financial instability and resulting loss of output and employment. The second view is based on the finance view or FSF approach (Black 1993; Black, Miller, and Posner 1978; Levine 2002; Merton and Bodie 1995, 2005). These two approaches are discussed in turn.

First, the official regulatory view argues that banks used financial innovation to arbitrage regulatory capital. The SIVs were off-balance sheet to avoid regulatory capital charges. The system of "originate to distribute" created incentives to lax standards in documentation and verification of mortgages because the originating party did not bear the risks of default. Mortgages were bundled in securities sold to ultimate investors but banks retained part of the risk to improve their earnings with not only high-return but also high-risk assets. Risk-management measurement, analysis and control lagged innovations in structured products. Banks and other financial institutions engaged in imprudent risk-taking by financing excessive volumes of assets in short-term SRPs without consideration of liquidity risk. The careless credit decisions at origination magnified through securitization to investors with imprudent leverage in complex CDOs, which were impossible to MTM. The uncertainty of the default risk of underlying mortgages in structured products increased the perception of counterparty credit risk. The financing of most financial assets paralyzed because of fear of losses of principal if the financed counterparty did not repurchase the financed security. Higher margins and haircuts in counterparty transactions reduced capital of financial institutions, causing fire sales in a collective movement of reducing leverage. The credit/dollar crisis was characterized by large, complex, and systemically important institutions with cross-border effects. The core of regulatory proposals consists of the creation of a systemic regulator with the powers to intervene in systemically important institutions. There are subsidiary proposals to tighten capital for trading and controls on leverage and liquidity exposures. The regulatory reform would be incomplete without tighter standards for credit contracts. Limits and regulation of executive compensation are contemplated to prevent excessive risks on short-term transactions.

The alternative approach claims that the credit/dollar crisis was caused by government intervention (Calomiris 2008, 2009Feb; Taylor 2008Nov). The critical policy impulse was the reduction of the fed funds rate to 1 percent during 2003–4 with the expressed intention that it would be maintained at that level or lower until required to prevent deflation (Peláez and Peláez 2005, 18–28, 2007, 83–95, 221–5, 2008a,b,c). The interest-rate subsidy by the central banks processed through the gigantic housing subsidy of the United States, amounting to $221 billion per year. The housing GSE, Fannie Mae and Freddie Mac, guaranteed or acquired $1.6 trillion of nonprime mortgages. The crucial entry of Fannie Mae and Freddie Mac in the nonprime market, staying until the peak in 2006, provided an implicit seal of approval by the full faith and credit of the US government. The discipline of calculating risks and rewards was eroded not only for financial institutions but also for the public. The low interest rate maintained by the Fed and the approval of the government through Fannie and Freddie created the impression that housing prices would increase forever. The only perceived risk to the mortgagor was to live in a better house for some time and then sell it for a higher price to pay the mortgage. The lender believed that the only risk was to sell the house in foreclosure to recover at least the principal and owed interest. An affordable house is a subsidized house in the presence of perennial scarcity of resources relative to unlimited wants by economic agents. Eventually, the Fed raised interest rates from 1 percent to 5.25 percent, almost as rapidly. The increase in interest rates triggered the nonprime crisis as the reset of adjustable rate mortgages and the end of teaser rates with no principal increased monthly mortgage payments beyond what the debtor could pay. The innovation in securitization had worked throughout decades and the problems were exacerbated in mortgages because of the housing subsidy and the unsound credit decisions of Fannie and Freddie.

The finance view or FSF does not propose entirely unregulated markets. The proposal is rather for balanced regulation that allows for innovation of financial products, risk management (Finger 2009Apr), and the efficient functions of banks and financial institutions. Economic prosperity has been created in economies with some market allocation by taking entrepreneurial decisions that require successful ex ante calculation of risk and returns. Regulation preventing or limiting entrepreneurial initiative can be as damaging as restrictions on health care innovation that have increased our life expectancy and participation in the labor force. Regulation needs sound weights for prosperity and stability. Excessive regulation and restrictions of financial innovation can limit future economic growth and employment.

Notes

1 The Theory of Regulation and Finance

1. Influential research has focused on finding the theoretical and empirical relationship of legal origin, financial development and economic growth. There have been also major research efforts in analyzing the principal/agent problem and the protection of minority shareholders. Some references in vast literature include: Djankov et al. (2002), Glaeser et al. (2001), Johnson et al. (2000), Kroszner (1999), La Porta et al. (1997, 1998, 1999, 2002a,b, 2003, 2006), Maurer and Haber (2007) and Shleifer and Vishny (1993).

2 Functions and Regulation of Deposit Banks

1. For the S&Ls see Brumbaugh and Carron (1987), Brumbaugh, Carron and Litan (1989), Brumbaugh and Litan (1991), DeGennaro Lang and Thomson (1993), Gupta and Misra (1999), Jackson (1993), Kroszner and Strahan (1996), Mester (1987) and Pantalone and Platt (1987). For the political economy of deregulation see Calomiris (1990, 2002), Economides, Hubbard and Palia (1996), Kroszner and Strahan (1999, 2001) and Laeven (2004).

3 Deposit Bank Market Power and Central Banking

1. Some representative works in the multiple sides of this debate include Alhadeff (1951), Alhadeff and Alhadeff (1976), Gilbert (1984), Heggestad (1977), Heggestad and Mingo (1976), Heggestad and Rhoades (1976), Peltzman (1968, 1984), Rhoades and Yeats (1974), Rhoades and Rutz (1981), Rose and Fraser (1976) and Smirlock (1985).

2. The proof of the first proposition is implicit in option pricing theory. Consider the expression of the put-call parity theorem (Miller 1988, 110):

$$S = C(K) + Ke^{-rt} - P(K)$$

The current price of the stock is S, $C(K)$ and $P(K)$ are the call and put prices at the same exercise price K, r is the riskless interest rate, t is time and exercise occurs at time T. There is an analysis of the capital structure in the option pricing contributions of Black and Scholes (1973) and Merton (1974). Default at time T occurs when the value of the assets, $A(T)$, is below the value of the firm's debt, D, or $A(T) \leq D$. The market value of the firm's assets follows a log-normal diffusion process (Duffie and Singleton 2003). Thus, the firm's equity is a call option on the total assets, A, with strike value at the firm's debt, D. The Black-Scholes formula can be used to obtain the value of the firm's debt by deducting the option price from the initial asset value. The value of the firm's debt without risk is Ke^{-rt}. If at maturity S were to be lower than K, the shareholders put the firm back to its creditors by appeal to limited liability. Thus, the present value of the debt less the put value of the shareholders, $Ke^{-rt} - P(K)$, is the actual market value of the debt. While the values of the equity and debt of the firm depend on the firm's leverage, the put-call parity theorem shows that their sum is independent of leverage. Miller (1988, 109) states that the option pricing results show new aspects of the Modigliani and Miller propositions that "is hardly surprising since [Modigliani and Miller] type arbitrage arguments were explicitly invoked by Black and Scholes in deriving their option valuation formula."

5   Securities Regulation

1. References on free cash flows include Halpern et al. (1999) and Hendershott (1996).
2. References on insider trading include Huddart et al. 2001, Kyle 1985 and Wilson 1978.
3. References on IPOs in vast literature include Aggarwal (2000), Aggarwal and Conroy (2000), Aggarwal et al. 2000, Aharony, Lee and Wong 2000, Arugaslan et al. 2004, Arugaslan et al. 2004, Benveniste and Busaba 1997, Bhuyan and Williams 2006, Benzoni and Schenone 2007, Berger and Hannan 1998, Bhuyan and Williams 2006, Biais et al. 2002, Bradley 2003, Bruner et al. 2004, Cai et al. 2004, Chemmanur and Fulghieri 1999, Chen and Ritter 2000, Cliff and Denis 2004, Cornelli and Goldreich 2003, Crutchley et al. 2002, Denis 1992, Derrien and Womack 2003, Gompers and Lerner 2003, Beatty and Welch 1996, Gale and Stiglitz 1989, Hertzel et al. 2002, Jenkinson and Jones 2004, Karolyi 1998, 2003, 2004, 2006, Krigman et al. 1999, Kutsuna and Smith 2004, Loughran and Ritter 2004, Michaely and Shaw 1994, Rajan and Servaes 1997, Ritter 1991, Ritter and Welch 2002, Subrahmanyam and Titman 1999, Teoh et al. 1998, Torstila 2003, Ljungqvist et al. 2003, Ljungqvist and Wilhem 2003 and Willenborg 1999.
4. More references in the vast literature on listing are Ammer et al. 2004, Bae, Stulz and Tan 2008, Bailey et al. 2006, Domowitz et al. 1998, Errunza and Miller 2000, Eun and Sabherwal 2003, Foucalt and Parlour 2004, Ljungqvist et al. 2003, Hail and Leuz 2006, Halling et al. 2007, Doidge et al. 2004, 2007, 2009, Foerster and Karyolyi 1993, 1999, 2000, Kryzanowski and Zhang 2002, Levine and Schmukler 2005, Li 2007, MacNeill and Lau 2001, Moulton and Wei 2005, Reese and Weisbach 2002, Saudagaran 1988, Saudagaran and Biddle 1995, Sundaram and Logue 1996 and, Werner and Kleidon 1996.

6   The Credit/Dollar Crisis and Recession Regulation

1. See Bernanke (2009Apr3, 2009Feb10); Fettig 2008; FOMC 2009Jan; FRBNY 2008Mar24, 2008Nov10, 2009Sep19, 2009Feb6; FRBO 2007Dec12, 2008Sep18, 2008Sep24 2008Oct28, 2008Oct29, 2008Nov10, 2008Nov23, 2008Dec12, 2009Jan16; FSOB (2009Jan).

References

Abrams, Burton A. and Russell F. Settle. 1992. What can regulators regulate? The case of bank entry. *Journal of Money, Credit and Banking* 24 (4, Nov): 511–8.

Aggarwal, Reena. 2000. Stabilization activities by underwriters after initial public offerings. *Journal of Finance* 55 (3, Jun): 1075–103.

Aggarwal, Reena, Isil Erel, René Stulz and Rohan Williamson. 2007. Differences in governance practices between US and foreign firms: measurement, causes and consequences. Columbus, OH: Dice Center WP 2007–14, Dec.

Aggarwal, Reena, Nagpurnanand R. Prabhala and Manju Puri. 2002. Institutional allocation in initial public offerings: empirical evidence. *Journal of Finance* 57 (3, Jun): 1421–42.

Aggarwal, Reena and Pat Conroy. 2000. Price discovery in initial public offerings and the role of the lead underwriter. *Journal of Finance* 55 (6, Dec): 2903–22.

Aharony, Joseph, Chi-Wen Jevons Lee and T. J. Wong. 2000. Financial packaging of IPO firms in China. *Journal of Accounting Research* 38 (1, Spring): 103–26.

Akerlof, George A. 1970. The market for "lemons": quality uncertainty and the market mechanism. *Quarterly Journal of Economics* 84 (3): 488–500.

Akerlof, George A. 2002. Behavior macroeconomics and macroeconomic behavior. *American Economic Review* 92 (3): 411–33.

Akerlof, George A. 2003. Writing "The Market for Lemons": a personal and interpretive essay. Berkeley, University of California, Nov 14.

Alhadeff, David A. 1951. The market structure of commercial banking in the United States. *Quarterly Journal of Economics* 65 (1, Feb): 62–86.

Alhadeff, David A. and Charlotee P. Alhadeff. 1976. Growth and survival of new banks, 1948–70. *Journal of Money, Credit and Banking* 8 (2, May): 199–208.

Allen, William R. 1993. Irving Fisher and the 100 percent reserve proposal. *Journal of Law and Economics* 36 (2, Oct): 703–17.

Almeida, Heitor, Murillo Campello and Crocker Liu. 2006. The financial accelerator: evidence from international housing markets. *Review of Finance* 10 (3, Sep): 321–52.

Ammer, John, Sara B. Holland, David C. Smith and Francis E. Warnock. 2004. Look at me now: the role of cross-listing in attracting US investors. Washington, DC, FRBO, Aug.

An, Xudong, Raphael W. Bostic, Yongheng Deng and Stuart A. Gabriel. 2007. GSE loan purchases, the FHA, and housing outcomes in targeted, low-income neighborhoods. *Brookings-Wharton Papers on Urban Affairs* 205–56.

Anand, Bharat N. and Alexander Galetovic. 2000. Information, nonexcludability and financial market structure. *Journal of Business* 73 (3, Jul): 357–402.

Andrade, Gregor, Mark Mitchell and Erik Stafford. 2001. New evidence and perspectives on mergers. *Journal of Economic Perspectives* 15 (2, Spring): 103–20.

Ambrose, Brent W. and Drew B. Winters. 1992. Does an industry effect exist for leveraged buyouts? *Financial Management* 21 (1, Spring): 89–101.

Arrow, Kenneth J. 1951. An extension of the basic theorems of classical welfare economics. In *Proceedings of the Second Berkeley Symposium on Mathematical*

Statistics and Probability. Berkeley: University of California Press, reprinted as Cowles Foundation Paper 54.

Arrow, Kenneth J. and Gerard Debreu. 1954. Existence of an equilibrium for a competitive economy. *Econometrica* 22 (3): 265–90.

Arugaslan, Onur, Douglas O. Cook and Robert Kieschnick. 2004. Monitoring as a motivation for IPO underpricing. *Journal of Finance* 59 (5, Oct): 2403–20.

Arzac, Enrique. 1992. On the capital structure of leveraged buyouts. *Financial Management* 21 (1, Spring): 16–26.

Asso, Pier Francesco, George A. Kahn and Robert Leeson. 2007. The Taylor rule and the transformation of monetary policy. Kansas City, Federal Reserve Bank of Kansas City, RWP 07–11, Dec.

Atkeson, Andrew and Patrick J. Kehoe. 2004. Deflation and depression: is there an empirical link. *American Economic Review* 94 (2, May): 99–103.

Bae, Kee-Hong, René M. Stulz and Hongping Tan. 2008. Do local analysts know more? A cross country study of the performance of local analysts and foreign analysts. *Journal of Financial Economics* 88 (3, Jun): 581–606.

Bailey, Elizabeth E. 1999. A regulatory framework for the 21st century. *Eastern Economic Journal* 25 (3): 253–63.

Bailey, Warren, G., Andrew Karolyi and Carolina Salva. 2006. The economic consequences of increased disclosure: evidence from international cross-listing. *Journal of Financial Economics* 81 (1): 175–213.

Bainbridge, Stephen M. 2000. Insider trading. In Boudewijn Bouckaert and Gerrit Gees, eds. *Encyclopedia of law and economics*, Volume III. Cheltenham, UK: Edward Elgar.

Baker, George P., Michael C. Jensen and Kevin J. Murphy. 1988. Compensation and incentives. *Journal of Finance* 43 (3, Jul): 593–616.

Banerjee, Ajeyo and E. Woodrow Eckard. 2001. Why regulate insider trading? Evidence from the first great merger wave (1897–1903). *American Economic Review* 91 (5, Dec): 1329–49.

Barclay, Michael and Clifford Holderness. 1989. Private benefits of control of public corporations. *Journal of Financial Economics* 25 (3): 371–95.

Barth, James R., Gerard Caprio, Jr. and Ross Levine. 2006. *Rethinking bank regulation*. Cambridge: Cambridge University Press.

Barth, James R., Dan Brumbaugh, Jr. and James A. Wilcox. 2000. The repeal of Glass-Steagall and the advent of broad banking. *Journal of Economic Perspectives* 14 (2, Spring): 191–204.

Bates, Thomas W., David A. Becher and Michael L. Lemmon. 2008. Board classification and managerial entrenchment: evidence from the market for corporate control. *Journal of Financial Economics* 87 (3): 656–77.

Bator, Francis M. 1958. The anatomy of market failure. *Quarterly Journal of Economics* 72 (3): 351–79.

Baumol, William J., John C. Panzar and Robert D. Willig. 1982. *Contestable markets and the theory of industry structure*. New York: Harcourt, Brace, Jovonovich.

Baumol, William J. and Robert D. Willig. 1986. Contestability: developments since the book. *Oxford Economic Papers* 38: 9–36.

Baumol, William J. and Kyu Sik Lee. 1991. Contestable markets, trade and development. *World Bank Research Observer* 6 (1): 1–17.

BCBS. 2004. Basel II: international convergence of capital measurement and capital standards: a revised framework. Basel: BCBS Publications No. 107, BIS, Jun.

BCBS. 2005. An explanatory note on the Basel II IRB risk weight functions. Basel, BIS, Jul.

BCBS. 2008Sep. Principles for sound liquidity risk management and supervision. Basel, BIS, Sep.

BCBS. 2009Jan. Proposed enhancements to the Basel II framework. Basel, BIS, Jan.

BCBS. 2009Econ. Range of practices and issues in economic capital frameworks. Basel, BIS, Mar.

BCBS. 2009Ins. Consultative document for core principles for effective deposit insurance systems. Basel, BIS, Mar.

Bean, Charles. 2003. Inflation targeting: the UK experience. *Bank of England Quarterly Bulletin* 43 (4, Winter): 479–94.

Beatty, Randolph P. and Ivo Welch. 1996. Issuer expenses and legal liability in initial public offerings. *Journal of Law and Economics* 39 (2, Oct): 545–602.

Bebchuk, Lucian Arye. 2007. Testimony to the House Committee on Financial Services. Washington DC, US House of Representatives, Mar 8.

Bebchuk, Lucian Arye and Alma Cohen. 2005. The costs of entrenched boards. *Journal of Financial Economics* 78 (22): 409–33.

Bebchuk, Lucian Arye and Jesse M. Fried. 2003. Executive compensation as an agency problem. *Journal of Economic Perspectives* 17 (3, Summer): 71–92.

Bebchuk, Lucian Arye and Jesse M. Fried. 2004. *Pay without performance: the unfulfilled promise of executive compensation.* Cambridge, MA: Harvard University Press.

Bebchuk, Lucian Arye and Yaniv Grinstein. 2005. The growth of executive pay. *Oxford Review of Economic Policy* 21 (2): 283–303.

Bebchuk, Lucian Arye, Jesse M. Fried and David I. Walker. 2002. Managerial power and rent extraction in the design of executive compensation. *University of Chicago Law Review* 69 (3, Summer): 751–846.

Bebchuk, Lucian Arye, John C. Coates IV and Guhan Subramanian. 2002a. The powerful antitakeover force of staggered boards: theory, evidence and policy. *Stanford Law Review* 54 (5, May): 887–951.

Bebchuk, Lucian Arye, John C. Coates IV and Guhan Subramanian. 2002b. The powerful antitakeover force of staggered boards: further findings and a reply to symposium participants. *Stanford Law Review* 55 (3, Dec): 885–917.

Beck, Thorsten, Asli Demirgüç-Kunt and Ross Levine. 2003. Bank concentration and crises. Washington, DC, World Bank Working Paper.

Beck, Thorsten, Asli Demirgüç-Kunt and Vojislav Maksimovic. 2004. Bank competition and access to finance: international evidence. *Journal of Money, Credit and Banking* 36 (3, Jun): 627–48.

Beck, Thorsten, Ross Levine and Norman Loayza. 2000. Finance and the sources of growth. *Journal of Financial Economics* 58 (1–2): 261–300.

Becker, Gary S. 1983. A theory of competition among pressure groups for political influence. *Quarterly Journal of Economics* 98 (3, Aug): 371–400.

Becsi, Zsolt and Ping Wang. 1997. Financial development and growth. *Economic Review – Federal Reserve Bank of Atlanta* 82 (4): 46–62.

Bencivenga, Valerie R., Bruce D. Smith and Ross M. Starr. 1995. Transaction costs, technological choice and endogenous growth. *Journal of Economic Theory* 67 (1): 53–177.

Benmelech, Efraim and Jennifer Dlugosz. 2008. The alchemy of CDO credit ratings. Cambridge, MA, Unpublished paper for the Carnegie-Rochester conference series.

Benmelech, Efraim, Jennifer Dlugosz and Victoria Ivashina. 2009. What lies beneath: an inside look at corporate CLOs collateral. Cambridge, MA, Harvard Business School, Jan.

Benston, George J. 1990. *The separation of commercial and investment banking: the Glass-Steagall Act revisited and reconsidered.* New York: Oxford University Press.

Benston, George J. 1994. Universal banking. *Journal of Economic Perspectives* 8 (3, Summer): 121–43.

Benston, George J. and George G. Kaufman. 1996. The appropriate role of bank regulation. *Economic Journal* 106 (436, May): 688–97.

Benston, George J. and George G. Kaufman. 1997. The FDICA after five years. *Journal of Economic Perspectives* 11 (3, Summer, 1997): 139–58.

Benston, George, Paul Irvine, Jim Rosenfeld and Joseph F. Sinkey, Jr. 2003. Bank capital structure, regulatory capital and securities innovation. *Journal of Money, Credit and Banking* 35 (3, Jun): 301–32.

Benveniste, Lawrence M. and Walid Y. Busaba. 1997. Bookbuilding vs. fixed price: an analysis of competing strategies for marketing IPOs. *Journal of Financial and Quantitative Analysis* 32 (4, Dec): 383–403.

Benzoni, Luca and Carola Schenone. 2007. *Conflict of interest and certification in the U.S. IPO market.* Chicago, Federal Reserve bank of Chicago, Jul.

Beny, Laura Nyantung. 2007. Insider trading laws and stock markets around the world: an empirical contribution to the theoretical law and economics debate. *Journal of Corporation Law* 32 (2, Winter): 237–300.

Beny, Lary Nyantung. 2006. Testimony on unlawful insider trading. Washington, DC, Senate Judiciary Committee, US Senate, Sep 26.

Berger, Allen N. 1995. The relationship between capital and earnings in banking. *Journal of Money, Credit and Banking* 27 (2, May): 432–56.

Berger, Allen N. 2003. The economic effects of technological progress: evidence from the banking industry. *Journal of Money, Credit and Banking* 35 (2, Apr): 141–76.

Berger, Allen N, Anil K. Kashyap and Joseph M. Scalise. 1995. The transformation of the US banking industry. *Brookings Papers on Economic Activity* (1995, 2): 55–218.

Berger, Allen N. and Loretta J. Mester. 1997. Inside the black box: what explains differences in the efficiencies of financial institutions? *Journal of Banking and Finance* 21 (7, Jul): 895–947.

Berger, Allen N. and Loretta J. Mester. 2003. Explaining the dramatic changes in the performance of US banks: technological change, deregulation and dynamic changes in competition. *Journal of Financial Intermediation* 12 (1): 57–95.

Berger, Allen N. and Timothy H. Hannan. 1998. The efficiency cost of market power in the banking industry: a test of the "quiet life" and related hypotheses. *Review of Economics and Statistics* 80 (3, Aug): 454–65.

Berger, Allen N., Asli Demirgüç-Kunt, Ross Levine and Joseph H. Haubrich. 2004a. Bank concentration and competition: an evolution in the making. *Journal of Money, Credit and Banking* 36 (3, Jun): 433–51.

Berger, Allen N., Seth D. Bonime, Lawrence G. Goldberg and Lawrence J. White. 2004b. The dynamics of market entry: the effects of mergers and acquisitions on entry in the banking industry. *Journal of Business* 77 (4): 797–834.

Berger, Allen N. and Astrid A. Dick. 2007. Entry into banking markets and the early-mover advantage. *Journal of Money, Credit and Banking* 39 (4, Jun): 775–807.

Bergson (Burk), Abram. 1938. A reformulation of certain aspects of welfare economics. *Quarterly Journal of Economics* 52 (2): 310–34.

Berle, Adolf and Gardiner Means. 1932. *The modern corporation and private property.* New York: Palgrave Macmillan.

Bernanke, Ben S. 1983a. Irreversibility, uncertainty and cyclical investment. *Quarterly Journal of Economics* 98 (1): 85–106.

Bernanke, Ben S. 1983b. Nonmonetary effects of the financial crisis in propagation of the Great Depression. *American Economic Review* 73 (3, Jun): 257–76.

Bernanke, Ben S. 2000. A crash course for central bankers. *Foreign Policy* 120 (Sep/Oct): 49.

Bernanke, Ben S. 2002. Deflation – making sure "it" doesn't happen here. Washington, DC, Speech before the National Economists Club, Nov 21.

Bernanke, Ben S. 2003. A perspective on inflation targeting. *Business Economics* 38 (3, Jul): 7–15.

Bernanke, Ben S. 2005. The global savings glut and the US current account deficit. Washington, DC, Board of Governors of the Federal Reserve Bank, Apr 14.

Bernanke, Ben S. 2007. Bank supervision in the United States. *Vital Speeches of the Day* 73 (2): 61–5.

Bernanke, Ben S. 2009Jan13. The crisis and the policy response. London, Stamp Lecture, London School of Economics, Jan 13. http://www.federalreserve.gov/newsevents/speech/bernanke20090113a.htm

Bernanke, Ben S. 2009Feb10. Federal Reserve programs to strengthen credit markets and the economy. Washington, DC, Testimony before the Committee on Financial Services, US House of Representatives, Feb 10. http://www.federalreserve.gov/newsevents/testimony/bernanke20090210a.htm

Bernanke, Ben S. 2009Feb24. Semiannual monetary policy report to the Congress. Washington, DC, Committee on Banking, Housing and Urban Affairs, US Senate, Feb 24.

Bernanke, Ben S. 2009Mar3. Current economic and financial conditions and the federal budget. Washington, DC, Committee on the Budget, US Senate, Mar 3.

Bernanke, Ben S. 2009Apr3. The Federal Reserve's balance sheet. Charlotte, NC, Federal Reserve Bank of Richmond Symposium, Apr 3, 2009.

Bernanke, Ben S. and Kevin Carey. 1996. Nominal wage stickiness and aggregate supply in the Great Depression. *Quarterly Journal of Economics* 111 (3, Aug): 853–83.

Bernanke, Ben S. and Cara S. Lown. 1991. The credit crunch. *Brookings Papers on Economic Activity* 2: 205–47.

Bernanke, Ben S. and Frederic Mishkin. 1992. Central bank behavior and the strategy of monetary policy: observations from six industrialized countries. *NBER Macroeconomics Annual* 7: 183–228.

Bernanke, Ben S. and Mark Gertler. 1995. Inside the black box: the credit channel of monetary policy transmission. *Journal of Economic Perspectives* 9 (4, Fall): 27–48.

Bernanke, Ben S. and Frederic S. Mishkin. 1997. Inflation targeting: a new framework for monetary policy? *Journal of Economic Perspectives* 11 (2, Spring): 97–116.

Bernanke, Ben S., Mark Gertler and Simon Gilchrist. 1999. The financial accelerator in a quantitative business cycle framework. In John B. Taylor and Michael Woodford, eds. *Handbook of macroeconomics, Volume 1C*. Amsterdam: Elsevier North Holland.

Bernanke, Ben S. and Vincent R. Reinhart. 2004AER. Conducting monetary policy at very low short-term interest rates. *American Economic Review* 92 (2, May): 85–90.

Bernanke, Ben S., Vincent R. Reinhart and Brian P. Sack. 2004BPEA. Monetary policy alternatives at the zero bound: an empirical assessment. *Brookings Papers on Economic Activity* 2 : 1–100.

Bhagat, Sanjai, Andrei Shleifer and Robert W. Vishny. 1990. Hostile takeovers in the 1980s: the return to corporate specialization. *Brookings Papers on Economics Activity* 1: 1–84.

Bhagwati, Jagdish N. 1982. Directly unproductive, profit-seeking (DUP) activities. *Journal of Political Economy* 90 (5): 998–1002.

Bhattacharya, Uuptal and Hazem Daouk. 2002. The world price of insider trading. *Journal of Finance* 57 (1, Feb): 75–108.

Bhuyan, Rafiqul and David L. Williams. 2006. Operating performance of the U.S. commercial banks after IPOs: an empirical investigation. *Journal of Commercial Banking and Finance* 5 (1/2): 69–95.

Biais, Bruno, Peter Bossaerts and Jean-Charles Rochet. 2002. An optimal IPO mechanism. *Review of Economic Studies* 69 (1, Jan): 117–46.

BIS. 2009Sep1. Addressing financial system procyclicality: a possible framework. Basel, BIS, Sep 1.

Black, Fischer. 1993. US commercial banking: trends, cycles and policy: comment. *NBER Macroeconomics Annual* 8: 368–71.

Black, Fischer and Myron Scholes. 1973. The pricing of options and corporate liabilities. *Journal of Political Economy* 81 (May/June): 637–54.

Black, Fischer, Merton H. Miller and Richard A. Posner. 1978. An approach to the regulation of bank holding companies. *Journal of Business* 51 (3, Jul): 379–412.

Black, Sandra E. and Philip E. Strahan. 2002. Entrepreneurship and bank credit availability. *Journal of Finance* 57 (6, Dec): 2807–33.

Blaug, Mark. 2007. The fundamental theorems of modern welfare economics, historically contemplated. *History of Political Economy* 32 (2): 186–207.

Bó, Ernesto Dal. 2006. Regulatory capture: a review. *Oxford Review of Economic Policy* 22 (2): 203–25.

Boadway, Robin. 2006. Principles of cost-benefit analysis. *Public Policy Review* 2 (1): 1–43.

Bolton, Patrick and David S. Scharfstein. 1998. Corporate finance, the theory of the firm and organization. *Journal of Economic Perspectives* 12 (4, Autumn): 95–114.

Boot, Arnoud W. A. 2000. Relationship banking: what do we know? *Journal of Financial Intermediation* 9: 7–25.

Boot, Arnoud W. and Anjan V. Thakor. 1993. Self-interested bank regulation. *American Economic Review* 83 (2, May): 206–12.

Bordo, Michael D. 2003. "The Great Depression and the Friedman-Schwartz hypothesis" by Lawrence Christiano, Roberto Motto and Massimo Rostagno. *Journal of Money, Credit and Banking* 35 (6, Dec): 1199–203.

Bordo, Michael D., Ehsan Choudhri and Anna J. Schwartz. 1995. Could stable money have averted the Great Contraction. *Economic Inquiry* 33 (3, Jul): 484–505.

Bordo, Michael D., Christopher J. Erceg and Charles L. Evans. 2000. *American Economic Review* 90 (5, Dec): 1447–63.

Boyd, John, Gianni De Nicoló and Bruce Smith. 2004. Crises in competitive versus monopolistic banking systems. *Journal of Money, Credit and Banking* 36 (3): 487–506.

Bradley, Daniel J., Bradford D. Jordan and Jay R. Ritter. 2003. The quiet period goes out with a bang. *Journal of Finance* 58 (1, Feb): 1–36.

Brumbaugh, Jr., R. Dan and Andrew S. Carron. 1987. Thrift industry crisis: causes and solutions. *Brookings Papers on Economic Activity* 1 (2): 349–88.

Brumbaugh, Jr., R. Dan, Andrew S. Carron and Robert E. Litan. 1989. Cleaning up the depository institutions mess. *Brookings Papers on Economic Activity* 1: 243–95.

Brumbaugh, Jr., R. Dan and Robert E. Litan. 1991. Ignoring economics in dealing with the savings and loan and commercial banking crisis. *Contemporary Policy Issues* 9 (1, Jan): 36–53.

Bruner, Robert, Susan Chaplinsky and Latha Ramchand. 2004. US-bound IPOs: issue costs and selective entry. *Financial Management* 33 (3, Autumn): 39–60.

Brunnermeier, Markus K. 2009. Deciphering the liquidity and credit crunch 2007–2008. *Journal of Economic Perspectives* 23 (1, Winter): 77–100.

Brunnermeier, Markus K. and Lasse Heje Pedersen. 2009. Market liquidity and funding liquidity. *Review of Financial Studies,* 22 (6): 2201–38.

Burns, Arthur F. 1958. *Prosperity without inflation.* New York: Fordham University Press.

Cai, Nianyun, Latha Ramchand and Arthur Warga. 2004. The pricing of equity IPOs that follow public debt offerings. *Financial Management* 33 (4, Winter): 5–26.

Calomiris, Charles W. 1990. Is deposit insurance necessary? A historical perspective. *Journal of Economic History* 50 (2, Jun): 283–95.

Calomiris, Charles W. 1993. Financial factors in the Great Depression. *Journal of Economic Perspectives* 7 (2, Spring): 61–85.

Calomiris, Charles W. 2002. Banking approaches the modern era. *Regulation* 25 (2, Summer): 14–20.

Calomiris, Charles W. 2008. The subprime turmoil: what's old, what's new and what's next. New York, Columbia University, Oct 2.

Calomiris, Charles W. 2009Feb. Financial innovation, regulation and reform. New York, Columbia University, Feb.

Calomiris, Charles W. and Gorton, Gary B. 1991. The origins of banking panics: models, facts and bank regulation. In R. Glenn Hubbard, ed. *Financial markets and financial crises.* Chicago: University of Chicago Press.

Calomiris, Charles W. and Joseph R. Mason. 2003. Consequences of bank distress during the Great Depression. *American Economic Review* 93 (3, Jun): 937–47.

Calvo, Guillermo. 1978. On the time consistency of optimal policy in a monetary economy. *Econometrica* 46 (6, Nov): 1411–28.

Cameron, Rondo. 1961. *France and the economic development of Europe, 1800–1914: conquests of peace and seeds of war.* Princeton: Princeton University Press.

Cameron, Rondo. 1967. *Banking in the early stages of industrialization*. Oxford: Oxford University Press.

Cameron, Rondo. 1972. *Banking and economic development*. Oxford: Oxford University Press.

Cameron, Rondo, V. I. Bovykin and Richard Sylla eds. 1992. *International banking 1870–1914*. Oxford: Oxford University Press.

Carney, William J. 2006. The costs of being public after Sarbanes-Oxley: the irony of going private. *Emory Law Journal* 55 (1): 141–60.

Carlton, Dennis W. and Daniel R. Fischel. 1983. The regulation of insider trading. *Stanford Law Review* 35 (5, May): 857–99.

CBO. 2009Jan. The budget and economic outlook: fiscal years 2009 to 2019. Washington, DC: CBO, Jan.

Cetorelli, Nicola and Philip E. Strahan. 2003. Finance as a barrier to entry: bank competition and industry structure in local US markets. Chicago, FRBC, WP.

Chandler, Jr., Alfred D. 1962. *Strategy and structure*. Cambridge, MA: MIT Press.

Chari, Varadarajan V. 1998. Nobel Laureate Robert E. Lucas, Jr.: architect of modern macroeconomics. *Journal of Economic Perspectives* 12 (1, Winter): 171–86.

Chemmanur, Thomas J. and Paolo Fulghieri. 1999. A theory of the going-public decision. *Review of Financial Studies* 12 (2, Summer): 249–79.

Chen, Hsuan-Chi and Jay R. Ritter. 2000. The seven percent solution. *Journal of Finance* 55 (3, Jun): 1105–31.

Cheung, Steven S. 1973. The fable of the bees: an economic investigation. *Journal of Law and Economics* 16: 11–33.

Choudhri, Ehsan U. and Levis A. Kochin. 1980. The exchange rate and the international transmission of business cycle disturbances: some evidence from the Great Depression. *Journal of Money, Credit and Banking* 12 (4, Nov): 565–74.

Christiano, Lawrence, Roberto Motto and Massimo Rostagno. 2003. The Great Depression and the Friedman-Schwartz hypothesis. *Journal of Money, Credit and Banking* 35 (6, Dec): 119–97.

Claessens, Stijn and Luc Laeven. 2004. What drives bank competition? Some international evidence. *Journal of Money, Credit and Banking* 36 (2, Jun): 563–83.

Clarida, Richard, Jordi Galí and Mark Gertler. 2001. The science of monetary policy: a new Keynesian perspective. *Journal of Economic Literature* 37 (4, Dec): 1661–707.

Cliff, Michael T. and David J. Denis. 2004. Do initial public offering firms purchase analyst coverage with underpricing? *Journal of Finance* 59 (6, Dec): 2871–901.

Coase, Ronald H. 1937. The nature of the firm. *Economica* 4 (16, Nov): 386–405.

Coase, Ronald H. 1960. The problem of social cost. *Journal of Law and Economics* 3 (1): 1–44.

Coase, Ronald H. 1998. The new institutional economics. *American Economic Review* 88 (2): 72–4.

Coates IV, John C. 2000. Takeover defenses in the shadow of the pill: a critique of the scientific evidence. *Texas Law Review* 79 (2, Dec): 271–382.

Coates IV, John C. 2007. The goals and promise of the Sarbanes-Oxley Act. *Journal of Economic Perspectives* 21 (1, Winter): 91–116.

Coffee, Jr., John C. 1999. Privatization and corporate governance: the lessons from securities market failure. *Journal of Corporation Law* 25 (1, Fall): 1–39.

Coffee, Jr., John C. 2002. Racing toward the top? The impact of cross-listings and stock market competition on international corporate governance. *Columbia Law Review* 102 (7): 1757–831.

Coffee Jr., John C. 2006. *Gatekeepers: the professions and corporate governance.* Oxford: Oxford University Press.

Cole, Harold L. and Lee E. Ohanian. 1999. The Great Depression in the United States from a neoclassical perspective. *Federal Reserve Bank of Minneapolis Quarterly Review* 23 (1, Winter): 2–24.

Cole, Harold L. and Lee E. Ohanian. 2000. Re-examining the contributions of money and banking shocks to the US Great Depression. *NBER Macroeconomics Annual* 15: 183–227.

Cole, Harold L. and Lee E. Ohanian. 2001. New deal policies and the persistence of the Great Depression: a general equilibrium analysis. Minneapolis, Federal Reserve Bank of Minneapolis, WP 957, May.

Cole, Margaret. 2007. The UK FSA: nobody does it better? *Fordham Journal of Corporate and Financial Law* 12 (2): 259–83.

Cooper, Russell and Thomas W. Ross. 2002. Bank runs: deposit insurance and capital requirements. *International Economic Review* 43 (1, Feb): 55–72.

COP. 2009Feb6. February oversight report. Washington, DC, US Congress. http://cop.senate.gov/documents/cop-020609-report.pdf

Cornelli, Francesca and David Goldreich. 2003. Bookbuilding: how informative is the order book. *Journal of Finance* 58 (4, Aug): 1415–43.

Cox, David R. 1972. Regression models and life-tables. *Journal of the Royal Statistical Society Ser B, (Methodological)* 34 (2): 187–220.

Cox, James, Thomas Lee Hazen and F. Hodge O'Neal. 2002. *Corporations.* New York: Aspen Publishers.

Cowen, David J., Richard Sylla and Robert E. Wright. 2006. Alexander Hamilton central banker. Helsinski, XIV International Economic History Congress, Aug.

Crutchley, Claire E., Jacqueline L. Garner and Beverly B. Marshall. 2002. An examination of board stability and the long-term performance of initial public offerings. *Financial Management* 31 (3, Autumn): 63–90.

Dahlquist, Magnus, Lee Pinkowitz, René M. Stulz and Rohan Williamson. 2003. Corporate governance and the home bias. *Journal of Financial and Quantitative Analysis* 38 (1, Mar): 87–110.

Debreu, Gerard. 1951. The coefficient of resource allocation. *Econometrica* 19 (3): 273–92.

DeGennaro, Ramon P., Larry H. P. Lang and James B. Thomson. 1993. Troubled savings and loan institutions: turnaround strategies under insolvency. *Financial Management* 22 (3, Autumn): 163–75.

Demirgüç-Kunt, Asli and Vojislav Maksimovic. 1998. Law, finance and firm growth. *Journal of Finance* 53 (6): 2107–39.

Demirgüç-Kunt, Asli, Luc Laeven and Ross Levine. 2004. Regulations, market structure, institutions and the cost of financial intermediation. *Journal of Money Credit and Banking* 36 (3, Jun): 593–622.

Demsetz, Harold. 1969. Information and efficiency, another viewpoint. *Journal of Law and Economics* 12: 1–21.

Demsetz, Harold. 1973. Industry structure, market rivalry and public policy. *Journal of Law and Economics* 16: 1–9.

Demsetz, Harold. 1986. Corporate control, insider trading and rates of return. *American Economic Review* 76 (May): 313–36.

Denis, David J. 1992. Corporate investment decisions and corporate control: evidence from going-private transactions. *Financial Management* 21 (3, Autumn): 80–94.

Dennis, Steven and Donald J. Mullineaux. 2000. Syndicated loans. *Journal of Financial Intermediation* 9 (4): 404–26.

Derrien, Francois and Kent L. Womack. 2003. Auctions vs. bookbuilding and the control of underpricing in hot IPO markets. *Review of Financial Studies* 16 (1, Spring): 31–61.

DeYoung, Robert. 2003. De novo bank exit. *Journal of Money, Credit and Banking* 35 (5, Oct): 711–28.

Diamond, Douglas W. 1984. Financial intermediation and delegated monitoring. *Review of Economic Studies* 51: 393–414.

Diamond, Douglas W. 1996. Financial intermediation as delegated monitoring: a simple example. *Economic Quarterly Federal Reserve Bank of Richmond* 82 (3): 51–66.

Diamond, Douglas W. 2007. Banks and liquidity creation: a simple exposition of the Diamond-Dybvig model. *Federal Reserve Bank of Richmond* 93 (2, Spring): 189–200.

Diamond, Douglas W. and Philip H. Dybvig. 1983. Bank runs, deposit insurance and liquidity. *Journal of Political Economy* 91 (3, Jun): 401–49.

Diamond, Douglas W. and Philip H. Dybvig. 1986. Banking theory, deposit insurance and bank regulation. *Journal of Business* 59 (1, Jan): 55–68.

Diamond, Douglas W. and Raghuram G. Rajan. 2000. A theory of bank capital. *Journal of Finance* 55 (6, Dec): 2431–65.

Diamond, Douglas W. and Raghuram G. Rajan. 2001a. Banks and liquidity. *American Economic Review* 91 (2, May): 422–5.

Diamond, Douglas W. and Raghuram G. Rajan. 2001b. Liquidity risk, liquidity creation and financial fragility: a theory of banking. *Journal of Political Economy* 109 (2, Apr): 287–327.

Djankov, Simeon, Rafael La Porta, Florencio Lopez-de-Silanes and Andrei Shleifer. 2002. The regulation of entry. *Quarterly Journal of Economics* 117 (1): 1–37.

Doidge, Craig, G. Andrew Karolyi and René Stulz. 2004. Why are foreign firms listed in the US worth more? *Journal of Financial Economics* 71: 205–38.

Doidge, Craig, G. Andrew Karolyi and René M. Stulz. 2007. Why do countries matter so much for corporate governance? *Journal of Financial Economics* 86 (1, Oct): 1–39.

Doidge, Craig, G. Andrew Karolyi and René M. Stulz. 2007Jul. Has New York become less competitive in global markets? Evaluating foreign listing choices over time. Columbus, OH, Dice Center WP 2007–9, Jul.

Doidge, Craig, G. Andrew Karolyi, Karl V. Lins, Darius P. Miller and René M. Stulz. 2009. Private benefits of control, ownership, and the cross-listing decision. *Journal of Finance* 64 (1): 425–66.

Domowitz, Ian, Jack Glen and Ananth Madhavan. 1998. International cross-listing and order flow migration: evidence from an emerging market. *Journal of Finance* 53 (6, Dec): 2001–27.

Dow, Sheila C. 1996. Why the banking system should be regulated. *Economic Journal* 106 (436, May): 688–97.

Dowd, Kevin. 1996. The case for financial laissez-faire. *Economic Journal* 106 (436, May): 679–87.

Duff and Phelps. 2009. Valuation report. Washington, DC, Congressional Oversight Panel, Feb 4. http://cop.senate.gov.

Duffie, Darrell and Hugo Sonnenschein. 1988. Arrow and general equilibrium. *Journal of Economic Literature* 27 (2): 565–98.

Duffie, Darrell and Kenneth J. Singleton. 2003. *Credit risk: pricing, measurement and management*. Princeton: Princeton University Press.

Duffie, Darrell and Haoxiang Zhu. 2009. Does a central clearing counterparty reduce counterparty risk? Palo Alto, Stanford University, Feb 19.

Dwyer, Jr., Gerald P. 1981. The effects of the banking acts of 1933 and 1935 on capital investment in commercial banking. *Journal of Money, Credit and Banking* 13 (2, May): 192–204.

Dyck, Alexander and Luigi Zingales. 2004. Private benefits of control: an international comparison. *Journal of Finance* 59 (2, Apr): 537–600.

Dyck, Alexander, Natalya Volchkova and Luigi Zingales. 2007. The corporate governance role of the media: evidence from Russia. Chicago, University of Chicago WP, Feb.

Easterbrook, Frank H. 2002. Derivative securities and corporate governance. *University of Chicago Law Review* 69 (3, Summer): 733–47.

Economides, Nicholas, R. Glenn Hubbard and Darius Palia. 1996. The political economy of branching restrictions and deposit insurance: a model of monopolistic competition among small and large banks. *Journal of Law and Economics* 39 (2, Oct): 667–704.

Edwards, Linda N. and Franklin R. Edwards. 1974. Measuring the effectiveness of regulation: the case of bank entry regulation. *Journal of Law and Economics* 17 (2, Oct): 445–60.

Eichengreen, Barry. 1992. The origins and nature of the great slump revisited. *Economic History Review* 45 (2, May): 213–39.

Eichengreen, Barry. 2004. Understanding the Great Depression. *Canadian Journal of Economics* 37 (1): 1–27.

Eichengreen, Barry and Jeffrey Sachs. 1985. Exchange rates and economic recovery in the 1930s. *Journal of Economic History* 45 (4, Dec): 925–46.

Eichengreen, Barry and Jeffrey Sachs. 1986. Competitive devaluation and the Great Depression. *Economic Letters* 22 (1): 67–71.

Eichengreen, Barry and Peter Temin. 1997. The gold standard and the Great Depression. Cambridge, MA, NBER WP 6060, Jun.

Eichengreen, Barry and Peter Temin. 2003. Counterfactual histories of the Great Depression. In Theo Balderston, ed. *The world economy and national economies in the interwar slump*. Basingstoke, UK and New York: Palgrave Macmillan.

Eisenberg, Melvin Aron. 1989. The structure of corporation law. *Columbia Law Review* 89 (7, Nov): 1461–525.

Elizalde, Abel and Rafael Repullo. 2007. Economic and regulatory capital. *International Journal of Central Banking* 3 (3, Sep): 87–117.

Engel, Ellen, Rachel M. Hayes and Xue Wang. 2007. The Sarbanes Oxley Act and firms' going private decisions. *Journal of Accounting and Economics* 44 (1–2): 116–45.

Errunza, Vihang R. and Darius P. Miller. 2000. Market segmentation and the cost of capital in international equity markets. *Journal of Financial and Quantitative Analysis* 35 (4, Dec): 577–600.

Eun, Cheol S. and Sanjiv Sabherwal. 2003. Cross-border listings and price discovery: evidence from US-listed Canadian stocks. *Journal of Finance* 58 (2, Apr): 549–75.

Faleye, Olumbunmi. 2004. Cash and corporate control. *Journal of Finance* 59 (5, Oct): 2041–60.

Fama, Eugene F. 1965a. The behavior of stock market prices. *Journal of Business* 38 (Jan): 34–105.

Fama, Eugene F. 1965b. Random walks in stock market prices. *Financial Analysts Journal* 21 (Sep–Oct): 55–9.

Fama, Eugene F. 1970. Efficient capital markets: a review of theory and empirical work. *Journal of Finance* 25 (May): 383–417.

Fama, Eugene F. 1991. Efficient capital markets: II. *Journal of Finance* 46 (Dec): 1575–617.

Fama, Eugene F. and Michael C. Jensen. 1983a. Agency problems and residual claims. *Journal of Law and Economics* 26 (2, Jun): 327–49.

Fama, Eugene F. and Michael C. Jensen. 1983b. Separation of ownership and control. *Journal of Law and Economics* 26 (2, Jun): 301–25.

Feenstra, Robert C. 1998. Integration of trade and disintegration of production in the global economy. *Journal of Economic Perspectives* 12 (4): 31–50.

Feenstra, Robert C. 2007. Globalization and its impact on labor. Vienna, Global Economy Lecture 2007, Vienna Institute for International Economic Studies.

Feenstra, Robert C. and Gordon H. Hanson. 1999. The impact of outsourcing and high-technology capital on wages: estimates for the US, 1979–1990. *Quarterly Journal of Economics* 114 (3): 907–40.

Ferguson, Thomas and Peter Temin. 2001. The German currency crisis of July 1931. Cambridge, MA, MIT WP 01–07, Feb.

Fernandes, Nuno, Ugur Lel and Darius P. Miller. 2008. Escape from New York: the market impact of SEC Rule 12h-6. Washington, DC, FRBO, Sep.

Ferris, Stephen P., Murali Jagannathan and A. C. Pritchard. 2003. Too busy to mind the business? Monitoring by directors with multiple board appointments. *Journal of Finance* 58 (3, Jun): 1087–111.

Fettig, David. 2008. The history of a powerful paragraph: Section 13(3) enacted business loans 76 years ago. *The Region*, Jun. http://www.minneapolisfed.org/publications_papers/pub_display.cfm?id=3485

FDIC. 2008Nov26. Temporary Liquidity Guarantee Program. 12 CFR Part 370. *Federal Register* 72 (229), Nov 26.

FDIC. 2009Jan12. Temporary Liquidity Guarantee Program Frequently Asked Questions. http://www.fdic.gov/regulations/resources/TLGP/faq.html

Finger, Christopher C. 2009Apr. VaR is from Mars, capital is from Venus. *RiskMetrics Group Research Monthly.* www.riskmetrics.com

Fischer, Stanley. 1990. Rules versus discretion in monetary policy. In Benjamin M. Friedman and F. H. Hahn, eds. *Handbook of monetary policy*, Vol. II Amsterdam: Elsevier Science Publishers: 1155–84.

Fisher, Irving. 1933. The debt-deflation theory of great depressions. *Econometrica* 1 (4, Oct): 337–57.

Fisher, Irving. 1936. *100% money,* rev. ed. New York: Adelphi Company.

FOMC. 2009Jan. Domestic open market operations during 2008. New York, FRBNY, Jan.

FRBNY. 2008Mar24. Summary of terms and conditions regarding the J P Morgan Chase Facility. http://www.newyorkfed.org/newsevents/news/markets/2008/rp080324b.html

FRBNY. 2008Sep19. Statement regarding planned purchases of agency debt. http://www.newyorkfed.org/newsevents/news/markets/2008/rp080919.html

FRBNY. 2009Feb6. MBS purchase program. http://www.newyorkfed.org/markets/mbs_faq.html

FRBO. 2005. The Federal Reserve System: purposes & functions 9th ed. Washington, DC: FRBO, Jun.

FRBO. 2007Dec12. Press release. http://www.federalreserve.gov/newsevents/press/monetary/20071212a.htm

FRBO. 2008BHC. *Bank holding company supervision manual.* Washington, DC: Board of Governors of the Federal Reserve, http://www.federalreserve.gov/BoardDocs/SupManual/bhc/200801/bhc0108.pdf

FRBO. 2008Sep18. Press release. http://www.federalreserve.gov/newsevents/press/monetary/20080918a.htm

FRBO. 2008Sep24. Press release. http://www.federalreserve.gov/newsevents/press/monetary/20080924a.htm

FRBO. 2008Oct28. Press release. http://www.federalreserve.gov/newsevents/press/monetary/20081028a.htm

FRBO. 2008Oct29. Press release. http://www.federalreserve.gov/newsevents/press/monetary/20081029b.htm

FRBO. 2008Nov10. Press release AIG. http://www.federalreserve.gov/newsevents/press/other/20081110a.htm

FRBO. 2008Nov23. Joint Statement by Treasury, Federal Reserve and the FDIC on Citigroup. http://www.federalreserve.gov/newsevents/press/bcreg/20081123a.htm.

FRBO. 2009Jan16. Treasury, Federal Reserve and the FDIC provide assistance to Bank of America. http://www.federalreserve.gov/newsevents/press/bcreg/20090116a.htm

FRBO. 2009Feb10. Information regarding recent Federal Reserve actions. http://www.federalreserve.gov/newsevents/recentactions.htm

FRBO. 2009Feb25. Agencies to begin forward-looking assessment. Washington, DC, Board of Governors of the Federal Reserve System, Feb.

FRBO. 2009Apr24. The supervisory capital assessment program: design and implementation. Washington, DC, FRBO, Apr 24.

Friedman, Benjamin. 1990. Targets and instruments of monetary policy. In Benjamin Friedman and F. H. Hahn, eds. *Handbook of monetary economics,* Vol. II (Amsterdam: Elsevier Science Publishers): 1185–230.

Friedman, Milton. 1957. *A theory of the consumption function.* Princeton: Princeton University Press.

Friedman, Milton. 1960. *A program for monetary stability.* New York: Fordham University Press.

Friedman, Milton. 1967. The monetary theory and policy of Henry Simons. *Journal of Law and Economics* 10 (Oct): 1–13.

Friedman, Milton. 1969. The euro-dollar market: some first principles. Chicago, University of Chicago Graduate School of Business, Selected Papers No. 34, 1969.

Friedman, Milton. 1970. Controls on interest rates paid by banks. *Journal of Money, Credit and Banking* 2 (1, Feb): 15–32.

Friedman, Milton. 1999. The business community's suicidal impulse. *Cato Policy Report* March/April: 6–7.

Friedman, Milton. 2005. A natural experiment in monetary policy covering three episodes of growth and decline in the economy and the stock market. *Journal of Economic Perspectives* 19 (4, Fall): 145–50.

Friedman, Milton and Anna Jacobson Schwartz. 1963. *A monetary history of the United States, 1867–1960*. Princeton: Princeton University Press.

FSF. 2008Enh. Report of the Financial Stability Forum on enhancing market and institutional resilience. Basel, BIS, Apr 7.

FSF. 2009Prov. Report of the FSF Working Group on Provisioning. Basel, BIS, Mar.

FSF-BCBS. 2009BankProc. Reducing procyclicality arising from the bank capital framework. Basel, BIS, Mar.

FSF-CGFS. 2009Val. The role of valuation and leverage in procyclicality. Basel, BIS, Mar.

FSF. 2009Comp. FSF principles for sound compensation practices. Basel, BIS, Apr 2.

FSF. 2009Coop. FSF principles for cross-border cooperation on crisis management. Basel, BIS, Apr 2.

FSF. 2009Procy. Report of the Financial Stability Forum on addressing procyclicality in the financial system. Basel, BIS, Apr 2.

FSF. 2009UpEnh. Report of the Financial Stability Forum on enhancing market and institutional resilience. Update on implementation. Basel, BIS, Apr 2.

Foerster, Stephen R. and G. Andrew Karolyi. 1993. International listings of stocks: the case of Canada and the US. *Journal of International Business Studies* 24 (4, 4th Qtr): 763–84.

Foerster, Stephen R. and G. Andrew Karolyi. 1999. The effects of market segmentation on asset prices: evidence from foreign stock listings in the United States. *Journal of Finance* 54 (3, Jun): 981–1013.

Foerster, Stephen R. and G. Andrew Karolyi. 2000. The long-run performance of global equity offerings. *Journal of Financial and Quantitative Analysis* 35 (4, Dec): 499–528.

Foucalt, Thierry and Christine A. Parlour. 2004. Competition for listing. *Rand Journal of Economics* 35 (2, Summer): 329–55.

FSA. 2009Turner. The Turner review: a regulatory response to the global banking crisis. London: FSA, Mar.

FSOB. 2009Jan. First quarterly report to Congress pursuant to section 104(g) of the Emergency Economics Stabilization Act of 2008. Washington, DC, US Treasury. http://www.ustreas.gov/initiatives/eesa/docs/FINSOB-Qrtly-Rpt-123108.pdf

Gale, Ian and Joseph E. Stiglitz. 1989. The informational content of initial public offerings. *Journal of Finance* 44 (2, Jun): 469–77.

Gande, Amar, Manju Puri, Anthony Saunders and Ingo Walter. 1997. Bank underwriting and debt securities: modern evidence. *Review of Financial Studies* 10 (4, Winter): 1175–202.

Geithner, Timothy. 2009Feb10. Remarks introducing the Financial Stability Plan. Washington, DC, US Treasury, Feb 10. http://www.treas.gov/initiatives/eesa/

Geithner, Tim. 2009Feb18. Statement by Secretary Tim Geithner on Treasury's commitment to Fannie Mae and Freddie Mac. http://www.ustreas.gov/press/releases/tg32.htm

Geithner, Tim. 2009Mar25. Remarks. New York, Council on Foreign Relations, Mar 25.

Geithner, Tim. 2009Mar26. Written Testimony. Washington, DC, House Financial Services Committee, Mar 26.

Gerschenkron, Alexander. 1962. *Economic backwardness in historical perspective: a book of essays.* Cambridge, MA: Harvard University Press.

Gilbert, R. Alton. 1984. Bank market structure and competition: a survey. *Journal of Money, Credit and Banking* 16 (4, Nov): 617–45.

Glaeser, Edward, Simon Johnson and Andrei Shleifer. 2001. Coase versus the Coasians. *Quarterly Journal of Economics* 116: 853–99.

Glaeser, Edward L. and Andrei Shleifer. 2003. The rise of the regulatory state. *Journal of Economic Literature* 41 (2, Jun): 401–25.

Glassman, Cynthia A. and Stephen A. Rhoades. 1980. Owner vs. manager control effects of bank performance. *Review of Economics and Statistics* 62 (2, May): 263–70.

Goldsmith, Raymond. 1969. *Financial structure and development.* New Haven: Yale University Press.

Gompers, Paul and Josh Lerner. 1999. Conflict of interest in the issuance of public securities: evidence from venture capital. *Journal of Law and Economics* 42 (1, Apr): 1–28.

Gompers, Paul A. and Josh Lerner. 2003. The long-run performance of initial public offerings: the pre-NASDAQ evidence. *Journal of Finance* 58 (4, Aug): 1355–92.

Goodhart, Charles A. E. 2008. The background of the 2007 financial crisis. *International Economics and Economic Policy* 4 (Feb): 332–46.

Gordy, Michael B. 2002. A risk-factor model foundation for ratings-based bank capital rules. Washington, DC, FRBO, Oct 22.

Grabowski, Richard, Ike Mathur and Nanda Rangan. 1995. The role of takeovers in increasing efficiency. *Managerial and Decision Economics* 16 (3, May): 211–23.

Graham, Frank D. 1936. Partial reserve money and the 100 per cent proposal. American *Economic Review* 26 (3, Sep): 428–40.

Granger, Clive W. J. 1969. Investigating causal relations by econometric models and cross-spectral methods. *Econometrica* 37 (3): 424–38.

Griffith, John M., Lawrence Fogelberg and H. Shelton Weeks. 2002. CEO ownership, corporate control and bank performance. *Journal of Economics and Finance* 26 (2, Summer): 170–83.

Grossman, Richard S. 1994. The shoe that didn't drop: explaining banking stability during the Great Depression. *Journal of Economic History* 54 (3, Sep): 654–82.

Grossman, Richard S. 2001. Charters, corporations and codes: entry restrictions in modern banking law. *Financial History Review* 8 (2, Oct): 107–21.

Grossman, Sanford and Oliver Hart. 1980. Takeover bids, the free rider problem and the theory of the corporation. *Bell Journal of Economics* 11 (1, Spring): 42–64.

G30. 2009. Financial reform: a framework for financial stability. Washington, DC: G30.

Gupta, Atul and Lalatendu Misra. 1999. Failure and failure resolution in the US thrift and banking industries. *Financial Management* 28 (4, Winter): 87–105.

Gurley, John G. and Edward S. Shaw. 1955. Financial aspects of economic development. *American Economic Review* 45 (4): 515–38.

Gurley, John G. and Edward S. Shaw. 1960. *Money in a theory of finance.* Washington, DC: Brookings Institution.

Haddock, David D. and Jonathan R. Macey. 1987. Regulation on demand: a private interest model, with an application to insider trading regulation. *Journal of Law and Economics* 30 (2, Oct): 311–52.

Hail, Luzi and Christian Leuz. 2006. Cost of capital effects and changes in growth expectations around US cross-listings. Philadelphia, Wharton School, Oct, in press *Journal of Financial Economics* available online May 2009 http://www.sciencedirect.com/science/journal/0304405X

Hall, Bronwyn H. 1990. The impact of corporate restructuring on industrial research and development. *Brookings Papers on Economic Activity: Microeconomics*: 85–124.

Hall, Simon. 2001. Credit channel effects in the monetary transmission mechanism. *Bank of England Quarterly Bulletin* 41 (4, Winter): 442–8.

Hall, Brian J. and Kevin J. Murphy. 2003. The trouble with stock options. *Journal of Economic Perspectives* 17 (3, Summer): 49–70.

Halling, Michael, Marco Pagano and Otto Randl. 2007. Where is the market? Evidence from cross-listings in the United States. *Review of Financial Studies* 21 (2): 725–61.

Halpern, Paul, Robert Kieschnick and Wendy Rotenberg. 1999. On the heterogeneity of leveraged going private transactions. *Review of Financial Studies* 12 (2, Summer): 281–309.

Hamilton, Alexander. 1780. National bank. In Henry Cabot Lodge, ed. *The works of Alexander Hamilton.* New York and London: G. P. Putnam & Son, 1904: 319–45. http://files.libertyfund.org/files/1380/0249-03_Bk.pdf

Hamilton, James D. 1987. Monetary factors in the Great Depression. *Journal of Monetary Economics* 19 (1, Mar): 145–69.

Hamilton, James D. 2008. Federal Reserve balance sheet, Dec 22 http://www.mrswing.com/articles/Federal_Reserve_balance_sheet.html

Hannan, Timothy H. and Ferdinand Mavinga. 1980. Expense preference and managerial control: the case of the banking firm. *Bell Journal of Economics* 11 (2, Autumn): 671–82.

Harberger, Arnold C. 1954. Monopoly and resource allocation. *American Economic Review* 44 (2): 77–87.

Harberger, Arnold C. 1971. Three basic postulates for applied welfare economics: an interpretive essay. *Journal of Economic Literature* 9 (3): 785–97.

Harberger, Arnold C. and Glenn P. Jenkins. 2002. Introduction. *Cost-benefit analysis.* Cheltenham, UK: Edward Elgar.

Harjoto, Maretno, Donal J. Mullineaux and Ha-Chin Yi. 2006. A comparison of syndicated loan pricing at investment and commercial banks. *Financial Management* 35 (4, Winter): 49–70.

Harvard Law Review. 1997. The new American universal bank. *Harvard Law Review* 110 (6, Apr): 1310–27.

Healy, Paul M. and Krishna G. Palepu. 2003. The fall of Enron. *Journal of Economic Perspectives* 17 (2, Spring): 3–26.

Hebb, Gregory M. and Donald R. Fraser. 2003. Conflict of interest in commercial bank security underwritings: United Kingdom evidence. *Quarterly Journal of Business and Economics* 42 (1/2, Winter): 79–95.

Hebb, Gregory M. and Gregory H. MacKinnon. 2004. Investment bank versus commercial bank underwriters. *Journal of Economics and Finance* 28 (1, Spring): 68–87.

Heggestad, Arnold A. 1977. Market structure, risk and profitability in commercial banking. *Journal of Finance* 32 (4, Sep): 1207–16.

Heggestad, Arnold A. and John J. Mingo. 1976. Prices, nonprices and concentration in commercial banking. *Journal of Money, Credit and Banking* 8 (1, Feb): 107–17.

Heggestad, Arnold A. and Stephen A. Rhoades. 1976. Concentration and firm stability in commercial banking. *Review of Economics and Statistics* 58 (4, Nov): 443–52.

Hendershott, Robert J. 1996. Which takeover targets overinvest? *Journal of Financial and Quantitative Analysis* 31 (4, Dec): 563–80.

Hertog, Johan den. 1999. *General theories of regulation*. Utrecht, Economic Institute/CLAV, Utrecht University.

Hertzel, Michael, Michael Lemmon, James S. Linck and Lynn Rees. 2002. Long-run performance following private placements of equity. *Journal of Finance* 57 (6, Dec): 2595–617.

Hicks, John R. 1935. Annual survey of economic theory: the theory of monopoly. *Econometrica* 3 (1): 1–20.

Hicks, John R. 1939. The foundations of welfare economics. *Economic Journal* 49 (196): 696–712.

Holmstrom, Bengt and Steven N. Kaplan. 2001. Corporate governance and merger activity in the United States: making sense of the 1980s and 1990s. *Journal of Economic Perspectives* 15 (2): 121–44.

Hori, Masahiro and Satoshi Shimizutani. 2005. Price expectations and consumption under deflation: evidence from Japanese household survey data. *International Economics and Economic Policy* 2: 127–51.

Hotelling, Harold. 1938. The general welfare in relation to problems of taxation of railway and utility rates. *Econometrica* 6 (3): 242–69.

Hotelling, Harold. 1939. The relation of prices to marginal costs in an optimum system. *Econometrica* 7 (2): 151–5.

HUD. 2008Jul30. Public Law 110–289 of July 30, 2008, Housing and Economic Recovery Act. http://www.hud.gov/offices/cpd/communitydevelopment/programs/neighborhoodspg/hera2008.pdf

HUD. 2009Feb. Housing and Economic Recovery Act of 2008 FAQ. http://www.hud.gov/news/recoveryactfaq.cfm

Huddart, Steven, John S. Hughes and Carolyn B. Levine. 2001. Public disclosure and dissimulation of insider trades. *Econometrica* 69 (3, May): 665–81.

IMF. 2009WEOApr. *World economic outlook: crisis and recovery* (Washington, DC: IMF, Apr)

Jackson, Howell E. 1993. The superior performance of savings and loan associations with substantial holding companies. *Journal of Legal Studies* 22 (2, Jun): 405–56.

Jaffee, Dwight M. 2009. Reforming Fannie and Freddie. *Regulation* 31 (4, Winter): 52–7.

Jaffee, Dwight M. and John M. Quigley. 2007. Housing subsidies and homeowners: what role for government-sponsored enterprises? *Brookings-Wharton Papers on Urban Affairs* : 103–49.

James, Harold. 1992. Financial flows across frontiers during the interwar depression. *Economic History Review* 45 (3, Aug): 594–613.

Jarrell, Gregg A. 1981. The economic effects of federal regulation of the market for new security issues. *Journal of Law and Economics* 24 (3, Dec): 613–75.

Jayaratne, Jith and Philip E. Strahan. 1998. Entry restrictions, industry evolution and dynamic efficiency: evidence from commercial banking. *Journal of Law and Economics* 41 (1, Apr): 239–73.

Jenkinson, Tim and Howard Jones. 2004. Bids and allocations in European IPO bookbuilding. *Journal of Finance* 59 (5, Oct): 2309–38.

Jensen, Michael C. 1986. Agency costs of free cash flow, corporate finance and takeovers. *American Economic Review* 76 (2, May): 323–9.

Jensen, Michael C. 1988. Takeovers: their causes and consequences. *Journal of Economic Perspectives* 2 (1, Winter): 21–48.

Jensen, Michael C. 1991. Corporate control and the politics of finance. *Journal of Applied Corporate Finance* 4 (2, Summer): 13–33.

Jensen, Michael C. 1993. The modern industrial revolution, exit and the failure of internal control systems. *Journal of Finance* 48 (3, Jul): 831–80.

Jensen, Michael C. 2005. Agency costs of overvalued equity. *Financial Management* 34 (1, Spring): 5–19.

Jensen, Michael C. and William H. Meckling, 1976. Theory of the firm: managerial behavior, agency costs and ownership structure. *Journal of Financial Economics* 3 (4): 305–60.

Jensen, Michael C. and Kevin J. Murphy. 1990. Performance pay and top-management incentives. *Journal of Political Economy* 98 (2, Apr): 225–64.

Jeon, Yongil and Stephen M. Miller. 2007. Births, death and marriages in the US commercial banking industry. *Economic Inquiry* 45 (2, Apr): 325–41.

Johnson, Simon, Rafael La Porta, Florencio Lopez-de-Silanes and Andrei Shleifer. 2000. Tunneling. *American Economic Review* 90 (2): 22–7.

Joskow, Paul L. 2006. *Regulation of natural monopolies.* Cambridge, MA, MIT, Aug 29.

Laffont, Jean-Jacques. 1994. The new economics of regulation ten years after. *Econometrica* 62 (3, May): 507–37.

Kahan, Marcel and Edward B. Rock. 2002. How I learned to stop worrying and love the pill: adaptive responses to takeover law. Philadelphia and New York, Institute for Law and Economics and Center for Law and Business, Apr.

Kaplan, Steven N. 1989. The effects of management buyouts on operating performance and value. *Journal of Financial Economics* 24 (Oct): 217–54.

Kaplan, Steven N. and Jeremy C. Stein. 1993. The evolution of buyout pricing and financial structure in the 1980s. *Quarterly Journal of Economics* 108 (2, May): 313–57.

Karolyi, G. Andrew 1998. Why do companies list shares abroad? A survey of the evidence and its managerial implications. *Financial Markets, Institutions and Instruments* 7 (1, Jan): 1–60.

Karolyi, G. Andrew. 2003. DaimlerChrysler AG, the first truly global share. *Journal of Corporate Finance* 9: 409–30.

Karolyi, George A. 2004. The role of ADRs in the development of emerging equity markets. *Review of Economics and Statistics* 86 (3, Aug): 670–90.

Karolyi, G. Andrew. 2006. The world of cross-listing and cross-listing of the world: challenging conventional wisdom. *Review of Finance* 10 (1): 99–152.

Kashyap, Anil K., Jeremy C. Stein and David W. Wilcox. 1993. Monetary policy and credit conditions: evidence from the composition of external finance. *American Economic Review* 83 (1, Mar): 78–98.

Kashyap, Anil K., Jeremy C. Stein and David W. Wilcox. 1996. Monetary policy and credit conditions: evidence from the composition of external finance: Reply. *American Economic Review* 86 (1, Mar): 310–4.

Kashyap, Anil K. and Jeremy C. Stein. 2000. What do a million observations on banks say about the transmission of monetary policy? *American Economic Review* 90 (3, Jun): 407–28.

Kashyap, Anil K, Raghuram Rajan and Jeremy C. Stein. 2002. Banks as liquidity providers: an explanation for the coexistence of lending and deposit taking. *Journal of Finance* 57 (1, Feb): 33–73.

Kashyap, Anil K., Raghuram G. Rajan and Jeremy C. Stein. 2008. Rethinking capital regulation. Jackson Hole, Wyoming, Symposium sponsored by the Federal Reserve Bank of Kansas City, Dec. http://search.yahoo.com/search?p=%22Rethinking+capital+regulation%22&fr=yfp-t-501&toggle=1&cop=mss&ei=UTF-8

Kaufman, Allen and Ernest J. Englander. 1993. Kohlberg Kravis Roberts & Co. and the restructuring of American capitalism. *Business History Review* 67 (1, Spring): 52–97.

Kehoe, Timothy J. and Edward C. Prescott. 2001. Great depressions of the twentieth century. Minneapolis, University of Minnesota, CP, Sep.

King, Robert G. and Ross Levine. 1993. Finance and growth: Schumpeter might be right. *Quarterly Journal of Economics* 108 (3, Aug): 717–37.

Kishan, Ruby P. and Timothy P. Opiela. 2000. Bank size, bank capital and the bank lending channel. *Journal of Money, Credit and Banking* 32 (1, Feb): 121–41.

Kiyotaki, Nobuhiro and John Moore. 2002. Balance sheet contagion. *American Economic Review* 92 (2, May): 46–50.

Knepper, William E. and Dan A. Bailey. 2002. *Liability of corporate officers and directors*, 7th ed.. New York: Lexis-Nexis.

Knight, Frank H. 1921. *Risk, uncertainty and profit*. New York: Houghton Mifflin Co.

Krigman, Laurie, Wayne H. Shaw and Kent L. Womack. 1999. The persistence of IPO mispricing and the predictive power of flipping. *Journal of Finance* 54 (3, Jun): 1015–44.

Kroszner, Randall S. 1999. *Is the financial system politically independent? Perspectives on the political economy of banking and financial regulation*. Chicago, University of Chicago, Jun.

Kroszner, Randall S. and Raghuram G. Rajan. 1994. Is the Glass-Steagall Act justified? A study of the US experience with universal banking before 1933. *American Economic Review* 84 (4): 810–32.

Kroszner, Randall S. and Raghuram G. Rajan. 1997. Evidence from commercial bank securities activities in the Glass-Steagall Act. *Journal of Monetary Economics* 39 (Aug): 475–516.

Kroszner, Randall and Philip E. Strahan. 1996. Regulatory incentives and the thrift crisis: dividends, mutual-to-stock conversions and financial distress. *Journal of Finance* 51 (4, Sep): 1285–319

Kroszner, Randall S. and Philip E. Strahan. 1999. What drives deregulation? Economics and politics of the relaxation of bank branching restrictions. *Quarterly Journal of Economics* 114 (4): 1437–67.

Kroszner, Randall S. and Philip E. Strahan. 2001. Obstacles to optimal policy: the interplay of politics and economics in shaping bank supervision and regulation reform. In Frederic S. Mishkin, ed. *Prudential supervision. What works and what doesn't*. Chicago: University of Chicago Press.

Krueger, Anne O. 1974. The political economy of the rent-seeking society. *American Economic Review* 64 (3): 291–303.

Kryzanowski, Lawrence and Hao Zhang. 2002. Intraday market price integration for shares cross-listed internationally. *Journal of Financial and Quantitative Analysis* 37 (2, Jun): 243–69.

Kurihara, Yutaka. 2006. The relationship between exchange rate and stock prices during the quantitative easing policy in Japan. *International Journal of Business* 11 (4): 375–86.

Kutsuna, Kenji and Richard Smith. 2004. Why does book building drive out auction methods of IPO issuance? Evidence from Japan. *Review of Financial Studies* 17 (4, Winter): 1129–66.

Kydland, Finn E. and Edward C. Prescott. 1977. Rules rather than discretion: the inconsistency of optimal plans. *Journal of Political Economy* 85 (3, Jun): 473–92.

Kyle, Albert S. 1985. Continuous auctions and insider trading. *Econometrica* 53 (6, Nov): 1315–35.

Ladenson, Mark L. and Kenneth J. Bombara. 1984. Entry in commercial banking, 1962–78. *Journal of Money, Credit and Banking* 16 (May): 165–74.

Laeven, Luc. 2004. The political economy of deposit insurance. *Journal of Financial Services Research* 26 (3): 201–24.

Laffont, Jean-Jacques. 1994. The new economics of regulation ten years after. *Econometrica* 62 (3, May): 507–37.

Lamont, Owen and Jeremy C. Stein. 1999. Leverage and house-price dynamics in US cities. *Rand Journal of Economics* 30 (3, Autumn): 498–514.

La Porta, Rafael, Florencio Lopez-de-Silanes, Andrei Shleifer and Robert W. Vishny. 1997. Legal determinants of external finance. *Journal of Finance* 52 (3): 1131–50.

La Porta, Rafael, Florencio Lopez-de-Silanes and Andrei Shleifer. 1998. Law and finance. *Journal of Political Economy* 106 (6): 1113–55.

La Porta, Rafael, Florencio Lopez-de-Silanes and Andrei Shleifer. 1999. Corporate ownership around the world. *Journal of Finance* 54 (2): 471–517.

La Porta, Rafael, Florencio Lopez-de-Silanes, Andrei Shleifer and Robert W. Vishny. 2000. Agency problems and dividend policies around the world. *Journal of Finance* 55 (1, Feb): 1–33.

La Porta, Rafael, Florencio Lopez-de-Silanes and Andrei Shleifer. 2002a. Government ownership of banks. *Journal of Finance* 57 (1): 265–301.

La Porta, Rafael, Florencio Lopez-de-Silanes, Andrei Shleifer and Robert Vishny. 2002b. Investor protection and corporate valuation. *Journal of Finance* 57 (3, Jun): 1147–70.

La Porta, Rafael, Florencio López de Silanes and Guillermo Zamarripa. 2003. Related lending. *Quarterly Journal of Economics* 118 (1): 231–68.

La Porta, Rafael, Florencio Lopez-de-Silanes and Andrei Shleifer. 2006. What works in securities laws? *Journal of Finance* 61 (1): 1–32.

Lee, Sang Whi and Donald J. Mullineaux. 2004. Monitoring, financial distress and the structure of commercial loan syndicates. *Financial Management* 33 (3, Autumn): 107–30.

Leibenstein, Harvey. 1966. Allocative efficiency vs. "X-efficiency". *American Economic Review* 56 (2, June): 392–415.

Leuz, Christian, Alexander Triantis and Tracy Yue Wang. 2008. Why do firms go dark? Causes and economic consequences of voluntary SEC deregistrations. *Journal of Accounting and Economics* 45 (2–3): 181–208.

Lev, Baruch. 2003. Corporate earnings: facts and fiction. *Journal of Economic Perspectives* 17 (2, Spring): 27–50.

Levine, Ross. 1991. Stock markets, growth and tax policy. *Journal of Finance* 46 (4, Sep): 1445–65.

Levine, Ross. 1997. Financial development and economic growth: views and agenda. *Journal of Economic Literature* 35 (2): 688–726.

Levine, Ross. 2002. Bank-based or market-based financial systems: which is better? *Journal of Financial Intermediation* 11 (4): 398–428.

Levine, Ross. 2005a. Finance and growth: theory and evidence. In Philippe Aghion and Steven N. Durlauf, eds. *Handbook of Economic Growth, 1A*. New York: North-Holland Elsevier.

Levine, Ross. 2005b. Law, endowments and property rights. *Journal of Economic Perspectives* 19 (3, Summer): 61–88.

Levine, Ross and Sara Zervos. 1998. Stock markets, banks and economic growth. *American Economic Review* 88 (3, Jun): 537–58.

Levine, Ross and Sergio Schmukler. 2005. Internationalization and stock market liquidity. Cambridge, MA, NBER WP 11894, Dec.

Li, Xi. 2007. The Sarbanes-Oxley Act and cross-listed private issuers. Miami, University of Miami, WP, Jan.

Lipsey, Richard G. and Kelvin Lancaster. 1956. The general theory of second best. *Review of Economic Studies* 24: 11–32.

Lipsey, Richard G. 2007. Reflections on the general theory of second best at its golden jubilee. *International Tax and Public Finance* 14: 349–64.

Lipton, Martin. 2002. Pills, polls and professors redux. *University of Chicago Law Review* 69 (3, Summer): 1037–65.

Lipton, Martin and Paul K. Rowe. 2007. The inconvenient truth about corporate governance: some thoughts on Vice-Chancellor Strine's essay. *Journal of Corporation Law* 33 (1, Oct): 63–71.

Litvak, Kate. 2007a. The effect of the Sarbanes-Oxley Act on non-US companies cross-listed in the US. *Journal of Corporate Finance* 13 (1): 195–228.

Litvak, Kate. 2007b. Sarbanes-Oxley and the cross-listing premium. *Michigan Law Review* 105 (8): 1857–98.

Ljungqvist, Alexander P., Tim Jenkinson and William J. Wilhem, Jr. 2003. Global integration in private equity markets: the role of US banks and US investors. *Review of Financial Studies* 16 (1, Spring): 63–99.

Ljungqvist, Alexander P. and William J. Wilhem, Jr. 2003. IPO pricing in the dot-com bubble. *Journal of Finance* 58 (2, Apr): 723–52.

Loughran, Tim and Jay Ritter. 2004. Why has IPO underpricing changed over time? *Financial Management* 33 (3, Autumn): 5–37.

Lucas, Jr., Robert E. 1976. Econometric policy evaluation: a critique. *Carnegie-Rochester Conference Series on Public Policy* 1 (1976): 16–46.

Lucas, Jr., Robert E. and Leonard A. Rapping. 1969. Real wages, employment and inflation. *Journal of Political Economy* 77 (3, Sep): 721–54.

Lucas, Jr., Robert E. and Leonard A. Rapping. 1972. Unemployment in the Great Depression: is there a full explanation. *Journal of Political Economy* 80 (1, Jan): 186–91.

MacNeill, Iain and Alex Lau. 2001. International corporate regulation: listing rules and overseas companies. *International and Comparative Law Quarterly* 50 (4, Oct): 787–810.

Maeda, Eiji, Bunya Fujiwara, Aiko Mineshima and Ten Taniguchi. 2005. Japan's open market operations under the quantitative easing policy. Tokyo, Bank of Japan WP, Apr.

Mahoney, Paul G. 1997. The exchange as regulator. *Virginia Law Review* 83 (7): 1453–500.

Mahoney, Paul G. 2001. The political economy of the Securities Act of 1933. *Journal of Legal Studies* 30 (1, Jan): 1–31.

McCall, Alan S. and Manferd O. Peterson. 1977. The impact of de novo commercial bank entry. *Journal of Finance* 32 (5, Dec): 1587–604.

Mamum, Abdullah Al, M. Kabir Hassan and Van Son Lai. 2004. The impact of the Gramm-Leach-Bliley Act on the financial services industry. *Journal of Economics and Finance* 28 (3, Fall): 333–47.

Manne, Henry G. 1966. *Insider trading and the stock market.* New York: Free Press.

Manne, Henry G. 2005. Insider trading: Hayek, virtual markets and the dog that did not bark. *Journal of Corporation Law* 31 (1, Fall): 167–85.

Marcus, Alan J. and Israel Shaked. 1984. The valuation of FDIC deposit insurance using option-pricing estimates. *Journal of Money, Credit and Banking* 16 (4, Nov): 446–60.

Margo, Robert A. 1991. The microeconomics of depression unemployment. *Journal of Economic History* 51 (2, Jun): 333–41.

Margo, Robert A. 1993. Employment and unemployment in the 1930s. *Journal of Economic Perspectives* 7 (2, Spring): 41–59.

Markowitz, Harry M. 2009. Proposals concerning the current financial crisis. *Financial Analysts Journal* 65 (1, Jan/Feb): 25–7.

Marosi, András and Nadia Massoud. 2008. You can enter but you cannot leave: US securities markets and foreign firms. Forthcoming in *Journal of Finance* http://www.afajof.org/journal/forth_abstract.asp?ref=473

Marshall, Alfred. 1890. *Principles of economics.* London: Macmillan & Co.

Maurer, Noel and Stephen Haber. 2005. *Related lending and economic performance: evidence from Mexico.* Stanford, Hoover Institute, Nov.

Maurer, Noel and Stephen Haber. 2007. Related lending: manifest looting or good governance: lessons from the economic history of Mexico. In Sebastian Edwards, Gerardo Esquivel and Graciela Márquez, eds. *The decline of Latin American economies: growth, institutions and crises.* Chicago: University of Chicago.

McCallum, Bennett T. 1990. Could a monetary base rule have prevented the Great Depression? *Journal of Monetary Economics* 26 (1): 3–26.

Meade, James E. 1952. External economies and diseconomies in a competitive situation. *Economic Journal* 62 (1): 54–67.

Mester, Loretta J. 1987. A multiproduct cost study of savings and loans. *Journal of Finance* 42 (2, Jun): 423–45.

Merton, Robert C. 1973. Theory of rational option pricing. *Bell Journal of Economics and Management Science* 4 (1, Spring): 141–83.

Merton, Robert C. 1974. On the pricing of corporate debt: the risk structure of interest rates. *Journal of Finance* 29 (2, May): 449–70.

Merton, Robert C. 1977. An analytic derivation of the cost of deposit insurance and loan guarantees. *Journal of Banking and Finance* 1 (Jun): 3–111.

Merton, Robert C. 1978. On the cost of deposit insurance when there are surveillance costs. *Journal of Business* 51 (3, Jul): 439–52.

Merton, Robert C. 1998. Applications of option-pricing theory: twenty-five years later. *American Economic Review* 88 (3): 323–49.

Merton, Robert C. and Zvi Bodie. 1992. On the management of financial guarantees. *Financial Management* 21 (4, Winter): 87–109.

Merton, Robert C. and Zvi Bodie. 1995. A conceptual framework for analyzing the financial environment. In Dwight B. Crane *et al.* eds. *The global financial system: a functional perspective.* Cambridge, MA: Harvard University Press.

Merton, Robert C. and Zvi Bodie. 2005. Design of financial systems: towards a synthesis of function and structure. *Journal of Investment Management* 3 (1): 1–23.

Michaely, Roni and Wayne H. Shaw. 1994. The pricing of initial public offerings: tests of adverse-selection and signaling theories. *Review of Financial Studies* 7 (2, Summer): 279–319.

Miller, Merton H. 1988. The Modigliani-Miller propositions after thirty years. *Journal of Economic Perspectives* 2 (4): 99–120.

Miller, Merton H. 1991. Leverage. *Journal of Finance* 46 (2, Jun): 479–88.

Miller, Merton H. and Franco Modigliani. 1961. Dividend policy, growth and the valuation of shares. *Journal of Business* 34: 411–33.

Mingo, John J. 1975. Regulatory influence on bank capital investment. *Journal of Finance* 30 (4, Sep): 1111–21.

Mishkin, Frederic S. 1992. An evaluation of the Treasury plan of banking reform. *Journal of Economic Perspectives* 6 (1, Winter): 133–53.

Mishkin, Frederic S. 2006. *The next great globalization: how disadvantaged nations can harness their financial systems to get rich.* Princeton: Princeton University Press.

Mitchener, Kris James. 2005. Bank supervision, regulation and instability during the Great Depression. *Journal of Economic History* 65 (1, Mar): 152–85.

Modigliani, Franco and Merton Miller. 1958. The cost of capital, corporation finance and the theory of investment. *American Economic Review* 48 (2): 261–97.

Morck, Randall, Andrei Shleifer and Robert W. Vishny. 1989. Alternative mechanisms for corporate control. *American Economic Review* 79 (4, Sep): 842–52.

Moulton, Pamela and Li Wei. 2005. A tale of two cities: cross-listed stock liquidity and the availability of substitutes. New York, NYSE, WP, Sep 14.

Murphy, Kevin J. 2002. Explaining executive compensation: managerial power versus the perceived cost of stock options. *University of Chicago Law Review* 69 (3, Summer): 847–69.

Murphy, Kevin J. and Ján Zábojník. 2004. CEO pay and appointments: a market-based explanation for recent trends. *American Economic Review* 94 (2, May): 192–6.

Murphy, Kevin J. and Ján Zábojník. 2007. Managerial capital and the market for CEOs. Los Angeles, USC Working Paper, Apr.

Muth, Mary, Walter N. Thurman, Randal R. Rucker and Ching-Ta Chuang. 2003. The fable of the bees revisited: causes and consequences of the U.S. honey program. *Journal of Law and Economics* 46 (Oct): 479–516.

North, Douglass C. and Barry R. Weingast. 1989. Constitutions and commitments: the evolution of institutional governing public choice in seventeenth-century England. *Journal of Economic History* 49 (4): 803–32.

Obama, Barack. 2009Jan8. Remarks of President-elect Barack Obama as prepared for delivery. Jan 8 http://www.whitehouse.gov/agenda/economy/

Olson, Mancur. 1965. *The logic of collective action*. Cambridge: Harvard University Press.

OMB. 2009. *A new era of responsibility: renewing America's promise*. Washington, DC: US Government Printing Office.

Opler, Tim and Sheridan Titman. 1993. The determinants of leveraged buyout activity: free cash flows vs. financial distress costs. *Journal of Finance* 48 (5, Dec): 1985–99

Pagano, Marco, Fabio Panetta and Luigi Zingales. 1998. Why do companies go public? An empirical analysis. *Journal of Finance* 53 (1, Feb): 27–64.

Pagano, Marco, Ailsa A. Roell and Josef Zechner. 2002. The geography of equity listing: why do companies list abroad. *Journal of Finance* 57 (6, Dec): 2651–94.

Pagano, Marco and Paolo F. Volpin. 2005. The political economy of corporate governance. *American Economic Review* 95 (4, Sep): 1005–30.

Panagariya, Arvind. 2002. Cost of protection: where do we stand? *American Economic Review* 92 (2, May): 175–9.

Pantalone, Coleen C. and Marjorie B. Platt. 1987. Predicting failure of savings & loan associations. *AREUEA Journal* 15 (2, Summer): 46–64.

Panzar, John C. and James N. Rosse. 1987. Testing for "monopoly" equilibrium. *Journal of Industrial Economics* 35 (4, Jun): 443–56.

Peek, Joe and Eric Rosengren. 1995. The capital crunch: neither a borrower nor a lender be. *Journal of Money, Credit and Banking* 27 (3, Aug): 625–38.

Peláez, Carlos A. 2008. The reform of Alexander Hamilton. Philadelphia, University of Pennsylvania Law School, unpublished manuscript.

Peláez, Carlos Manuel. 1968a. A balança commercial, a Grande Depressão e a industrialização brasileira. *Revista Brasileira de Economia* 22 (1, Jan/Mar): 15–47.

Peláez, Carlos Manuel. 1968b. The state, the Great Depression and the industrialization of Brazil. New York, unpublished PhD dissertation, Columbia University.

Peláez, Carlos Manuel. 1972. *História da industrialização brasileira*. Rio de Janeiro: APEC.

Peláez, Carlos M. and Carlos A. Peláez. 2005. *International financial architecture: G7, IMF, BIS, debtors and creditors*. Basingstoke, UK: Palgrave Macmillan.

Peláez, Carlos M. and Carlos A. Peláez. 2007. *The global recession risk*. Basingstoke, UK: Palgrave Macmillan.

Peláez, Carlos M. and Carlos A. Peláez. 2008a. *Globalization and the state: volume I*. Basingstoke, UK: Palgrave Macmillan.

Peláez, Carlos M. and Carlos A. Peláez. 2008b. *Globalization and the state: volume II*. Basingstoke, UK: Palgrave Macmillan.

Peláez, Carlos M. and Carlos A. Peláez. 2008c. *Government intervention in globalization: regulation, devaluation and trade wars*. Basingstoke, UK: Palgrave Macmillan.

Peltzman, Sam. 1965. Entry in commercial banking. *Journal of Law and Economics* 8 (Oct): 11–50.

Peltzman, Sam. 1968. Bank stock prices and the effects of regulation of the banking structure. *Journal of Business* 41 (4, Oct): 413–30.

Peltzman, Sam. 1970. Capital investment in commercial banking and its relationship to portfolio regulation. *Journal of Political Economy* 78 (1, Jan): 1–26.

Peltzman, Sam. 1976. Toward a more general theory of regulation. *Journal of Law and Economics* 19 (Aug): 211–40.

Peltzman, Sam. 1984. Bank market structure and competition: comment. *Journal of Money, Credit and Banking* 16 (4, Nov): 650–6.

Peltzman, Sam. 1989. The economic theory of regulation after a decade of deregulation. *Brookings Papers on Economic Activity*: 1–41.

Pigou, Arthur C. 1932. *The economics of welfare* 4th ed. London: Macmillan & Co.

Pinto, Edward J. 2008. Statement. Washington, DC, US House of Representatives, Committee on Oversight and Government Reform, Dec 9.

Piotroski, Joseph D. and Suraj Srinivasan. 2008. Regulation and bonding: the Sarbanes-Oxley Act and the flow of international listings. *Journal of Accounting Research* 46 (2): 383–425.

Pittman, Mark and Bob Ivry. 2009. Financial rescue nears GDP as pledges top $12.8 trillion. New York, Bloomberg, Mar 31. www.bloomberg.com

Posner, Richard A. 1974. Theories of economic regulation. *Bell Journal of Economics and Management Science* 5 (2, Autumn): 335–58.

Posner, Richard A. 1975. The social cost of monopoly and regulation. *Journal of Political Economy* 83 (Aug): 807–27.

Posner, Richard A. 2000. An economic analysis of the use of citations in the law. *American Law and Economics* Review 2 (2): 381–406.

Posner, Richard A. 2009. Re-regulating the banking industry. Apr 4, www.becker-posner-blog.com

Prescott, Edward C. 1999. Some observations on the Great Depression. *Federal Reserve Bank of Minneapolis Quarterly Review* 23 (1, Winter): 25–31.

Prescott, Edward C. 2002. Prosperity and depression. *American Economic Review* 92 (2, May): 1–15.

Raines, Franklin D. 2008. Testimony. Washington, DC, US House Committee on Oversight and Government Reform.

Rajan, Raghuram G. 1998. The past and future of commercial banking viewed through an incomplete contract lens. *Journal of Money, Credit and Banking* 30 (3, Aug): 524–50.

Rajan, Raghuram G. 2005. Has financial development made the world riskier? Jackson Hole, Wyoming, Symposium sponsored by the Federal Reserve Bank of Kansas City, Aug. http://www.kc.frb.org/publicat/sympos/2005/PDF/Rajan2005.pdf

Rajan, Raghuram G. and Henri Servaes. 1997. Analyst following of initial public offerings. *Journal of Finance* 52 (2, Jun): 507–29.

Rajan, Raghuram G. and Luigi Zingales. 2000. The governance of the new enterprise. In Xavier Vives, ed. *Corporate governance, theoretical and empirical perspectives*. Cambridge, UK: Cambridge University Press.

Rajan, Raghuram G. and Luigi Zingales. 2001. The influence of the financial revolution on the nature of the firm. *American Economic Review* 91 (2): 206–11.

Rajan, Raghuram G. and Luigi Zingales. 2003. *Saving capitalism from the capitalists: unleashing the power of financial markets to create wealth and spread opportunity*. New York: Crown Business.

Rajan, Uday, Amit Seru and Vikrant Vig. 2008. The failure of models that predict failure: distance, incentives and default. Chicago, CGB Research Paper 08–19, Dec.

Raynold, Prosper, W. Douglas McMillin and Thomas R. Beard. 1991. The impact of federal government expenditures in the 1930s. *Southern Economic Journal* 58 (1, Jul): 15–28.

Rees, Albert. 1970. On equilibrium in labor markets. *Journal of Political Economy* 78 (2, Mar): 306–10.

Reese, William A. and Weisbach, Michael S. 2002. Protection of minority shareholder interests, cross-listing in the United States and subsequent equity offerings. *Journal of Financial Economics* 66 (1, Oct): 65–104.

Rhoades, Stephen A. 1982. Welfare loss, redistribution effect and restriction in output due to monopoly in banking. *Journal of Monetary Economics* 9 (3): 375–87.

Rhoades, Stephen A. and Alexander J. Yeats. 1974. Growth, consolidation and mergers in banking. *Journal of Finance* 29 (5, Dec): 1397–1405.

Rhoades, Stephen A. and Roger D. Rutz. 1981. A reexamination and extension of the relationship between concentration and firm rank stability. *Review of Economics and Statistics* 63 (3, Aug): 446–51.

Ritter, Jay R. 1991. The long-run performance of initial public offerings. *Journal of Finance* 46 (1, Mar): 3–27.

Ritter, Jay R. and Ivo Welch. 2002. A review of IPO activity, pricing and allocations. *Journal of Finance* 57 (4, Aug): 1795–828.

Robbins, Lionel. 1935. *An essay on the nature and significance of economic science*. London: Palgrave Macmillan.

Rock, Edward B. 1997. Saints and sinners: how does Delaware corporate law work? *UCLA Law Review* 44:1009–107.

Rockoff, Hugh. 1993. The meaning of money in the Great Depression. Cambridge, MA, NBER WP No. H0052, Dec 1.

Roe, Mark J. 1991. A political theory of American corporate finance. *Columbia Law Review* 91 (1, Jan): 10–67.

Rogoff, Kenneth. 2006. Impact of globalization on monetary policy. Jackson Hole, Wyoming, FRBKC Symposium, Aug 24–6.

Romano, Roberta. 1991. The shareholder suit: litigation without foundation? *Journal of Law, Economics & Organization* 7 (1, Spring): 55–87.

Romano, Roberta. 2005. The Sarbanes-Oxley act and the making of quack corporate governance. *Yale Law Journal* 114 (7): 1521–611.

Romer, Christina D. 1990. The great crash and the onset of the Great Depression. *Quarterly Journal of Economics* 105 (3, Aug): 597–624.

Romer, Christina D. 1992. What ended the Great Depression? *Journal of Economic History* 52 (4, Dec): 757–84.

Romer, Christina D. 1993. The nation in depression. *Journal of Economic Perspectives* 7 (2, Spring): 19–39.

Romer, Christina D. 1999. Why did prices rise in the 1930s? *Journal of Economic History* 59 (1, Mar): 167–99.

Romer, Christina D. 2009Mar9. Lessons from the Great Depression for economic recovery in 2009. Washington, DC, Brookings Institution, Mar 9.

Romer, Christina D. 2009Mar31. Lessons from the New Deal. Washington, DC, Senate Committee on Banking, Housing and Urban Affairs, Mar 31.

Romer, Christina D. and David H. Romer. 2004. A new measure of monetary shocks: derivation and implications. *American Economic Review* 94 (4, Sep): 1055–84.

Rose, Peter S. 1992. Agency theory and entry barriers in banking. *Financial Review* 27 (3, Aug): 323–53.

Rose, Peter S. and Donald R. Fraser. 1976. The relationship between stability and change in market structure: an analysis of bank prices. *Journal of Industrial Economics* 24 (4, Jun): 251–66.

Ross, Stephen A. 1976. The arbitrage theory of capital asset pricing. *Journal of Economic Theory* 13 (3): 341–60.

Roten, Ivan C. and Donald J. Mullineaux. 2005. Equity underwriting spreads at commercial bank holding companies and investment banks. *Journal of Financial Services Research* 27 (3): 243–58.

Samuelson, Paul A. 1965. Proof that properly anticipated prices fluctuate randomly. *Industrial Management Review* 6 (Spring): 41–9.

Samuelson, Paul A. 1947. *Foundations of economic analysis.* Cambridge, MA: Harvard University Press.

Sarkissian, Sergei and Michael J. Schill. 2004. The overseas listing decision: new evidence of proximity preference. *Review of Financial Studies* 17 (3, Autumn): 769–809.

Saudagaran, Shahrokh M. 1988. An empirical study of selected factors influencing the decision to list on foreign stock exchanges. *Journal of International Business Studies* 19 (1, Spring): 101–27.

Saudagaran, Shahrokh M. and Gary C. Biddle. 1995. Foreign listing location: a study of MNCs and stock exchange in eight countries. *Journal of International Business Studies* 26 (2, 2nd Qtr): 319–41.

Saunders, Anthony and Ingo Walter. 1994. *Universal banking in the United States: what could we gain? What could we lose?* New York: Oxford University Press.

Schnabel, Isabel. 2004. The German twin crisis of 1931. *Journal of Economic History* 64 (3, Sep): 822–71.

Schumpeter, Joseph A. 1911. *The theory of economic development: an inquiry into profits, capital, credit, interest, and the business cycle.* Translated by Redvers Opie. Cambridge, MA: Harvard University Press.

Schumpeter, Joseph. 1942. *Capitalism, socialism and democracy.* New York: Harper and Brothers.

SEC. 2006. The investor's advocate: how the SEC protects investors, maintains market integrity and facilitates capital formation. http://www.sec.gov/about/whatwedo.shtml.

Senior Supervisors Group. 2009Mar. Observation on management of recent credit default swap credit events. Basel, BIS, Mar 9.

Shapiro, Fred R., 2000. The most-cited legal scholars. *Journal of Legal Studies* 29 (1): 409–26.

Shiller, Robert J. 2002. *The new financial order: risk in the 21st Century.* Princeton: Princeton University Press.

Shleifer, Andrei. 2000. *Inefficient markets.* New York: Oxford University Press.

Shleifer, Andrei and Robert W. Vishny. 1986. Large shareholders and corporate control. *Journal of Political Economy* 94 (3, Jun): 461–88.

Shleifer, Andrei and Robert W. Vishny. 1988. Value maximization and the acquisition process. *Journal of Economic Perspectives* 2 (1, Winter): 7–20.

Shleifer, Andrei and Robert W. Vishny. 1990. The takeover wave of the 1980s. *Science* 249 (Aug): 745–9.

Shleifer, Andrei and Robert W. Vishny. 1991. Takeovers in the '60s and '80s: evidence and implications. *Strategic Management Journal* 12 (Winter): 51–9.

Shleifer, Andrei and Robert W. Vishny. 1993. Corruption. *Quarterly Journal of Economics* 108 (3, Aug): 599–617.

Shleifer, Andrei and Robert W. Vishny. 1997. A survey of corporate governance. *Journal of Finance* 52 (2, Jun): 737–83.

Simon, Carol J. 1989. The effect of the 1933 Securities Act on investor information and the performance of new issues. *American Economic Review* 79 (3, Jun): 295–318.

Smirlock, Michael. 1985. Evidence on the (non) relationship between concentration and profitability in banking. *Journal of Money, Credit and Banking* 17 (1, Feb): 69–83.

Smith, Adam. 1776. *The wealth of nations.* Chicago: University of Chicago Press, reprinted in 1976.

Spence, Michael A. 1973. Job market signaling. *Quarterly Journal of Economics* 87 (3): 355–74.

Spence, Michael A. 2002. Signaling in retrospect and the informational structure of markets. *American Economic Review* 92 (3): 434–59.

Stein, Jeremy C. 1998. An adverse selection model of bank asset and liability management with implications for the transmission of monetary policy. *Rand Journal of Economics* 29 (3, Autumn): 466–86.

Simons, Henry C. 1948. *Economic policy for a free society.* Chicago: University of Chicago Press.

Sloan, Jr., Alfred P. 1963. *My years with General Motors.* New York: Doubleday & Company.

Stigler, George J. 1955. Mergers and preventive antitrust policy. *University of Pennsylvania law Review* 104 (2, Nov): 176–84.

Stigler, George J. 1964. Public regulation of the securities markets. *Journal of Business* 37 (2, Apr): 117–42.

Stigler, George J. 1971. The theory of economic regulation. *The Bell Journal of Economics and Management Science* 2 (1): 3–21.

Stigler, George J. and Claire Friedland. 1962. What can regulators regulate? The case of electricity. *Journal of Law and Economics* 5 (Oct): 1–16.

Stigler, George J. and Claire Friedland. 1983. The literature of economics: the case of Berle and Means. *Journal of Law and Economics* 26 (2, Jun): 237–68.

Stiglitz, Joseph E. 1987. Technological change, sunk costs and competition. *Brookings Papers on Economic Activity* 3: 883–937.

Stiglitz, Joseph E. 1994. The role of the state in financial markets. *Proceedings of the World Bank Annual Conference on Development Economics 1993.* Washington, DC: World Bank.

Stiglitz, Joseph E. 2002. Information and the change in the paradigm in economics. *American Economic Review* 92 (3); 460–501.

Stiglitz, Joseph E. and Andrew Weiss. 1981. Credit rationing in markets with imperfect information. *American Economic Review* 81 (3): 391–401.

Stiroh, Kevin J. and Philip E. Strahan. 2003. Competitive dynamics of deregulation: evidence from US banking. *Journal of Money, Credit and Banking* 35 (5, Oct): 801–28.

Stout, Lynn A. 2003. The shareholder as Ulysses: some empirical evidence on why investors in public corporations tolerate board governance. *University of Pennsylvania Law Review* 152: 667–712.

Stulz, René. 1999. Globalization, corporate finance and the cost of capital. *Journal of Applied Corporate Finance* 12 (3, Fall): 8–25.

Stulz, René M. 2005. The limits of financial globalization. *Journal of Finance* 60 (4, Aug): 1595–638.

Subrahmanyam, Avanidhar and Sheridan Titman. 1999. The going-public decision and the development of financial markets. *Journal of Finance* 54 (3, Jun): 1045–82.

Suda, Mikayo. 2003. The effects of "quantitative monetary easing" when the nominal short-term interest rate is zero. Tokyo, Bank of Japan, Apr 2.

Sufi, Amir. 2004. Agency and renegotiation in corporate finance. Cambridge, MA, unpublished paper, MIT, Oct.

Summerhill, III, William R. 2007a. Inglorious revolution: political institutions, sovereign debt and financial underdevelopment in Brazil. New Haven, Yale University Press, forthcoming.

Summerhill III, William R. 2007b. Sovereign credibility with financial underdevelopment: the case of nineteenth-century Brazil. Palo Alto, Hoover Seminar on Collective Choice, Mar 6.

Sundaram, Anant K. and Dennis E. Logue. 1996. Valuation effects of foreign company listings on US exchanges. *Journal of International Business Studies* 27 (1, 1st Qtr): 67–88.

Svensson, Lars E. 2003. What is wrong with Taylor rules? Using judgment in monetary policy through targeting rules. *Journal of Economic Literature* 41 (2 Jun): 426–77.

Taylor, John B. 1993. Discretion versus policy rules in practice. *Carnegie-Rochester Conference Series on Public Policy* 39 (1993): 195–214.

Taylor, John B. 1999. An historical analysis of monetary policy rules. In John B. Taylor, ed. *Monetary policy rules*. Chicago: University of Chicago Press.

Taylor, John B. 2007. Housing and monetary policy. In Housing, housing finance and monetary policy. Jackson Hole, WY: Symposium by the Federal Reserve Bank of Kansas City. http://www.kc.frb.org/home/subwebnav.cfm?level=3&theID=10982&SubWeb=10658

Taylor, John B. 2008Nov. The financial crisis and the policy responses: an empirical analysis of what went wrong. Palo Alto, CA, Stanford University, Nov. http://www.hoover.org/research/globalmarkets?section=publications

Taylor, John B. 2009. *Getting off track: how government actions and interventions caused, prolonged and worsened the crisis*. Stanford: Hoover Institution Press.

Taylor, John B. 2009Feb. How government created the financial crisis. *Wall Street Journal*, Feb 9.

Taylor, John B. and John C. Williams. 2009. A black swan in the money market. *American Economic Journal Macroeconomics* 1 (1, Jan): 58–83.

Temin, Peter. 1976. *Did monetary forces cause the Great Depression?* New York: W.W. Norton.

Temin, Peter. 1989. *Lessons from the Great Depression.* Cambridge: MIT Press.

Temin, Peter. 1993. Transmission of the Great Depression. *Journal of Economic Perspectives* 7 (2, Spring): 87–102.

Teoh, Siew Hong, Ivo Welch and T. J. Wong. 1998. Earnings management and the long-run market performance of initial public offerings. *Journal of Finance* 53 (6, Dec): 1935–74.

Throop, Adrian W. 1975. Capital investment and entry in commercial banking: a competitive model. *Journal of Money, Credit and Banking* 7 (2, May): 193–214.

Tirole, Jean. 2001. Corporate governance. *Econometrica* 69 (1, Jan): 1–35.

Tobin, James. 1982. The commercial banking firm: a simple model. *Scandinavian Journal of Economics* 84 (4): 495–530.

Torstila, Sami. 2003. The clustering of IPO gross spreads: international evidence. *Journal of Financial and Quantitative Analysis* 38 (3, Sep): 673.

Treasury. 2008Sep17. Treasury announces supplementary financing program. http://www.ustreas.gov/press/releases/hp1144.htm

Treasury. 2009Feb10. Financial Stability Plan fact sheet. Washington, DC, US Treasury, Feb 10. http://www.treas.gov/initiatives/eesa/

Treasury. 2009Feb18. Homeowner affordability and stability executive summary. http://www.ustreas.gov/news/index2.html

Treasury. 2009Feb25. Treasury white paper. Washington, DC, US Treasury Department, Feb 25. http://www.financialstability.gov/

Treasury. 2009 Mar4. Home affordable modification program guidelines. Washington, DC, US

Treasury. http://www.ustreas.gov/press/releases/reports/modification_program_guidelines.pdf

Treasury. 2009RRProposal. Treasury proposes legislation for resolution authority. Washington, DC, US Treasury Mar 25.

Treasury. 2009RRFrame. Treasury outline framework for regulatory reform. Washington, DC, US Treasury, Mar 26.

Treasury. 2009Mar30. Public-Private Investment Program. Washington, DC, UST, Mar 30. http://www.financialstability.gov/roadtostability/publicprivatefund.html

Tullock, Gordon. 1967. The welfare costs of tariffs, monopolies and theft. *Western Economic Journal* 5 (3): 224–32.

Tullock, Gordon. 2003. The origin of the rent-seeking concept. *International Journal of Business and Economics* 2 (1): 1–18.

Ugai, Hiroshi. 2006. Effects of the quantitative easing policy: a survey of empirical analysis. Tokyo, Bank of Japan WP, July.

Vafeas, Nikos, James F. Waegelein and Maria Papamichael. 2003. The response of commercial banks to compensation reform. *Review of Quantitative Finance and Accounting* 20 (4, Jun): 335–54.

Vander Vennet, Rudi. 2002. Cost and profit efficiency of financial conglomerates and universal banks in Europe. *Journal of Money, Credit and Banking* 34 (1, Feb): 254–82.

Vasicek, Oldrich Alfons. 2002. The distribution of loan portfolio value. *Risk* 15 (12, Dec): 160–2.

Vernon, J. R. 1994. World War II fiscal policies and the end of the Great Depression. *Journal of Economic History* 54 (4, Dec): 850–68.

Vives, Xavier. 2001. Competition in the changing world of banking. *Oxford Review of Economic Policy* 17 (4): 535–48.

Walras, Leon. 1870. *Elements of pure economics*. London: Allen and Unwin, 1954.

Wellink, Nout. 2009Mar. Basel Committee initiatives in response to the financial crisis. Brussels, Remarks before the Committee on Economic and Monetary Affairs of the European Parliament (ECON), Mar.

Werner, Ingrid M. and Allan W. Kleidon. 1996. UK and US trading of British cross-listed stocks: an intraday analysis of market integration. *Review of Financial Studies* 8 (2, Summer): 619–64.

White, Eugene M. 1990. The stock market boom and crash of 1929 revisited. *Journal of Economic Perspectives* 4 (2, Spring): 67–83.

White, Lawrence J. 1989. The reform of federal deposit insurance. *Journal of Economic Perspectives* 3 (4, Autumn): 11–29.

Willenborg, Michael. 1999. Empirical analysis of the economic demand for auditing in the initial public offerings market. *Journal of Accounting Research* 37 (1, Spring): 225–38.

Williamson, Oliver E. 1963. Managerial discretion and business behavior. *American Economic Review* 53 (Dec): 1051–3.

Williamson, Oliver E. 1975. *Markets and hierarchies*. New York: Free Press.

Williamson, Oliver E. 1984. Corporate governance. *Yale Law Journal* 93 (7, Jun): 1197–230.

Williamson, Oliver E. 1985. *The economic institutions of capitalism*. New York: Free Press.

Williamson, Oliver E. 1988. Corporate finance and corporate governance. *Journal of Finance* 43 (3, Jul): 567–91.

Williamson, Oliver E. 1994. Evaluating Coase. *Journal of Economic Perspectives* 8 (2): 201–9.

Williamson, Oliver E. 1998. The institutions of governance. *American Economic Review* 88 (2): 75–9.

Williamson, Oliver E. 2000. The new institutional economics: taking stock, looking ahead. *Journal of Economic Literature* 38 (3): 595–613.

Williamson, Oliver E. 2002. The lens of contract private ordering. *American Economic Review* 92 (2, May): 438–43.

Wilson, Robert. 1978. Information, efficiency and the core of an economy. *Econometrica* 46 (4, Jul): 807–16.

Winston, Clifford. 1998. US industry adjustment to economic deregulation. *Journal of Economic Perspectives* 12 (3, Summer): 89–110.

Winston, Clifford. 2006. *Government failure versus market failure*. Washington, DC: AEI/Brookings Joint Center for Regulatory Studies, Brookings Institution Press.

Zerbe Jr., Richard O. and Howard McCurdy. 1999. The failure of market failure. *Journal of Policy Analysis and Management* 18, 4 (Fall): 558–79.

Zerbe Jr, Richard O. and Howard McCurdy. 2000. The end of market failure. *Regulation* 23 (2): 10–4.

Zingales, Luigi. 1995. Insider ownership and the decision to go public. *Review of Economic Studies* 62 (3, Jul): 425–48.

Zingales, Luigi. 1998. Corporate governance. In Peter Newman, ed. *The new Palgrave dictionary of economics and the law*. Basingstoke, UK: Palgrave Macmillan.

Zingales, Luigi. 2000. In search of new foundations. *Journal of Finance* 55 (4, Aug): 1623–54.

Zingales, Luigi. 2007. Is the US capital market losing its competitive edge? Bruxelles, European Corporate Governance Institute, Finance WP 192, Nov.

Index